VLADIMIR JABOTINSKY'S RUSSIAN YEARS, 1900–1925

JEWS IN EASTERN EUROPE

Jeffrey Veidlinger

Mikhail Krutikov

Geneviève Zubrzycki, *editors*

VLADIMIR JABOTINSKY'S RUSSIAN YEARS, 1900–1925

Brian J. Horowitz

INDIANA UNIVERSITY PRESS

This book is a publication of

Indiana University Press
Office of Scholarly Publishing
Herman B Wells Library 350
1320 East 10th Street
Bloomington, Indiana 47405 USA

iupress.indiana.edu

© 2020 by Brian Horowitz

All rights reserved

No part of this book may be reproduced or utilized in any form or by any means, electronic or mechanical, including photocopying and recording, or by any information storage and retrieval system, without permission in writing from the publisher. The paper used in this publication meets the minimum requirements of the American National Standard for Information Sciences—Permanence of Paper for Printed Library Materials, ANSI Z39.48-1992.

Manufactured in the United States of America

Cataloging information is available from the Library of Congress.

ISBN 978-0-253-04767-0 (hardback)
ISBN 978-0-253-04768-7 (paperback)
ISBN 978-0-253-04771-7 (web PDF)

1 2 3 4 5   25 24 23 22 21 20

CONTENTS

Acknowledgments vii

Introduction *1*

1 A Zionist in Odessa, circa 1900–1903 *14*

2 Zionism before 1905 *33*

3 In Revolution and Counterrevolution, 1905–1906 *52*

4 The Decade between the Revolution of 1905 and World War I, 1907–1914 *77*

5 Political Alliances Break; Jabotinsky Goes His Own Way, 1907–1914 *101*

6 The Jewish Legion's Russian Inspiration, 1915–1917 *124*

7 Postwar Disappointments, Palestine 1918–1922 *156*

8 Russian-Jewish Emigration and the Path to Zionist Revisionism, 1923–1925 *187*

9 Russia in the Life and Work of Jabotinsky after 1925 *215*

Conclusion *234*

Bibliography *239*

Index *259*

ACKNOWLEDGMENTS

I WANT TO ACKNOWLEDGE THE HELP OF MANY people who deserve thanks for financial and intellectual aid. I want to thank Tulane University and its Provost's Office, the Lavin-Bernick family, and the Dean's Office at Tulane University. I also want to thank the Frankel Center at the University of Michigan and the Kertész Institute at the University of Jena, as well as the Hebrew University and the Israeli National Library. A special thank you to the Vladimir Jabotinsky Institute for access to archives.

I want especially to thank Dee Mortensen of Indiana University Press for shepherding this book through the hoops of publication and through the process of improving it. I also thank Ashante Thomas of Indiana University Press, who is the consummate professional.

Several individuals have given generously of their time and talent; these include William Craft Brumfield, Scott Ury, Alex Orbach, Inna Shtakser, Jesse Tisch, Susan Johnson, and Vladimir Levin, and the editors of the series, Professors Jeffrey Veidlinger, Mikhail Krutikov, and Geneviève Zubrzycki. Additionally, I acknowledge the help of Michael Ralph Cohen, Shaul Stampfer, Zvi Gitelman, Andrew Sloin, Heinz Dietrich-Loewe, Israel Bartal, Mikhail Beizer, Yigit Akin, Michael Cohen, Ari Ofengenden, Maxim Shrayer, Zoya Kopelman, Dmitry Shumsky, Moshe Naor, Sarah Cramsey, Joachim Puttkamer, Ronna Burger, Ilan Fuchs, Antony Polonsky, and Colin Shindler, as well as a number of individuals who were involved with the project but did not live to see its publication: Avram Greenbaum, Jonathan Frankel, Ezra Mendelsohn, Hugh McLean, and John Klier, z.l.

VLADIMIR JABOTINSKY'S
RUSSIAN YEARS, 1900–1925

INTRODUCTION

* * *

THIS STUDY OF VLADIMIR JABOTINSKY IN RUSSIA, AND the Russian theme in Jabotinsky's life and works, offers a portrait of the development of the Zionist leader from his beginnings as a young journalist in 1900 to the establishment of HaTzoHar (Brit Ha-Tsionim Ha-Revizionistim), the Revisionist party, in 1925. The name Jabotinsky has been mythologized in the Israeli political sphere—lionized on the right, demonized on the left—but here he is shown not as something finished and polished, but in development, changing, and becoming. My goal has been to sketch the contexts that shaped him, to show readers the discourses in which he participated and the politics in Russia that helped shape his views.

This story tracks Jabotinsky as a young man, an apprentice to Menachem Ussishkin and Avram Idel'son, and shows how he gradually gained confidence to chart his own path. The research collides with the myths of Jabotinsky as a born leader who emerged prepared and ready from the first moment to battle with the ossified Zionist leadership. Instead I found that Jabotinsky's vaunted uniqueness and independence are relative, he weaved between cooperation with and rejection of his elder colleagues. The reader will discover that he learned from many people who left their stamp on his thoughts in ways large and small. Most of all, this book recovers the Russian Jabotinsky, who came of age in a specific time and place and, despite the physical disappearance of that original world (tsarist Russia), harkened back to it with unexpected frequency.

My choice of Jabotinsky was not random. In today's Israel, followers of Jabotinsky cart his image around to legitimize a political and social platform—settlements in the West Bank, inequality of income, and an aggressive struggle with the Palestinians. The question of what Jabotinsky really stood for and how he came to be associated with the political right wing of Zionism—these are questions that still await an answer.

In my research I discovered a contradictory person, a fox who wanted, but failed, to become a hedgehog (to use Isaiah Berlin's well-known dichotomy). But I also found a brilliant political tactician who played the weak hand of Zionism in the early twentieth century astoundingly well. Whatever one's politics, it is undeniable that Jabotinsky made a successful career as a political leader with little in the way of connections or advantage. Much of what he attained was the result of relentless commitment and shrewd tactics. Although he found himself in a crowded race, he was not afraid of change or contradiction, and he had a gift for changing tactics and outwitting rivals. His rise was neither quick nor easy, but by the mid-1930s, he stood among Zionism's top leaders, with Ben-Gurion and Chaim Weizmann.

Although he was the head of his party, HaTzoHar (Zionist Revisionists), one should ask what he really achieved, since he never became head of state or held operative political power. His outsize image deflates considerably when one compares him to Ben-Gurion, for example. At the same time, many have claimed that his struggles for Jewish sovereignty and Jewish dignity changed real people in innumerable ways.[1] He became a popular figure worldwide, but especially in Poland and Palestine in the mid- to late-1930s.

I became interested in this subject because I wanted to answer important questions. Was Jabotinsky a liberal posing as a reactionary, a reactionary with liberal residue, a democrat with dictatorial leanings, or a dictator with a nostalgia for democracy? I have tried to explain his zigzag trajectory by claiming that Jabotinsky should be understood as a political actor in the early decades of the twentieth century. In fact, we must connect Jabotinsky, and Zionism more generally, to the political history of that period, with its displays of power, political performances, cultural innovations, and emphasis on destruction of the old world. We should shift the focus from coincidence—Jabotinsky's policies happen to share qualities with the radical right—to an acknowledgement that he consciously shaped his self-image and conceived his own trajectory.[2]

Jabotinsky's right-wing politics stimulated my curiosity: how did the young man, a committed liberal, become associated with the political right? After dismissing the initial falsehood that antisemitism prevents Jews from supporting the political right, I wondered about Jabotinsky's shift. When, where, and how did he move from the left of center, from liberalism, to militant Zionism, and almost Jewish fascism? What was the connection with his experience in Russia?

I discovered that he was strongly influenced by the Russian context. In "Reactionary," an article from 1912, Jabotinsky confesses that he learned a great deal from Polish ethno-nationalists.[3] While such extremists were intolerant, they nevertheless provided lessons in how to liberate one's own nation from the yoke of another. In addition, Jewish weakness taught him lessons. To be a sovereign nation, one needs strength—an army prepared to use force—as well as a majority status in the population. Jabotinsky remembered these truths in his pronouncements about Jewish Palestine ("The Iron Wall" [1923]) while also expressing "liberal" principles, such as political autonomy for national minorities.

Jabotinsky differed in profound ways from Ben-Gurion and the Second Aliyah representatives in Palestine, so one naturally wonders what might explain the difference. It seems that Jabotinsky's Zionism emerged from a different experience than Labor Zionism. Jabotinsky's political views were bound up with a European urban cultural experience, not the pastoral dreams of the Second Aliyah. The additional years he spent in tsarist Russia inculcated a different position toward Palestine, British rule, and the Arabs; he took a tougher line on all three. By comparison, Second Aliyah members left Russia around 1905. Jabotinsky's extra years in Russia affected who he became, because he saw the rise of nationalism throughout Europe.

Nonetheless, I show that Jabotinsky was not the embodiment of the statist idea (*mamlachiut*), as was Ben-Gurion. In fact, his pronouncements on the role of the state and minority rights come closer to Russian populism (belief in the Jewish people) or American-style civic engagement. He maintained that the Jewish right to Palestine would be secured on the basis of a Jewish majority, not absolute control over the state's political apparatus. From this it followed that minority nations have certain rights and responsibilities. Since Jews were not a majority, and he accepted (at least potentially) the need for violence to attain his goals, Jabotinsky appears different, further to the political right, than the liberal that he imagined himself to be.

Moral questions also whetted my interest. Can Revisionist Zionism be morally defended? How? As I read and researched, I came to see that many of Jabotinsky's pronouncements and attitudes seemed ethically questionable. However, the historical events of World War II and the Holocaust complicate judgments regarding Jabotinsky's belligerence vis-à-vis the Palestinian Arabs. The fact that the world closed its doors to Jewish immigration in the 1930s, when Eastern European Jewry needed a refuge, and that England largely bowed to Arab wishes to halt Jewish immigration to Palestine, contributed to the deaths of many thousands.[4] In a crisis like that unfolding in Europe of the 1930s, Jabotinsky's struggle for open immigration to Palestine feels appropriate. Facing such a dilemma, how do moral experts distinguish right from wrong?

Posing the problem in such a way suggests a related question: were there other alternatives for Jews in Palestine besides building a nation state? Here, one should recall that Jabotinsky planned for Palestinian Arabs to remain in Eretz Yisrael, but under the condition that they were a minority. They would have civic rights, perhaps even national rights, but they would lack sovereignty. They would lose their former majority status and have a subordinate political position, though their lives might improve economically. Again, what would a moral philosopher say? Should such a fate be regarded as an earth-shattering tragedy for a people, or something less terrible? These turned out to be difficult questions.

In addition, the history of the period inspired me. Scholars have written so much about contemporary Zionism, but few delve into its origins in Russia. In fact, there are only a few reliable books about Russian Zionism, all written decades ago.[5] Can we expand that knowledge by consulting new sources? Moreover, scholars of Jabotinsky usually focused on the later period of his political life (1925–1940), and neglected his development as a Zionist in Russia. Maybe they lacked Russian (Jabotinsky's primary linguistic instrument) or knowledge of Russian culture. In any case, as someone who has been studying Russia for decades, I thought I could go deeper than the superficial platitudes about Russia that one hears repeated in any Jabotinsky biopic. It seemed worth remembering that Russia was one of the centers of European culture in the epoch before World War I. Russia was at the forefront in dance, music, poetry, and art. But what about politics? There, too, the revolutionary atmosphere produced a plethora of thinkers and theories. Jewish national life existed in the Russian Empire: the masses lived there; the rabbis, laymen, and women had created a Jewish civilization, with schools, synagogues, clubs, and organizations. It was a large, organized community, well aware of its potential and vulnerabilities. Indeed, all that was needed for the emergence of a national movement was a spark. Western education and acculturation, combined with an awareness of antisemitism, ignited it.

Jabotinsky's Russia was very different from the Russia portrayed in Cold War propaganda and in Jewish religious sources. Russia acquainted

Jabotinsky with writers from around the world—Shakespeare, Dante, Edgar Allen Poe, the Russian classic poets, Pushkin, Lermontov, Nekrasov, and many more. Jabotinsky himself was a writer of some repute, a poet of considerable talent. Russia was also the site of Russian-Jewish journalism, the home of *Odesskie Novosti*, *Evreiskaia Zhizn'* (*Rassvet*), *Russkie Vedomosti*, and the other journals where Jabotinsky got a political education and learned the discourse of politics and Zionism. Russia was the home of fellow Zionists, friends and foes, with whom he became involved and from whom he learned a great deal. Any attempt to understand Jabotinsky without Russia will be futile.

* * *

The story of Jabotinsky's development in Russia begins in Odessa, situated on the Black Sea. It was an ethnically mixed town populated primarily by Greeks, Italians, Ukrainians, Russians, and Jews. It boasted a rich cultural tapestry that included Western opera and literatures in Southern Russian dialect, Polish, Ukrainian, Yiddish, and Hebrew. The city's Jews were involved in a variety of businesses—Jabotinsky's father bought and sold grain. In a sense, Odessa represents a paradox. The city was a multilinguistic universe where religion was widely ignored; at same time, it was the leading center of Zionism and the revival of modern Hebrew—the home of Ahad-Ha'am, Moshe Leib Lilienblum, Yehoshua Ravnitsky, Semyon Dubnov, and Joseph Klausner.[6] There was a sizeable Jewish intelligentsia involved in journalism, politics, and culture. Like many young people of the fin de siècle, Vladimir was not initially attracted to politics; his first love was literature. In his teens, he translated Edgar Allan Poe's "The Raven" into Russian. Just before finishing high school, Jabotinsky left for Bern and then Rome, where he spent three years studying at the university, while supporting himself by writing for Odessa's newspapers. In 1900, at age twenty, he returned to Odessa. That is where his life as a Zionist began.

In 1904, Jabotinsky moved to St. Petersburg, the capital city in the northwest. It was a very different place, with a smaller Jewish population due to special anti-Jewish restrictions. The Jews who had permission to live there—rich notables and highly educated professionals—gave Jabotinsky a perspective on class levels and power. Jabotinsky lived there illegally from 1904 to 1907, and during the critical Revolution of 1905 he wrote and edited Russia's first Zionist newspaper in Russian, *Rassvet* (known also at times as *Evreiskaia Zhizn'*).

During this "Petersburg period," Jabotinsky and other nonsocialist Zionists were drawn to Russian liberalism. He witnessed the rise of Russian and Polish nationalism, and observed how difficult it was for minorities to gain power via the democratic process, through elections to the First and Second Dumas (parliaments) (1906–1907). He tried to design a system of autonomy for Jews and other minorities, a system that would guarantee social control over resources, and innovations in education. He was involved in the League for the Attainment of Full Rights for the Jews of Russia, and participated in the so-called Cherikov Affair (1907–1909), in which some Russian intellectuals singled Jews out as alien to Russian culture. From 1909 to 1910, Jabotinsky traveled to Istanbul to work as an editor of Zionist journals during the Young Turk Revolution. He returned to Russia in time to witness the Mendel Beilis Affair (1911–1913), in which the government put Beilis, a Jewish factory worker, on trial for ritual murder.

During World War I, Jabotinsky joined Joseph Trumpeldor, Pinkhas Rutenberg, and Meir Grossman, all Russian Jews, and formed the Jewish Legion, a Jewish fighting unit under British command. The Legion brought him to Palestine in 1918, but Britain decommissioned his unit shortly afterward, and he was left unemployed. In 1920, he was arrested for defending Jerusalem during the Arab Riots. The British government sentenced him to three years in the Acre prison, but he was soon released, and shortly afterward, Chaim Weizmann appointed him to the Zionist Executive and then sent him to America as a representative of Keren Hayesod, the Zionist fund for the purchase of land in Palestine. After Jabotinsky's resignation from the Zionist Executive in 1923, he moved to Berlin and then Paris. From 1923 to 1925, he traveled around Europe giving talks and laying the groundwork for his own political party, HaTzoHar, which he started in 1925. Though small at first, with few members, it grew into a popular opposition party within Zionism. In 1935, as much out of frustration as hope, Jabotinsky withdrew his party from the World Zionist Organization and established the New Zionist Organization (NZO). Jabotinsky died in 1940, in Hunter, New York, where he was inspecting a Betar camp.

* * *

For the intellectual historian, this project has opened many paths: Russia with its great literary tradition, the 1905 Revolution, and its period of democratic experimentation (1907–1916), Zionism and Jewish politics, the Russian emigration, and then the explosive historical contexts of the first half of the twentieth century (World War I, the interwar period, and then World War II). It seemed to me that no one yet had been able to bring all these dimensions together properly or find the right emphasis.

This book's genre is intellectual biography. It traces the development of Jabotinsky's Zionism in the context of his ideological, personal, and political experiences. In the history of Zionist thought, I view Jabotinsky as representing the end of one phase of Zionism and the beginning of another. He comes to the movement at the close of the age of theoretical Zionism, which had its origins in the Russian Empire and produced such inspired thinkers as Leon Pinsker, Ahad-Ha'am, and Micah Yosef Berdichevsky. In the next period, Jabotinsky joined Yehiel Chlenov, Avram Idel'son, Menachem Ussishkin, and others who dealt with practical politics in Russia. He began organizing Zionist groups, publishing literature about Zionism, running for a Duma seat, and participating in various political conferences.

What I have not done in this book is recount Jabotinsky's thoughts and actions as they evolved day by day. Two biographies, one by Joseph Schechtman and the other by Shmuel Katz, do exactly that.[7] Instead, I provide arguments and evidence to explain the arc of Jabotinsky's development. Therefore, although the facts of his life matter, this book is not strictly speaking a biography. Ideas and contexts take precedence; I include details about his family, but sparingly, and only when they are relevant to his ideas.

In terms of sources, this book draws heavily on Jabotinsky's large Russian-language oeuvre, which, though once thought to be lost, is now available.[8] Similarly, I have immersed myself in Russian-language publications by and about Zionism in Russia. In this context one may mention the Russian-language Zionist newspaper *Rassvet*.[9] There are also large archival holdings in the Jabotinsky Institute in Tel Aviv, as well as many sources on Jabotinsky in Hebrew, Yiddish, German, Polish, and English. Another deep well of materials is the extensive secondary scholarship on Jewish politics in Russia, especially scholarship that has appeared since the opening of Soviet archives.

My project relies on Michael Stanislawski's earlier book, *Zionism and the Fin de Siècle*. Professor Stanislawski shows that Jabotinsky knew little about nationalism, much less Zionism, until he was nearly twenty years old. But Professor Stanislawski left it to others to figure out Jabotinsky's development once he did embrace Zionism. That has been my task, and it drew my attention to a body of rare and unused sources about Russian Zionism and Zionists. Those sources have fueled this book.

Disagreements among historians are common and perhaps inevitable. Although Michael Stanislawski's insights are important—that Jabotinsky's autobiography diverged from the historical facts, that his Jewish education occurred belatedly, and that he was influenced by the fin de siècle culture that he encountered in Rome—they should not be overestimated.[10] If we are interested in Jabotinsky primarily because of his Zionist ideas and activities, we need to focus on the history of Zionism in Russia and Russian politics and culture at the time when he participated in the Zionist movement. The cosmopolitan culture that influenced him before he joined the movement is of secondary significance. However, we should pay attention to Stanislawski's insight that in his autobiographical writings, Jabotinsky mixed true events with myths.[11] It cannot be doubted that Jabotinsky had a penchant for exaggeration. For these reasons, I use his autobiography with caution. However, rather than reject Jabotinsky's fabrications, I analyze them as part of his political strategy, and I locate Jabotinsky within narratives that are larger and more complex than his sympathizers would allow. His stories are useful in helping to piece together a composite understanding of Jabotinsky against the backdrop of twentieth-century events.

For many years, ideology and tendentiousness characterized scholarship on Jabotinsky and Revisionism.[12] Recently, however, a number of serious scholars of Zionism and Jewish history have attempted to go beyond the polemics of popular political history (Labor versus Revisionism) and take seriously Jabotinsky's complicated position in the Russian ferment. Avi Bareli and Pinhas Ginossar have assembled a fine book of essays, *In the Eye of the Storm* (2004). Leonid Katsis and Elena Tolstaya have also published a collection of essays on the Russian Jabotinsky (2013), while Dimitry Shumsky, a professor of Zionism at the Hebrew University, has written a good deal about Jabotinsky's theories of national autonomy.[13] In his latest book, *Beyond the Nation-State: The Zionist Political Imagination from Pinsker to Ben-Gurion* (2018), Shumsky argues in favor of a tradition of Jewish autonomism, which endorsed sharing Palestine with its Arab inhabitants. Jabotinsky's contradictory pronouncements, especially about the relevance of political autonomy for minorities, can be compiled to show his respect for tolerance and giving full rights to the Arabs in Palestine.[14]

Svetlana Natkovich, a young Israeli scholar, has also written about the Russian Jabotinsky. In *Among Radiant Clouds: The Literature of Vladimir (Zeev) Jabotinsky in its Social Context* (2015), she examines Jabotinsky's psychology, political dreams, and creative ambitions, attempting to grasp his politics through his artistic imagination.[15] By contrast, another Israeli scholar, Amir Goldstein, sees antisemitism as the unifying thread in *Zionism and Antisemitism in the Thought and Action of Ze'ev Jabotinsky* (2015).[16] Daniel Heller, a Canadian scholar, recently published his dissertation, *Jabotinsky's Children: Polish Jews and the Rise of Right-Wing Zionism*, which deals with the formation of Betar, the Revisionist youth group, and the popularity of Revisionism among Polish Jews in the 1930s.[17]

Besides these books, there are several works devoted to the Israeli political right with major sections devoted to Jabotinsky's role as inspiration or father figure. Among these books are Colin Shindler's *The Triumph of Military Zionism*, Ami Podazhur's *The Triumph of Israel's Radical Right*, and Eran Kaplan's *The Jewish Radical Right*.[18] Recently, a debate broke out over the authorship of Jabotinsky's texts and his use of pseudonyms. Leonid Katsis argues for a more generous incorporation of texts that might belong to Jabotinsky, whereas Alexander Frenkel criticizes the former's approach.[19]

My book differs from these. Unlike Natkovich, I set aside Jabotinsky's dreams and concentrate on his Zionist writings, downplaying the gap between the writer and the politician. For me, the politician takes precedence. After all, if Jabotinsky had remained only a journalist and creative writer, he wouldn't be the subject of a biography.[20] My project shares common elements with Amir Goldstein's, but his concentration on antisemitism pushes him in a different direction. I follow Jabotinsky's path in Zionism; to me, antisemitism is only a part of the picture. Additionally, most books about Israel's radical right deal with the later period in Jabotinsky's life, and see his rightward drift as inevitable. This approach examines his ideological endpoint and wants only to know "how he got there." I see this approach as overdetermined. I emphasize the potentialities and contingencies of Jabotinsky's life and the contradictions in his views, showing that his path was hardly unidirectional. Indeed, he entertained multiple and contradictory choices along the way, and his fate was hardly inevitable.

Recently, scholars have become interested in Jabotinsky's literary oeuvre and in the contrast between fiction and politics.[21] In truth, his politics and creative writing rarely addressed the same themes at the same time. In this context, it is something of a conundrum that Jabotinsky wrote a novel *(The Five)* about tsarist Russia in the late 1930s, when the Nazis were gaining power in Europe and antisemitism was growing. However, while he was remembering the past, he became extremely active politically in the present. He withdrew his party from the World Zionist Organization and created the New Zionist Organization, and he negotiated with the Polish government to facilitate the mass evacuation of Polish Jewry.[22] His newspaper articles in the last years of the 1930s concentrated on "evacuation," which he defined as a strategically prudent act of retreat.[23]

Although Jabotinsky left Russia permanently in 1915, I have added two chapters on his relationships with Russians abroad and the story of the emigration of Jews and Russians from the Soviet Union. As I see it, the creation of a Revisionist Zionist Party in 1925 was entirely a Russian-Jewish phenomenon: its leaders and original members were Jews from Russia. Thus, the period 1915 to 1925 is part of my story. Even when Jabotinsky was outside its borders, Russia followed him everywhere: he established the Jewish Legion with colleagues from Russia, and the reason for a Legion was to entice the Jewish immigrants from Russia to volunteer for military service in Britain. In his Palestine period (1918 to 1920); in his work as a fundraiser for the Keren Hayesod; and as a member of the Zionist Executive, Jabotinsky was linked with Chaim Weizmann, another Jew from Russia. From 1920 to 1925, Jabotinsky befriended and worked with a group of Russian émigrés—Joseph Schechtman, Shlomo Gepstein, Alexander Kulisher, Yuly Brutskus, and Meir Grossman—in publishing *Rassvet*, the Russian-language newspaper. All were Zionists.

Because the Russian chapter of Jabotinsky's life did not end in 1925, I have added a postscript about Russian thematics, which played an important role in Jabotinsky's later career. One might expect the Russia theme to vanish from Jabotinsk's life in the 1930s, especially since he was busy with Revisionist party matters, but, surprisingly, he wrote a great deal about Russia, and with rose-tinted glasses. He idealized his friends and experiences, and painted a self-portrait of a moderate liberal, a person who stands for individual freedom, the democratic process, and minority rights. In his final years, Jabotinsky linked memories of Russia with his defense against charges of fascism. Russia symbolized a happier time, unlike the anxious present, when the Nazi threat loomed on a dark horizon.

Nonetheless, the Revisionist party changed rapidly after it was officially established. Russian émigrés left its ranks, and Palestinian and Polish Jews joined, as Revisionism turned more radical. The story of Jabotinsky's evolution after 1925 belongs to a different narrative. In this context, the trajectory and the chronological bookends of 1900 to 1925 make sense.

The large and growing literature on Jabotinsky reveals enormous popular interest in him. Perhaps the fascination stems from the ideological parallels between the present-day Likud party and Jabotinsky.[24] Some journalists have linked Benjamin Netanyahu to Jabotinsky through Bibi's father, Benzion Netanyahu, who was involved in the Revisionist movement. Benzion devoted a chapter in his book on Zionism to Jabotinsky.[25] Menachem Begin, also a Likud forefather, invoked Jabotinsky to enhance his own political legitimacy, although one should acknowledge that Begin distorted Jabotinsky's image to serve his own interests.[26]

For many Israelis today, Jabotinsky's greatest achievement was the establishment of a Zionism of the political right.[27] Likudniks like to recall that Jabotinsky opposed Mapai (socialism) and promoted capitalist investment to expand Jewish employment. Jabotinsky disliked the Histadrut (labor exchange), so he established a parallel Revisionist labor exchange. As early as the mid-1920s, Jabotinsky rejected labor strikes in Palestine, arguing that they frightened away investment. When workers brought legitimate grievances, Jabotinsky suggested arbitration, his reasoning being that the Yishuv was a society in the making: at this early point in its development, it simply couldn't endure economic dislocations caused by class conflict.

History has been both generous and cruel to Jabotinsky. Generous in that there is an institute devoted entirely to his legacy in Tel Aviv, and numerous scholars are occupied with him. Cruel because, even though he is remembered, it is often not for what he accomplished, but primarily for what he has signified for Israeli politics in the years since his death.[28]

Notes

1. Brian Horowitz, "Was Vladimir Jabotinsky a 'Good' Politician?," *Frankel Center Yearbook*, 2012.
2. Jan Zouplna, "Revisionist Zionism: Image Reality and the Quest for Historical Narrative," *Middle Eastern Studies* 44, no. 1 (2008): 5.
3. Vladimir Jabotinsky, *Fel'etony* (St. Petersburg, 1913), 264–274.
4. Dvora Hacohen, "British Immigration Policy to Palestine in the 1930s: Implications for Youth Aliyah," *Middle Eastern Studies* 37, no. 4 (October 2001): 216.
5. For example, *Katzir: Kovets le-korot ha-tenuah ha-tsionit be-rusya*, 2 vols. (Tel Aviv: Masada, 1964); Yizhak Maor, *Ha-Tenuah ha-tsionit be-rusya* (Jerusalem: Magnes & Hebrew University, 1986); Yossi Goldshtein, *Bin tsionut medinit le-tsionut ma'asit: Ha-tenuah ha-tsionit be-rusya ba-reshitah* (Jerusalem: Magnes, 1991).
6. Patricia Herlihy, "Port Jews of Odessa and Trieste: A Tale of Two Cities," *Jahrbuch des Simon-Dubnow Institut* II (2003): 183–198; Steven J. Zipperstein, "Odessa," in The YIVO

Encyclopedia of Jews in Eastern Europe, ed. Gershom Hundert, vol. 2 (New Haven, CT: Yale University Press, 2008): 1277–1282.

7. Joseph B. Schechtman, *The Vladimir Jabotinsky Story*, 2 vols. (New York: Thomas Yoseloff, 1956); Shmuel Katz, *Lone Wolf: A Biography of Vladimir (Ze'ev) Jabotinsky*, 2 vols. (New York: Barricade Books, 1996).

8. Vladimir Jabotinsky, *Polnoe sobranie sochinenii v deviati tomakh* (Minsk: Met, 2007); up to now only four volumes have appeared.

9. *Rassvet* appeared in St. Petersburg (Petrograd), 1904–1917, and Berlin, Paris, 1922–1934. At times appeared with the title, *Evreiskaia Zhizn'*.

10. Michael Stanislawski, *Zionism and the Fin de Siècle: Cosmopolitanism and Nationalism from Nordau to Jabotinsky* (Berkeley: University of California Press, 2001), 116–149.

11. Michael Stanislawski, *Autobiographical Jews: Essays in Jewish Self-Fashioning* (Seattle: University of Washington Press, 2004), 3.

12. Ya'acov Vainshel, *Jabo: Sirtutim le-dmuto shev Ze'ev Z'abotinski* (Tel Aviv: Ha-Matmid, 1954).

13. *Ish be-sa'ar: Masot u'mekharim 'al Ze'ev Z'abotinski*, ed. Avi Bareli and Pinhas Ginossar (Ber-Sheva: Universitat Ben-Guryon ba'Negev, 2004); *Zhabotinskii i Rossiia: sbornik trudov Mezhdunarodnoi konferentsii 'Russian Jabotinsky: Jabotinsky and Russia,' posveshchennoi 130-letiiu V. E. Zhabotinskogo*, ed. Leonid Katsis and Elena Tolstaya (Evreiskii Universitet v Ierusalime, iiul' 2010) (Palo Alto: Department of Slavic Languages and Literatures, Stanford University, 2013); Dmitry Shumsky, "Tsionut ve-medinat ha-leum: Ha'araha me-hadash," *Zion* 1/2 (January 2012).

14. Dmitry Shumsky, *Beyond the Nation-State: The Zionist Political Imagination from Pinsker to Ben-Gurion* (New Haven, CT: Yale University Press, 2018).

15. Svetlana Natkovich, *Ben aneney zokhar: Yetsirato shel Vladimir (Ze'ev) Z'abotinski ba-heksher ha-hevrati* (Jerusalem: Magnes, 2015).

16. Amir Goldstein, *Derekh rabat-panim: Tsiyonuto shel Ze'ev Z'abotinski le-nokhah ha-antishemiyut* (Kiryat Sedeh-Boker: Jabotinsky Institute, 2015).

17. Daniel Heller, *Jabotinsky's Children: Polish Jews and the Rise of Right-Wing Zionism* (Princeton, NJ: Princeton University Press, 2017).

18. Colin Shindler, *The Triumph of Military Zionism: Nationalism and the Origins of the Israeli Right* (London: I. B. Tauris, 2009); Ami Pedahzur, *The Triumph of Israel's Radical Right* (Oxford: Oxford University Press, 2012); Eran Kaplan, *The Jewish Radical Right: Revisionist Zionism and its Ideological Legacy* (Madison: University of Wisconsin Press, 2005).

19. Leonid F. Katsis, *'Russkaia vesna' Vladimira Zhabotinskogo* (Moscow: Rossiiskii Gosudarstvennyi Gumanitarnyi Universitet, 2019); Aleksandr Frenkel', "Falsifikatsii Zhabotinskogo non-stop," *Narod Knigi v Mire Knig* (August 2014): 1–3.

20. Hillel Halkin, *Jabotinsky: A Life* (New Haven, CT: Yale University Press, 2014).

21. Dan Miron, *Ilan metsak ba-gai: Ze'ev Z'botinski ve shirato* (Tel Aviv: Ha-msidar'a sh. Ze'ev Z'abotinski, 2005); Marat Grinberg, "Was Jabotinsky the Zionist Nabokov?" *Tablet Magazine*, August 4, 2014.

22. Heller, *Jabotinsky's Children*, 18.

23. Vladimir Jabotinsky, "The Evacuation Problem, Humanitarian Zionism," *Jewish Herald* 30, no. 9 (March 11, 1936): 4.

24. Nonetheless, Colin Shindler warns against using history to answer today's political questions. *The Rise of the Israeli Right: From Odessa to Hebron* (Cambridge: Cambridge University Press, 2015), ix.

25. Benzion Netanyahu, *The Founding Fathers of Zionism* (Jerusalem: Balfour Books, 2012).

26. Yechiam Weitz, *Bin Ze'ev Z'abotinski le-Menachem Begin: Kovets ma'amarim al ha-tenua ha-revizionistit* (Jerusalem: Magnes Press, 2012), 15–33. Begin portrayed Jabotinsky as the father of a Jewish paramilitary underground. In fact, Jabotinsky favored public displays of armed force that acted as a deterrent to violence.

27. Shindler, *Rise of the Israeli Right*; also Benzion Netanyahu, "Z'abotinski ki-medinai u'kemannig le-amo: Keitsad haya magiv al ba'ayot zmanenu," in *Ish be-Sa'ar: Masot ve-Mekhkarim al Ze'ev Z'abotinski* (Ber-Sheva: Ben-Gurion, 2004); Eran Kaplan, "A Rebel with a Cause: Hillel Kook, Begin and Jabotinsky's Ideological Legacy," *Israel Studies* 10, no. 3 (Fall 2005): 87–103.

28. Weitz, *Bin Ze'ev Z'abotinski le-Menachem Begin*, 15–33.

1

A ZIONIST IN ODESSA, CIRCA 1900–1903

* * *

> I found that Russia had a new face. Instead of "tedium and longing," there was a nervous unrest, a general expectancy of something, a mood of spring. During my stay abroad, important events had taken place—the revolutionary parties had come out of the underground, and one or two ministers were killed; here and there disorders broke out among workers or farmers; and in particular there was excitement in the student milieu.
>
> —Vladimir Jabotinsky in *Story of My Life*

THE STORY OF VLADIMIR JABOTINSKY'S TRANSFORMATION INTO A Zionist is somewhat confusing because, as we will see, claims from a later period give the impression of an early attraction to the movement. However, documents from the time show his intense desire to integrate into Russian culture. It would be wrong to concentrate on one event, such as his experiences in Italy in 1897–1900 (when he supposedly learned about Garibaldi and Italian nationalism), as motivating his attraction to Zionism or focusing only on Kishinev and the 1903 pogrom that occurred there, which radicalized an entire generation.[1] In contrast, I propose examining his commitment to Zionism as part of a personal and intellectual evolution.

The trajectory of his development, then, was a two-stage process in which Jabotinsky struggled for recognition in a purely Russian environment, and then, having succeeded as a Russian journalist, turned his energies to Zionism. Later, in his autobiography, he revised history, making it seem like he embraced Zionism earlier than he actually did. Perhaps he wanted to make himself seem more precocious or more zealous. But the truth was that the Kishinev Pogrom, in 1903, was the precipitating event.

At the time, both Jabotinsky and other authors described the pogrom as a profoundly frustrating event that compelled them to endorse and participate in Zionism. Jabotinsky's later claims were a crafty revision, as I hope to demonstrate through a close examination of the earlier documents.

* * *

Writing about the Kishinev Pogrom in 1936, Jabotinsky confesses: "It is a strange thing: I do not remember the impression this event made on me, the turning point in our whole life as a nation. In general, it made no impression. I was already a Zionist before it happened; I had also thought about [the possibility of a pogrom] before. Neither was the Jewish cowardice revealed in Kishinev a discovery for me, no more than for any Jew or Christian. I always had the feeling that there is nothing to learn from pogroms; they hold no surprise." Then he adds, "I had always known that such would be the case, and it was."[2]

The assertion "I was already a Zionist" piques one's curiosity. In his autobiography Jabotinsky testifies to a commitment to Zionism long before he joined the movement. His evidence consists of conversations he reports he had with his mother, which he sentimentalizes: "One more decisive thing I learned from her brief answers: I was about seven years old or even younger when I asked her: 'Shall we Jews also have a kingdom in the future?' And she replied: 'Of course, we shall—you silly boy!' From then until today I did not ask anymore; I already knew."[3] Although this exchange seems trivial, it is intended to show that the absence of a traditional Jewish education was not necessarily a hindrance to his choice of political loyalties. He did not know much about Judaism, Hebrew, or Yiddish, but he imbibed his Zionism with his mother's milk; Zionism was part of his upbringing.

In another attempt to give himself a Jewish pedigree, Jabotinsky tells the reader that at the time of his bar mitzvah, he studied Hebrew with Yehoshua Ravnitzky, one of the greatest Hebrew writers of the day and a Zionist, who happened to be a neighbor. It is hard to determine how much Hebrew he studied with Ravnitzky, but he repeated the claim many times, including in 1936, when he published *Story of My Life*.[4] In a footnote the original editor, Shlomo Zal'tsman, writes that it was Ravnitzky's "fate to be Z[eev] Jabotinsky's first teacher of Hebrew, and he . . . helped us with useful and trustworthy advice in Hebrew in the first edition of Zeev Jabotinsky's selected works."[5]

In *Story of My Life* Jabotinsky continued to strain to provide tangible antecedents for his future as a Zionist leader. He focused his efforts on a speech he made in 1898 in Bern, when he was a university student. No transcript survives; all we have by way of documentation are Jabotinsky's impressions of the reactions of the audience, which consisted of Jewish socialists.

> But I remember that discussion well, because I gave the first speech of my life then, and it was a "Zionist" speech. I spoke in Russian, and the gist of it was as follows: I do not know whether I am a socialist—I didn't know that doctrine well enough—but I am a Zionist, no doubt about that, because the situation of the Jewish people is very bad. Their neighbors hate them, and the neighbors are right: in the end the Jews in the Diaspora are bound to experience a general Bartholomew's Night, and their only salvation is mass immigration to Eretz Yisrael.⁶

No evidence can be found that Jabotinsky made such a speech, so it is naturally difficult to ascribe significance to it. It is noteworthy that for the next few years, Jabotinsky apparently made no effort to acquaint himself with Zionism. These were important years for the movement, when Theodor Herzl promoted his book, *The Jewish State*, and annual Zionist congresses were convened for the first time, starting in 1897. During these years, debates broke out between Herzl and the Russian Zionists over political Zionism and Hibbat Tsion's preference for infiltration into Palestine: Should Jews try to reclaim land in Palestine now, even without a charter from the Sultan?⁷ In 1898, Jabotinsky lived in Rome, a little over nine hundred kilometers from Basel. Had he felt the urge, he could have attended the Zionist congresses. Jabotinsky's first attendance was registered in 1903. But, as he notes when describing his life in Rome at the time, he was occupied with other matters: socialism, anarchism, democracy—anything but specifically Jewish problems. In 1902, a congress of Russian Zionists was held in Minsk. Already back in Odessa, Jabotinsky did not attend and did not comment on it.

This was the time, one should recall, when many Jews in Russia embraced russification in the hope that they could find a place in Russian society and a respectable livelihood for themselves even if the government imposed legal disabilities on them. There was no fear at this time of Russian nationalism. In fact, Russian culture was seen as reflecting universal values. Some people denied the idea that Jews composed a separate nation because Jews had no land to call their own and no common language uniting all of them, and their future appeared linked with the majority populations among whom they lived. The only realistic option was integration into the majority society and patience.[8] Therefore Jews could either emigrate (usually to the United States) or acculturate and fight for improvements in their status. Progress, almost a substitute for religion in Europe's nineteenth century, was viewed as inevitable; reason could be thwarted, delayed, ignored, but it would ultimately succeed and bring with it equality for Jews. Few knew of, understood, or accepted Zionism.

We can learn about Jabotinsky's pre-Zionist attitudes from his writings in 1903, when he discussed the earlier years of 1898–1900. For example, although the majority of the people he knew in Rome were Jews, they had neglected to acknowledge the fact. He writes, "But during these three years I never recognized any Roman Jews, because they hid their Jewishness and avoided any mention of their ethnicity. During these three years I literally did not encounter the word *ebreo* a single time, either in print or in conversation, although I know now that the articles that I read were often written by Jews, and that there were Jews among the gentlemen with whom I discussed matters."[9]

Jabotinsky's recasting of his Italian period as connected with his Jewish identity seems exaggerated. In 1897, he went to Bern and then to Rome without any particular plan, and in neither city, it seems, did he seek out other Jews. His readings at this time were disparate: action novels, symbolist dramas, and works on socialism and Russian politics, among others. Nowhere in his writings of the time does he indicate an interest in Jewish religious texts or Yiddish fiction, although he grew up in the city where Mendele Mocher Sforim, Moses Leib Lilienblum, Ahad-Ha'am, and many others wrote their classic works. Thus, Jabotinsky could be said to embody cosmopolitanism; his Jews did not forget who they were, but they imagined that, outside of government oppression, being a Jew did not greatly matter.

In *Story of My Life*, Jabotinsky casts his transformation into a Zionist as a reclamation of identity. He argues that Italy's Jews debated questions of universal significance while their own Jewish identity remained invisible. "And nonetheless, if there is no antisemitism, there is 'something,' some kind of indestructible tiny seed—not of evil or hate, but of discord, frigidity, and alienation—and this tiny seed, like the pea under the mattress, despite its size, does not let one rest comfortably and peacefully."[10] A fascinating coda to this acknowledgement of the vague presence of Jewish identity is that Jabotinsky describes his high-school Russian friends in the same way:

Jews who discuss everything under the sun but never consciously recognize their Jewish identity.

> It is nevertheless my duty to acknowledge that the spirit of antisemitism was almost entirely absent from these government schools: perhaps because in those days public opinion generally was dormant in Russia, left-wing as well as right; that is why the entire period up to the last years of the nineteenth century is referred to in Russian as "Bezvremennye"—a faceless epoch. We Jewish students suffered no persecution on the part of either the teachers or our classmates. The most astonishing thing about it was that, all this notwithstanding, we always kept apart from our Christian environment. There were about ten Jews in our class; we sat together, and if we met in a private house to play or to read or just to chat, all this was always and strictly among ourselves. At the same time several of us also had friends in the Russian camp. For example, I was bound by faithful friendship to Vsevolod Lebedintsev, a very fine fellow, whose name will appear in the course of this story. I visited him many times at his home, and he also came to mine, but it never occurred to me to introduce him to our separate circle, and neither did he introduce me to his group; I do not even know if he had a group. Stranger still was the fact that even inside our Jewish circle there was no Jewish spirit. When we read together, it was foreign literature, and discussions were concerned with Nietzsche and moral problems, morals in general or sexual morals—not the fate of Jewry, not even the Jewish situation in Russia, which was bothering every one of us.[11]

Although Jabotinsky apparently gave little thought to his Jewish identity, nonetheless he projects his alienation from the Russian environment. As much as they tried, he and his schoolmates were not "cosmopolitans"; something like *russified* Jews is more appropriate. However, during the 1890s, Jews in Russia fell into a feeling of false security. There had not been pogroms since 1882, and although quotas for Jews in Russian schools and universities had been imposed in 1887, and Jewish economic life had become significantly worse for many, for Odessa's Jews, life was predictable, and for wealthy Jews, there were still ways to avoid restrictions. To be sure, Jews were the objects of official discrimination, but life was not easy for others either.

In 1897, Jabotinsky went to Bern, Switzerland, for a few months and then traveled on to Rome, Italy, where he stayed three years. Although his motives are not entirely clear, adventure, experience, culture, and education played a role in his decision.[12] In the final years of the nineteenth century, Jabotinsky habitually published his reports from Italy in Odessa's local press. He was also a budding playwright. However, as he describes it, he was unable to get his literary work published, and therefore he complained to the doyen of Russian literature, Vladimir Korolenko, in the hope of receiving help. Korolenko and other leading writers received hundreds of letters a year from provincial writers seeking advice and publishing opportunities. Here is a passage from Jabotinsky's letter, dated 1898:

> But here in Odessa, not only am I unable to get my story published, I did not even try—I cannot even find a competent person who would agree to read it and give me his opinion. Meanwhile, forgive me my overconfidence, but I cannot help but see in it a modicum of originality.... But, at least, having received your valuable review, I would know what I should do with it, and, if your evaluation is positive, I will try to send it to a journal.... A thousand times I beg your pardon. I have no right to bother you, but what else can I do?![13]

He played the provincial card—"I cannot even find a competent person"—but that was just a gambit. No doubt he was hoping that Korolenko would invite him to write for his important thick journal, *Russkoe Bogatstvo*. However, in a letter to Korolenko a little over a year later, Jabotinsky suggested that his problems stemmed from the fact that his writings were out of step with the leading fashions; he did not fulfill the social demands of "critical realism"—that is, he was not sufficiently politically engaged. Even specialized journals, such as *Mir Bozhii*, rejected him for ideological reasons. Jabotinsky continues,

> For two years the liberal journals in the cities have been regularly returning my works to me, mainly poems, rejecting them. . . . And what is more, *Mir Bozhii* sent one poem back to me only because "its idea was deeply false from the sociological point of view." I considered such a treatment of the issue to be *sui generis*—and a very dangerous kind of censorship; so I wrote an open letter about it to *Novosti*. But since this letter is another of my works, it too was not printed. [As they say,] "They beat them and don't even let them scream."[14]

However, there is something disingenuous in Jabotinsky's complaints, since he was a popular journalist with a decent salary, and his articles appeared regularly in *Odesskie Novosti*. Maybe he considered popularity in provincial Odessa beneath him, although he acknowledged that he enjoyed the attention he received from the locals, including the young ladies of the town.[15]

Jabotinsky had more luck as a journalist and dramatist with the Decadent crowd that was forming in the last decade of the nineteenth century than with populists like Korolenko. Already in 1892, Dmitry Merezhkovsky had shocked Russia's elite with his lecture, "The Causes for the Decline of Contemporary Russian Literature and New Trends in It," which inaugurated the Decadent movement in Russia.[16] With Merezhkovsky came other writers, such as Zinaida Gippius and Akim Volynsky, whose work was published in the journal *Northern Flowers (Severnye Tsvety)*.[17] These and other writers condemned populism, social criticism, and the judgment of literature strictly for its political value. In contrast, these authors defended the individual's right to ignore society's problems and to give expression to beauty, love, and a person's internal emotions—eros, joy, or sadness.

Jabotinsky strongly identified with this new movement. Although in his autobiography he insisted that he preferred adventure novels—apparently he was trying to give the impression that in his youth he was not an egghead or budding intellectual, but rather a "can-do" person—in fact, he read highbrow literature: Shakespeare, Cervantes, and Pushkin, as well as Maxim Gorky and Anton Chekhov. Chekhov apparently had a huge influence on young Russians in the 1890s. Kornei Chukovsky, later a famous Soviet poet and a friend of Jabotinsky's in Odessa, describes Chekhov's omnipresence: "Chekhov's books seemed the only truth about everything that was happening around us. You read a Chekhov story and then look out of the window and see a continuation of what you have just read. All the inhabitants of our city, all of them without exception, were, for me, characters from Chekhov. . . . And I perceived every cloud, every tree, forest path, every landscape, in the city or the countryside, as quotations from Chekhov. I had never before observed such an identification of literature with life; even the sky above me was Chekhovian."[18]

While in Rome, Jabotinsky introduced Chekhov to an Italian audience.[19] In all, Jabotinsky published a few articles in the Italian press, but in this, his first serious publication of literary criticism, he wanted to give a taste of the latest currents in Russia. Published in the literary journal *Nuova Antologia* (1901), the article concentrates on Maxim Gorky and Chekhov. In an article that pays tribute to "Hamlet and Don Quixote," Ivan Turgenev's famous portrayal of the intellectual's dilemma in Russia, Jabotinsky portrays Chekhov as offering a diagnosis of society's problems while Gorky provides the solution.[20] For Turgenev, both Hamlet and Don Quixote had embodied positive and negative qualities: Hamlet was plagued by contemplation and fear of action, while Don Quixote shot off into action without thinking.

Naming the new trend a "literature of moods," Jabotinsky contrasts Chekhov and Gorky. Chekhov is the "singer of pain, preeminent creator of that grey and depressing emptiness that contemporary life has become."

Jabotinsky continues, "In Chekhov we have only a single feeling, a single note, to which all the melodies of his plays are attuned. . . . Real boredom will catch up with you later and you will be tortured for several days as if by a nightmare, by the terrible thought: 'What is the damn point of life in this world!'"[21]

In contrast to the Chekhovian Hamlet, Jabotinsky presents Gorky's protagonist, the barefoot wanderer (*bosiak*). "For Maxim Gorky's tramps, morality does not exist. His wanderers do not shrink from committing crimes, even crimes that are savage—yet by no means petty in intent and execution."[22] Jabotinsky points out that the wanderer is misunderstood by many who want Gorky's hero to represent their own political viewpoint. They interpret him as a member of the proletariat or representative of the simple people. In fact, the wanderer is neither. He is an individual, but one entirely indifferent to social issues or the problems of others. Nonetheless, the character's appearance is timely because "the time has not come for contemplation, but for constructive action; yet in order to build, one must struggle. And to be able to struggle, one needs to have desire, passionate and bold desire."[23] Jabotinsky prefers Don Quixote to Hamlet.

According to Jabotinsky's biographers, when he returned to Odessa in 1901, he intended to return to Rome to finish his law degree.[24] However, he was offered a full-time position with *Odesskie Novosti*, a job that included a significant salary increase. Furthermore, he became the paper's theater critic, a role that gave him access to the city's opera and theaters free of charge. Though still a young man, he attained a prized status among Odessa's bourgeoisie. He describes this position: "The sense of being popular . . . was sweet and pleasant at the age of twenty-one. 'Journalist' was an important title in the Russian provinces in those days. It was pleasant to enter the city theater, one of the most beautiful in the country, for free, with the usher dressed in the solemn attire of the time of Marie Antoinette, bowing and accompanying you to a seat in the fifth row, which was adorned with a bronze plaque engraved with 'Mr. Altalena.'"[25] Only a few years earlier Jabotinsky's theatergoing had entailed waiting many hours for a low-cost seat in the upper rows.

The themes of individuality and creativity that appealed to him in Italy found expression in his talks at the Literary Club in Odessa, in his newspaper columns, in his stories, and in the plays that he wrote and produced at the City Theater.[26] In all of these venues, he found different readers, but his message was the same: individualism. Two of his dramas were staged at the

Odessa City Theater, *Blood* (*Krov'*, 1901) and *It's All Right* (*Ladno*, 1902).²⁷ A typical monologue from *It's All Right* conveys the timbre of his voice and the content of his thinking. The play is not rooted in any plot but patched together in monologues. The protagonist, Korol'kov (whose name comes from the Russian for "small king"), expresses the author's preoccupations, especially the assertion that the individual has priority over the collective and has a right to purely personal goals. A typical monologue expresses Jabotinsky's radical individualism:

> I acknowledge one sole right
> for myself alone—only one, but for all that,
> vast, without limits. No one
> must. There is no obligation. A child involuntarily
> comes into the world, and life hits him cruelly and painfully,—
> so is he not right to consume his whole life
> in the struggle for happiness, for his own personal happiness? ...
> the right to oneself is given to all at birth.
> No obligation to anyone. Chase after pleasure,
> be happy, greedily believe your desire—
> and be afraid to sacrifice yourself, because
> never from sacrifice has
> happiness been sown. Light your holy candle
> before desire, call it your leader, wherever it would take you: for love,
> art, knowledge, idleness, like a stone into the water
> or on the old path of serving the people—
> but you—bring onto the old road
> your spirit, your new spirit, and again proclaim:
> "In my struggle I respect not obligation, not an order—
> I celebrate my sovereign desire!"²⁸

This message, embodied in such phrases as "no obligation to anyone," or "greedily trust your own desire," underlines the right of the individual to clear any obstacles to his happiness. Here we not only see Jabotinsky's affirmation of Gorky's heroes, but his commonality with Nietzsche, as well as with the heroes of such Decadent writers as Fyodor Sologub, Vasily Briusov, and Vasily Rozanov.²⁹ There is also a similarity with Sanin, the hero of Mikhail Artsybachev's novel of the same name and a popular figure with the Decadent crowd. The novel, *Sanin*, which appeared in 1907, came to exemplify the Decadent worldview in which the will of the individual for personal gratification permitted one to transgress all moral prohibitions.³⁰

Needless to say, this message of individual freedom sharply strayed from the themes of conventional Russian-Jewish theater. Regarding these works, the scholar Viktoriia Litvina has commented, "In both these plays there is no national idea. Both are interesting only as signposts of Jabotinsky's spiritual development."[31] According to Litvina, plays by Jewish authors ordinarily reflected the collective Jewish "problem":

> Take any Jewish play—they are astoundingly typical. In the fate of the characters is the fate of the people, in the plots are the conflicts of reality. The family of a cobbler killed in a pogrom; a son goes off to the revolution, a daughter is forced to become a prostitute.... The drama of a revolutionary who gives all his strength to the liberation of the Russian people, who see in him only a 'kike.'... Night-time ambushes of Jews... the apartments of conspirators... tears... blood... death.... The heroes' thoughts are occupied by the highest problems of the life of their people. Their main anxiety, their life task is the search for a way out of this unendurable situation.[32]

Jabotinsky's commitment to individualism has additional support in his autobiography, where he notes that when he was arrested and imprisoned in the Alexandrovsk Fortress outside Odessa in 1903 for the possession of illegal literature, he gave lectures to his fellow prisoners on Decadence and individualism.[33] Incidentally, in autobiographical stories written about this period of his life, Jabotinsky described aesthetic problems and erotic and psychological issues—anything but politics.[34] Despite the overwhelming evidence of Jabotinsky's affiliation with Decadence, some scholars still try to connect Jabotinsky with Marxism and political radicalism.[35] After all, he was arrested, and a police dossier on him exists.[36] However, if there is one thing we know about the tsarist police, it is that their investigations were as likely to mystify as enlighten. In fact, a police file should not constitute the sole proof of political allegiance. Furthermore, although Jabotinsky was a close friend of Vsevolod Lebedintsev (1881–1908), a leader in the Socialist Revolutionary (SR) movement who was executed by tsarist authorities, SRs were anti-Marxist. Additionally, this same Lebedintsev was also an opera buff and a science student. Ties going back to their school days united the two men. In short, Jabotinsky may have sympathized with Marxism, but party affiliation has not been noted in his own writings or in the memoir literature. On the other hand, the body of evidence connecting him in his youth to Decadence, Nietzscheanism, and literary modernism is overwhelming.

Journalism provides another source for tracing Jabotinsky's development in his early years, and we find a similar pathway. He reveals his struggle for fame and then his boredom in Odessa's Russian-language culture (in Odessa he could have joined other language groups—Hebrew, Yiddish, Ukrainian). In his autobiography he says that his journalistic pieces were often inspired by mockery and jest. However, he underestimates the role of journalism in shaping his worldview. One might come to the mistaken conclusion that his journalistic efforts were insignificant from the following account.

> Most of the readers of [Odesskie] Novosti enjoyed reading my articles, but not one of them gave them serious attention, and I was aware of that. The only one of all my articles of that period that deserves to be saved from oblivion is the one in which I openly, in black and white, called myself and all the rest of my fellow journalists "jesters." I devoted one of my articles to one of the writers of a rival newspaper—a decent, quiet, "neutral" man, neither clever nor stupid, anonymous in the full sense of the expression—of whom I had made a kind of dummy, and who I used to ridicule at every opportunity and even without one, just for the fun of it. That time I addressed myself directly to him, and I said: "Of course I have persecuted you without any reason or necessity, and I shall continue, because we are jesters for the reading public. We preach, and they yawn; we write with the bile of our heart's blood, and they say, 'Well written; give me another glass of compote.' What is there for a buffoon to do in the circus but to slap the cheek of his fellow buffoon?"[37]

The other journalist in the passage was likely A. E. Kaufman, who wrote for Jewish and Russian newspapers.[38] Jabotinsky apparently did write such an article, but in fact his depiction of it in his autobiography does not give a truthful rendering either of the importance of journalism in Russia at that time or of his own contribution to literary, political, and social discourse in Odessa and throughout Russia's southwest in the early 1900s.

In that time period, journalists, and especially popular writers, were considered the conscience of society. Because there was no legally recognized political opposition to the tsarist government, journalists adopted this role. In fact, one definition of an "intelligent," a member of the "intelligentsia," encompassed the notion of political opposition.[39] The job of journalist resembled that of the muckrakers in the United States of the same era: to hold the government accountable, to expose corruption and immorality, and to use examples from real life to provide a model of proper thought and behavior. Although Jabotinsky did not express a party line, he did articulate an idea of morality and the ideals of humanism, while standing up for the independent value of art and creativity.

* * *

The real change in his life trajectory occurred sometime in 1902, when Jabotinsky began to make occasional allusions to Zionism. In his autobiography he observes:

> My Zionism was also considered something frivolous. True, I did not join any group, nor did I even know who the Zionists were in the city, but several times I devoted one or two fragments in a *feuilleton* to the subject. In a big and decent monthly published in St. Petersburg, an article by a certain Bickerman appeared, couched in the style that was then called scientific, in which he demolished Zionism, demonstrating that Jews were a happy people, satisfied with their fate. I wrote a lengthy answer, using arguments that would satisfy me even now. The next day I met one of my acquaintances, [Yehoshua] Ravnitzky, also a "Lover of Zion," no doubt, and he said to me, "What is this new plaything you are toying with?"[40]

The article that Jabotinsky criticized had appeared in *Russkoe Bogatstvo* and was the work of Iosif (Joseph) Bickerman, who introduced a number of arguments to conclude that Zionism was utopian, and therefore unatttainable. He claimed that Palestine was far away and the Jewish masses—living traditional lives in the towns of Eastern Europe—were traders and artisans with no experience of farming. Thus, Zionism amounted to mere dreaming.

In his response Jabotinsky threw all he had against the article's alleged pseudoscientific tone. He discussed Bickerman's arguments as an example of the "cheapening of science." As science became associated with convenience, it lost its value. For example, a book that costs half a penny cannot be esteemed, however brilliant it may be. Bickerman's pseudoscience was like that—dirt cheap. Then Jabotinsky turned to the utopian claim, mocking Bickerman's voice:

> Whatever has not happened yet can never occur.
> —That is,
> —All the laws of historical development are known to us and whatever we have
>   not yet seen or predicted, should therefore not happen.
> I do not think that this could be scientific.[41]

Jabotinsky contrasted pseudoscience with "real" science. He pointed to millions of people who had traveled across the sea to new lands on ships with motors—that phenomenon would have seemed utopian a few decades earlier. Jabotinsky remarked that Zionism contained two main elements: "The first is mass emigration, which is hardly an innovation. The second is the guarantee of self-rule, also hardly an innovation."[42] About history, he writes,

> Much that seemed utopian a hundred years ago has now become established fact—and it marches and attacks and conquers.
> History does not know of utopias.
> History is made not by the will of man, but by the force of events.
> And when a mass of people is gripped, all in unison, by a single ideal, it means that it wasn't the *feuilleton* writers who were whispering it to them.
> It was the force of things that whispered to them.
> Those ideals that are whispered by the force of things are not utopia. They are real necessity.
> They are future reality.[43]

At the end of his article, Jabotinsky waxes poetic about Zionism.

> One can argue against Zionism, think it unattainable or undesirable.
> But to speak about its reactionary nature, to see in its statesmen the traitors of the ideals of humanity's well-being, this means not to argue against it, but to sully it, roughly and carelessly to sully a dream that was born from all the sobs, from all the sufferings of the Jewish people; this means to lure people into your gang by hook or by crook; this means to respond with curses to the tearful prayer of long-suffering Agaspher and blacken with torment and blasphemy his centuries-long protected ideal.
> Curse it! Ideals stand above torment and do not fear blasphemy.[44]

It is hard not to feel like Ravnitzky: What is this novice doing? Why of all people is he rallying to Zionism's cause? What motivates him, someone who has never shown previous interest? Is it just the desire to mock specious arguments? Although one can hear an echo of Herzl's faith in progress, one senses sincerity in his article. However, the question remained: was his interest in Zionism a one-off, or was it the start of something new?

Although Jewish issues had not bothered him earlier, something changed. Others gave it a sociological definition: a different Russia.[45] Jews and other minorities were no longer prepared to tolerate their low status but sought ways to show their discontent. Opposition groups were forming throughout the country. In the Northwest, the Bund gained popularity; in the Southwest, Zionism attracted support. Israel Trivus, a Zionist from Odessa, writes, "The beginning of the '90s in Russia was a time of public awakening. Underground student groups, worker strikes, intellectual circles of diverse varieties, plays with 'Aesopian language,' tea-parties with endless political conversations, the unexpected 'tsarism be gone!' in the theater or at a concert. . . . The press came alive, despite strict censorship, and the tone of the protests became ever more decisive and sharp." Trivus continues, "The average Jew caught the bug of the public mood of optimism and belief in a better future. But in the Jewish milieu still other factors were at work that transformed the average Jew into a citizen: the development of Zionism, and a bit later, the Bund."[46]

Jabotinsky too faced new questions about ethnic and political affiliation. By 1903, acculturated Jews were confronted with urgent questions: *Who are you?* Are you a Russian or a Jew? The disarming confidence that "the Russian people" included everyone, even those who felt oppressed, had disappeared; the age of cosmopolitanism was over. Although there was much hand-wringing and complaining, one had to choose. If you were Russian, that meant Russian language, Russian society, and perhaps even conversion to Russian Orthodox Christianity. If one answered "Jewish," then other consequences followed: even if one had no religious affiliation to Judaism and cared little about identity, a Jew was the object of social and governmental discrimination. Some russified Jews reacted by taking an interest in Jewish life and culture: Alexander Goldstein, Yuly Brutskus, Israel Trivus, Boris Goldberg, and others went in this direction. A russified intellectual and an atheist, Jabotinsky set his sights on politics.

Jabotinsky became actively involved with Zionists in early 1903. Rumors were circulating in Odessa that a pogrom would occur, and in response to the threat, Jabotinsky apparently sent letters to Odessa's wealthiest Jews, requesting a secret meeting to decide how to meet the crisis. No one answered. His friend Israel Trivus explained to him that those to whom he wrote would never act, and besides, a self-defense organization was already in operation.[47] Trivus invited him to join the group, and Jabotinsky quickly became "indispensable." Trivus describes Jabotinsky's activities during the weeks before the Kishinev pogrom:

> For entire days at a time, V[ladimir] E[vgenievich] Jabotinsky, together with M[eir] Ia. Dizengoff, drove around the city to collect money for the unusual task. Then came the worries about how to acquire arms and the like. V. E. took on all this work like a devoted soldier: he showed up, he asked what was needed and he fulfilled the task he was given without questions.... He studied intensively Hebrew language, history, literature, the history of various national movements, and the colonial systems of different peoples—everything that, directly or indirectly, might pave the way to overcoming exile. Few are aware what an enormous task he set for himself. He did not rely on his own natural talent, did not engage in irresponsible improvisations. Impossibly demanding of himself, he did not stop studying and it would not be an exaggeration to assert that there was no one in the Zionist ranks as prepared as he was for the role of leader of the people.[48]

Although it is difficult to separate hagiography from biography, the memoir literature provides details about an early period where few other sources exist. In contrast to his belittling of Kishinev in his autobiography, others acknowledge the intense feelings elicited by the pogrom.

According to Kornei Chukovsky, "That savage event which horrified the civilized world marked the turning point in his life." "Jabotinsky," Chukovsky recalls, "stormed into the *Odesskie Novosti* offices late one spring afternoon and angrily upbraided us, the non-Jewish members of the staff, accusing us of indifference to that terrible crime. He blamed the whole Christian world for the Kishinev pogrom. After his bitter outburst he left, slamming the door behind him."[49] Chukovsky gives more information to the poet Rakhel' Margolina in 1965. "Volodya Zhabotinsky had completely changed. He started to study Hebrew, broke with his former environment, stopped his involvement in the Russian press. Previously I looked at him from the ground up: he was the most educated, most talented of my acquaintances, but now I grew even more attached to him. Earlier he tried to impress with his knowledge of English, and he brilliantly translated Edgar Allen Poe's 'The Raven,' but now he devoted himself to Hebrew literature and began to translate Bialik."[50]

The Kishinev pogrom had multiple echoes in Jabotinsky's life and work. It became very important for Jabotinsky later, in 1911, with the appearance of the volume of his Russian translations of Bialik's poetry, including "In the City of Slaughter."[51] The translations and the famous preface did a great deal to cement a connection in the public perception between Jabotinsky and Zionism.

Perhaps the entire point of diminishing the significance of Kishinev is to remove the suggestion, promoted by Chukovsky, that the pogrom "changed his life forever." In this case, rather than acknowledging antisemitism as the stimulus for his Zionism, Jabotinsky prefers to emphasize other influences. For example, he attributes his initial acquaintance with Zionism to Shlomo Zal'tsman, a fellow Odessan Jew.

Zal'tsman is first described in the autobiography as an "elegant gentleman with a black moustache and Western manners."[52] The two were introduced by Lebedintsev at an Italian opera that Zal'tsman attended as "the special correspondent for a Milanese review of music and opera."

> Afterward I met him at the house of Miss Degli Abbati. We spoke French, and when we left together, I continued the conversation in the same language.

"We can speak Russian, too," he told me. "I too am from Odessa, like you, although born in Lithuania."

I knew already that he was a Jew—"Signor Zal'tsman." It was clear who and what he was. Now he suggested that I call him Solomon Davidovich; he revealed that his position as correspondent with the Italian magazine was only a hobby, and that his main occupation was commerce, as was every Jew's. He also told me that he was a Zionist.[53]

Zal'tsman, with his Italian credentials, his command of French, and his Russian-Jewish origins seemed the ideal friend for Jabotinsky. Zal'tsman was also a publisher. Jabotinsky describes how Zal'tsman introduced him to a Zionist circle of wealthy Jewish businessmen in Odessa, and how he arranged for Jabotinsky to represent the group at the Sixth Zionist Congress in Basel in 1903, where the famous Uganda issue would be discussed. Incidentally, Zal'tsman's version of these events differs from Jabotinsky's; Zal'tsman reports that the invitation to meet the members of the Zionist club was not immediately accepted. Jabotinsky apparently consulted with Lebedintsev about whether he should join the national Jewish cause so far from general Russian problems.[54] Lebedintsev gave his blessing, and Jabotinsky went to Basel.

Vsevolod Lebedintsev, who was hanged in 1908 for revolutionary activity, appears to be much closer to Jabotinsky and more influential in his early political development than Zal'tsman. But in the long run, Zal'tsman would become a central figure in Jabotinsky's life, coming to the rescue any number of times with cash, publication opportunities, and advice; he was instrumental in the publication of Jabotinsky's translation of Bialik's poetry in 1911.[55] Zal'tsman apparently masterminded the plan to recruit this well-known, talented, and interesting young man to serve the Zionist cause. At the same time, Zal'tsman played many other roles in Jabotinsky's life; a Pygmalion, he helped Jabotinsky realize wide-ranging and ambitious plans.

Thus, it is something of a conundrum that the handmaiden to bring Jabotinsky to Zionism was not a Jew, but a Russian aristocrat and revolutionary. But perhaps there is logic in it; many Jews came to feel alienated from Russian culture and attracted to their own people. In fact, such Jewish artists as Mark Antokol'sky or Ilya Ginzburg were directed to Jewish culture by Vladimir Stasov. Ultimately, however, Zal'tsman played the greater role. Jabotinsky provided his energy, his knowledge of literature, and his vision to Zal'tsman, who contributed his capital and organizational acumen. Despite his attempt to give himself a longer Zionist pedigree, his Jewish feelings before 1903 were unformed, generalized, and spliced with others; after 1903, they took shape and became his life credo.

Notes

1. Steven Zipperstein, *Pogrom: Kishinev and the Tilt of History* (New York: Liveright, 2018); Arye Naor, "Mavo," in *Leumiut liberalit*, ed. Ze'ev Z'abotinski (Tel Aviv: Jabotinsky Institute, 2013), 11–56.
2. Vladimir Jabotinsky, *Story of My Life*, eds. Brian Horowitz and Leonid Katsis (Detroit: Wayne State University Press, 2017), 66.
3. Ibid., 42.
4. Michael Stanislawski has discovered that *Story of My Life* has a problem with facts. At times the autobiography departs from fact altogether, while in other instances Jabotinsky manipulates facts to score various political points. However, it is not unusual that political autobiographies reflect the time they were written as much as—and in some cases more than—the times they describe. Nonetheless, I caution the reader not to jettison this text as a factual source because it provides information that often corresponds with reliable sources and adds to our overall knowledge.
5. Vladimir Jabotinsky, "Sippur yamai,"in *Golah ve-hitbolelut* (Tel Aviv: Sh. Zal'tsman, 1936), 16.
6. Jabotinsky, *Story of My Life*, 49.
7. Israel Klausner, *Opozitsiya le-Herzl* (Jerusalem, 1960). Hibbat Tsion refers to the organization in the Russian Empire that offered support for settlement in Palestine between 1882 and 1897. They stood for "infiltration" and small-scale colonization of Jews in Palestine.
8. Jewish liberals envisioned integration as the ultimate solution for Jews in Russia. Brian Horowitz, *Jewish Philanthropy and Enlightenment in Late-Tsarist Russia* (Seattle: University of Washington Press, 2009), 81–86.
9. Vladimir Jabotinsky, "Vskol'z: Antisotsial'noe uchrezhdenie," *Odesskie Novosti*, November 2, 1903, 4.
10. Ibid.
11. Jabotinsky, *Story of My Life*, 43.
12. Stanislawski, *Zionism and the Fin de Siècle: Cosmopolitanism and Nationalism from Nordau to Jabotinsky* (Berkeley: University of California Press, 2001), 127, 132.
13. Vl. Jabotinsky to Vl. Korolenko from April 26, 1898, in V. Zhabotinskii, "Pis'ma russkim pisateliam," *Vestnik Evreiskogo Universiteta v Moskve* 1 (1992): 203.
14. Vl. Jabotinsky to Vl. Korolenko from August 28, 1899, ibid., 204–205.
15. Jabotinsky, *Story of My Life*, 58.
16. Dimitry Merezhkovskii, "O prichinakh upadka i o novykh techeniiakh sovremennoi russkoi literatury," *O prichinakh upadka i o novykh techeniiakh sovremennoi russkoi literatury* (Moscow: Direkt-Media, 2010).
17. Helen Tolstoy, *Akim Volynsky: A Hidden Russian-Jewish Prophet*, trans. Simon Cook (Leiden: Brill, 2017), 6–8.

18. Kornei Chukovskii, "Kak ia stal pisatelem," *Zhizn' i tvorchestvo Korneiia Chukovskogo: Sbornik* (Moscow, 1978), 143.

19. Vladimir Jabotinsky, "Anton Cekhof e Massimo Gorki: L'Impressionismo nella literature russa," *Nuova Antologia* (1901): 96. See also S. Gardzonio, "Zhabotinskii ital'ianskogo perioda," in V. (Z.) Zhabotinskii, *Polnoe sobranie sochinenii v 9 tomakh* (Minsk: Met, 2008), 2:6–18.

20. Ivan Turgenev, "Gamlet i Don-Kikhot," *Polnoe sobranie sochinenii i pisem v tridtsati tomakh*, 2nd ed. (Moscow: Nauka, 1980), 5:330–348.

21. Vladimir Jabotinsky, "Anton Chekhov i Maksim Gor'kii," in V. Jabotinsky, *Polnoe sobranie sochinenii v deviati tomakh* (Minsk: Met, 2008), 2:676–678.

22. Ibid., 683.

23. Ibid., 686.

24. Joseph B. Schechtman, *The Life and Times of Vladimir Jabotinsky: Rebel and Statesman, The Early Years* (Silver Springs, MD: Eshel Books, 1986), 64.

25. Altalena in Italian means "seesaw"; it was Jabotinsky's nom de plume.

26. Jabotinsky, *Story of My Life*, 56.

27. "The first pacifist play, *Blood* (in three short scenes) was staged in 1901 by one of the best provincial theaters, the Odessa theater, and gave two performances with no particular success. The next play (in one act), infelicitously named 'Ladno' by the author, was passed by the censor on October 16, 1902. It was shown in the same theater, only a single time, which was a scandal, on November 5, 1902." Viktoriia Litvina, "*. . . i evrei, moia krov'*": *Evreiskaia drama—russkaia stsena* (Moscow: Vozdushnyi Transport, 1991), 239.

28. Ibid., 260–261.

29. Viktor Kel'ner, ed., "Vladimir Jabotinsky i russkie pisateli," *Vestnik Evreiskogo Universiteta v Moskve* 1 (1993): 215–255.

30. Mikhail Artsybashev, *Sanin* (Moscow: Zhizn', 1907).

31. Litvina, "*. . . i evrei, moia krov'*," 239.

32. Ibid., 51.

33. "I too was invited to lecture on my professional subjects—the Decadents, Italian revival (in honor of the aforementioned 'Garibaldi'), and of course individualism. But after this lecture they did not invite me to speak anymore." Jabotinsky, *Story of My Life*, 72.

34. Jabotinsky, *Story of My Life*, 61–63.

35. Natal'ia Pasenko, "Zhabotinskii i politicheskie partii," *Moriia* 12 (2011): 6–20.

36. Mitiyahu Mintz, "Al shum ma hitehakta ha-Ohrana' ha-tsarit al tse'avdav shel Jabotinsky?," *Ish be-sa'ar: Masot u'mekhkarim 'al Ze'ev Z'abotinski*, ed. Avi Bareli and Pinhas Ginossar (Ber-Sheva: Universitat Ben-Guryon ba'Negev, 2004), 449–457.

37. Jabotinsky, *Story of My Life*, 60.

38. Abram Evgen'evich Kaufman (1855–1921), who grew up in Odessa, was a noted Jewish journalist and editor. For more about him, see Viktor Kel'ner, "Redaktsionnyi chernorabochii," in A. E. Kaufman, *Za kulisami pechati: Iz vospominanii starogo zhurnalista* (St. Petersburg: Rossiiskaia Natsional'naia Biblioteka, 2011), 5–18.

39. Isaiah Berlin, *Russian Thinkers* (New York: Penguin Classics, 2008), 2–3.

40. Jabotinsky, *Story of My Life*, 60. The term "lover of Zion" refers to Hovevei Tsion, the name of the adherents of Hibbat Tsion, the proto-Zionist group organized in post-1882 Odessa. Iosif Menassievich Bickerman (1867–1942) was the author of the article, "O sionizme i po povodu sionizma," *Russkoe Bogatstvo* 7 (1902): 27–69. Jabotinsky answered Bickerman in

an article, "O sionizme," *Odesskie Novosti* (September 8, 1902). Jabotinsky characterized him as an assimilationist.

41. Vladimir Jabotinsky, "O sionizme," *Polnoe sobranie sochinenii*, 2b:367–368. Original in *Odesskie Novosti*, (September 8, 1902).

42. Ibid.

43. Ibid., 367.

44. Ibid., 373.

45. There are many books on Russia in the period leading up to the 1905 Revolution. These include Terrence Emmons, "Russia's Banquet Campaign," *California Slavic Studies* 10 (1977), 45–86; Shmuel Galai, *The Liberation Movement in Russia, 1900–1905* (Cambridge: Cambridge University Press, 1973); A. Kizevetter, *Narubezhe dvukh stoletii, Vospominaniia, 1881–1914* (Prague, 1929), 167–171; Gregory Freeze, "A National Liberation Movement and the Shift in Russian Liberalism, 1901–1903," *Slavic Review* 28 (March 1969): 81–91.

46. Israel Trivus, "Pervye shagi," *Rassvet* 42 (October 19, 1930): 17.

47. Jabotinsky, *Story of My Life*, 65.

48. Trivus, "Pervye shagi," 19.

49. Quoted in Shmuel Katz, *Lone Wolf: A Biography of Vladimir (Ze'ev) Jabotinsky*, (New York: Barricade Books, 1996), 1:46.

50. Rakhel Margolina, *Rakhel Pavlovna Margolina i ee perepiska s Korneem Ivanovichem Chukovskim* (Jerusalem: Stav, 1978), 11. In the same letter, Chukovsky describes meeting Jabotinsky in London in 1916: "The last time I saw Vladimir was in London in 1916. He was dressed in a military uniform entirely engrossed in his ideas—completely different from the person I knew in my youth. Concentrated, despondent, but he embraced me and spent the entire evening with me." Ibid., 14.

51. Vladimir Jabotinsky, "Vvedenie k pesniam i poemam Bialika," *Pesni i poemy Bialika* (St. Petersburg: S. D. Zal'tsman, 1911), 7–55. Jabotinsky published the poem in his translation, along with an introduction, in *Evreiskaia Zhizn'*, November 11, 1904, 160–62. The poem was published many times thereafter, including in a collection of Bialik's poems in Russian translation: Kh. N. Bialik, *Pesni i poemy: Avtorizovannyi perevod s evreiskogo i vvedenie Vl. Zhabotinsky* (St. Petersburg: S. D. Zal'tsman, 1911).

52. Jabotinsky, *Story of My Life*, 64.

53. Ibid.

54. Shlomo Zal'tsman, *Min he-avar: Zichronot u'reshumot* (Tel Aviv: Sh. Zal'tsman, 1943), 241.

55. Bialik, *Pesni i poemy: Avtorizovannyi perevod s evreiskogo i vvedenie Vl. Zhabotinsky*.

2

ZIONISM BEFORE 1905

* * *

THE SIXTH ZIONIST CONGRESS, THE FIRST JABOTINSKY ATTENDED, had a powerful effect on him. There he encountered Herzl, and the influential meeting drew him deeper into the movement. The conference, Herzl's last, took place in Basel in 1903, and became known for the debate over the Uganda proposal.¹ Although Jabotinsky insisted in his autobiography that he voted against Herzl and the Uganda proposal "just so," because he felt like it, in fact he understood the issues very well. We can gauge the extent of his knowledge in three articles that he published in August 1903, reporting from the conference for *Odesskie Novosti*.² The first article contained a general discussion of Britain's Uganda offer and its significance for the Zionist movement; the second was devoted to the Mizrachi, religious Zionists; and the last to Herzl and the Russian opposition to Uganda. The last article also contained Jabotinsky's own credo.

The Sixth Congress was extremely contentious. The British government's offer of a colony for Jews in Uganda (land within the borders of present-day Kenya), split the movement into those who thought Eastern European Jews needed an asylum (these were the days following the murders in Kishinev), and those focused solely on the struggle for Palestine. Herzl defended the need for an alternative to Palestine, since it was not available for mass immigration due to Ottoman opposition, when Britain invited him to consider a Jewish center in Uganda. Max Nordau, second in the movement, argued in favor of Uganda as a "Nachtasyl," an asylum for the Jewish people until a Palestine charter could be attained.³ Significantly, there was opposition to Uganda from those who did not want to compromise on the main precept of Zionism, settlement in Palestine. Many of the so-called Nein-Sagers came from Russia.

Two issues frame Jabotinsky's experience of the Congress: his observations about Herzl and his own position. He began by lauding Herzl as the sole authority in the movement. "The entire administration, the entire leadership, and the entire responsibility for the movement rests with Theodor Herzl. When they talk about Zionism, they think of him."[4] Herzl's presence stimulated Jabotinsky to give thought to leadership qualities.

> I know all the good and all the bad that those around Herzl think of him, and I look at him entirely coldly and soberly, and I think that in his person there stands before us one of the most wonderful individuals of our time. It is difficult to define what constitutes his strength. He is not at all a first-class writer, but he is a fine stylist and transmits clearly and incisively what he needs to say, and precisely in the way that is needed. He is amazingly harmonious and controlled; he gives the impression of a person incapable of a falsely calculated gesture—a person who of course can lose his way, but cannot stumble. He is never sharp, but always gets his way. Many claim that he hypnotizes them. In every detail this gentleman is an average man, but on the whole he is a great figure, a great individual who needs great levers—maybe not talented, but also, maybe, a genius.[5]

This is a typical description of Herzl at the time.[6] Many wrote about his unsuspecting genius, his amazing success in creating a movement seemingly out of nothing. Jabotinsky watched and analyzed Herzl and was astounded by the latter's success in resolving the split in the movement. After a small majority sided with Herzl in favor of funding an investigation of East Africa, many of the Nein-Sagers burst into tears. Their emotional response, a symbolic allusion to the Jews of ancient Babylonia, who were described as weeping for the loss of Jerusalem, reflected the degree of their alienation from their own movement.[7] Zionism, which once embodied all their dreams, had now betrayed them. Jabotinsky, having voted with the Nein-Sagers, was present at the meeting where the group was deciding how to proceed. Jabotinsky's article provides a transcript of sorts of what happened at the meeting, and also presents his own perspective.

At the time when "angry Russians" were fulminating at Herzl and considering various tactics to delay the colonization of East Africa, Herzl arrived and demanded the opportunity to explain.[8] He spoke about his failure with the Ottoman Sultan and the lack of support among the wealthy and powerful Jews. When everything looked grim, hope burst out in the form of an offer from Great Britain. Uganda was not a retreat from Zion, Herzl exclaimed, but a detour. In fact, who knows, maybe this initiative would help the movement gain a foothold in Palestine. In any case, Herzl said that he would resign outright if he ever gave up on Palestine; he wouldn't need this group to help him understand that. In the moment at hand, however, it would be impolite and impolitic to reject Britain's offer without proper consideration. The opposition felt pacified, and the threat of a break had passed. The leaders and the rank and file decided to remain in the movement and continue the struggle for Palestine together.

Jabotinsky was deeply impressed by Herzl's poise, control, and delivery, as well as his sentiments. He understood Herzl's attempt to appear one among equals.

> It was precisely here, where he appeared without his formal jacket, without the gavel and the stage and the whole pompous apparatus that separates him from the public, that he appeared simply as a delegate from one of the Kishinev clubs to explain himself and almost to justify himself. Precisely here, it piqued my curiosity to find out how he would behave, how he would win over his audience, whether he would lose control of his tone, whether he would stumble. Herzl spoke, as always, calmly, expressively, without any rhetorical devices, entirely in control of himself. In each word one could hear self-assurance, and standing before his opponents, he did not hesitate to speak to them sharply, and at the same time with condescension, as one in power, almost as an elder with a child. There were moments when I thought that now the protesting voices would break in, but the voices didn't. Starting from his first words, from the expression that appeared on almost every face in this hall, in the extraordinary quiet that had now taken shape, I understood the entire meaning of Lomonosov's historic utterance: "It would be easier to take the Academy from me than to take me from the Academy."[9]

Lomonosov, the great figure of the Russian Enlightenment of the eighteenth century, represented for Jabotinsky an original thinker who gave his life to the Russian Academy that was founded by Peter I. Herzl showed the same complete identification with his institution, the Zionist movement. Of course, his readers at *Odesskie Novosti* would know Lomonosov and therefore could understand what Herzl meant to the Zionist movement.

Jabotinsky was convinced that, despite his apparent push for Uganda, Herzl had not changed. In contrast to others, Herzl was persuasive not because he showed goodwill or had experienced some kind of psychological transformation in recent years, as Yehiel Chlenov, the Moscow Zionist leader, maintained.[10] In contrast, Jabotinsky thought that it was Herzl's personal ambition that drove him to Palestine. "I am convinced that Zion is terribly important for this person, more important than for many, many others, precisely because the prospect of Zion's rebirth is far more tempting and infinitely more grandiose than the simple colonization of the first secluded corner that one finds. The rebirth of Zion would not have a precedent in history: to settle East Africa would mean to repeat Baron Hirsch."[11]

But Jabotinsky felt that Herzl's East Africa gambit, even if forced, had a certain logic. Diplomacy made up his sole strength, and although diplomacy was not necessarily the best method, if one played that card, then Herzl was right to exploit every opportunity. Fate always depended on chance, but a great leader, Jabotinsky concluded, prepared for the moment when fortune might strike. Cultivating a relationship with Great Britain, the world's greatest power, made sense. "History has its own laws, but to us, observing it from below, it will seem for a long time yet a chain of chance events. The same chance event that gave Herzl East Africa today might give him Palestine tomorrow. Politics is a game of 'chance events' in which the strong, smart person always has at least a fifty-percent chance, if only he wants to win."[12]

It is hard to read this article without feeling surprised that the prediction came true—indeed, today, Uganda, but tomorrow, maybe, Palestine. Who knows the gifts Britain could bestow, like fate, on the leader ready to accept and exploit the moment? Lord Balfour's letter in November 1917 was such a moment.

In his third article from Basel, Jabotinsky expressed his own views. He repeated Ahad-Ha'am's division between "Western" and "Eastern" Jews: he disdained the Jews of Western Europe for craving comfort; but admired the Jews of Russia for retaining a strong collective identity. The Westerners, those "eminent professors,"[13] thought that Jerusalem was equal or inferior to Wiesbaden, he wrote. But the East Europeans were different. They sought in Zionism spiritual goals—nothing less than the creation of a new Jewish civilization. "There is a different kind of Zionism in Russia. I consider Russia an amazing country: the best of the Slavs live here, and the best of the Jews: 'best' in the sense of the strongest and the least resigned to the submissiveness that Ahad-Ha'am called slavery in freedom among the Western 'Izraelites.' That is precisely why the Jewish masses in Russia are especially crowded together, why their desires and dreams—beneath the appearance of hopelessness—are so bold."[14]

The sentiment about Russia having the "best" Jews and Slavs belongs to Vladimir Solov'ev, the Judeophile Russian thinker who belonged to the Slavophile tradition and repeated the claim that the material West was spiritually corrupt, whereas the East still embodied religious purity.[15] The Eastern Europeans retained their Jewish complexion; they would not sell their Judaism or their love for Zion. That is why the Eastern Europeans stood with the Nein-Sagers, the representatives of artisans, various traders, workers, and students.[16] For these people Zionism without Zion was unthinkable.

Jabotinsky adopted the position of Nein-Sager, but he based his decision on a populist premise. Instead of viewing himself as a novice who followed the more experienced and popular figures in the Russian camp, he imagined himself as a representative of the Jewish people in their steadfast unity for Zion. Jabotinsky explained, "In days of sorrow, in a foreign land, what can people dream of if not their homeland, glorified and blessed in all the holy books, endowed with miracle tales, preserving the ruins of the sacred places given to the ancestors, taken from the grandfathers and promised to the grandchildren? One has *to want not* to understand in order not to understand the necessity, the inevitable elemental necessity of this national dream."[17]

In the months following the conference, Jabotinsky would join two seemingly contradictory positions, those of Herzl and Ahad-Ha'am, political and spiritual Zionism, politics and culture. He was attracted to Ahad-Ha'am's view that Palestine had the potential to transform all of the Jewish people through the cultivation of a new Jewish society, economy, and culture in Palestine. At the same time, Jabotinsky wanted to spur emigration to Palestine. Other Russian Zionists—Yehiel Chlenov, Menachem Ussishkin, and Yaakov Bernstein-Kogan—supported infiltration, emigration, and land purchases in Palestine. At the same time Jabotinsky still romanticized Herzl and dreamed of attaining a legal charter through diplomacy.

Nonetheless, having come closer to the "Russian" position on Herzl, Jabotinsky revised his view of the great leader. In the first article, he affirmed that the movement had put all its money on a single bet: Herzl. At the end of the series, he took a different tack: if Herzl were to abandon the end goal of Zion, the "movement would simply walk over him" and "continue along its old path."[18] The movement superseded Herzl and would keep him only as long as he articulated its dreams.

In these articles Jabotinsky wanted his readers to view him not as a mere observer, but as someone who was involved, potentially a leader. He analyzed what it takes to be a leader and expressed respect, awe, surprise, and affection for Herzl. In this indirect way, Jabotinsky linked himself to Herzl, beginning a lifelong metonymic relationship meant to lend Jabotinsky credibility and political legitimacy.

His reportage reflected enthusiasm, but his private correspondence was more critical of the movement at that moment. A letter to his close friend Kornei Chukovsky presented a different perspective altogether, one grounded in the material reality of Basel. He complained about the wasteful expenditures for transportation, how he was harangued when he gave his short speech and almost got arrested for having sex in public. "I took the trip and it was boring and stupid and I wasted 500 rubles doing it. At the congress I got whistled at; however, I did not leave. And the next day, that is, at night, I was caught by a policeman *in flagrante delicto* with a Zionist lady on the cathedral grounds. I was almost given a summons!"[19] Apparently Zionist congresses, like congresses everywhere, were characterized by extracurricular entertainments that often do not make it into the history books.

Jabotinsky had the opportunity to deepen the connection between himself and Herzl at the time of the latter's death a year later in 1904. The event affected the entire movement.[20] Chlenov wrote:

> The completely unexpected news about his illness reached the organization and then the death of the beloved leader. We all experienced this blow with our heart and mind, and it was useless to speak about its significance. Now, it seems, everyone understood, how much we have lost in him. But only a close and objective study will show us how much we had in life, so much beauty, strength, truth, and purity. Doctor Herzl's death revealed still more clearly how strongly attached the organization was to him. Many people have entirely loosened their grip, faith in success is broken, and energy for work has weakened.[21]

Herzl's death made an indelible impression on Jabotinsky. In 1904, in a literary response, Jabotinsky described his unshakable love and admiration. He devoted a poem, "Hêsped," and an article, "Sitting on the Floor" ("Sidia na polu"), to the event. Incidentally, Jabotinsky carefully shaped these works to produce the appearance of a personal connection with the leader. Both appeared in *Evreiskaia Zhizn'* (*Jewish Life*) in April 1905.

In "Hêsped," Jabotinsky immortalized Herzl. The first lines compare him to Moses, a trope that was gaining relevance at the time:

> He did not disappear like ancient Moses,
> On the edge of the promised land;
> He did not reach his desired homeland
> Far from her pining children;
> He burned himself and gave his life to a sacred cause,
> And "If I forget you, Jerusalem,"—

> But he did not reach it and fell while still in the desert,
> And on the best day, to our native Palestine
> We will commit just the ashes of the tribune.²²

The link with Moses, who led the people to the holy land, reflects Jabotinsky's image of a prophet to whom a promise has been made. Hêsped as a generic type is a poem of mourning and a conventional hagiography. Formally, the poem appears conventional in the Russian context, although at the same time, there are distinct details from Herzl's own life that Jabotinsky transfers into poetry, such as the famous line from the 1903 Zionist Congress, "I won't forget you, Jerusalem." Although there is much one could say about the poem, perhaps its most striking feature is its similarity with the "Lay of Igor" ("Slovo o polku igoreve"), the most important East Slavic saga written in the fourteenth century. For example, the following comparison of Herzl with an eagle is almost lifted from the epic tale.

> Sometimes he was a titan with granite shoulders,
> Sometimes he was an eagle with eagle eyes,
> On his forehead an eagle's sorrow.

By comparing Herzl and Igor, the author underscores the victory inherent in both texts. The defeat of ancient Rus' leads to the realization that the East Slavic people constitute the Russian nation. Similarly, Herzl's death contains a promise: the people will join together to regain their homeland. Despite the title, the poem diverges from a traditional Jewish memorial, but resembles a Russian ode.²³

In "Sitting on the Floor," a prose essay published in the same issue of *Evreiskaia Zhizn'*, Jabotinsky alludes to *shiva*, a week of mourning following the death of a close relative. Jabotinsky describes Herzl's formidable talent: "His genius was not of an exclusive sphere, like the genius of an orator or writer or statesman: his genius was focused deeper, internally—in his great heart, a heart of tremendous sensitivity that could understand the spirit of each moment and prompted the orator, the writer and the leader with the necessary word. His primary and essential talent, perhaps, consisted in this amazing art of finding the necessary word at the right time."²⁴

Attachment to Herzl was a tactic that Jabotinsky used to enhance his own image in the Zionist movement. He depicted himself as altered forever by Herzl. He wrote, "We became different people, we came alive from touching the ground that he placed beneath our feet. Only recently have I truly felt the ground under my feet, and understood only from that minute what it means to live and breathe. And if tomorrow I would awaken and suddenly see that it had all been a dream, that my former self and the ground under my feet did not exist and never had existed, I would kill myself, because one who has breathed the air of the mountaintop cannot return in resignation and sit beside the ditch."[25]

Throughout his life, Jabotinsky tried to draw parallels between himself and Herzl. Herzl appears numerous times in *Story of My Life* in various treatments, narrated in a serious as well as a jocular tone. For example, Jabotinsky relates what would appear to be an embarrassing scandal: Herzl threw him off the stage at the Congress. In the letter to Chukovsky cited above, Jabotinsky records the negative reception of his speech ("they 'whistled' at me").

What Jabotinsky says transpired was the following: Jabotinsky devoted his speech at the Congress to a defense of Herzl's travels to Russia and his meeting with Count Plehve, the hated interior minister. According to Jabotinsky's account in *Story of My Life*, it was taboo to speak on the subject, and everyone knew it. When he raised the issue, a general tumult arose. In response to the noise in the hall, Herzl came out from the back and asked Weizmann what the young man was saying in Russian. Weizmann responded, "Quatsch. [Nonsense.]" And Herzl announced, "Ihre Zeit ist um. [Your time is up.]"[26]

Of course, the story reflects Jabotinsky's preoccupations in 1936: his competition with Weizmann and his desire to underscore his love for Herzl, even facing the latter's wrath in doing so. Nonetheless, it seems possible that Jabotinsky invented the story "from whole cloth," as Michael Stanislawski has argued, although his letter to Chukovsky accurately describes the catcalls that he received.[27]

But Jabotinsky did not stop there. He continues in *Story of My Life*, solemnly announcing that

> Herzl made a colossal impression on me—this word is no exaggeration, no other description would fit: colossal. And I am not one of those who will easily bow to any personality—in general, I do not remember, out of all the experiences I had in my life, any man who impressed me either before Herzl or after him about whom I felt that, truly, there stands before me a man of destiny, a prophet and leader by the grace of God deserving to be followed even through error. . . . And even today it seems to me that I hear his voice ringing in my ears, as he swore to all of us: "Im eshkahech Yerushalayim . . ." ("If I forget thee, Jerusalem . . .").[28]

Jabotinsky never stopped trying to appropriate Herzl's authority, often asserting that he alone retained a commitment to Herzl's political Zionism, with its emphasis on a political breakthrough. Though in 1904 he embraced "Synthetic Zionism," which included support for both political Zionism and practical settlement, by 1925 he was emphasizing his attachment to Herzl and calling his new party Revisionism (HaTzoHar), meaning a revision of Herzl's original "Basel" Zionism. In a 1926 policy statement, *What Do Revisionists Want?*, Jabotinsky explicitly announced that he had embraced Herzl's legacy. "With a firm belief, we call on the Zionist public to renew Herzl's tradition—the energetic, systematic and peaceful political struggle to attain our demands."[29] And what were these demands? "The first goal of Zionism is the creation of a Jewish majority in Palestine, East and West of the Jordan [River]. That is not the last final goal of the Zionist movement which has several broader ideals, such as the solution of the Jewish Question in the whole world and the creation of a new Jewish culture."[30]

In different ways Jabotinsky developed the image of father-son, mentor-student, and leader and successor, as though he photoshopped a picture of himself standing next to Herzl. In all these permutations, Jabotinsky conceived Herzl as a Nietzschean, one who exploited every moment and embodied the qualities of the ideal man. Although Herzl was superhuman and therefore impossible to emulate fully, nonetheless Jabotinsky believed that it was our task to try to do so. In fact, Herzl is the Nietzschean figure who inspires precisely because his example is unattainable. The virtues he possesses include confidence, discipline, ambition, prophetic vision, an ability to convince and inspire, and a sense that the real and unreal are not far apart.

Today we may be used to adulation of Herzl, but it is worth recalling that Russian Zionists in 1903 had ambivalent feelings toward him.[31] They did not begrudge him his greatness as an organizer and genuine leader, nor did they deny his brilliance as an orator, but they faulted Herzl for a lack of Jewish spirit, a complaint first raised by Ahad-Ha'am.[32] They also opposed his exclusive emphasis on political Zionism, preferring the expansion of settlements and pioneers. The democratic faction within the camp (including Martin Buber, Weizmann, and many Russian Zionists) criticized Herzl's authoritarian approach to guiding the movement. For example, most Russian Zionists expressed anger at Herzl's trip to Russia to meet Viacheslav Plehve, which they felt was unseemly after the events in Kishinev.

If the meeting with Plehve without proper consultation with his Russian colleagues showed insensitivity, Russian Zionists were more shocked by Herzl's Uganda proposal. Chlenov writes that "[Uganda] brought in our ranks an extremely strong tumult, from which the movement has not yet calmed down. Not just one of the foundation stones has been shaken, but the whole building has cracked."[33] It seemed to take the movement in the direction of Territorialism and away from Zionism. Furthermore, they had long expressed skepticism about Herzl's dream of a quick diplomatic breakthrough and maintained that his public proclamations harmed the cause because they brought unwanted attention and raised suspicions among the Ottomans.

These debates harkened back to the East-West divide in which Herzl wanted to employ diplomacy to secure for the Jews a charter, or the legal right to immigrate to Palestine.[34] The East-European Jews often found Herzl's go-it-alone attitude naïve and self-destructive. Far more could be achieved, they maintained, if one harnessed the collective efforts of the entire movement.

Though he admired Herzl, Jabotinsky was less enamored of his politics than his personality. Jabotinsky would remember that the leader's personality, his effect on others, did not always coincide with the wisdom of his politics. In fact, Jabotinsky counted himself among those who favored the Russian position:

> We will create a beautiful program consolidating our influence in our irredentist land, and we will realize this program day after day, step by step, stubbornly and relentlessly. The work for Palestine will revive in us an ancient organic connection with the beloved little homeland of a great tribe, and even those among us today who once subscribed to the ranks of those indifferent to their origins will love her once again. This is the only path that can unify the disparate elements that nothing can unify, except for the living work on the living task dear to our heart.[35]

This and other expressions of sympathy for Palestine won him friends among the Russian leaders, Ussishkin, Chlenov, and Bernstein-Kogan.

* * *

In 1904, Jabotinsky decided to leave Odessa for St. Petersburg, where he had been invited to join the editorial board of *Evreiskaia Zhizn'*. He arrived in time to contribute to the paper's inaugural issue. At the same time, he was also invited to write for *Rus'*, a liberal newspaper edited by Aleksei Suvorin Jr., the son of the conservative publisher Aleksei Suvorin. In his autobiography, Jabotinsky claims that he fled to St. Petersburg in order to escape an arrest warrant in Odessa.[36] Although the police in Odessa did seek his arrest (Svetlana Natkovich described Jabotinsky's fear of imprisonment), like so many provincials he also yearned for fame and a bigger stage in the capital city.[37]

Jabotinsky's stay in St. Petersburg was problematic because as a Jew, he did not have a legal right to live in the capital. Only so-called "privileged Jews" had the right to live in St. Petersburg—for example, Jewish members of the first merchant guild, Jews with a diploma, and certain other categories of "useful Jews."[38] Nikolai Sorin, the editor of *Evreiskaia Zhizn'*, found Jabotinsky a hotel where it was possible to bribe the police so that he could live without fear of arrest. Jabotinsky lived in St. Petersburg on and off for the next several years.

To understand Jabotinsky at this time, we need to examine *Rassvet*, also known as *Evreiskaia Zhizn'*. One can not exaggerate the importance of the newspaper for the propagation of Zionist ideas in Russia. It was printed in the Russian language and was expressly devoted to the idea of Zionism, a Jewish home in Palestine. Its readership rivaled the most popular newspapers in Russia.[39]

In contrast to the hands-on experience of the Second Aliyah figures—Ben-Gurion, Berl Katsenelson, Yitzhak Tabenkin, and others who went to Palestine to promote agricultural settlements—the character of *Rassvet* (*Evreiskaia Zhizn'*) was elitist, urban, and intellectual. Nikolai Sorin, a wealthy businessman, founded the journal by paying the government a fee for a license and then set about attracting a team to help him run it. The contributors were talented individuals: Yuly Brutskus, Daniil Pasmanik, Shlomo Gepstein, Alexander Goldstein, Vladimir Jabotinsky, Arye Babkov, Arnold Seiderman, Max Soloveichik, and an engineer, Moshe Zeitlin.[40] This group acquired the name Halastra, which means "group" or "club" in Polish, reflecting the bohemian assembly of young intellectuals.

Admittedly, the newspaper was something of a strange bird, a Zionist weekly in the Russian language, published in the country's capital, a city that most of the contributors could not live in, at least not lawfully.[41] The first editor, Moisei Margolin, articulated the goals of the journal, declaring, among other things, the right to Jewish self-consciousness, self-preservation, and a land of their own.[42] "Enough! It is time to finish our wanderings, time for the landless Jewish people to get its own piece of land, time for the European peoples to acknowledge the heavy guilt of their millennia-long persecutions of the wandering people, and give them the opportunity to stop being a foreign body in an alien organism and to live freely on their own land."[43] Margolin continued his argument: for the past two thousand years, the Jews had devoted themselves to the well-being of other countries and peoples; now they had to change course and concentrate on themselves.

Zionist theory was important, but praxis—what was happening today—was paramount for a weekly newspaper. And the watchword of the moment was "crisis." The political shake-up in Russia itself was leading to excitement and political awareness. Yehiel Chlenov predicted positive changes on the horizon. Externally things seemed negative, but Zionism was growing stronger and building a broader constituency:

> In the last two years, life has been far from normal. It abandoned direct practical questions because forces passed over to the ideological struggle, spiritual work. Zionism turned inward, into itself; it experienced and experiences to this day a period of internal birth, the formation of new ideas, new foundations and new forces. It would therefore be wrong to define the true pulse of Zionist life only by means of external indicators. One should go deeper, examine the internal life of the clubs. And we will see in almost all the regions three analogous phenomena: the weakening, in places the death of existing forms, the strengthening of those who survived, and the planting of new kinds of new forces.[44]

In 1905, the number of shekel-payers in Russia surpassed seventy thousand, which was significantly lower than earlier, although in his calculations Chlenov acknowledged that communication with the provinces was unreliable, and therefore membership numbers could be higher.[45]

After two issues, the editorship of *Evreiskaia Zhizn'* passed to Avram Idel'son, who was more dynamic and envisioned a vital, popular, and intellectually vibrant paper. Idel'son decided to face the crisis directly in order to solve it. But first one needed a diagnosis. What was the crisis?

According to Idel'son, Herzl had directed the movement singlehandedly, but his imperious attitude had thwarted grassroots and local initiatives. For one thing, the total dependence on diplomacy hindered efforts to colonize Palestine. Also, Herzl's conception of his own role left little space for developing new leaders from among the younger generation. Finally, Herzl had not attained a charter or a promise of rights to a Jewish homeland in Palestine. Thus, Zionism found itself at a crossroads: the political movement Herzl had established was exhausted. If it was to be revitalized, it would need to pursue new directions. Idel'son had some idea of how to escape the cul-de-sac.

As is well known, Ahad-Ha'am formulated the idea that the Galut (Jewish Diaspora) was objectively negated, although subjectively there was no escaping the fact that millions of Jews lived and would continue to live outside of Eretz Yisrael. Therefore, theory had to surrender to praxis; it was unclear when or if the Diaspora would ever come to an end.[46]

Calling his idea Synthetic Zionism, Idel'son advocated a reevaluation of the Galut, asking whether participation in the political life of host societies should be encouraged.[47] Idel'son argued that Diaspora life was far from merely a wasteland. At a minimum, it offered educational opportunities and preparation for life in Palestine.

Idel'son's style of argumentation was paradoxical. He started with an antinomy—for example, that Marxism denied the reality of nationalism. Then he claimed that Marxism was wrong because nationalism was a powerful force that energized capitalism. Capitalism, however, competed with nationalism and sought the assimilation of minority nations because a single unified nation-state provided the most effective means of producing and consuming products and services. Assimilation was therefore inevitable. Concretely, the Jews of Russia would ultimately be forced to integrate due to economic pressures. For Jews, therefore, the only solution was emigration to Palestine, where Jews would compose the hegemonic culture to which others would need to assimilate.[48] Paradoxically, in Idel'son's view, Jews in Russia must fight to promote Jewish interests, all the while knowing that efforts to retain Jewish difference in the Diaspora were doomed to failure.[49]

Jabotinsky described Idel'son's position this way:

> Our ideal consisted in preserving only what is alive in Judaism, the energy that at one time was transferred into our workshops; i.e., they shook the dust of the Diaspora from their feet. That [ideal] is still true. But now we bend down and pick up from the ground the clumps of this 'dust' and try to analyze them. We immediately see that it is full of valuable organic ingredients that turn out to be productive when used properly. Let us analyze the ghetto. A terrible institution that has poisoned us physically and morally—but at its base is found the healthy principle of estrangement, and it is worth cultivating this principle [albeit] in a different form. At the same time, take assimilation: an indisputable illness, moral gangrene—but it put into our hands the whole cultural arsenal of modernity without which we would not even be able to dream of any building. Take the Jew's cowardliness and physical passivity, his response to a pogrom, "the dark cellar." It is shameful and an invitation to other pogromists, but in certain conditions it is precisely the very best method for a weak minority's self-defense.[50]

While Jabotinsky promoted the conclusion that one needed to empty the Galut and move the Jewish people to Palestine to create a Jewish majority there, the other parts of Idel'son's program appealed to him too. Jabotinsky was strongly tethered to the Galut and well prepared to engage in Russian politics with his expert knowledge of Russian language and culture. In fact, this was a vital point because Jabotinsky was weak in Jewish subjects—Hebrew and Jewish ritual practice. However, his knowledge of Western culture gave him "the arsenal" with which to dream of liberation. Jabotinsky began to espouse Synthetic Zionism and engagement with political life in the Diaspora.

Idel'son played a vital role in Jabotinsky's career as an ideological lodestar and mentor. Everyone who met Idel'son acknowledged his brilliance. Jabotinsky lauded Idel'son as a rare genius.

> I am sure that it is no exaggeration if I say that to describe the value of Idel'son the word "talent" is inadequate—that man stood on the border of "genius." "Acid all-corroding brain"—[Osip] Gruzenberg once said to me speaking of Idel'son, and he was right. But that was merely one face of a multifaceted crystal. His "acidity" consumed only the shells; into the kernels he knew to inject vivifying magic fluids. The curse of his destiny, the fate of a pauper—as were most of the members of our circle—or perhaps also, and to a certain extent, the self-neglect originating in the same "acidness," prevented him from explicating his ideas in the form of a definite treatise.... But to us youngsters, even without his "works" his company was like a university.[51]

In early 1905 the Revolution erupted, and Jabotinsky, like many others, got caught up in the political wave. In "Sketches without a Title," Jabotinsky wrote:

> But when *we* grow old, and the question is raised for us by the next generation—how will *we* justify ourselves and on what will we rely? Our time is not like that of our fathers. A somnolent quiet enveloped them, while we are surrounded by noise and rumbling: something is falling apart, something is being built, thousands of guides seek thousands of new paths, new banners are flashing in the air and new words are rattling—"the ice is coming," thundering, striking, breaking into pieces everything that succumbs to pressure. Whoever has been fated to live in this roar of life and nevertheless lives to old age, what will he say on Passover night with empty hands to both his children in response to their questioning and justified "*Ma*"? ["What?"][52]

At this time Jabotinsky called on young men and women to devote three years to service in Palestine, coining for the first time the name, "Monism," which he defined as the obligation of a Zionist to devote all one's strength and energy exclusively to the Zionist project.⁵³ Jabotinsky compared this commitment with army service. "This is military duty. For many centuries the Jewish people did not have their own soldiers; now the time has come for them. He who becomes a soldier in times of war, if he loves his homeland, he will not ask questions about whether he will be well fed and warm during the campaign. We are in wartime too, and let our warriors be ready for heavy work and for hunger and cold."⁵⁴ One can hear the voice of the future recruiter for the Jewish Legion here. Regarding the comment that the Jewish people did not have soldiers, it is essential to note that Jews were not only enlisted in the Russian army but were overrepresented at this time.⁵⁵

Jabotinsky's early articles in *Evreiskaia Zhizn'* showed the influence of Menachem Ussishkin, who emphasized total sacrifice for the sake of practical achievements in Palestine. Ussishkin was an important model since he was the leader of the practical camp, a builder of institutions in Odessa who effectively organized people and money.⁵⁶ In 1905, Ussishkin published "Our Program," a manifesto that outlined his solution to the crisis of Zionism. Ussishkin called for synthesis, intense movement on all fronts—practical, theoretical, and diplomatic. He pleaded for the fulfillment of the Basel program, including the resurrection of Hebrew as a living language, diplomacy with the Sultan and the European powers, and the purchase of tracts of land in Palestine to house the growing Jewish population. His main innovation, however, was the formulation of a "Jewish University Society of Workmen" (*Weltarbeitergenossenschaft*). He called on young men to devote three years of their lives to the cultivation of land in Palestine. A group of volunteers, "unmarried young men, physically and mentally sound, must be formed. It should be the duty of every member of this society to go to Palestine for three years, in order to perform his military duty to the Jewish people, not with musket and sword, but with plow and sickle. These thousands of young people will be obliged to present themselves in the colonies, in order to offer their services as laborers at the same wages that Arabs receive."⁵⁷

Ussishkin's goal was to instill a "bond between the Jews of Palestine and the Jews of the lands of the exile [so that it] will cease to be a paper one (prayers, books, periodicals), and ... become a living one."⁵⁸ He maintained that this experience would cultivate a new prophet, a new Herzl,

> whose appearance our people has awaited for thousands of years. Neither the unemancipated nor the spiritual Ghetto of the lands of the exile will rear him, but the free spirit of the mountains of Judea and Galilee. He will open

unto us the gates of our home not from without, but from within. He will unite in himself the courage and might of old Bar Kochba with the spirit and the charm of our contemporary Herzl. Boldly and proudly will he plant in the sight of the whole world the blue and white banner of liberated Israel upon Mount Zion.[59]

By promoting similar practical efforts to Judaize Palestine, Jabotinsky borrowed from Ussishkin. Jabotinsky's relationship to Ussishkin went beyond a shared love for active settlement of the land. In fact, Jabotinsky worked as a kind of apprentice, helping Ussishkin conduct his extensive schedule of meetings and serving as his personal ambassador. As their correspondence from 1904–05 shows, Jabotinsky kept Ussishkin abreast of his activities, where he went and whom he met.[60]

It is worth mentioning that in Herzl, Ahad-Ha'am, and Ussishkin, Jabotinsky had created for himself a combination of three spiritual fathers—political, intellectual, and practical. Although he was still a novice in politics, he modeled himself on strong men who had a great deal to teach him.

Notes

1. Michael Heymann, ed., *The Uganda Controversy: Minutes of the Zionist General Council*. 2 vols. (Jerusalem: Hassifriya Haziyonit, 1977).
2. Vladimir Jabotinsky, "Bazel'skie vpechatleniia: Congress sionistov. Ot nashego korrespondenta," *Odesskie Novosti* (August 19, 1903); "Bazel'skie vpechatleniia: 'Mizrakhi.' Ot nashego korresp.," *Odesskie Novosti* (August 20, 1903); "Bazel'skie vpechatleniia: Gertsl' i Neinsager'y," *Odesskie Novosti* (August 23, 1903).
3. Gur Alroey, *Zionism without Zion: The Jewish Territorial Organization and Its Conflict with the Zionist Organization* (Detroit: Wayne State University Press, 2016), 31–44.
4. Vladimir Jabotinsky, "Bazel'skie vpechatleniia: Shestoi kongress sionistov" in Jabotinsky, *Polnoe sobranie sochinenii v deviati tomakh* (Minsk: Met, 2007), 3:376–377.
5. Ibid., 377.
6. Yehuda Slutzky, *Ha-itonut ha-yehudit-rusit be-reshit be-mea ha-esrim (1900–1918)* (Tel Aviv: Ha-aguda le-haker toldot ha-yihudim, 1978), 204–218.
7. Yehiel Chlenov, *Sion i afrika na shestom kongresse* (Moscow: Poplavskii, 1905), 28.
8. A somewhat different impression was given by Yehiel Chlenov. See note 7.
9. Jabotinsky, "Bazel'skie vpechatleniia: Gertsl'," 399.
10. Ibid., 400.
11. Ibid., 402–403.
12. Ibid., 402.
13. Ibid., 391–92.
14. Jabotinsky, "Bazel'skie vpechatleniia: Gertsl'," 392.

15. There are many articles on Vladimir Solov'ev and the Jews, see Brian. Horowitz, "Vladimir Solov'ev and the Jews: A View from Today," *The Russian-Jewish Tradition: Intellectuals, Historians, Revolutionaries* (Boston: Academic Studies, 2017), 198–214.
16. Jabotinsky, "Bazel'skie vpechatleniia: Gertsl'" 393.
17. Ibid.
18. Ibid., 403.
19. Letter of Vladimir Jabotinsky to Kornei Chukovsky, December 10, 1903. Jabotinsky Institute Archives.
20. Yitzhak Greenbaum, "Me-Varsha ad Helsingfors (shalosh veidot rishonot shel tsionim be-rusya)," *Katsir: Kovets le-Korot* 1:33.
21. Yehiel Chlenov, *Polozhenie sionizma v Rossii: k vii-mu kongresu* (St. Petersburg: Ts. Kraiz, 1905), 21.
22. Vladimir Jabotinsky, "Hêsped," *Evreiskaia Zhizn'* 13 (April 3, 1905): 8. "*Im eshkahech Yerushalayim*"—the line in Hebrew from Psalm 137:5, "If I forget you Jerusalem." The psalm continues, "May my right hand forget its cunning." Herzl made this the cornerstone of his speech at the Sixth Zionist Congress in order to undercut those who accused him of indifference to Palestine for promoting East Africa as a possible place of settlement.
23. Jabotinsky called his 1927 memoir about the Jewish Legion *Slovo o polku*, again using the East Slavic saga for his own purposes.
24. Vladimir Jabotinsky, "Sidia na polu . . . ," *Evreiskaia Zhizn'* 6 (June 1904): 15.
25. Ibid., 17.
26. Jabotinsky, *Story of My Life*, 23.
27. Michael Stanislawski, *Zionism and the Fin de Siècle: Cosmopolitanism and Nationalism from Nordau to Jabotinsky* (Berkeley: University of California Press, 2001), 119.
28. Jabotinsky, *Story of My Life*, 23–24.
29. Vladimir Jabotinsky, *Was wollen die Zionisten-Revisionisten* (Paris: Polyglotte, 1926), 16.
30. Ibid., 3.
31. Israel Klausner, *Opozitsiya le-Herzl* (Jerusalem: Akhiever, 1960), 6–7.
32. Chlenov, *Sion i Afrika*, 28.
33. Jabotinsky, *Polozhenie sionizma*, 19. Information on Yehiel Chlenov can be found in *Yehiel Tchlenov: Perkei hayav u'feulato, zichronot, ktavim, neumim, mikhtavim, 1863–1918* (Tel Aviv: Eretz Israel, 1937).
34. Shlomo Avineri, *Herzl's Vision and the Foundation of the Jewish State* (New York: BlueBridge, 2017), 12.
35. Vladimir Jabotinsky, "Sionizm i Palestina," *Evreiskaia Zhizn'* 2 (February 1904): 219.
36. Jabotinsky, *Story of My Life*, 73.
37. Svetlana Natkovich, *Ben aneney Zohar: Yetsirato shel Vladimir (Ze'ev) Z'abotinski ba-heksher ha-hevrati* (Jerusalem: Magnes, 2015), 95. It is worth wondering why the Petersburg police did not have authorization to arrest and send him to Odessa. The tsarist secret police, Okhrana, had a file on Jabotinsky that apparently continued until 1915. In 1905, Jabotinsky was tracked, as were other Zionists and revolutionaries. Matityahu Mintz, "Al shum ma hithakta ha-Okhrana' ha-tsarit al tse'avdav shel Z'abotinski?," in *Ish be-sa'ar: Masot u'mekharim 'al Ze'ev Z'abotinski*, ed. Avi Bareli and Pinhas Ginossar (Ber-Sheva: Universitat Ben-Guryon ba'Negev, 2004), 450–455.
38. Benjamin Nathans, *Beyond the Pale: The Jewish Encounter with Late Imperial Russia* (Berkeley: University of California Press, 2004), 17.

39. Slutzky, *Ha-itonut ha-yehudit rusit be-mea ha-esrim*, 203–267. On subscriptions to Jewish newspapers see Vladimir Levin, "Verbreitung jüdischer Zeitschriften in Rußland: Sprache versus Geographie," in *Die jüdische Presse im europäischen Kontext, 1686–1900*, ed. Susanne Marten-Finnis and Marcus Winkler (Bremen: Edition lumière, 2006), 101–116.

40. Jabotinsky, *Story of My Life*, 74.

41. It might be noted that a Yiddish newspaper, *Der Fraynd*, began publishing in 1903 in St. Petersburg.

42. M. M. Margolin, *Osnovnye techeniia v istorii evreiskogo naroda: etiud po filosofii istorii evreev* (St. Petersburg: Severnaia Skoropechatnia, 1900).

43. M. M. Margolin, "O zadachakh Evreiskoi Zhizni," *Evreiskaia Zhizn'* 1 (1904): 1.

44. Chlenov, *Polozhenie sionizma*, 17.

45. Ibid., 9.

46. "Negation of the *Galut*" means the idea that Jews needed to leave the Diaspora and form a new commonwealth in their historic homeland. Robert Seltzer, "Ahad-Ha'am and Dubnow: Friends and Adversaries," *At the Crossroads: Essays on Ahad-Ha'am*, ed. Jacques Kornberg (Albany: State University of New York Press, 1983), 67.

47. Although Idel'son is hardly remembered now, émigrés published two volumes dedicated to him. *Sefer Idelsohn: Divre ha-arakhah ve-zikhronot, toldot hayav u'khetavav* (Tel Aviv: Omanut, 1946); Yu. D. Brutskus et al., ed., *Sbornik pamiati A. D. Idel'sona* (Berlin: Lutse & Bogt, 1925).

48. Avram Idel'son, "Marksizm i evreiskii vopros," *Evreiskaia Zhizn'* 8 (August 1905): 86.

49. Certainly this differed from Ber Borochov's position that neither assimilation nor equal rights are possible since a loss in economic competition is foreordained.

50. Vladimir Jabotinsky, "U kolybeli Gel'singforskoi programmy," in Brutskus, *Sbornik pamiati A. D. Idel'sona*, 90. "Ma" refers, of course, to the first of the Hebrew "Four Questions," recited on Passover.

51. Jabotinsky, *Story of My Life*, 75.

52. Vladimir Jabotinsky, "Nabroski bez zaglaviia," *Khronika Evreiskoi Zhizni* 14 (February 10, 1905): 8.

53. The concept comes from Leibniz and refers to a closed system, such as a person whose perception of the world is limited to the five senses.

54. Jabotinsky, "Sionizm i Palestina," 69.

55. Yochanan Petrovsky-Shtern, *Jews in the Russian Army, 1827–1917: Drafted into Modernity* (Cambridge: Cambridge University Press, 2014), 202.

56. At this time Ussishkin headed the Zionists in Odessa, having recently relocated from Yekaterinoslav. Yossi Goldshtein, *Ussishkin biografiya: ha-tekufa ha-rusit, 1853–1919*, 2 vols. (Jerusalem: Magnes Press, 2000), 1:211.

57. M. Ussischkin, *Our Program: An Essay*, trans. D. S. Bondheim (New York: Federation of American Zionists, 1905), 27.

58. Ibid., 28.

59. Ibid., 36–37.

60. See, for example, this letter from Jabotinsky to Ussishkin from May 28, 1906: "Regarding the congress: a) a large one in Odessa is impossible; b) a medium-size congress is almost impossible, c) a small, private conference by invitation is not necessary. But as commissioners they are simply obliged to hold a congress of the Union [of Zionist

journalists]. It was acknowledged that the initiative should not come from the official leaders. The commissioners will unanimously bless us (*Evreiskaia Zhizn'* and *Glos Żydowski*) to sign the invitation." See Jabotinsky's letters to M. Ussishkin, located in Jabotinsky Institute Archives. Some of these letters are also available in Zeev Zabotinski, *Igorot*, ed. Daniel Carpi (Jerusalem: Hassifriya Haziyonit, 1995), vol. 2.

3

IN REVOLUTION AND COUNTERREVOLUTION, 1905–1906

* * *

THE 1905 REVOLUTION PRODUCED A GROWTH SPURT IN Jabotinsky. He developed as a Zionist theorist, a thinker on nationalism, and a leader in the movement. He rightfully calculated that the revolution could help him promote his role as a propagandist and also a devoted activist, and he worked hard on his self-presentation to attain a new status in the eyes of Russian Zionists and, without exaggerating, Russian politicians too. The upheaval in the country was breaking down ossified hierarchies and advancing new leaders. Chlenov stated, "Zionism has ceased being a hobby, fashion, and has become a question of life, shapes one's worldview."[1]

In later days, Jabotinsky described himself as part of the generation shaped by the Revolution of 1905.[2] Known as "Russia's first revolution," it began as a struggle for political reform among liberals, but then passed into the hands of radicals. Russia's defeat in the 1904 Russo-Japanese War had shaken the entire system and elicited calls for change that intensified after Bloody Sunday in January 1905.[3] The revolution was extinguished thanks mainly to the tsar's concession in October 1905, his *Manifesto on the Improvement of the State Order*, in which he outlined political reforms, including elections to a parliament, dubbed the State Duma, and the rights to political assembly and public expression without censorship.[4] Some of these rights were ignored in reality and were partially reversed in 1907.

The year 1905 offered unexpected opportunities for the establishment of democratic politics generally and Jewish politics in particular. For decades, the government had resisted political change. It jailed revolutionaries and battled liberals; anyone who wanted change was targeted as an enemy. The government of Nicholas II had little trust in society; it censored the press and expected submission from the people.[5] Regarding Jews, the government continued, and at times intensified, discriminatory decrees. To deal with Jews, government officials were comfortable with the traditional institution of Jewish intercession (*Shtadlanut*)—wealthy Jews made private requests and deals with government officials on behalf of the Jewish community.[6]

However, in the years before 1905, a new kind of politics was emerging, led by the intelligentsia. Lawyers tried to use trials as public forums to show the injustice of the current system and embarrass the government.[7] Scholars and writers had long used cryptic, or "Aesopian," language to express their discontent. Gradually a new politics broke with the past: instead of private requests or trading favors, a system of pressure politics was taking shape. The revolutionary parties and public opinion began to matter more. Although the revolution failed to attain all its goals, the October Manifesto extended the franchise (voting) to Jews, and that concession triggered legal Jewish political activism across a broad spectrum. In 1906, elections to the First Duma took place.

The revolution transformed people. Jabotinsky followed the same emotional arc as many other Russians: ecstasy in the spring of 1905, cautious hope after the publication of the tsar's manifesto in October, and distrust after the dispersal of the First Duma in June 1906. Like other Jews, Jabotinsky was appalled by the anti-Jewish pogroms, including a major one in his native Odessa, in October 1905. These were particularly painful: hundreds were killed; Jews were singled out for violence; the revolution, which had promised to unify the multiethnic population, had failed to do so. In October 1905 especially, it appeared to many Jews that the revolutionaries would accept a bargain with the government: liberation for Russians, but the denial of rights for others.

The revolution made an indelible impression on Jabotinsky because it showed that reactionary forces, while powerful, would not necessarily win. The possibility of a different Russia, characterized by freedom, equality, democracy, and unity between Russians and the country's national minorities, had emerged, and now that it had emerged, it would be hard to put the genie back in the bottle.[8]

In *Story of My Life*, Jabotinsky poetically describes the general attitude at the time. "Youth was not only inside us—it was in the air; the youth of the entire country, the youth of the whole of Europe. Such periods in the history of the world do not occur often—periods when many peoples quiver with hopeful expectancy, like a young boy waiting for his girl. Such was the case for Europe before the year 1848, as it was also at the beginning of the twentieth century, that deceitful century that frustrated so many of our hopes."[9] Now comes his self-conscious confession:

> To say that we were naïve then, without experience, that we believed in easy and cheap progress—like an instantaneous leap from darkness to light—would be incorrect. We had already witnessed murder on the cusp of the holiday [the October pogroms of 1905], and especially then, precisely that winter, we already knew that all the reactionary elements were shaping their ranks into a huge, mighty, and powerful army. But in spite of all these facts, faith, the charm of the nineteenth century, had not died in our hearts. We were certain in our belief in abstract principles, in sacred slogans—freedom, fraternity, justice—and despite everything, we were certain that the day of their triumph had come and would overcome all obstacles.[10]

It is important to remember that Jews were a small minority in Russia, just 4 percent of the population; despite being overrepresented in the revolutionary movement, they were still only minor partners. Although Zionist revolutionary groups were emerging at this time, most Zionists, especially non-Marxists, aligned themselves with Russian liberals.[11] They viewed themselves as struggling for essential rights that could be attained only through the transformation of the tsarist regime from a monarchy with limitless powers to a government restrained by a constitution. Therefore, although previously Zionists tended to regard Jewish members of the Kadet (Constitutional Democratic) party as "assimilators" (a word they bandied about to disparage their opponents), now there was reconciliation.[12] Zionists realized that, to have any impact, they would need allies, and liberals were the best they could find, since the Kadets supported equal rights for Jews. In fact, they supported equal rights for all the national minorities in Russia.

During the revolution not only the Zionists but all the Jewish political organizations to the right of the Bund joined liberal Russia. Viktor Kel'ner has written, "By the beginning of the new century a considerable part of the Jewish intelligentsia fully associated itself with the general Russian liberal movement. They saw the fate of the Jews of Russia only through the prism of their active, shared participation in the political struggle with autocracy."[13]

During 1905, Jabotinsky was active on a number of fronts. In addition to advocating a political struggle, he also defended Jewish rights.[14] During

1905 and 1906, Jabotinsky participated in the League for the Attainment of Full Rights among the Jews of Russia, the body that sought to unify the Jewish political parties to the right of the Bund into a single coalition that could influence political life in the Duma. At the same time, he wrote about a future Jewish politics in Russia, modifying ideas of "autonomy" that he gleaned from Austro-Marxists such as Otto Bauer, Karl Renner, and Max Adler, who sharply critiqued capitalism and advanced ideas of national autonomy.

* * *

During the revolution, the Jewish Workers' Party of Russia, Poland, and Lithuania—the Bund—was the most popular Jewish political organization. It had a membership of fifty thousand; its sympathizers were many times that. Formed in 1897, its mission was to represent the Jewish worker by organizing strikes for higher wages and by promoting revolutionary political activity.[15] Bund leaders sought to overthrow the tsarist regime and construct a new society based on socialism. The Bund had been part of the Russian Social Democrats until 1903, but they decided to leave the party because of the attacks on the Bund's national dimension and the claim that non-Bundists could not understand the true needs of the Jewish worker.[16]

The Bund had advantages over Zionism. For a time, its alliance with the revolutionary parties seemed to promise political transformation and the end of tsarism. Additionally, the Bund had come to be associated with Jewish self-defense. That helped its popularity during the summer and especially the fall of 1905, when Jews were under attack by elements hostile to the revolution.

The Bund's success appeared to mirror Zionism's failure. Fewer people were paying the single shekel membership. With Russia up in arms, Zionism, with its emphasis on settlement in Palestine, seemed irrelevant. It also did not help that Zionism was considered a plaything of the well-to-do that had little in common with the working class. Jabotinsky responded by reaching out to workers and explaining to them that Zionists were the original defenders of Jewish interests and remained uncompromising advocates, whereas Bundists were divided in their loyalties.

In *The Bund and Zionism* (1906), Jabotinsky presented a simple argument. Instead of belittling the Bund, he praised its work, but compared it to a step on an evolutionary ladder in which Zionism represented a higher rung. To justify this hierarchy, Jabotinsky claimed that Zionism provided the Bund with its original inspiration: the consciousness of a Jewish nation and the desire to serve the nation's interests. Later, Bundist leaders grew that original seed into something different: a Jewish workers' party. However, Zionism differed from the Bund because the latter inevitably veered toward "assimilation"; "inevitably," because its calls for national self-renewal were subordinate to socialist unity and the denial of Jewish separatism. According to Jabotinsky, even the announcement in favor of national autonomy at the Bund's Fourth Conference (1901) reflected a promise that the leaders could not keep.

Comparing the Bund with the government's program to allow wage strikes but not politically motivated work stoppages (*Zubatovshchina*), Jabotinsky writes: "I do not place an equal sign between the Bund and the agents of autocracy, but the proclamation of national autonomy at the Bund's 4th Conference was an act of national *Zubatovshchina*. And in the same way that real *Zubatovshchina* was conceived subjectively for the elimination of Social Democracy, but objectively signified the subordination of aristocracy under the impact of Social Democracy—in exactly the same way the nationalization of the Bund program, undertaken for a struggle with Zionism, was in reality a concession to Zionism."[17]

"*Zubatovshchina*," named after the tsarist official who designed it—Sergei Zubatov—was a government policy intended to separate legitimate economic demands from revolutionary activity, and thereby isolate the revolutionaries from the ordinary workers. In the government's view, the policy was successful as a political strategy but went against its own economic goals. Simultaneously, many believed that the policy was dangerous since the success of "economic" strikes might whet a desire for increased political rights. Jabotinsky's point was that the Bund initiated the national policy in order to stave off Zionism, the party truly devoted to Jewish national interests. Jabotinsky further claimed that there was no need to compromise between Jewish nationalism and socialism. Only Zionism was designed to advance national politics without compromise or half-measures.

One should not get the impression from Jabotinsky's argumentation that he actually respected the Bund. His argument hung on the premise that the Bund and Zionists were not antipodes, as Bundists argued, but rather "two plants with a single root," each operating according to its own inner logic.[18] Thus, the Bund actually promoted Zionism's ideals. Jabotinsky writes, "When the future scholar writes a comprehensive history of the Zionist movement, one chapter in his work, perhaps, will draw the reader's special attention. It will immediately follow the chapters about Palestine immigration and Ahad-Ha'am's philosophy. At the beginning, its reader will encounter a repetition of Pinsker's ideas, at the end, the first proclamation of Poale Tsion. In this chapter, one of the episodes of Zionism will be recounted, and this chapter will be entitled 'Bund.'"[19] Incidentally, it is hard not to recall here the argument of Grigory Plekhanov that "Bundists are Zionists who fear sea sickness."[20]

However, for Jabotinsky the tactic of connecting the Bund and Zionists made sense since support taken from the Bund was a net win for Zionism. In the context of the Bund's boycott of the elections to the First Duma, Jabotinsky's Zionism filled the absence. He was saying, in essence: If you care about Jewish interests, you need not worry about the Bund's boycott of the Duma, since Zionism has stepped into the space that belonged to the Bund. Therefore, a vote for Zionism was actually a vote for Jewish nationalism in its superior form.

In his criticisms, Jabotinsky unabashedly pilfered from the enemy. Jonathan Frankel explains, "It was typical of the period that, in attacking the socialists, Jabotinsky tended to adopt their historico-philosophical modes of thought and even their vocabulary. He, too, spoke of the inevitably unfolding of historical necessities; of the logical development from revolution to Jewish national autonomy in Russia and from autonomy as a penultimate stage to final and maximal goals. This ideological framework was shared by all the Jewish socialist parties in 1906. More specifically, Jabotinsky adopted the incrementalist or quasi-evolutionist approach to revolution and territorialism first advanced in coherent ideological form by the Vozrozhdentsy in the years 1903–4."[21]

Jabotinsky's polemic against the Bund also reflected a degree of cynicism, since the two organizations clashed on every issue. Bundists rejected Jabotinsky's arguments as entirely divorced from reality because he willfully ignored the main differences: class conflict, coalitions with Russian parties, integration in Russia, and the question of Palestine. To a degree, the two movements appealed to different constituencies. The Bund courted the working class and intellectuals who supported the workers. Zionists rejected class conflict and stressed collective national unity. The Bund maintained that "unity" concealed the true interests of the Jewish bourgeoisie: to exploit the workers.[22] In addition, the Bund desired to link the Jewish masses to the international workers' movement, and asserted that Jews would remain in Eastern Europe.[23] For their part, Zionists rejected the Diaspora and envisioned a new society in Palestine. They also clashed on the language issue: the Bund embraced Yiddish and Jewish folk culture, whereas Zionists valorized Hebrew, the language of the Bible and the upper class (rabbis and the elite, for example).[24]

Bund representatives did not ignore Jabotinsky's attacks. At the Bund's Fourth, Fifth, and Sixth Conferences, representatives denounced Zionism as "bourgeois politics" that distracted the Jewish working class from its proper role.[25] In fact, the Bund apparently used its conflict with Zionism to score points with Russian radicals. Jabotinsky took note of the struggle. In response to a pro-Bund article in *Iskra*, he wrote: "The 'Bund' responded to this with an unprecedented intensification, so to speak, of repression against Zionists of every stripe. Every scrap of printing paper was to be utilized for the 'struggle.'"[26]

Apparently hostilities between the Bund and the other Jewish parties grew to such a degree that a Bund member killed a fellow Jew on ideological grounds.[27] Jabotinsky feigned disbelief, expressing hope that the killer had another motivation. "I would like to believe that a personal hatred existed between Bussel (the victim) and the gentleman from the 'Bund,' so that, actually, the confrontation was motivated by some secondary reason. Let it be a bad one, even dirty—just let it not turn out to be true that one person killed another person because of a difference in political beliefs. That would be too disgusting."[28]

Jabotinsky expressed his disdain for the Jewish political left in 1905–6, and held them in contempt in later years as well. Generally speaking, he distrusted left-wing leaders who were committed to Jewish nationalism; they would betray the people, he thought, if a deal were brokered to join a non-Jewish revolutionary party. Vladimir Medem, the Bund leader, admitted as much.[29] Despite what one would expect, Jabotinsky was not against socialism in theory—in fact, he admired syndicalism, another economic system based on what he considered collective consent—but he maintained that the Bund's national program was only an anodyne front for its real goal: assimilation in the international workers' movement.[30]

Although the Zionist-Bund feud continued, the pogrom violence unleashed in October 1905 showed the Jews' essential weakness. Jabotinsky used the violence to launch an attack. Making an allusion to Bundist position that Jews were part of Russia, Jabotinsky questioned worker cohesion:

> We live in a foreign country, we are in the hands of a foreign people. If they wish it, there will be pogroms, and we can die as courageous fighters, but we

cannot interfere. If they do not wish it, they will not give us even a basic measure of civic equality, and we cannot force them to because we make up a tiny minority. But one thing is in our power: we can summon the Jewish people, separate them from the surrounding peoples, and shape the people into a beautiful unity and cultivate a consciousness of national necessity and work.[31]

Highlighting anti-Jewish attitudes within the Russian working class, which precluded solidarity, Jabotinsky hoped to exploit the pogroms on behalf of Zionism.

* * *

When political assembly became possible, some Jewish leaders in Russia organized a coalition of political groups to the right of the revolutionaries. The organization called itself The League for the Attainment of Full Rights for the Jewish People in Russia, or the "League" for short.[32] The League was formed in spring 1905, impelled by the belief that Jews, as a small minority, had little influence over the country's political path. Thus, it made sense for Jewish political groups to join together. Of course, even a coalition could not attain power on its own— Jews would still need non-Jewish allies—but the goal was to make the best of a politically weak position. With regard to specific issues, coalitions could produce powerful lobbies. In fact, some Kadets complained about "unreasonable Jewish demands."[33]

Although other ethnic and religious groups faced government discrimination, Jews were the worst off. Thus, they had much to gain from political reforms that granted them the right to vote. Although the government had failed them, perhaps they could attain equal rights through democracy by lobbying among other (voting) groups in society.

However, the organization's leaders chose to use the appellation "full rights" in the League's title because, in addition to equal rights as citizens, they hoped to acquire additional national rights.[34] Those included government schools for Jews in a Jewish language, and other institutions: a Jewish theater, libraries, and so forth. Leaders wanted the government to fund these from general tax revenues in addition to the special Jewish taxes.

The League reflected an alliance of liberals and nationalists that was not uncommon. From the mid-1890s through the second Duma, Jewish non-Marxists made common cause with Russian liberals. Marxists were the internal political enemy. The goal of the League was to offer the Jewish masses an alternative to Marxism (the Bund as well as the Russian Socialist Democratic Labor Party). Thus the first meeting in Vilna brought together uncomfortable allies and produced a platform that was reluctantly agreed to in the face of the common foes.

Until October 1905, the word on the street had been "no enemies on the left"—everyone fought tsarism. Nicholas II drove a wedge into the broad camp in October with his manifesto. Jewish liberals (Maxim Vinaver) and Zionists (Shmarya Levin) stayed with the Kadets, but broke over the question of whether the twelve Jews elected to the first Duma would be a single, united faction, or merely an interest group, each member free to vote as he wished on any issue. Still, Kadets were seen as supporting Jewish rights. For example, Kadet leaders wanted to send a delegation to Bialystok in the summer of 1906 to investigate the pogrom that had taken place there but were thwarted by the government.

Because its members had different goals, the League was vulnerable to dissolution. Indeed, the breakup occurred in late 1906, when it became clear that the organization's basic goals could not be fulfilled.[35] The mission to find common cause ran aground on the shoals of ideological and tactical disagreement. For starters, the parties to the left of the Trudoviki (a small non-Marxist, pro-agrarian party) such as the Bund, did not participate because they opposed any non-class-based political actions. But even without them, liberals and so-called nationalists (including Zionists) faced challenges. Foremost was the question of compromise: What kinds of compromises could be justified, and which issues would lead to endless squabbles that risked the life of the League?

The League met four times in the course of nearly two years, and its membership rose from five thousand to almost ten thousand. The first meeting, in Vilna, in March 1905, set the tone for the future. Sixty-seven Jewish representatives from over thirty different Jewish communities gathered "to participate in organizing a Jewish political lobby that would advocate Jewish interests and concerns before the bar of progressive Russian opinion."[36] Alexander Orbach explains the organization's two goals: "(1) The relationship of the Jews to general society—here, of course, the need for full and equal rights for Jews became the central plank of the League's program—and (2) The nature of Jewish identity and Jewish communal structure within a newly democratized, reformed Russia."[37]

The largest group in the League, Jewish liberals, emphasized the need for unity under their leadership. The revolution was proceeding apace, and since liberals appeared to have the most popular support, it made sense to follow their lead. The liberal position was best articulated in the speeches and writings of the Jewish leader Maxim Vinaver. According to Viktor Kel'ner, "During the course of his entire life he defended the idea that Russian Jewry could attain equal rights only on condition of the complete support of Russian liberalism."[38]

However, by the League's second meeting, in November 1905, much had changed. Although Nicholas II's manifesto on October 15, 1905, had confirmed new political rights for the state's subjects, including the establishment of a legislative Duma, mass pogroms had broken out in the Pale of Settlement. A description is offered by Nahum Sokolow:

> [It] was one of the *ans terribles* in the annals of Jewish history. It was a year of bloodshed and terror. Not even the dark ages extracted so heavy a toll of Jewish blood: something like 1,400 pogroms took place all over the Ghetto. In many districts the Jewish population was completely exterminated. The number of persons directly affected, that is to say of those whose houses, shops, or factories were the objects of attack and pillage, reached a total of some 200,000 to 250,000. To this number must be added that of the clerks, workmen, etc., indirectly affected by the destruction of factories and shops, which could not be ascertained. The casualty list was estimated at approximately 20,000 murdered and 100,000 injured.[39]

The violence led many Jews to question the value of an alliance with Russians, even with Russian liberals. Orbach describes the atmosphere: "Emotions were running high, and the mood was extremely bitter and angry as some seventy representatives from thirty different locations gathered in St. Petersburg for the second Congress of the League for the Attainment of Full Rights for the Jews of Russia on November 22, 1905 (O.S.). In fact, the expectation was that many more delegates would have come, but the fear of traveling through the countryside in those violent days kept attendance down."[40]

Jabotinsky's attitude toward liberals was mixed. During the revolution he had complained that the Russian intelligentsia had abandoned Jews. Although Jews had supported the liberals in the struggle against the ruling power, they had received little in return. In fact, as Ahad-Ha'am had claimed, it seemed that the tsarist government had offered the Russian people a deal: they were permitted to beat Jews in exchange for withdrawing demands for political reform.[41] Semyon Dubnov agreed, saying that 1905 resembled 1648 more than 1848.[42] (1648 was the tragic year of the Chmelnitsky rebellion in Ukraine; 1848 was the year of the Spring of Nations, the partially successful revolutions in France, Germany, and Hungary.) In this complicated time, Jabotinsky gave a talk in St. Petersburg, where he chastised the Russian intelligentsia.[43] He said that he could bear the violence against Jews by the reactionaries but was disturbed by the workers' abandonment.[44] "People have tried to comfort us by telling us that there were no workers among those who murdered us. Perhaps. Perhaps it was not the proletariat who made pogroms on us. But what the proletariat did to us was something worse than that: they forgot us. That is the real pogrom."[45]

Once again Jabotinsky tried to separate Jews and non-Jews, to break the domination of the workers' movement, and point out that the promises of the proletariat were empty because the interests of Jews and non-Jews differed. However, it was something of a topos to claim, as Jews often did, that the lack of support from liberal Russia hurt more than the actual violence committed by antisemitic thugs and political reactionaries.[46] Incidentally, the revolutionary press of the time wrote a lot against the pogroms; they assumed that this would stop the revolution. The intelligentsia protested as well. Some non-Jewish revolutionary workers took a very active part in self-defense. On the other hand, there was a general feeling of embarrassment, since the pogromists were in fact mainly workers and peasants, who also attacked students, revolutionary workers, and anybody wearing glasses.

This speech presaged the soon-to-be screaming matches over the Jewish-liberal alliance. At the League's second meeting, in November 1905, Jabotinsky proposed negotiating a new compact to reflect the realization that Russian society had promoted pogroms. He described a trade-off: "The Russian Revolution will cost us a river of Jewish blood; we do not want to buy Russian freedom at such an expensive price! And what then? Are there really those among you, respectable people and friends, who are honest, who are unafraid to look at truth directly and have the courage to announce that this has not happened?"[47] According to Jabotinsky, the relationship of Jews and the revolution could be compared to two works of Russian literature, "Attalea Princeps" by Vsevolod Garshin and Mikhail Saltykov-Shchedrin's *The Golovlev Family*.

In the Garshin story, the protagonist, Attalea Princeps, has a dream of freedom, but when she shatters the glass ceiling, she is stung with thousands of shards. "For years we ran towards the light, towards open space, into the sunshine. And when the dawn of liberation flickered for the Russian people, an overcast and gloomy day met us Jews. Before us appeared dark and bloody clouds, eclipsing the last ray of the sun."[48] The Saltykov-Shchedrin tale is a little different and depicts a suicide pact in which Yudushka's cousins take poison, while the other backs out. The Jews, in this conceit, are like the latter: they do not commit suicide despite having promised to do so. In both of these stories, Jabotinsky expresses the view that the alliance with Russians and support for the revolution have left Jews worse off than they were before.

Jews were indeed paying a high price, but they were not a sacrificial lamb. The situation was more complex, and I suspect Jabotinsky knew this. For one thing, his interpretation makes the Jews unwitting victims of the revolution and denies the fact that Jews willingly joined, hoping to attain freedom. Additionally, part of his approach was calculated to gain political advantage for Zionism from whatever circumstances arose. If the Jewish public lost confidence in the revolutionaries, perhaps they would defect to the Zionists.

On the question of political direction, the main difference was that now, after the October pogroms, Jabotinsky rejected the position that only a coalition with Russians would ameliorate the Jewish condition. Jabotinsky proposed an "internal politics," a go-it-alone strategy to improve those aspects of life that Jews do, in fact, control. "Our main and primary task is to assemble and come to an agreement to receive orders from the whole Jewish people. We need to focus our entire strength on the only brand of politics accessible to us, internal politics. I do not insist upon a name, but above all we need a genuine, nationwide Jewish assembly, not a surrogate. The call for the constituent assembly must come first and must be, perhaps, the only task that we need to lay before the new central bureau."[49]

Jabotinsky conceived of Jewish political autonomy as a voluntary institution in which members would fulfill essential state functions. In contrast to cultural autonomy, as understood by the Bund, Jabotinsky's was closer to national "self-management."[50] Jewish autonomy enjoyed popularity, and every Jewish political group took a stab at constructing its own ideas. Semyon Dubnov, the Jewish historian and leading theorist of the Folkspartey, had his version, the Bund had their version, and the Vozrozhdentsy had theirs.[51] Jabotinsky, inspired by fellow Zionists—Idel'son, Ussishkin, Shmarya Levin—offered his as well.[52]

At the February 1906 meeting, discussions circled around the question of whether Jews should participate in elections to the first Duma. The leftist parties boycotted the elections. What would the League do? Despite his refrain about "internal politics," Jabotinsky favored participation because he believed that it would be wrong not to try to win power.[53] After all, Jews made up 4 percent of the population: they had a right to representation. With the Duma containing over five hundred seats, if Jews won proportionately, the number of Duma seats would be over twenty. At the same time, Jabotinsky reported the threats of antisemites in Odessa, who promised pogroms if Jewish candidates ran and if Jews came out to vote. But, he noted, they might use violence in any case. Therefore, he saw nothing to gain by yielding to threats. Jabotinsky was in the majority; most, if not all, of the leaders concurred, and League members encouraged Jews to vote.

The Jewish representatives elected to the Duma in 1905–6 were faced with a more divisive issue. Of course, they should consult on questions affecting Jews, but were they free to vote their conscience on other legislation? And what about alliances with parties of the right; would those be permitted? A heated debate ensued, with liberals aghast at the idea of Jewish collaboration with "pogrom-makers" and Zionists defending any alliance that would produce positive results. Zionists justified their position by noting that the real goal was not to form permanent relationships, but to leave Russia and build a national home in Palestine. The controversy died down somewhat when the results of the elections to the First Duma appeared, showing that Jews had finished with only twelve seats. Moreover, not a single Jew was elected from Congress Poland.[54]

The liberals were blamed for the lackluster results, since they dominated the League and had pushed hard for a Russian-Jewish alliance. At the League's last meeting, in November 1906, after the tsar's closing of the First Duma, Zionists called for the abrogation of the Russian-Jewish pact, insisting on going it alone. The League fell apart.

In the historical literature, most scholars have accused Zionists of seeking the League's dissolution until they attained it.[55] Zionists launched the "fatal" blow to the Union for Full Rights when, at their congress in Helsingfors, they decided to act independently in Russian political life—and in elections as well.[56] However, according to Viktor Kel'ner, a historian of Russian liberalism, the Zionists were merely a symptom; the League was breaking apart because all the groups chose party interests over collective goals. He writes, "Zionist tactics only nudged the League towards dissolution. In fact, at its core there had long been several groups that had their own conception of the correct path for the struggle to attain equal rights. Practically at the same time, the Jewish People's Group, the Jewish Democratic Group, and the Volkspartei were formed." In other words, "The split was caused by general political tendencies inherent . . . in the period of the defeat of democracy during the events of 1905–07."[57] As a result of the League's failure to achieve its goals, each group lost interest in the coalition and went its own way. In contrast, Vladimir Levin argues that the prospects to win elections to the second Duma caused Zionists to go it alone, and liberals could not allow Zionists to speak in the name of Russian Jews and began to organize as well. This led to the final split in the League.[58]

The breakup of the League, however, did not end Zionist-Kadet cooperation, because in campaigns for seats in subsequent Dumas, Zionists would have to coordinate with liberals to maximize their chances of getting elected. For example, as already mentioned, Jabotinsky ran for a seat in the second Duma from Rovno, Ukraine, but was asked by Ussishkin to withdraw his candidacy to enable a non-Jewish liberal to get elected.[59] Incidentally, neither Jabotinsky nor the liberal won the seat.

In his study, Kel'ner exaggerated the League's significance, asserting that it made a legacy that mattered. "The activities of the Union for the Attainment of Full Rights of the Jewish People in Russia became a colorful page in the history of Russian Jewry.[60] [These] activities reflected all the contradictions of the national development of Jews in Russia. At the same time, it became a political school for the generation that would be fated to play an important role in the future history of the Jewish people, and in the history of Russia as a whole."[61]

It is hard to agree. Jewish liberals, and liberals generally, became weaker after 1910. However, it would be wrong to characterize the liberals as "assimilators," as Zionists often did. Liberals had a national program that was close in spirit to Dubnov's cultural nationalism, offering a vision of a future Russia based on law, democracy, and equality for the national minorities.[62] One can acknowledge that Jabotinsky learned a great deal from the liberals, especially his vision of democracy as a powerful tool for change. Moreover, his, and the Zionists', struggle with the liberals should not imply a rejection of liberalism as much as a demand to reshape liberalism for national purposes.

In an article from January 1906, Jabotinsky expressed skepticism about the revolution, noting that, at least for Zionists, little had been achieved, and it was already over. Nonetheless, he expressed the positive side. "Without a doubt, the Revolution gave me one victory. That victory deals with morality. The role of our youth in the historic events of the Russian Revolution stimulated an entirely new opinion about our people, especially in

Europe."⁶³ But that advantage paled before the more significant one, the change within Jews themselves:

> There is nothing to hide: certainly a change occurred not only in the way others viewed our nation—a change occurred within ourselves as well. A Jew today no longer resembles a Jew of 25 years ago or even of 10 years ago. Of course, it would be comical to think that the Russian Revolution caused this advance. It was born in the course of Jewish life, which led to an awakening of national independence, of active historical creativity. But the Russian Revolution was a school for this new spirit. It taught the Jew "through fire," as army men express it, and this instruction will prove necessary for us again and again in the future.⁶⁴

What is interesting is what Jabotinsky left unsaid. He undoubtedly uttered under his breath that the revolution was not a worthy goal, that a victory might not benefit Zionism, and that Jews could now leave the Bund knowing in full conscience that they had given the revolution their best shot and lost. The future, therefore, begged for reorientation. Jews should not rely on others but should commit themselves to an internal struggle and focus their energies on achieving Zionism's goal of a national home in Palestine.

It is interesting to note that most liberals at the time (in January 1906, before the first Duma had met) were optimistic. Pavel Miliukov had high hopes that a Kadet majority would lead to serious reforms.⁶⁵ Additionally, the revolution had promised a good deal, such as the legalization of political parties, the end of prepublication censorship, and the Duma itself. But some things Jabotinsky wished for had not come into being, such as the Jewish Congress called for by the League in March 1905. But the paradox was that Jabotinsky realized that even the achievement of a democratic and prosperous Russia would not benefit Zionism.

* * *

Since the League had showed itself powerless to achieve its goals through the ballot box, Jabotinsky pondered how Jews could attain rights without a democratic majority. During the summer of 1906, Jabotinsky penned "Our Tasks," an article that was serialized in several consecutive issues of *Evreiskaia Zhizn'*. He questioned the extent to which Jews in Diaspora had cultural rights, and asked: "What do we mean when we speak of national autonomy?" He went on: "National autonomous rights are defined as a sanctioned form of organized independence, a logical consequence and generalization that naturally arises from the restoration of our national-territorial government. But what should be the character of these rights? In what [kinds of] questions and areas of our life should and can diaspora Judaism achieve autonomy?"[66] What kind of autonomy would best serve the Jews of Russia? It was hardly a simple question. This was a people, after all, who lived in a monarchy that was (perhaps) morphing into a democracy, an empire that pretended to be a nation-state, although, in fact, it consisted of a mélange of nations and ethnicities. Usually national rights were understood in terms of cultural institutions—schools, libraries, and theaters—that made use of the people's native language.

Although Jabotinsky compared Jews to other nations—the Poles, Czechs, and others, for whom the idea of national-cultural rights was territorially focused—Jews in the Russian Empire had no territory to claim as their own. Thus, not only did Jabotinsky need to define what he meant by nation; he needed to conceive of rights for Jews in terms of a nonterritorial group.

For several reasons, Jabotinsky did not like the term "autonomy"; instead, he preferred "national self-governance," because he centered his thinking on communal administration—social and religious institutions, law courts, and cultural bodies. However, like cultural nationalists such as Dubnov, he emphasized national identity over territory. Nonetheless, Jabotinsky tried to balance Diaspora interests and a focus on Palestine; only there, he claimed, would Jews have genuine political sovereignty. He explained, "Whatever the examples of diasporic autonomy there would be regarding the number of functions involved in it, this autonomy cannot possess a political character. In essence, therefore, the very word 'autonomy' is not even appropriate, because when one speaks about the autonomy of Poland, Georgia, or any region generally, one has in mind, as I already pointed out, a purely political construction distinct from apolitical self-administration."[67]

To understand minority rights and autonomy as they might apply in Russia, he turned to Austro-Marxism. In 1906, Jabotinsky published Karl Renner's *State and Nation* in Russian translation with his own introduction.[68] Although Jabotinsky admired Renner, he drew attention to several flaws. Primarily, Jabotinsky found that Renner focused exclusively on the application of legal rights for minorities in the case where one nation had clear majority status. This did not correspond to the situation in Russia's Western borderlands in which many nations lived side-by-side. Jabotinsky wrote, "When applied to conditions in Russia, his conclusions necessarily require development. National differences in Russia are much deeper, forms of national infighting much sharper: to answer Jewish pogroms or the slaughter of Armenians with 'cultural' autonomy is simply a joke. Nationalities should possess the means really to attain mutual inviolability. But even leaving aside this sensitive question, it is impossible to forget the fact, for example, that nations as nations routinely possess their own understanding of law, worked out historically, not only in the form of common law, but in written form too."[69]

Jabotinsky also judged the ideas of Semyon Dubnov, the leading theorist of Jewish politics in Russia. In his collection of articles, *Letters on Old and New Jewry*, Dubnov promoted "autonomy," the idea that Jews should have independent Jewish cultural rights in addition to political rights as citizens.[70] Based in democratic principles, such as the volition of the governed, autonomy included such rights as the establishment of schools in Yiddish or Hebrew, Jewish cultural activities, and the adjudication of inter-Jewish affairs through special courts.

Jabotinsky favored more flexibility in the relations of minorities to the state. He believed that different nationalities had their own conceptions of law and legal procedures, and that these differences should be preserved as much as possible. This approach would permit different nationalities to maintain their own ways of life and give nations a modified form of self-determination. Breaking with Renner, Jabotinsky conceived of national rights even for individuals who lived in areas with few conationalists. Territorial unity was not as important as national identity.

However, Jabotinsky applied different principles to his conception of national autonomy. Instead of a centralized government with an area designated for cultural independence, Jabotinsky favored a decentralized state in which autonomy was the reigning institutional form and the central government served fewer functions.

> The task of settling the national question in Russia—if it is fated that, at some point, this solution should come to pass—cannot be immediately accomplished by the all-Russian constituent assembly, no matter its composition and prevailing attitude. In such questions the center—even if it is democratic—cannot be competent. The questions are subject to answers "on site." Regular and legitimate national assemblies of all nationalities should be convened both in densely populated territories and in areas with scattered populations. Each of these nationalities will define in its own national assembly the full extent of its national demands, and then a special council of delegates

from all these national assemblies, comparing the various applications, will reconcile the contradictions between them and work out a truly reliable modus vivendi. Only in such a way can the principle of self-determination of nationalities that is put forward in all the leading programs be realized in the full legal sense of this word.[71]

These proposals did not elicit a great deal of interest at the time because they seemed unrealistic, and later, in 1930, Alexander Kulisher, a historian and sympathizer of Revisionism, gently mocked them. "In the field of ideological study V. E. Jabotinsky was, to his own credit, not an author, but only a follower and a passionate preacher of one of the most unsuccessful ideas (in my opinion) of recent times: the idea of the national-personal collective—an idea that, in contrast to Jabotinsky himself, did not play any historical role and—again in contrast to Jabotinsky himself—did not clarify, but only obscured many political questions."[72]

Back in 1906, Jabotinsky embraced an expansive conception of autonomy that was different from the ideas bandied about by Dubnov and others. He imagined membership in a collective to surpass conventional ideas of space, geographic cohesion, and population concentration. In 1906, these ideas were abandoned, but Jabotinsky would return to these paradigms in his efforts to organize Jewish life in Eastern Europe (for example in Ukraine in 1917, Lithuania in 1918, and Palestine in the 1920s).

* * *

Since the League was not able to help Jews attain rights, Zionists needed to recalibrate and revise their direction in the post-1905 reality. Their new program found its expression in the Helsingfors Zionist Conference on November 6–8, 1906.[73] The Helsingfors Conference was originally the brainchild of Abram Idel'son, though Idel'son was unable to attend.[74] His absence proved useful to Jabotinsky, who led delegates to approve the proposal to participate in Russian politics and reject the principle of the "negation of the *Galut*."[75] Although the long-term goal of a Jewish home in Palestine remained unchanged, the group voted to support "Synthetic Zionism." They believed that Jews in the Diaspora had to devote themselves to self-realization, especially since there were now opportunities to gain national rights in addition to civic and individual rights.

Helsingfors represented a sharp break with earlier Russian Zionism going back to BILU and Hibbat Tsion, in which some Zionist leaders explicitly abjured any form of political activity in Russia. For Hibbat Zion, the goal had always been raising funds to help Russian Jews leave for Palestine. The moment Zionists began to advance ideas focused on the future of Russia and the place of non-Russians in that configuration, they became, in the eyes of the authorities, revolutionaries, and were treated as others with incendiary views.

Jabotinsky considered the Helsingfors Conference one of the most important events of his life. In his autobiography, he announces:

> My conscience compels me to make a bold and impudent confession here: in my heart's inner depths, I feel I am the author of the Helsingfors Program. Of course I am aware that the individual who directed our thinking was not me, but Idel'son; and I also know that all the details of the program—all of them, bar none—were worked out and took shape in many conversations during the conference, including those with the members of the Warsaw group and the Odessa group with whom we had permanent contact (Israel Trivus, Nahum Sirkin, Shalom Shwartz, and Hayim Grinberg). Nevertheless, if I did not curb my enthusiasm, I would not hold back, and would fill this page with evidence proving that precisely me, and nobody else, had the privilege of formulating the final text. However, it is best that I hold back, since those others—and there are perhaps two or even four of them—also feel the same certainty deep in their hearts, and maybe even carry the same page of evidence and the same right.[76]

The conference's pro-Diaspora platform aligned with Jabotinsky's own needs. Although committed to Zionism, the Jabotinsky of 1906 showed no interest in moving to Palestine (in that, he was like the majority of Zionists). Thus, he supported a policy that gave him concrete tasks in the Diaspora. Additionally, the Helsingfors Conference helped boost his status. According to the historian Yossi Goldstein, Jabotinsky's proposals at the conference won every time, even though another man, Yehiel Chlenov, served as the conference chairman.[77]

It is possible to agree with Alexander Orbach that Helsingfors represented a continuation of the League's politics, minus the baggage it had to carry in order to satisfy all constituents—i.e., Vinaver, Sliozberg, and Leon Bramson.[78] In any case, the foundation was already set for Zionists to influence Russian politics, and the conference merely ratified what was already taking place.

Helsingfors carried weight because it fused two contradictory dimensions: the Diaspora, with its struggle for political representation, and a "national home" in Palestine as the ultimate solution for the Jewish nation.

Gegenwartsarbeit, the conference's mantra, was based on the idea that one could unite Herzl and Ahad-Ha'am; political solutions and on-the-ground infiltration; international diplomacy and day-to-day cultural revitalization.[79] Another motivation for Helsingfors was the demand to democratize Russia and offer full and equal rights, including national rights, to Jews. The appeal emerged from the realization that Russia was not a nation-state with a couple of non-Russian minorities, as the government and some spokesmen on the political right claimed. In fact, Russians composed less than 50 percent of the population. Since Russia was a multinational state with no national majority, Jews were entitled to self-government (as was every nation), their own schools, and their own cultural institutions.[80]

With the call for a democratized Russia, an echo resounded for the democratization of Jewish politics. Jabotinsky spoke in favor of creating a Jewish parliament that would govern the internal affairs of Russia's Jews. He wrote, "As a person with a definite viewpoint, I strongly believe that Jewish people will unanimously acknowledge the ideal of Zionism as their own ideal. The day this acknowledgement is proclaimed will be a great holiday for my colleagues and me. But a new era of Jewish history will not begin that day. The revolutionary moment in the history of the Jews will occur only when for the first time after many centuries—although in Russia alone—a parliament of the Jewish people will gather under the flag of national self-reliance."[81] Significantly, this was one of the major planks agreed to, reluctantly, in March 1905, in Vilna. According to Yossi Goldstein, the parliament "would have executive and legislative rights only with regard to the community. However, the scope of this mandate would not be insignificant. Recognition and support of Jewish organizations connected with national education, Jewish culture, health, mutual aid (social and economic), the marriage and divorce process, questions touching on the Jewish religion, and the right to impose taxes for national Jewish purposes, would all be within the sphere of its jurisdiction."[82]

The Helsingfors Conference left open the possibility of finding new collaborators, but as Jabotinsky explained in mid-1906, only groups who suffered similar conditions would properly empathize with Jews. "Our question is a question of nationhood, which is always and everywhere in the minority. Therefore, our natural allies—these are not nationalities in their entirety, but only their parts, those 'detached pieces' that find themselves in the same position with us—the position of a national minority.

We do not need a union of autonomists, not a union of non-Russians, but a union of national-minority groups."[83] In other words, collaboration was possible among similar groups, although one would have to guess what non–territorially based groups he had in mind.

Jabotinsky was comfortable collaborating with non-Zionists. In fact, the general optimism about Russia's transformation into a constitutional state, with equal rights for Jews and special national rights, too, animated the entire conference. The majority agreed that radicalism was not the answer. In November 1906, many still believed in a continued struggle through parliamentary means to realize the goals of the revolution. Jabotinsky in particular expressed optimism that Zionism would find a place in the new political alignment, if only as a party singularly devoted to political self-sufficiency. He wrote of "the platform that includes a full system of rights—both national-autonomous and national-civic—for internal and external independence. This platform should provide Russian Jewry—which is a cell of world Jewry—the freedom of national evolution, and for us, a synthetic expression of national will, the true opportunity to lead this evolution on the path of Zionism."[84]

If one needed proof that Zionism could mean different things in different places for different people, one need only turn to the group of Russian Jews in Palestine at the same time: Ben-Gurion, Yitzhak Tabenkin, and Berl Katzenel'son. In Palestine, they started organizing the politics of Poale Tsion and Ha-Poel Ha-Tsair, with the newspaper *Ha-Davar*, dealing with issues of security and agricultural settlements. The events in Palestine under Ottoman rule characterized their reality.

Things were different in Russia, where the Senate's decree of June 1, 1907, made Zionism illegal and subject to police repression and arrests. The decree thwarted dreams of changing politics and empowering Jews. Although David Vital believed that the goals articulated in Helsingfors became futile almost immediately, it is possible to disagree.[85] In fact, the ideas endured, even if application in Stolypin's Russia was out of the question. Jabotinsky could not know how long the repression against Zionists would last, but he admired the elegance of the theoretical principles in Synthetic Zionism. Simultaneously, he understood that he too should leave Russia as a precaution, since the police were arresting Zionists without justification. Indeed, the police had already stopped him in 1906, just before the Helsingfors Conference. It was only thanks to Henrik Sliozberg, a liberal lawyer, that he was released.[86]

Notes

1. Chlenov, *Polozhenie sionizma v Rossii: k vii-mu kongresu* (St. Petersburg: Ts. Kraiz, 1905), 44.
2. Vladimir Jabotinsky, *Story of My Life*, eds. Brian Horowitz and Leonid Katsis (Detroit: Wayne State University Press, 2017), 79–80.
3. Shmuel Galai, *The Liberation Movement in Russia* (New York: Cambridge University Press, 1973), 74.
4. Abraham Ascher, *The Revolution of 1905: Russia in Disarray* (Palo Alto: Stanford University Press, 1988).
5. Abraham Ascher, *The Revolution of 1905: A Short History* (Palo Alto: Stanford University Press, 2004), 10.
6. On *Shtadlanut*, see Brian Horowitz, *Jewish Philanthropy and Enlightenment in Late-Tsarist Russia* (Seattle: University of Washington Press, 2009), 17–19.
7. A. A. Gol'denveizer, "Pravovoe polozhenie evreev v Rossii," *Kniga o russkom evreistve, ot 1860-kh godov do revoliutsii 1917 g.: Sbornik statei*, 2nd ed. (Minsk: Met, 2002), 115–158.
8. The best description of Jewish politics during the Revolution is Jonathan Frankels, *Prophecy and Politics: Socialism, Nationalism and the Russian Jews, 1862–1917* (Cambridge: Cambridge University Press, 1981), 134–170.
9. Jabotinsky, *Story of My Life*, 89.
10. Ibid.
11. Christoph Gassenschmidt, *Jewish Liberal Politics in Tsarist Russia, 1900–1914: The Modernization of Russian Jewry* (New York: New York University Press, 1995), 10.
12. On the battles between Jewish nationalists and Jewish Kadets in the struggle for Jewish schools, see Horowitz, *Jewish Philanthropy*, 161–177.
13. Viktor Kel'ner, "'Ikh tseli mogut byt' vysokim, no oni – ne nashi tseli' (M. M. Vinaver-anti-tsionist)," *Judaica Petropolitana* 1 (2013): 114.
14. In part of the summer and autumn of 1905, Jabotinsky was in Switzerland. He returned after the issuance of the October Manifesto, Nicholas II's promise to establish a democratically elected parliament.
15. There are many books on the Bund during this period. Among the best are Ezra Mendelsohn, *Class Struggle in the Pale: The Formative Years of the Jewish Workers Movement in Tsarist Russia* (Cambridge: Cambridge University Press, 1970) and Joshua Zimmerman, *Poles, Jews, and the Politics of Nationality: The Bund and the Polish Socialist Party in Late Tsarist Russia, 1892–1914* (Madison: Wisconsin University Press, 2004).
16. It would return to the alliance in 1906. The reasons were mainly political and, if you will, emotional. Many Bundists yearned to be part of the general Russian revolutionary movement. See Frankel, *Prophecy and Politics*, 246–256; Henry Tobias, "The Reassessent of the National Question," *Essential Papers on Jews and the Left*, ed. Ezra Mendelsohn (New York: New York University Press, 1997), 109–110.
17. Vladimir Jabotinsky, *Bund i Sionizm* (Odessa: Kadima, 1906), 25.
18. Ibid., 48.
19. Ibid.
20. Colin Shindler, *The Rise of the Israeli Right: From Odessa to Hebron* (Cambridge: Cambridge University Press, 2015), 47.
21. Frankel, *Prophesy and Politics*, 165.

22. Ibid.
23. Ibid.
24. Emanuel Nowogrodzki, *The Jewish Labor Bund in Poland, 1915–1939: From Its Emergence as an Independent Political Party until the Beginning of World War II* (Rockville, MD: Shengold, 2001), 175.
25. Zimmerman, *Poles, Jews*, 229–230.
26. Vladimir Jabotinsky, "Pole 'brani'," *Rassvet* 50 (December 30, 1905): 6. "Despite the stylistic outbursts found in the Bundist polemics against *Iskra*, the general tone of these polemics is without a doubt the tone of the self-justifying subordinate. On the contrary, attacks on Zionism have become more and more intense, as reproaches appear in *Iskra* ever more frequently regarding the Bund's capitulation to the Zionists."
27. Ibid., 4.
28. Ibid.
29. Yosef Gorny, *Converging Alternatives: The Bund and the Zionist Labor Movement, 1897–1985* (Albany: State of New York University Press, 2006), 43.
30. On Jabotinsky's syndicalism, see Stanislawski, *Zionism and the Fin de Siècle*, 213.
31. Vladimir Jabotinsky, "Nabroski bez zaglaviia," *Rassvet* 1 (January 10, 1906): 15.
32. On the League, see Galai, *The Liberation Movement*, 245–72.
33. Gassenschmidt, *Jewish Liberal Politics*, 108–109.
34. Alexander Orbach, "The Jewish People's Group and Jewish Politics in Tsarist Russia," *Modern Judaism* 10, no. 1 (February, 1990): 7.
35. On the dissolution of the League see Vladimir Levin, *Mi-mahapeha le-milhama: Ha-politika ha-yehudit be-rusya, 1907–1914* (Jerusalem: Zalman Shazar Center for Jewish History, 2016), 130–137.
36. Alexander Orbach, "Zionism and the Russian Revolution of 1905: The Commitment to Participate in Domestic Political Life," *Bar-Ilan University Annual* 24–25, no. 5749 (1989): 11.
37. Ibid., 12.
38. Kel'ner, "'Ikh tseli mogut byt' vysokimi," 2.
39. Nahum Sokolow, *History of Zionism*, 2 vols. (London, 1919), 2:li. The casualty numbers are not as certain as Sokolow insists. See John Klier, "Pogroms," in *The YIVO Encyclopedia of Jews in Eastern Europe*, 2 vols. (New Haven, CT: Yale University Press, 2008), 2:1378–1379.
40. Orbach, "Zionism and the Russian Revolution," 18.
41. "Vtoroe ocherednoe obshchee sobranie Odesskogo Obshchestva Prosveshcheniia, 6 marta," *Nedel'naia Khronika Voskhoda* 16 (1905): 18.
42. Semyon Dubnov, "Uroki strashnykh dnei," *Voskhod* 47–48 (December 1, 1905): 9.
43. Joseph B. Schechtman, *The Life and Times of Vladimir Jabotinsky: Rebel and Statesman, The Early Years* (Silver Spring, MD: Eshel Books, 1986), 95.
44. Ibid., 94–95.
45. Ibid., 94.
46. Elias Tcherikover, "Peter Lavrov and the Jewish Socialist Émigés," *Yivo Annual of Jewish Social Science* 7 (1952): 132–45.
47. Vladimir Jabotinsky, "Evreiskii miting v S.-Peterburge," *Khronika Evreiskoi Zhizni* 46 (November 25, 1905): 10.
48. Ibid.
49. Vladimir Jabotinsky, "Vopros o sozyve evreiskogo uchreditel'nogo sobraniia," *Khronika Evreiskoi Zhizni* 46 (November 25, 1905): 36.

50. Yossi Goldshtein, "Jabotinsky and Jewish Autonomy in the Diaspora," *Studies in Zionism* 7, no. 2 (1986): 224–225.

51. On the variety of autonomism, see David E. Fishman, *The Rise of Modern Yiddish Culture* (Pittsburgh: University of Pittsburgh Press, 2005), 62–82; On the spread of the autonomist idea, see Vladimir Levin, "Ha-folks-partey shel Shimon Dubnov - sipur shel kishalon?," *Zion* 77 (2012): 359–68.

52. Fishman, *Rise of Modern Yiddish*, 68.

53. Viktor Kel'ner, "Nesostoiavshiisia soiuz (Soiuz dostizheniia polnopraviikh evreiskogo naroda v Rossii v dokumentakh i memuarakh)." Unpublished manuscript.

54. Vladimir Levin, "Russian Jewry and the Duma elections, 1906–1907," *Jews and Slavs* 7 (2000): 233–258.

55. Gassenschmidt, *Jewish Liberal Politics*, 40–41. Orbach, "The Jewish People's Group," 7.

56. Orbach, "The Jewish People's Group," 7.

57. Ibid.

58. Vladimir Levin, "Politics at the Crossroads—Jewish Parties and the Second Duma Elections, 1907," *Leipziger Beiträge zur jüdischen Geschichte und Kultur* 2 (2004): 129–46.

59. Kel'ner, "Nesostoiavshiisia soiuz."

60. Ibid.

61. Ibid.

62. Semyon Dubnov, *Pis'ma o starom i novom evreistve* (St. Petersburg: Obshchestvennaia pol'za, 1907).

63. Vladimir Jabotinsky, "Evreiskaia revoliutsiia," *Khronika Evreiskoi Zhizni* 3 (January 24, 1906): 5.

64. Ibid.

65. Alexander Orbach, "Between Liberal Integrationists and Political Segregationists: The Zionism of Asher Ginsberg (1889–1907)," *Studia Judaica* 6 (1997): 61–70.

66. Vladimir Jabotinsky, "Nashi zadachi," *Khronika Evreiskoi Zhizni* 25 (June 29, 1906): 7.

67. Ibid., 9.

68. Karl Renner, *Gosudarstvo i natsiia* (Odessa: Kadima, 1906). Original German title, *Staat und Nation*.

69. Vladimir Jabotinsky, "Predislovie," in Renner, *Gosudarstvo i natsiia*, 4.

70. Dubnov, *Pis'ma o starom i novom evreistve*. The articles that were collected and published in a single volume began appearing in the 1890s.

71. Ibid., 7.

72. Alexander Kulisher, "Politicheskii vozhd'," *Rassvet* 42 (October 19, 1930): 5.

73. Jabotinsky was involved in organizing the Helsingfors Conference already in the spring of 1906.

74. Yossi Goldshtein, "Jabotinsky and Jewish Autonomy in the Diaspora," *Studies in Zionism* 7, no. 2, (1986): 230.

75. Joseph Klausner, "Real'nye zadachi russkogo evreistva," *Evreiskaia Zhizn'* 3 (1906): 125.

76. Jabotinsky, *Story of My Life*, 90–91. Hayim Grinberg (or Greenberg [1889–1953]), theorist of Labor Zionism, was head of Poale Zion in the United States. Sholem (Ben-Baruch) Shwartz (1887–1965) was a journalist and editor of the *Palestine Daily Bulletin*. He was born in Russia and moved to Palestine in 1920. He is the author of such works as *The Arab Problem, The Poetry of Tchernichovsky*, and *Herzl in His Diaries*.

77. Goldshtein, "Jabotinsky and Jewish Autonomy," 225.

78. Orbach, "The Jewish People's Group," 10.

79. Abram Idel'son was the editor of the Russian-language Zionist newspaper *Rassvet* (*Evreiskaia Zhizn'*). See Brian Horowitz, "What Is Russian in Russian Zionism? Synthetic Zionism and the Fate of Avram Idel'son," in *Russian Idea-Jewish Presence: Essays on Russian-Jewish Intellectual Life* (Boston: Academic Studies, 2013), 54–71; Idel'son and Jabotinsky had a falling out by the decade's end. Yehuda Slutzky, *Ha-itonut ha-yihudit-rusit ba-mea estrim (1900–1918)* (Tel Aviv: Ha-aguda le-haker toldot ha-yihudim, 1978), 205–206.

80. Vladimir Jabotinsky, "O iazykakh i prochem," *Fel'etony*, 2nd ed. (Berlin, 1922), 157. The article originally appeared in *Odesskie Novosti* (January 25, 1911): 2.

81. Viktor Kel'ner, "Tak govoril Zhabotinskii: Iz protokolov s''ezda soiuza dlia dostizheniia polnopraviia evreiskogo naroda v Rossii," *Vestnik Evreiskogo Universiteta v Moskve* 4 (1993): 167–168.

82. Goldstein, "Jabotinsky and Jewish Autonomy," 225.

83. Jabotinsky, "Nashi zadachi," 9–10.

84. Ibid., 12.

85. David Vital, *Zionism: The Crucial Phase* (Oxford: Clarendon, 1987), 47.

86. Jabotinsky describes this event in *Story of My Life*, 89.

4

THE DECADE BETWEEN THE REVOLUTION OF 1905 AND WORLD WAR I, 1907–1914

* * *

THE YEARS 1907 TO 1914 WERE CRITICAL TO Jabotinsky's development as a Zionist activist and theorist. He had acquainted himself with theories of nationalism, but in Russia he saw firsthand an entire Empire swing to the right—from the Revolution of 1905 to control by a conservative Duma. Even the Constitutional Democrats (Kadets) lurched rightward, which surprised Jabotinsky when they too became infected with Russian nationalism. In Congress Poland, things were worse: the Democratic Nationalists, known as Endeks, expressed a blanket hostility toward ethnic minorities, including Jews, declaring them an illegitimate presence. Antisemitism, formerly the exclusive purview of the government, became widespread. The government now shared hate not only with the gutter press, but with the intelligentsia.[1]

The disappointment of 1905 included the failure to challenge tsarist power in the two first Dumas. The first Duma lasted a mere seventy-two days before Tsar Nicholas II disbanded it. After its closure, representatives of the Kadets, Trudoviki, and other liberal groups met in Vyborg, Finland, to sign a declaration calling for the population to refrain from paying taxes or voting in future Duma elections.[2] The police arrested the signatories, who were imprisoned for three months and prohibited from serving in a future Duma. The second Duma was also closed on June 3, 1907. After that debacle, the government carefully neutered subsequent Dumas by reducing voter enfranchisement.[3] The third Duma with a center-right Octobrist domination functioned from 1907 to 1912. There were only two Jewish representatives out of over five hundred delegates. Thus, demands for Jewish equality had the appearance of publicity stunts with no chance of success.[4]

Because political change was impossible, many intellectuals shifted their interests from politics to culture. Once people realized that the tsarist government had survived, it took time to reorient themselves. If radicalism had failed, what was now worth striving for? In Russia, the *Landmarks* (*Vekhi*) volume that appeared in 1909 offered an option that garnered a good deal of attention.[5] The seven authors, liberals mainly, argued that the 1905 Revolution had failed because radical politics was not the answer. According to the editor, Mikhail Gershenzon, political action had created human cripples. Instead of concentrating on the most important parts of life—work, friends, and family—revolutionaries had devoted themselves solely to politics for fifty years.[6] Gershenzon, Nikolai Berdiaev, and Sergei Bulgakov called for a turn to spiritual concerns, an investigation of oneself and the search for harmony with society.

In the Jewish environment, the swerve away from politics led to local initiatives in education, culture, and philanthropy. The former center of organized Jewish culture, the Society for the Promotion of Enlightenment, became transformed and revitalized through its partial disintegration. Its core—commissions for education, teachers, heders, and culture—spun off into independent units: a Jewish university of sorts was established in St. Petersburg, a historical society was founded, and teacher training programs and new schools were opened in cities and towns in the Pale of Settlement.[7] Additionally, the Kovno Conference in 1909 was an important expression of the Jewish focus on community building before the next opportunity to reconfigure the Russian Empire.[8] The conference included a number of Zionists—Chlenov, Ussishkin, and Yuly Brutskus—but not Jabotinsky, who was in Istanbul at the time. Although infighting was fierce, especially by the Orthodox rabbis, an agreement was reached that conceived of the Jewish community, as Christoph Gassenschmidt writes, "as a democratic and modernized organization which would have allowed all elements of Jewish society to participate."[9]

Another feature of the period was full-blown antisemitism. Though its rise was, in some ways, predictable, Jabotinsky was surprised by the wave of antisemitism that accompanied Duma democracy.[10] Antisemitism expressed itself in a variety of contexts: culture, politics, and daily life.[11] There were calls in Poland to hire only Poles; in Russia, Jews were required to use their Jewish (as opposed to russified) names in business and on store signs. The quotas for Jews in Russian schools remained in place. As a journalist and Zionist propagandist, Jabotinsky polemicized, mocked, and argued with antisemites, despite his conviction that one could not reason with them. He surprised many readers with the nihilistic claim that pogroms have nothing to teach, no moral lesson or secret insight to impart.[12]

Zionists had their own problems. Zionism was in a weakened state, and the cause was not solely 1905. The bitter legacy of Uganda and Herzl's death had fractured the World Zionist Organization. Adding insult to injury, many Zionists regretted the appointment of David Wolffsohn, Herzl's successor, who moved the organizational center from Vienna to Cologne and presided over the movement's stagnation. Zionism in Russia suffered a setback when government restrictions hobbled the movement after Helsingfors. In 1907, tsarist officials officially disbanded the organization and prohibited donations abroad and the purchase of the Shekel, or membership fee.[13] The government viewed Zionism as a menace in league with radicalism, although the political affinities of the Zionists were closer to the center than government officials supposed. However, the experience of Russian Zionists post-1905 was hardly unique; one might compare it with the situation of other Jews and many non-Jews in Russia. Emigration to the United States and other countries was rising. Revolutionaries hid from military courts with the right to order summary hangings (Stolypin's necktie) during 1906–07. In subsequent years, Jewish liberals fell into depression, finding themselves in the hopeless position of permanent opposition.

One central fact of Jabotinsky's biography has escaped historians: he was a member of the disappointed generation—those who placed their hopes in the Revolution of 1905 and were bitterly betrayed. Like many others, Jabotinsky left Russia. From 1907 to 1910, Jabotinsky crossed the world, traveling to Vienna, Istanbul, and Eretz Yisrael. By the time of the Mendel Beilis trial in 1911–13, Jabotinsky no longer viewed liberals as natural allies. He had clashed with Pyotr Struve, Vasilii Maklakov, and Maxim Vinaver, as well as with conservative nationalists Roman Dmowski and Vladimir Purishkevich. He had fallen out with his mentor and friend, Avram Idel'son. Over the course of the decade, the struggle with antisemitism weakened his hope in Diaspora politics—that Jews could collaborate with non-Jews for mutual benefit.

During the campaign for the second Duma, Jabotinsky busied himself in election politics, even buying a home in Rovno, Ukraine, in order to run for a seat. His chances of winning were slim, however, because he needed support from non-Jews. In such cases, the political right skillfully instrumentalized prejudice, and the center and center left often could not amass the needed support. Indeed, Ussishkin asked Jabotinsky to resign his candidacy to increase the chances of a certain liberal running in the same election (to no avail: the liberal lost as well). Although Jews constituted 4 percent of the population, as a minority it could not win 4 percent of the seats. Not a single Jewish candidate was elected from Congress Poland to the second Duma. The result in Poland diminished Jabotinsky's belief in representative democracy.[14]

But the experience offered insights. Primarily, he now saw how allies, Russian liberals, could quickly switch and embrace nationalism. He also understood that sympathy for Jews and other minorities disappeared when juxtaposed with sectarian interests. Finally, and perhaps most importantly, he gained firsthand experience of how Polish nationalists could manipulate public opinion by demonizing minorities. He also noticed that in Russia, where the national minorities actually constituted a majority, they were unable to translate their numbers into political power. Russian nationalism, which had been suppressed, was unleashed paradoxically by democracy, and with nationalism came the expression of antisemitism. All in all, Jabotinsky became acquainted with the tools of the radical right.

His transformation into a leader was manifest in subtle ways. To be sure, he was elected as a delegate in the League for the Attainment of Full Rights for the Jews of Russia, and he was assigned a leadership post in Istanbul, but a real change occurred when he returned to Russia in 1910. He distanced himself from Ussishkin and Idel'son and wrote less for *Rassvet*. He pursued his own interests, organizing lectures around the Pale of Settlement and traveling to Europe to study the organization, structure, and finances of universities. He conceived of a publishing house for Hebrew translations, and he involved himself in school creation and design. These practical enterprises lacked the theoretical dimension of his thinking on autonomy, but they showed greater commitment to effecting real, albeit small, change among Russia's Jews.

* * *

In 1907, Jabotinsky went to Vienna, where he decided to continue his study of national autonomy and ethnic rights.[15] His research became the basis for a thesis that earned him a diploma from Demidov College in Yaroslavl in 1913.[16] He published his research as a long article entitled "Political Autonomy of a National Minority," which appeared in two installments in the legendary Russian "thick journal" *Vestnik Evropy* (*Messenger of Europe*) in 1913.[17]

As Jabotinsky described it in his autobiography, in 1907 he felt the need for intellectual replenishing. Instead of portraying his disappointment as collective ennui, he expressed personal angst. "And I, where am I? What has become of me? I give but do not receive. I am preaching to the public—me, an ignoramus—teachings that I do not know. Ever since I left the university [in Rome], I did not learn a thing but just taught others. Every journalist knows this hunger of the brain that he empties every day, pouring its contents onto the readers. He has no time to replenish the empty vessel. '*Basta!*' ['Enough of that!']"[18] Maybe intellectual replenishing was the ostensible reason, but with the police arresting Zionists and revolutionaries, it made little sense to wait around. Since his wife was leaving Russia to study agriculture in France, Jabotinsky left as well.

Vienna was the capital of the multinational Hapsburg Empire and the center of experimental thinking on minority nations within empires. Jabotinsky read Max Adler, Otto Bauer, and Karl Renner (all Austrian Marxists), and he studied the national question in various contexts. He summarized his activities:

> I spent about a year in Vienna. I did not meet anyone, nor did I go to Zionist meetings, except for once or twice. I devoured books. In those days Austria was a real school for studying "the problem of nationalities." I would spend the whole day at the university library or at the library of the Reichstag. I learned to read Czech and Croatian (I've since forgotten, of course); I studied the history of the Ruthenians and the Slovaks, and even the story of the forty thousand Romanians in the canton of Grisons in Switzerland, the customs of the Armenian church (there is a Michitar cloister in Vienna that also has a library), and the life of the gypsies in Hungary and Romania. I made notes from every book and pamphlet; I wrote them down in Hebrew in order to train myself in our language, which I also did not know sufficiently well. By the way, I became accustomed to writing Hebrew in Latin letters, a style of writing that is easier for me than the Assyrian square script.[19]

Jabotinsky came to conclusions similar to those he had described in his introduction to Renner's *State and Nation* and in his articles on national autonomy that appeared in *Evreiskaia Zhizn'* in 1905–06. He still sought answers to the basic questions that haunted him in Russia, post-1905: how to protect the rights of national minorities in a democracy, and how to ensure democratic representation for small groups that could not win in winner-take-all elections.[20]

From Vienna, he traveled to Istanbul in 1909, where he monitored the Young Turk Revolution on behalf of Odessa's Zionists.[21] After waiting so long without result from the sultan, the Young Turk Revolution offered real hope.[22] As one historian put it, "It is hard to imagine any other event in the late history of the Ottoman Empire that created such high expectations for change and triggered so many political and social processes as did the Young Turk Revolution of 1908."[23] The new leaders were relatively young, and some had studied in Western Europe. Since the government seemed to lean in the liberal direction, some in Odessa, such as Ussishkin, felt that the opportunity to influence the future should not be missed.[24] In Istanbul, Jabotinsky monitored several newspapers that received subsidies, and tried to introduce pro-Zionist sentiments wherever possible.[25]

Despite the appearance of liberalism, the Young Turk leaders jealously guarded the interests of the Turks in their empire. For Zionists, that meant that reforms affected personnel rather than ideology. Jabotinsky presumed that these new rulers, as open as they were, showed the same hostility to Zionism or any attempt to develop an autonomous national culture in the Ottoman Empire. Their slogan sent the message: "We are all Ottomans"— that is, we favor the full assimilation of all the nations in our empire.

Nonetheless, Jabotinsky accepted Ussishkin's offer to go to Istanbul and edit a group of newspapers. These papers received subsidies from the World Zionist Organization, in exchange for which, they allowed positive press on Zionism. This activity should not be equated with propaganda; it was more subtle. According to Yaron Ben Naeh, these efforts made sense, since newspapers were respected by both the public and the Turkish leaders.[26] The goal was to influence public opinion on Zionism; to enable intercession with the Ottoman authorities; to win over the Jewish elite; and encourage leading personages in the community to join the Zionist ranks."[27] Vladimir Levin stresses that Russian Zionists imagined that their program of Gegenwartsarbeit, which failed in Russia, had become viable in postrevolutionary Turkey, and therefore sent Jabotinsky, one of the main authors of the program.[28]

In his articles from Istanbul in 1909, Jabotinsky argued that the new rulers were blinded by ideological dreams of unity that would shatter when they collided with reality. He considered "reality" the national question in the Ottoman Empire, the fact that the Armenians and Arabs would not surrender their higher cultures to join the Turkish. Jabotinsky predicted that the threat to Turkish rule would arise from Arabs. "Simple arithmetic spurs the Arabs to the natural thought that will develop in the course of time into the central motif of their politics—the idea that if hegemony must belong to someone, then it must belong to them and not the Turks. If the role of other ethnic groups with regard to the Turks amounts to self-defense, then the Arab-Turkish relationship becomes more and more similar to a kind of competition between equally strong rivals."[29] According to Jabotinsky, the Arabs and Turks would attempt to control the religious element of the struggle so as to not appear weak before non-Muslims. At the same time, the Young Turks would try to repel any attempt by Arab leaders to break away or directly challenge Turkish power.

This political configuration was likely to dampen support for Zionism, since thwarting Jewish emigration to Palestine could be used by the government as a pay-off for Arab support. Jabotinsky looked to Sephardic Jews for help. He considered Sephardic Jews the most loyal of all the national minorities in the Ottoman Empire, because they had no internal alliance with other states, as did Christians (or foreign Jews, for that matter). For their safety and prosperity, Ottoman Jews could rely only on their relationship with the Turks.[30]

Despite everything, Jabotinsky maintained that the Jewish-Turkish relationship could benefit Zionism: "The interests of Zionism completely coincide in this regard with the interests of this part of Ottoman Jewry: the national politics of the Sephardim must clearly carry a staunchly Turkophilic character, the preservation of political dominance must be [the politics'] leading principle."[31] Interestingly both David Ben-Gurion and Berl Katzenelson, who went to Istanbul to study law at the start of World War I, came to the same conclusion, as did Eliezer Ben-Yehuda (Eliezer Yitzhak Perlman), who took a Turkish passport at the expense of his Russian citizenship.[32]

Jabotinsky claimed that Ottoman authorities had erred by not exploiting Jewish nationalism to create an ally who would support them in the contest between the empire and the Arab majority. Yosef Gorny explains that Jabotinsky "argued that the unitary nationalist nature of the new regime would soon cause it to clash with any national entity of similar characteristics within the Ottoman Empire, i.e., with the 'Arab nation.' There were more Arabs than Turks in the Ottoman Empire; they had a long cultural tradition and a spiritual center in Egypt. Jabotinsky doubted whether an Arab national movement already existed, but he was convinced that all the conditions were ripe for the development of 'a strong national movement in the not too distant future.'"[33]

His reasoning led him to a paradoxical conclusion. Repopulating Palestine with Jews would strongly benefit the Turks, as they "could employ the Zionist movement as an instrument for diluting the overwhelmingly Arab character of Palestine." Therefore, "Turkish fears of national territorial concentrations need not apply to Palestine."[34]

Such ideas should be labeled utopian: it was unrealistic to imagine that Turkey would enlist a small minority to deal with a major structural problem in the empire. Jabotinsky argued that Turkish officials should promote Jewish emigration to Palestine because Jews could provide economic relief in that undeveloped region. In this vision, the Sephardim could bridge conflicts between the Ashkenazi Jews who wanted to settle in Palestine and the Ottoman authorities.

Jabotinsky was fully aware of the Arab rejection of assimilation into Ottoman identity. But he also saw an opening for Jews through supporting the ruler rather than the rebel. This is the opposite of his suggestion to link Jewish aspirations with other minorities in Russia (for example, with Ukrainians), and has nothing to do with ideas of personal autonomy. Before calling for mass immigration, Jabotinsky demanded political security for Jews, such as a legal charter, thereby showing himself to be a follower of Theodor Herzl.[35] At the same time, Jabotinsky discussed the meaning of the Basel formula. As he noted in 1909, a sovereign state was not necessary; the territory, however, was nonnegotiable. It appears that he still sympathized with Ahad-Ha'am:

> Therefore, the pathos of our ideal lay not in the idea of sovereignty, but in the idea of territory, of a compact Jewish society in a single, unified space. This was always the essential idea of our movement and we saw in it the main, even the exclusive factor for the normalization of the Jewish people. Theoretically speaking, Zionism as such would be entirely realized for us if on one fine day Jews found themselves in the position of the Poles of Poznań with regard to Russian Latvians—in the position of a people that not only lacks sovereignty, and is even oppressed, but nevertheless has its own territory.[36]

The experience in Istanbul made one thing clear: Turkey's new regime was as unrealistic as the old regime with regard to national liberation. It could have strengthened itself by decentralizing and granting autonomy to its Arab subjects; it could have bolstered its position by courting Jews as allies; but since it was unable to reform, it was likely to crumble at the first sign of stress. Jabotinsky gained important insights into Arab nationalism, its ambitions, self-awareness, and religious extremism. These insights would prove vital during World War I.

His sojourn in Istanbul ended due to a scandal involving Jacobus Kahn, second in command of the Zionist movement. In 1909, Kahn published *Erez Israel, das jüdische Land*, demanding that a Jewish state in Palestine be created immediately.[37] Although Jabotinsky agreed "with every word," he had to repudiate the book because it threatened to bring disaster to Istanbul's Zionists. Over several months, Jabotinsky exchanged recriminations with David Wolffsohn, Herzl's successor as the head of World Zionism, but for all practical purposes the incident passed without notice.[38] Jabotinsky's sponsors (Ussishkin) ran out of money, and he returned to Russia.

* * *

Perhaps the most important event in Jabotinsky's life during these years was his "first visit" to Palestine in 1909. The sparse evidence that he was in Palestine includes a short interlude in *Story of My Life*. Although his journalism gives a broad portrait of his stay in Istanbul in 1908 and 1909, the Palestine trip is buried in secrecy; little is known about his experiences there; he did not publish his usual feuilletons about it. His personal letters, at least those that are preserved, are silent about the journey.

The portrayal in *Story of My Life* of the two months he spent in the Yishuv is notable for its reticence. It occupies a single, long paragraph, focusing on three scenes: the first relates a visit to Meir Dizengoff, the future mayor of Tel Aviv and a fellow Odessan, and describes Dizengoff's wife, Zina, on the "sands north of Yaffo." Jabotinsky attentively sympathizes with Zina's daily hardship of getting water from a pump with her "delicate hands," while Dizengoff expounds, "We bought the land here, and if the Lord is with us, we will build a Jewish city, and in the center we will erect a building for a school; I mean, if we can find somebody to provide the money."[39]

Jabotinsky shifts to his next portrait—meetings with workmen in the agricultural settlements up north. The workers complain, "Why is there no immigration from Russia?" Jabotinsky describes the men as *Shomrim*, guards, who carry rifles slung over their shoulders.[40] One of them relates a story of his encounter with an Arab Bedouin who asks for help lighting his cigarette. Instead of approaching the man, the Jew puts his own cigarette in the barrel of his rifle and passes it in front of the Arab's face. This way he avoids being a victim of a robbery or even murder. The last scene depicts a conversation in Tiberias with a Jewish boy of fourteen, whom Jabotinsky addresses with the question, "Do you speak Hebrew?" The boy answers in Yiddish: "My rabbi says: 'Who speaks Hebrew? Non-believers speak Hebrew.'" Jabotinsky ends his description of Palestine—one long paragraph—with the sentence, "And from the top of Mount Tabor, I saw the Jezreel Valley, at that time a desert."[41]

The most surprising aspect of the narrative is its terseness. Jabotinsky neglects to provide a general itinerary, and withholds details about the people he met. He defends his silence: "As this is a book that will appear in Tel Aviv, there is no need for me to describe the Hebrew Yishuv as it was in 1908. I will mention only some details that may have been forgotten, and some of which will perhaps surprise you, owing to the tremendous difference between the past and present."[42] Perhaps Jabotinsky is right: in 1936, the reader is not interested in Palestine circa 1908, but in Jabotinsky's impressions, feelings, thoughts, contemplations, and meditations. But these vignettes and their relationship to one another appear to be presented at random. I would argue, however, that the three examples in fact tell us what Jabotinsky remembered about his trip and what he wanted his readers of 1936 to remember.

The stories are vivid representations of emigration, power, Arab-Jewish encounters, and the question of Hebrew. These were the central themes in Jabotinsky's early political vision of the formation of the Jewish Yishuv. In Zina's parable of suffering, she tells the story of a commitment, which of course resonated with Jabotinsky. Indeed, the story embodies Jabotinsky's idea of Monism, as Zina and Meir Dizengoff are blind to everything but their dedication to creating a Jewish city. The second story illustrates his obsession with immigration, his belief that world politics means little in comparison with boots on the ground. The description of the Arab-Jewish encounter portrays a tough Jew who is physically able to defend himself. He illustrates the idea that Jewish security lies in the hands of the Jews themselves. The last story, of the boy and the Jezreel Valley, is offered as a metaphor. The boy, who belongs to the old Yishuv, is linked with the Jezreel Valley, then a desert, but in time it will become an oasis. Jabotinsky wants us to consider that, although the boy is presently an opponent of the Hebrew settlers, he too will become transformed. It seems that Jabotinsky chose or created his stories with deliberation, withholding many events and impressions in order to focus on a few colorful and meaningful messages.

* * *

Back in Russia, political fires were once again flaring, though not with revolution, but reaction. In 1907, a scandal broke out in St. Petersburg: "The

Cherikov Affair" ("Cherikovskoe Delo") concerned the implicit right of Jews to join the Russian intelligentsia. Identifying himself as a legitimate Russian intellectual and a Jew, Jabotinsky could not resist getting involved.[43]

The facts are relatively simple: in 1907, during a meeting of writers, Sholem Asch, the Yiddish playwright, asserted that Russian writers could not accurately portray Jewish experience. He maintained that only Jews can truly understand Jewish life under tsarist oppression and express this pain in artistic form. Evgenii Cherikov, a well-known Russian playwright, was stunned by the reproach, because he had written a play, *Jews* (1904), from a Jewish point of view. He was furious: How could Asch claim that Jews were entitled to express their national identity, but Russians were not? To Asch and others, it was unseemly for Russian writers to take pride in their identity, since only antisemites or the government expressed Russian pride. Good intellectuals were supposed to internalize cosmopolitanism and sympathize with the oppressed non-Russians—as did Cherikov.[44]

Asch's disgraceful manners shattered restraint among the Russian intelligentsia. For over two years, different writers took a stand on Jewish participation in Russian culture. The Younger Symbolists—Andrey Bely, Emilii Metner, Alexander Blok, and even Jabotinsky's friend, Kornei Chukovsky—asked Jews "respectfully" to withdraw from Russian literature. The Older Symbolists—Maxim Gorky, Vladimir Korolenko, and Fyodor Sologub—tried to calm the situation. However, the debate inspired Jabotinsky to take a radical position on Russian-Jewish cooperation.

This apparent division between Jews and Russians appeared strange: Jews had long considered Russian culture a refuge. Certainly, one could not expect the tsar to like Jews, but one could trust Russian culture. After all, it inspired feelings of unity, idealism, and morality; it gave Jews hope in a future multicultural Russia.

As a Zionist, Jabotinsky was not surprised and even pleased that the lid had popped off, revealing people's real feelings, but as a Russian author, a master of the Russian language, he felt tension. The debate convinced him again that compromise was impossible; Russian-Jewish identity was a lie, and dreams of attaining unity were absurd. In this spirit, he decided to awaken Jews from their illusion and expose Russians' unconscious chauvinism. He shocked his readers with "On Jews in Russian Literature" and "Russian Gentleness."

Instead of dealing directly with Asch and Cherikov, Jabotinsky explored the attitudes of Russia's greatest nineteenth-century authors, who, although known for their universalism and idealism, felt differently about Jews, Poles, and other undesirables. For example, Jabotinsky analyzed the image of Jews in Nikolai Gogol's historical novella *Taras Bulba*: "No other great literature contains anything as cruel. One cannot even call it antipathy or sympathy for the Cossack revenge on the kikes. It is worse, a kind of careless, transparent joy, not spoiled by the notion that the feet that are comically swinging in the air are the feet of living people."[45]

Jabotinsky exposed the fact that Russia's leading writers—Pushkin, Turgenev, Dostoevsky, and Chekhov—peddled anti-Jewish stereotypes.[46] Even writers considered Judeophilic, such as Leskov and Korolenko, did not depict Jews positively; rather, they merely acknowledged that Russians can act as immorally as Jews. According to Jabotinsky, negative stereotypes did not represent actual Jews, but were products of the imagination. Gogol "did not discover and could not discover anything like it in real life, but made it up, just as he made up ghost tales."[47] Jabotinsky extended his critique to all of Russian literature. He claimed that the lack of interest in the real Jew explained why Russian authors had not produced literature on par with the great works of Western culture, such as *The Merchant of Venice* or *Nathan the Wise*.[48]

The Cherikov Affair hit close to home, forcing Jabotinsky to consider his own role as a writer. In "On Jews in Russian Literature" (1908), Jabotinsky explored ways to define Jewish literature. Interestingly, he rejected the central role of language, arguing that language and subject matter were less important than the ideological orientation of the author, his/her purpose in writing, and the audience's expectations. Years before the appearance of "reader response theory," Jabotinsky would write: "Here the decisive moment is not language and at the same time not the author's background or the plot. The decisive moment is the author's *attitude—for whom* [he is writing]; many people will read you, but you either remain inside the border or outside it. To serve your people, speak to them and write for them to the best of your abilities, you do not have to know Yiddish and certainly not desert the [Jewish] camp. The issue here is not language, but exclusively intention."[49] (Italics in original)

Jabotinsky conceived of literature as an expression of national spirit, and although he admired Russian literature, he refused to conflate morality and aesthetics. Russian literature was extraordinary in its aesthetic quality, but many of its leading authors disliked Jews. It was time to draw a clear line, to define who belonged where. Jabotinsky disavowed his membership in Russian literature. In contrast, he pledged allegiance to Jewish literature and declared his loyalty to Hebrew, although paradoxically he was not fluent in the language.[50] The sacrifice that he allegedly made had added significance because he was russified through and through. According to Michael Stanislawski, "His entire linguistic and ideational world was Russian, and his aspiration in life, from his early teens on, was to become a Russian writer and a contributor to Russian literature."[51]

One might stop here to examine Jabotinsky's long drama in verse, *Abroad* (*Na chuzhbine*), written in 1909 but not published until 1922.[52] According to Svetlana Natkovich, the poem was "the fruit of the experience that combined the creative and the personal."[53] *Abroad* was doubtless written in the heat of the Cherikov Affair; the plot deals with Jewish revolutionaries who conceive of themselves as "Russian," but who learn through a pogrom who they really are and what Russians really think of them. The "fabula" takes place during the 1905 Revolution in a forest outside a city in Southern Russia, where revolutionaries gather to hear talks by their leaders. Jabotinsky inserts a romantic subplot, a love affair between a Russian woman, Natasha, and Gont, a Jewish revolutionary who pretends to be Russian. The lines are written in blank verse.[54]

One message of Jabotinsky's long drama is that a Jew cannot impersonate a Russian; in the end, the antisemitic Natasha rejects the Jewish Gont. Just as he did in 1906, Jabotinsky concludes that Jews miscalculated. They flew to the fires of revolution, hoping to help others, and themselves got burnt. Gont says it best in one of his speeches before the crowd:

> Our struggle is a mirage, we are shadow, we have no role.
> Events rush past our will,
> Both our senseless labor and all our sacrifices—all of this pearl,
> Bloodied, but small—
> History will equate with the scurryings of a squirrel
> In a wheel that serves no purpose.[55]

The play was read in public in 1910 but was not well received.[56] Most of the attendees considered it tendentious rather than artistic; it transmitted Jabotinsky's political views, and used language skillfully, but was lacking in overall merit. There is doubtless truth to these claims and similar claims against other writers. When Shimon An-sky, David Aizman, and Semyon Yushkevich addressed Jewish issues, they, too, were accused of tendentiousness and artistic clumsiness.[57]

The plot of *Abroad* shares a common theme with Jabotinsky's story "Edmée," which appeared in 1912.[58] The plot of "Edmée" features an older German-Jewish doctor, an assimilated Jew who, in an inner monologue, describes his erotic feelings for a twelve-year old girl, Edmée, the daughter of a French diplomat. The location is an island in the Bosporus Straights. The short tale abruptly ends with Edmée disparaging the island's Jews as "crass and cheap."

Marina Mogilner calls the story an example of "colonial distance." "This 'I cannot stand it' that has crushed the doctor was not the result of a Jewish education and socialization; after all Edmée was socialized precisely where Europe ends and where 'the home country' begins that has been rejected by the Europe of the doctor. Disgust for Jews appeared in Edmée on the instinctual level, literally came to her through her blood."[59] Mogilner's reading juxtaposes conceptual antipodes (Europe versus Asia), but one may interpret the story differently, noting the doctor's unexpected shock at Edmée's hostility to Jews. In the story, the decadent theme (pederasty) is joined somewhat awkwardly to the theme of antisemitism. Nonetheless, the story reiterates Jabotinsky's ideological conviction that Jews misinterpret their status. Their imagination, like the doctor's, leads them to invent relationships and feelings, but a few words from a partner throw cold water on them, making the doctor, or Gont, or the Jews in the Cherikov Affair, realize that non-Jews don't like them, want them, or need them.

* * *

During these years (1910 and 1914), Jabotinsky published several of the early stories that later appeared in a collected volume, called, simply, *Stories* (1930).[60] Although scholars have tried to connect Jabotinsky's literary oeuvre with the political writings, it seems impossible to draw any convincing conclusions from his early stories.[61] In his fiction, Jabotinsky dealt with nonpolitical issues, subjects that had no obvious connection to Zionism. Stories about his student days in Odessa, his university years in Italy, failed romances, and other escapades of youth remind one of other Russian prose writers of the time: Ivan Goncharov, Anton Chekhov, and Ivan Bunin.

It is impossible to take a wonderful story, such as "Diana," and link it to Jabotinsky's politics. The story is set in Rome and features a character named Vladimir Jabotinsky, who is involved in a complicated relationship with Diana, a young Italian woman who is his intellectual and emotional equal. Since she is engaged to someone else, it is unseemly and even dangerous for Diana and Vladimir to meet. So the question is: how to break off their friendship without ruining Diana's reputation. If one wanted to analyze the story in terms of Jabotinsky's political career, one could note a parallel with a Betarist who acts chivalrously. Jabotinsky acts chivalrously with Diana. He knows, as does she, that he cannot marry her, and therefore he steps aside. The final meeting recalls Italian opera, but no one dies, and one feels that the first-person narrator has learned a great deal about life from his experience.

It's a riveting story, but what does it say about Zionism, Jewish politics, and antisemitism? A symbolic reading suggested to me by Alexander Orbach identifies Diana with Russia—a love-object that cannot be possessed and so must be abandoned honorably. Orbach's creativity, not Jabotinsky's, finds expression in this operatic tale.

Similarly, "Squirrel," another fine piece of fiction, also somewhat autobiographical, has nothing to say about Jabotinsky's politics. From these stories, one can hone in on the fiction-versus-politics problem. According to some literary aficionados, politics was guilty of stealing a great talent. The writer Leonid Gershovich expresses the position best when he writes, "Precisely what stopped Jabotinsky from becoming a significant force in Russian literature was his leadership of the 'Jewish barracks.' But his gifts as a writer had greater value than his talent as a politician. Therefore, for us Jabotinsky is above all else a writer."[62] The émigré Mikhail Osorgin conveyed the same thought when he said that "for him and many Russians, Jabotinsky was and remained a Russian writer, novelist and journalist, a Jewish colleague who mastered Russian better than many native Russian writers . . . whose exit from literature into political activism was a kind of wound for his fellow wordsmiths."[63]

Jabotinsky's status as a writer in relation to his political work raises numerous issues, especially when one considers that many of the political leaders of the era, especially on the right, practiced creative art and writing. The Italian futurists (inventors of Fascism) were artists: Charles Maurras and Léon Daudet (leaders of the Action Française) and Benito Mussolini were writers. Literary dabbling, and even professional writing, served to legitimize political activity. For one thing, writers enjoyed celebrity status. Additionally, writers were often viewed as representatives of the nation, and their voices had authority, which gave them influence in the political sphere.[64]

It seems right to say that Jabotinsky's authority was enhanced by his journalism, which had lent him a celebrity status in Odessa at the start of the twentieth century. But his was a local Odessa popularity, and the writers of *Evreiskaia Zhizn'* were hardly household names outside of the relatively small pro-Zionist reading public. Moreover, Jabotinsky was known for his political activity and polemical writings more than his literary work.

Nonetheless, it is worth asking whether the publication of his stories reflected a desire for stature in the Russian literary pantheon. We know that in his earlier days, Jabotinsky had sought inclusion in Russian literature. Thus, one wonders whether Jabotinsky was still keeping his options open and whether, if he had been celebrated as a writer, he might have chosen that alternative path.

* * *

Although scholars have tried to connect the two parts of Jabotinsky's life—his literary work and his political activism—this has proven difficult. Even more difficult is connecting his universalist individualism and his sectarian Zionism. The best attempt, by Michael Stanislawski, compares Jabotinsky with Theodor Herzl, who also strayed far from Judaism as a religion and even from the Jewish people, but "returned" (in David Roskies' term) to the Jewish people through Zionism. For Stanislawski, the key that opens the mystery is the Weltanschauung that prevailed at the turn of the twentieth century, which emphasized individual potential and dreams of future greatness, combined with national aspirations. This certainly applies to Jabotinsky, if somewhat vaguely, since that Weltanschauung includes contradictory qualities: individualist-nationalist, aesthete-politician, Jewish apologist-militarist. On the face of it, Jabotinsky swallowed whole the Symbolist mystique—its ideas, modes of writing, and behavioral norms; then he adopted Zionism. What or where is the bridge between the two?

On the question of how to understand Jabotinsky's status as a writer and politician, the reader might consider daring language in Jabotinsky's feuilletons. Among the few things that Jabotinsky-the-decadent took with him when he became Jabotinsky-the-Zionist, the feuilleton was one. In fact, the feuilleton played a direct role in the development of Jabotinsky's political style. Feuilleton writing and the feuilleton genre actually have little to do with political tactics, yet Jabotinsky succeeded in breaking the rules and shaping it into an instrument for his personal use. The fundamental element is "daring"—breaking rules and disputing conventions, provoking others, and energizing one's supporters.

The feuilleton occupied a large place in Jabotinsky's oeuvre. He employed it early in his career and never stopped. It shaped him as a writer, a thinker, and politician. A letter to Maxim Gorky in 1903 reveals Jabotinsky's anguished pride in his accomplishments as a feuilletonist:

> I got pulled into the newspaper and it appears that I will never get out. Therefore, people who earlier predicted great things for me, now think I am dead. I do not want to think that way because I know that I have put a great deal of passion and fury into some of my feuilletons. It would be painful for me to reconcile with the idea that, because of their origins in the newspaper, they are destined for oblivion.... After multiple hesitations, I decided to send you, as the director of the publisher, Znanie, the collection of my newspaper feuilletons with a request to publish them as a volume.[65]

Though Gorky did not publish the collection, it did appear in 1913, issued in St. Petersburg by the publishing house of Shlomo Zal'tsman. The initial volume was republished under the same title in Berlin in 1922 but with additional articles. All the essays in the volumes concerned Jewish themes.

To get closer to the original purpose of the feuilleton in its day, let us turn to a definition of the genre from his biographer, Joseph Schechtman, who writes that it

> is not exactly an essay, neither is it precisely a short story, not necessarily a topical article, nor timely criticism—yet it partakes of all of them.... Feuilletons were almost completely non-political. Most of them dealt with subjects of minor, often local and passing, significance. Altalena would write on the deficiencies of the city's communications system run by a Belgian company, or of limitations of the rights of university students; of citizens' demands that the city fathers improve streets and parks, or of current performances in the municipal theater. He would discuss the new public library, but also topics of more essential and lasting interest: problems of youth, of ethics, art, literature. All of them, irrespective of their content, were remarkable specimens of brilliant writing, done with a light and provocative touch; more often than not they were bubbling with the exuberance of youth, with the irrepressible urge to proclaim truth, beauty, and justice, whenever the writer felt those values to be involved.[66]

Jabotinsky's feuilletons exemplified the genre. His narrator shifts between topics and also tones, from serious to humorous, sardonic, ironic, melancholy, pathetic, desperate, confident, and factual. To add to Schechtman, feuilletons are defined by a degree of self-conscious artifice; the author knows that he is producing a literary construct, in which content is less important than context, and the author's imagination is less important than social issues. Also central is the mutually dependent relationship of author and reader—the author alludes to shared values even when he/she tries to convince. Finally, the purpose is as much entertainment as edification.

We might examine a few examples. This one appeared on December 21, 1901, and was published in *Odesskii Listok*. Here Jabotinsky, writing as Altalena, discusses women's education in response to a new school for women in Odessa. He writes,

> It is easy for a specialist to write three volumes to prove that a women's brain proves her incapacity for science.
> It is equally easy to write three volumes to prove that a woman's brain proves her capacity for scientific activity.
> It is easier to proclaim that science distracts a woman from her motherly duties and kills femininity in her.
> And still easier to disprove that and prove the opposite—that science "in no way" distracts a woman from her motherly duties and "in no way" robs her of her femininity.[67]

The voice here uses irony to reach his conclusion: "support women's schools!" Incidentally his sister, Tamara Jabotinskaia-Kopp, was a schoolteacher and principal in Odessa and Eretz Yisrael.

On July 7, 1903, Altalena employed a self-conscious voice:

> My soul is unhappy, reader.
> I look at my colleagues and at myself.
> We could bring a lot of benefit.
> After all, several tens of thousands of people generally read us.
> We could speak with them about the things that interest them.
> Sometimes, perhaps, we would succeed in explaining to them those things they misunderstood. . . .
> Instead of this, we deceive them.
> We never give them what they expect.
> Sometimes we do not raise subjects that interest them.
> We are not conscientious, we are dishonest, crafty: we do not write what we think, do not write about the things that concern us.[68]

There is more than a whiff of self-deprecation in the assertion that we journalists could bring edification, but, alas, we cannot, because we are too shallow. This is a Russian topos of morally beating one's breast.

Incidentally, Jabotinsky used a variety of pseudonyms with his feuilletons. Why? Certainly the author's identity involves the genre's artifice; the author is not the real person but also not hidden; the author's identity both matters and doesn't. What matters is that he is one of us, a person just like you and me, because he presents shared values and the common response to injustice, moral turpitude, and government incompetency.

There are many more examples. In almost every one, the generic definitions hold: Jabotinsky's use of the feuilleton reflects the domination of a moral voice, the concern with righting wrongs. But this concern with morality differs from political engagement. Schechtman is right: the absence of politics characterizes the feuilleton, and for good reason: an essential feature is its playful discourse; a political message would clash with the author's light, mocking treatment.

If politics has no place in the Russian feuilleton, nothing was less feuilleton-ish than Jabotinsky's Zionist writings, which are unapologetically political, ideological, and polemical? Take, for example, Jabotinsky's essay from 1911, "Instead of an Apology," written in reaction to the arrest of Mendel Beilis. Beilis, we remember, was arrested for the crime of using a Christian's blood to make matza. With this essay, Jabotinsky writes exclusively for a sympathetic audience. "How much longer will this go on? Tell me, my friends, are you not tired by now of this rigmarole? Isn't it high time, in response to all of these accusations, rebukes, suspicions, smears, and denunciations—both present and future—to fold our arms over our chests and loudly, clearly, coldly, and calmly put forth the only argument which this public can understand: why don't you all go to hell?"[69]

The author is anything but factual, neutral, or mocking. Jabotinsky is leveling a polemic, knocking down people's arguments. In her general description of Jabotinsky's rhetoric, Anita Shapira writes: "Jabotinsky's style was inseparable from his personality. When one of his disciples, Yehoshua Klinov, wished to try to bring the revisionists closer together with the camp of Labor, he suggested to Jabotinsky that he should express himself in a more cautious and circumspect way. Jabotinsky replied that his strength as a journalist was not in writing about some objective truth. Rather, he bent the stick, in a figurative sense, all the way to the opposite side in order to accentuate and sharpen the point he wished to emphasize. 'This is the only journalistic method I can use,' he remarked."[70]

A similar point is made by Yosef Gorny, who argues that Jabotinsky's exaggerations have political value insofar as they control the conversation: Jabotinsky's opponents are so busy responding, they can't promote their own ideas. Additionally, Jabotinsky's provocations have the benefit of dividing readers into allies or rivals; therefore, the rhetoric sharpens the discourse and leaves no room for compromise. Gorny writes that Jabotinsky began to use his political proclamations of "the true nature of Zionism" in order "to exert pressure on the opponent so as to force him, in turn, to clarify his own aims and to be clearly aware of what lay ahead. Such pressure might not change the opinions of opponents or persuade those who were vacillating, but it would force the Jews to open their eyes to facts and to prepare the instruments for the confrontation with reality."[71]

It is easy to agree with Shapira and Gorny that Jabotinsky's Zionist rhetoric cannot be separated from his personality. The striking way he linked his Revisionist political style with his own voice is evident in his early feuilletons, where he persuaded readers through sarcasm, cajoling, pathos, and personal appeal. The difference between ordinary feuilletons and Jabotinsky's feuilletons comes down to daring—upsetting norms, going beyond the conventional. Alexander Kulisher, a Revisionist colleague, writes about Jabotinsky with the help of an allusion to Danton and the French Revolution: "Victor Hugo says in one place.... In order to make the French Revolution it was not enough that Diderot predicted it, that Voltaire prepared it, that Rousseau pointed to its ideal, that Sieyès appealed for it, that Mirabeau proclaimed it—it was necessary that Danton did it. 'Daring' has a particular meaning here: the sense of word and 'gesture,' what one says and does in the moment when the situation demands something new. Novelty makes them 'daring,' it fits the profound forces of history that turn them into historical action."[72] Kulisher views Jabotinsky as the Danton of our own day.

Perhaps Literary Structuralism can help us here. The language of Jabotinsky's behavior is characterized by shifts and breaks; resignations and change of direction; retreating from one group and starting anew with another. Creating new organizations, new parties—all this mirrors the language of the feuilleton with its multidirectional voices. If the feuilleton draws attention to its quality of literariness, Jabotinsky's political behavior does the same—it draws attention to its strangeness. If Anita Shapira is right that Jabotinsky's style is his personality, then both his feuilleton writing and political behavior reflect the use of daring language—to rouse, to challenge, to provoke.

Perhaps a bigger question should be posed: Why was feuilleton writing a productive path to Zionist politics for Herzl, Nordau, and Jabotinsky? For starters, we should examine the social component of the author-reader relationship. In the feuilleton, authors came into contact with reality, and some realized that it is not enough to describe problems; one should prescribe solutions. Recall Jabotinsky's feuilleton from 1903—"we could do more to help people." Furthermore, the feuilleton, with its emphasis on entertainment, turns the author into a kind of celebrity who could use his/her writing as a platform for a political career. Herzl certainly was guilty. Jabotinsky, too, exploited his fame as a journalist to launch his career in politics. Employing an urgent style and language, Jabotinsky agitated for change. That desire shaped his political style and became his signature as a Zionist.

What we may wonder, when discussing Jabotinsky, is whether the writer's mentality influenced the politician's. In his work on Jabotinsky's poetry, Dan Miron depicts a writer whose artistic choices are based on his literary education in late Russian realism.[73] If there is a connection between the writer and the political activist, perhaps it is in the realm of aesthetics. Jabotinsky sought wholeness, order, logic, in himself and in others. He would articulate the idea of Monism, a commitment to a single goal: Zionism. However, it is easy to claim, as many have, that Jabotinsky was not as serious in his writing as he was in his politics. In truth, creative writing would take a distinct second seat to politics.

Notes

1. Hans Rogger, *Jewish Policies and Right-Wing Politics in Imperial Russia* (London: Macmillan Press, 1986), 189.
2. Maksim Vinaver, *Istoriia vyborgskogo vozzvaniia (vospominaniia)* (Moscow, 1913), 75–76.
3. Vladimir Levin, *Mi-mahapeha le-milhama: Ha-politika ha-yehudit be-rusya, 1907–1914* (Jerusalem: Zalman Shazar Center for Jewish History, 2016), 46–47.
4. L. N. Nisselovich, *Evreiskii vopros v 3-ei Gosudarstvennoi Dumy: Otchet chlena Gosudarstvennoi Dumy* (St. Petersburg: Ts. Kraiz, 1908), 20. Since Nisselovich's is an apologetic booklet that sought an understanding with the Octobrists, one should also turn to Levin, *Mi-mahapeha le-milhama*, 66–68.
5. *Vekhi: Sbornik statei o russkoi intelligentsii* (St. Petersburg, 1909).
6. Mikhail Gershenzon, "Tvorcheskoe samosoznanie," *Vekhi*, 82.
7. Brian Horowitz, *Jewish Philanthropy and Enlightenment in Late-Tsarist Russia* (Seattle: University of Washington Press, 2009), 190–205.
8. Christoph Gassenschmidt, *Jewish Liberal Politics in Tsarist Russia, 1900–1914: The Modernization of Russian Jewry* (New York: New York University Press, 1995), 84–93.
9. Ibid., 91.
10. Rogger, *Jewish Policies*, 32–33.
11. Ibid., 36–39.
12. Vladimir Jabotinsky, "V traurnye dni (1906)," *Fel'etony* (1912), 21–23.

13. Yitzhak Maor, *Sionistskoe dvizhenie v Rossii*, trans. O. Mints (Jerusalem: Biblioteka Alia, 1977), 267–279.

14. Gregorz Krzywiec describes the Endek philosophy toward Jews in the second Duma. "During the elections to the Russian Duma in the spring of 1907, the Endeks became even more radical in their attitude toward the Jews and began using political antisemitism as an instrument for combating any opposition. The Jews as a metaphor of 'the enemy within' began epitomizing all kinds of aggression against 'Polishness,' and the ND Party appointed itself, during the first campaign in 1906 and even in a more aggressive way in 1907 in the campaign to the second Duma, the sole depository and defender of Polish values." "Eliminationist Anti-Semitism at Home and Abroad: Polish Nationalism, the Jewish Question and Eastern European Right-Wing Mass Politics," in *The New Nationalism and the First World War*, ed. Lawrence Rosenthal and Vesna Rodic (New York: Palgrave, 2015), 69.

15. Vladimir Jabotinsky, *Story of My Life* (Detroit: Wayne State University Press, 2017), 94.

16. A diploma gave him the right to live in Russia proper, a right that had eluded him earlier. Despite the myriad discriminatory decrees and laws against Jews, one privilege from the time of Alexander II remained in force: the right to live anywhere in the Russian Empire.

17. Vladimir Jabotinsky, "Samoupravlenie natsional'nogo men'shinstva," *Vestnik Evropy* 9 (September 1913), 10 (October 1913).

18. Jabotinsky, *Story of My Life*, 94.

19. Jabotinsky suggested that modern Hebrew be written in Latin script. See Vladimir Jabotinsky, *Taryag Milim: 613 (Hebrew) Words—Introduction into Spoken Hebrew (in Latin Characters)* (New York: Jabotinsky Foundation, 1949).

20. The results of Duma elections tell the story. In the first Duma (April 27–July 8, 1906) there were twelve Jewish deputies, but in the following Dumas, this number significantly diminished, to four deputies in the Second Duma (February 20–June 2, 1907); two deputies in the third Duma (November 1, 1907–June 9, 1912); and three deputies in the fourth Duma (November 12, 1912–October 6, 1917). See Vladimir Levin, "Russian Jewry and the Duma Elections, 1906–1907," *Jews and Slavs* 7 (2000): 233.

21. Yossi Goldshtein, *Ussishkin biografiya: Ha-tekufa ha-rusit, 1853–1919* (Jerusalem: Magnes Press, 2000), 1:225.

22. David Vital, *Zionism: The Crucial Phase* (Oxford: Clarendon, 1987), 23–24.

23. Yuval Ben-Bassat, "Rethinking the Concept of Ottomanization: The Yishuv in the Aftermath of the Young Turk Revolution of 1908," *Middle Eastern Studies* 45, no. 3 (2009): 462.

24. On the enthusiasm of Russian Zionist leaders and on collection of fifty thousand rubles for establishing newspapers in Istanbul, see Levin, *Mi-mahapeha le-milhama*, 202–203, 209.

25. Jabotinsky uses the word "Politcom"—i.e., political commissar—in his autobiography. *Story of My Life*, 97.

26. Yaron Ben Naeh, "The Zionist Struggle as Reflected in the Jewish Press in Istanbul in the Aftermath of the Young Turk Revolution, 1908–18," in *Late Ottoman Palestine: The Period of Young Turk Rule*, ed. Yuval Ben-Basssat and Eyal Ginio (London: I. B. Tauris. 2011), 246.

27. Ibid.

28. Levin, *Mi-mahapeha le-milhama*, 209.

29. Vladimir Jabotinsky, "Novaia Turtsiia i nashi perspektivy," *Rassvet* 5 (February 1, 1909): 2.

30. Vladimir Jabotinsky, "Politicheskaia rol' Sefardov," *Rassvet* 10 (March 8, 1909): 4.
31. Ibid.
32. Jonathan Mark Gribetz, *Defining Neighbors: Religion, Race, and the Early Zionist-Arab Encounter* (Princeton, NJ: Princeton University Press, 2014), 91.
33. Yosef Gorny, "To Understand Oneself: Does It Mean to Understand the Other?," *Israel Studies* 19, no. 2 (Summer 2013): 52.
34. Ibid.
35. Vladimir Jabotinsky, "Politicheskaia rol' Sefardov," *Rassvet* (March 22, 1909): 3.
36. Ibid.
37. Jacobus Kahn, *Erez Israel, das jüdische Land* (Köln: Jüdischer Verlag, 1909). This incident is treated by Vital, *Zionism*, 55–56.
38. Jabotinsky described this incident in his autobiography. See *Story of My Life*, 110.
39. Jabotinsky, *Story of My Life*, 96.
40. The guard movement (Ha-shomrim) had officially become established in 1907.
41. Jabotinsky, *Story of My Life*, 96.
42. Ibid., 96.
43. Viktor Kel'ner, "Dva intsidenta: Iz russko-evreiskikh otnoshenii v nachale XX v." *Vestnik Evreiskogo Universiteta v Moskve* 3, no. 10 (1995).
44. See Kornei Chukovskii, "Evrei v russkoi literature," *Rassvet* 3 (January 18, 1908): 8–10.
45. Vladimir Jabotinsky, "Russkaia laska," *Fel'etony* (Berlin, 1922), 125–26. (First publication 1909.) The "feet" refer to Nikolai Gogol's novel, *Taras Bulba*.
46. Amir Goldstein, *Derech rebat-panim: Tsionuto shel Zeev Z'abotinski le-nokech ha-antishemiut* (Tel Aviv: Jabotinsky Institute, 2015), 142–48. Svetlana Natkovich treats this material in her book, *Ben aneney zohar: Yetsirato shel Vladimir (Ze'ev) Z'abotinski ba-heksher ha-hevrati* (Jerusalem: Magnes, 2015), 117–18.
47. Vladimir Jabotinsky, *Fel'etony*, 2nd ed. (Berlin, 1922), 126.
48. Ibid., 128.
49. Ibid., 102–103.
50. In 1907, Jabotinsky still maintained that the two parts of his identity—Russian Jew—could be made whole through a synthesis of the two.
51. Michael Stanislawski, *Zionism and the Fin De Siècle: Cosmopolitanism and Nationalism from Nordau to Jabotinsky* (Berkeley: University of California Press, 2001), ix.
52. "In the winter of 1907, while in Vienna, Jabotinsky conceived the idea of and started working on a drama in verse, *Extern Abram*, devoted to the spiritual crisis of Russian Jewry. In 1908, Jabotinsky read this play, which he renamed *Chuzhbina* (*The Alien Land*)—a comedy in five acts, before a select gathering of St. Petersburg writers. The opinions of those present were divided. Some praised it very highly, others questioned its literary value and saw in it a 'publicistic feuilleton in rhymes or rhythmic prose.' Nevertheless, the manuscript was sent to the printers and proof sheets were submitted to the censor. The latter started making difficulties: he demanded substantial cuts and changes and threatened to confiscate the work upon its appearance. The publication of the play was therefore suspended for fourteen years; it was not before 1922 that S. D. Salzman published it in Berlin. In Russia, extensive excerpts from *Chuzhbina* appeared in 1910 in *Rassvet*, where S. Gepstein devoted to it an extensive review, 'based on a set of proof sheets salvaged from the censor's clutches.'" Joseph Schechtman, *The Life and Times of Vladimir Jabotinsky: Rebel and Statesman, The Early Years* (Silver Spring: Eshel Books, 1986), 139.

53. Natkovich, *Ben aneney zohar*, 97.

54. See Mikhail Weiskopf's article, "Predislovie," in Vladimir Jabotinsky (Vladimir Zhabotinskii), *Chuzhbina (P'esa)* (Jerusalem: Gesharim, 2000), 5–14.

55. Jabotinsky, *Chuzhbina*, 223.

56. Weiskopf, "Predislovie," 12.

57. Zsuzsa Hetényi, *In a Maelstrom: The History of Russian-Jewish Prose, 1860–1940* (Budapest: Central European University Press, 2008), 115–168.

58. "Edmée," *Odesskie Novosti* (June 17, 1912).

59. Marina Mogilner, "Fin de siècle imperii: Ostrovnaia utopia Vladimira Zhabotinskogo," *NLO* 1 (2018): 9.

60. Vladimir Jabotinsky, *Razskazy* (Paris: Voltaire, 1930).

61. Yehuda Friedlander, "He-arot le-yitsirato ha-sifrutit shel Ze'ev Z'abotinsky," in *Ish be-sa'ar: Masot u'mekhkarim 'al Ze'ev Z'abotinski*, ed. Avi Bareli and Pinhas Ginossar (Ber-Sheva: Universitat Ben-Guryon ba'Negev, 2004), 283–98; See also Barry Scherr, "An Odessa Odyssey: Vladimir Jabotinsky's *The Five*," *Slavic Review* 70 (2011): 94–115; Marat Grinberg, "Was Jabotinsky the Zionist Nabokov?" *Tablet Magazine*, August 4, 2014, tabletmag.com/jewish-arts-and-culture/books/180735/jabotinsky-the-zionist (August 4, 2014).

62. Quoted in Mikhail Veiskopf, "Liubov' k dal'nemu: literaturnoe tvorchestvo Vladimira Zhabotinskogo," *Vestnik Evreiskogo Universiteta v Moskve* 29, no. 11 (2006): 196.

63. Quoted in I. Galperin, "V. E. Zhabotinskii (biograficheskii ocherk)," *Evreiskii mir: Sbornik* (New York: Union of Russian Jews, 1944), 2:220.

64. Jacob Golomb, *Nietzsche and Zion* (Ithaca, NY: Cornell University Press, 2004), 8.

65. Vladimir Jabotinsky to Maxim Gorky, in Vladimir Jabotinsky, "Pis'ma russkim pisateliam," *Vestnik Evreiskogo Universiteta v Moskve* 1 (1992): 216.

66. Schechtman, *Rebel and Statesman*, 65.

67. Vladimir Jabotinsky, "Vskol'z," *Polnoe sobranie socheinenii v deviati tomakh* (Minsk: Met, 2007), 2:658.

68. Jabotinsky, "Vskol'z," *Polnoe sobranie sochinenii*, 3:354.

69. Vladimir Jabotinsky, "Vmesto apologii," *Fel'etony*, 3rd ed. (Berlin: Zal'tsman, 1922), 13.

70. Anita Shapira, *Land and Power: The Zionist Resort to Force, 1881–1948* (Stanford, CA: Stanford University Press, 1999), 162.

71. Gorny, *Zionism and the Arabs, 1882–1948: A Study of Ideology*, trans. Chaya Galai (Oxford: Clarendon Press, 1987), 162.

72. Aleksandr Kulisher, "Politicheskii vozhd'," *Rassvet* 42 (October 19, 1930): 5.

73. Dan Miron, "Trumato shel Ze'ev Z'abotinski le-shira ha-ivrit ha-modernit in *Ish be-sa'ar*, 187–252.

5

POLITICAL ALLIANCES BREAK; JABOTINSKY GOES HIS OWN WAY, 1907–1914

* * *

IN 1909, ON THE HEELS OF THE CHERIKOV Affair, new expressions of Russian nationalism appeared that affected politics generally and the liberal camp in particular. Unlike earlier times, when the state monopolized politics and—with the exception of radicals—few people dared challenge it, now there were independent political parties, which disseminated their views (more or less) independent of government involvement. Earlier, the state and the yellow press had a monopoly over Russian nationalistic and jingoistic expression. Now it came from many quarters. In this climate, the Kadet Party (Constitutional Democrats) moved rightward. At the same time, Poland seethed with antisemitism.

This was the time of the third Duma (1907–1912), which the center-right Octobrists dominated. The Octobrists were confident that their perceived ideological unity with the government would lead to successful reforms.[1] Although the actual results were meager, a conservative spirit dominated the Duma. A pronationalist attitude led such Kadets as Pyotr Struve, Pavel Miliukov, and Vasilii Maklakov—individuals who had sought a coalition with opposition parties in 1905—to move from the left-center toward a compromise with the political center-right.[2]

One significant example was Pyotr Struve, whose article, "The Intelligentsia and the Face of the Nation" (1909), defended the domination of Russian culture in the empire. Struve drew a distinction between the culture of the state (*gosudarstvennost'*), which he thought lacked distinct qualities, and the culture of the Russian nation. Struve was proud of Russian culture and rejected accusations that its domination over others was shameful. "In the difficult trials of the last years our national Russian feeling has appeared. It has changed, become more complex and refined, and at the same time more courageous and strong. Let us stop pretending and stop hiding our [national] face."[3] Dismissing the conception of the Empire as a cosmopolitan whole, he asserted the primacy of Russia. Regarding Jews, Struve praised individual Jews who embraced Russian culture (his best example was the painter Isaac Levitan), while Zionists and other Jewish nationalists earned his opprobrium.[4] But he set strict conditions: only Jews who integrated in Russian culture would be accepted.

Jewish Constitutional Democrats, such as the lawyers Maxim Vinaver and Osip Gruzenberg, found themselves in a difficult position. They could not ignore that Struve seemed to have arrived at an accommodation with the tsarist regime. Vinaver defended Struve as a patriotic Russian who had not abandoned fundamental principles, including equal rights for national minorities.[5] Vinaver reasoned that "Russian" in this context did not exclude national minorities, and that Struve and the Kadet Party remained committed to the principle of equality for all of Russia's citizens.

One might be cautioned here not to label the Kadet party antisemitic. To a degree, antisemitism infected the party, but the motivation was largely pragmatic. The strident and explicit hostility to Jews persuaded Kadet leaders not to identify themselves publicly with the Jewish plight. Struve, Miliukov, and Maklakov refrained from advancing any measure that would give the impression that they were "Jew lovers" or had been bought off by Jewish "wealth"—two common accusations at the time.[6] Nonetheless, in 1911, Kadets did support a bill to abrogate the Pale of Settlement. One of the two Jewish deputies, L. N. Nisselovich, introduced the legislation and even managed to get all the opposition members behind him. However, because the majority opposed it, it could not pass.[7] Overall, confidence in the Kadet party's commitment to Jewish equality fell, especially because the party had achieved so little of substance for the national minorities.[8]

Semyon Goldin, a historian at Hebrew University, has shrewdly observed that Struve's viewpoint paralleled the Enlightenment position that Jews should receive full rights as individuals, but not as a collective.[9] It might be noted here that Semyon Dubnov, the widely respected Jewish historian in Russia, described the French Revolution as a betrayal because Jews traded their collective identity for the sake of individual rights.[10]

Jabotinsky claimed that the liberals' newfound devotion to Russian nationalism was motivated by antisemitic attitudes that were concealed beneath prettified political principles. Jabotinsky mocked the liberals, calling them "a bear out of his lair"—that is, the freedom to insult Jews had awoken them. Struve appeared to represent higher principles, but when he encountered the Jewish Question, he was revealed to be no more enlightened than politicians further to the right, since he too rejected Jewish separatism. Jabotinsky, making an allusion to Alexander Herzen's famous remark that the Decembrist movement was a "shot in the silent darkness"—a sign of protest at a time of political passivity—wrote about liberal antisemitism: "What was going on—[was it] a chance wayward bullet flying who knows from where, or a first and even premature shot from a strong camp that was ready to adopt a military footing?"[11] For Jabotinsky, the joke involved a comparison with the Decembrists; either this shot represented an aimless and haphazard effort without a clear origin or it was the start of something potentially very dangerous. In any case, the liberal's shot against Russian Jewry was undignified, if only because Jews were already oppressed by the government and other political parties.

Jabotinsky went further. He not only repudiated Struve's claims that the empire must have a Russian national character; he faulted the decent liberal Russians who ignored antisemitism. He was more pained by their non-response than by antisemitism itself, he wrote:

> Five years have passed since the Kishinev Pogrom. During this time pamphlets and broadsheets that advocate tribal slaughter have flooded Russia, dozens of gutter newspapers are distributed on all corners that incite passionate hate toward Jews. Nearly the entire ideology of the reactionary movement leads to hate and it would seem that the liberal Russian press should intercede on behalf of the persecuted if only because of a chivalrous need to defend the oppressed and fight this propaganda. The liberal Russian press did not do anything like this. Indeed, forgive me a sharp word: I found more nails driven into the dead pupils of [the eye] of one of the victims of the Bialystok Pogrom than articles about this pogrom in the liberal Russian press.[12]

Did Jabotinsky really think that Struve and other Kadet leaders were antisemitic? It's difficult to say. Clearly, he wanted to argue that Jews had little to gain from cooperation with them. That lumping together of everyone who couldn't advance the cause of Jewish equality or support Zionism was almost a conventional attitude among Zionists. At the same time, there was little to gain from repudiating the only alliance with Russians that had any realistic hope of success. However, if his goal was to radicalize Jews and turn them away from the dream of a Kadet-Zionist alliance, then his efforts made sense.

Still, one should not criticize Jabotinsky too harshly. To be sure, Jabotinsky purposely misrepresented Struve in order to radicalize Jews, but the Kadets also played their own political game. Jabotinsky and others accused the Kadets of moving to the political right, thus signaling that they were not puppets of Jewish interests.[13] However, it is also possible to view the rightward shift as an attempt to distance the party from the Jewish Question, which was then intractable. But it is also possible that a tension existed between two principles: the prohibition of state antisemitism, and allowing individuals to discriminate. David Vital puts it well when he writes about Vasily Maklakov, a right-wing Kadet:

> Even declared and committed liberals found the subject tricky, if not distasteful. When in 1911, the noisily reactionary antisemitic Third Duma was forced by a handful of courageous deputies, led by one of its two Jewish members, to debate a proposal to abolish the Pale of Settlement in which the greater part of Russian and Polish Jewry was confined, the liberal and generally decent Kadet party reluctantly resolved to support the motion. They had, indeed, no choice. But their spokesman, Vasily Maklakov, an eminent and respectable attorney, was careful to take the line that antisemitism in itself was permissible. Those now, for whatever reason, liberal Russians were fully entitled to ostracize them socially and boycott them in their business dealings, to avoid looking at works of art they had produced or listening to music they had written. What was impermissible was for the state to engage in discrimination.[14]

Jabotinsky found himself in an awkward position. He had been educated among liberals and believed in Russian liberalism. The principles of justice, democracy, and protection for minorities made up the bedrock of his spiritual being. That explains why he could pay scant attention to the government and self-professed antisemites like the members of the Black Hundreds, while obsessing over Russian liberals. The liberals mattered, because they alone interfered with the construction of a Zionist monopoly within the Jewish community on the center and right of center. At this time, intra-Jewish politics flared up when the Bund agreed to run for Duma seats. Now there were alternatives to Zionism both among the left and the center—the Jewish People's Party, the Jewish National Group, representatives of Orthodox Jewry—which raised questions regarding Zionist claims to be the authentic spokespersons of Russian Jewry. Jabotinsky guessed correctly that the Kadets represented the biggest threat, and therefore he wrote a series of articles on liberal antisemitism in order to neutralize them.[15]

It was bad enough that Struve would betray the principle of equality, but even worse was the case of Maxim Vinaver, the Jewish Kadet leader, who in Jabotinsky's eyes was a traitor who humiliated himself through craven subservience to his Russian masters.[16] In 1911, Jabotinsky commented in the liberal journal *Rech'*: "Mr. Vinaver . . . nonetheless offers now and for the future Jewish support warmed with mutual love, 'precisely love.' Let it be. A lovely calf sucks two udders. We would like to offer Mr. Vinaver and such lovely people [the chance] to live Malthusian lifetimes in the curious position where they, looking into each other's eyes, sweetly say, 'After all, you love us!' but Mr. Struve and Mr. Miliukov answer, 'Mm . . . not really.'"[17] The image accompanying the text showed a calf squeezed uncomfortably beneath two cow udders, with the face of Vinaver below and those of Struve and Miliukov above.

Here is still another example of the kind of character assassination in which Jabotinsky indulged. According to Jabotinsky, Vinaver's subservience amounted to self-hatred because he sold out Jewish interests to gain his colleagues' affection. But that's not all: Jabotinsky demonized Vinaver, putting into his mouth the idea that Kadets will only accept Jews who renounce Jewish interests. "This was as bad as the Bund that also asked Jews to deny Jewish interests in order to be liked."[18]

* * *

Although he wrote a great deal about antisemitism among non-Jews, especially in politics, it was Jewish self-hate that drew Jabotinsky's strongest ire. Russian-Jewish journalists had a long history of criticizing real apostates and near apostates—those who sold out fellow Jews or abased themselves to gain advantage. However, Jabotinsky had a political agenda. Since his Zionism was that of Helsingfors (i.e., political activity in the Diaspora) and not emigration to the future Jewish state exclusively, he could offer Zionism as the panacea for any problem at home.

Jabotinsky blamed Jews for tolerating antisemitism rather than accusing non-Jews of provoking it. But he faced certain rhetorical constraints: How to shame Jews without appearing a scold? Perhaps Jabotinsky borrowed the approach from Hayim Nachman Bialik when he pointed to the phenomenon of Jewish humiliation. Unlike Bialik, however, he used Struve's term, "asemitism," which the latter had used in his essay "The

Intelligentsia and the Face of the Nation" (1909).[19] Like Struve, Jabotinsky insisted that asemitism should be defined as "legitimate" indifference to the Jewish minority. Non-Jews who do not hate Jews, but also don't want them around, or want to socialize with them, or have their children attend the same schools as Jews, do not deserve condemnation. According to Jabotinsky, there is justification for this view. In fact, one can derive from asemitism Jabotinsky's later position in which he divides antisemitism into two types: the antisemitism of things and the antisemitism of men.[20]

The antisemitism of things reflects a normal society, where the majority discriminates against minorities not out of malice, but to aid one's own family or nation. If a Pole hires another Pole over a Jewish candidate, is that antisemitism? Perhaps, but it is natural and justified by the understandable desire to aid one's brother, son, or neighbor. However, the other kind of antisemitism, malevolent and disturbing, is the antisemitism of men. Here, hate is entirely unprovoked and unjustified. The antisemite singles out the Jew and instrumentalizes hate for various reasons, including political gain. In Jabotinsky's interpretation, in the 1930s Poland embodied the antisemitism of things: there were too many Jews in Poland, which led to unemployment among Poles. In contrast, Nazi Germany practiced the antisemitism of men. The government employed racial discrimination as a kind of sugar pill to push through harmful policies that would never win approval without provocations against Jews.

As an example of asemitism, Jabotinsky offered the withdrawal of Russians from literary clubs. In 1912, he noticed that the audience of literary clubs in the Pale of Settlement consisted entirely of Jews. As he tells it, Russian literary enthusiasts start a literary club. At first there are only Russians, then a few Jews come, and by the second month many more Jews join, but all the Russians have disappeared. Defenders assert that without Jews, these clubs would close due to a lack of patrons. Jabotinsky argued otherwise. "Allow me to ask: if there were no Jews at all in Petersburg or Odessa, would literary clubs really never crop up here and there? My modest opinion is that, not only would they appear, but they would flourish no less than those today—only the people in them would be Russian."[21] Could it be, he asks, that Russians just don't want to socialize with Jews when they celebrate their favorite writers? "They simply do not 'feel comfortable' with Jews, and when they see that, at their own holiday celebrations, too many Jews are dancing, then even the best of them prefer to celebrate at home; and if this is the case, then is it incumbent upon Jews to continue to assume the honored role of being the sole musicians at a stranger's wedding when the bride and groom have departed?"[22] Isn't this in fact an example of Jabotinsky's ideal of segregationism: ethnically or religiously different enclaves living together but kept apart from one another?[23]

Jabotinsky noticed that Jews in Russia suffered from an inferiority complex. He strongly criticized Jews who were embarrassed by their ethnic origins and therefore overpaid in order "not to appear stingy."

> The Jew of today loves to pay a premium for everything. For example, he gives an idiotic tip to a waiter that even the most generous Russian would never give; he's afraid of what "they might think." I know intellectuals who are fully incapable of bargaining in a store. Ten rubles are demanded for something whose price is clearly nine; a Russian, German, Pole would complain without any embarrassment. But an educated Jew feels uncomfortable, he is afraid that "they might think"—that he is economical and exacting, that he is (oh, no!) a cheapskate. And his entire life he tries to demonstrate that God forbid, he is not a cheapskate at all.[24]

"Asemitism" represents an attempt to use shaming as a weapon. Jabotinsky reports that Jews make non-Jews uncomfortable, letting the reader draw his/her own conclusion: alliances with non-Jews in politics, literature, or socializing do not work. The only way for Jews is separatism—that is, Zionism.

In "Our Everyday Event" (1910), Jabotinsky dealt with the issue of Jewish self-hate and betrayal. He reported that his position condemning converts had elicited angry letters. In fact, he argued that Jews who deserted Judaism in order to seize economic opportunity discredited the Christian society to which they now belonged.[25] If young Jews thought they could convert, but remain ethnically Jewish, Jabotinsky disabused them of that notion.

> To this day, those who leave our religion also leave our nationality. And in Europe, moreover, there is a saying: "Grandpa is an assimilator, father is baptized, the son is an antisemite." This is entirely natural. The "father" still possesses, nevertheless, a warmth in his soul from his memories of childhood connected with the Sabbath, or at least from the tears of his mother on the day he went to see the priest. But his son really cannot feel anything but a profound irritation toward all Jews because people sometimes still curse at him anyway and call him a kike. They won't let him forget that's he's a Jew, he is unable to love Judaism, and one thing remains: to hate it.[26]

Jabotinsky understood why Jews were inclined to hate themselves. Take Russian schools, for instance: despite debilitating quotas, Jews were rushing to get into these institutions as a means of acquiring basic civil rights.

A good example of his attitude is this passage from "On National Education" (1910):

> The children of our people hear the word "Jew" from their parents only with the connotations of contempt and fear. Bringing her son out onto the street, his mother says to him, "Remember that you are a Jew, and walk on the edge of the sidewalk so that you don't bump into anyone. . . ." Leaving him at school, his mother tells him, "Remember that you are a Jew, and be as quiet as a church-mouse. . . ." Thus, for him, the word "Jew" is involuntarily connected with the idea of the slave's lot and nothing more. He does not know a Jew, he knows a kike; he does not know Solomon, but only Shylock; he does not know the proud Syrian horse that our people once were—he knows only the pathetic "nag" of today.[27]

In his articles from this period, Jabotinsky focused on acculturated, even integrated, Jews, like himself. And there was much that he disliked. Such Jews were guilty of many things, but above all, they were guilty of wanting to be Russian, which meant sacrificing another Jew for the sake of material gain. Inculcating Jewish pride in such people, and making them aware of what they lost when they rejected Judaism, was the panacea. Having seen Bialik's success with "The City of Slaughter," Jabotinsky used shame to blame Jews for their own enslavement. Objecting to the antisemite was ineffective, Jabotinsky argued; it egged him on. The only solution was to embrace one's Jewish identity, to proudly and openly declare oneself a Jew.

This line of reasoning led to the authentic Jew, a better person, who cannot "pass" for a Russian and who is not ashamed of who he is. In his autobiography, Jabotinsky recalls his first trip to Western Europe as a youth in 1897 and his alienation from the pious Jews whom he encountered on the train traveling through Galicia. In contrast, he described an Orthodox Jew around 1905, unable to pass for a non-Jew and thus defend himself.

> At one of the markets where there were many people, an old Jew caught my eye, wearing payes and a long caftan. He moved carefully through the crowd, and you could tell from his face that he understood the danger and was frightened. But looking at him I realized that, although he was frightened, he did not and could not attempt to obscure his Jewish traits. He knows that his appearance is noticeable and draws attention from the hostile crowd, but it would not even enter his mind that he should not appear to be a Jew. From an early age he grew up with the idea that he was a Jew and should be a Jew, and now he could not even imagine that he could not look like a Jew, even in a moment of extreme danger. That is why he, in his fright, felt himself at that moment internally freer than we are, we who are perhaps not afraid in the simple meaning of this word, but nevertheless instinctively hid what he was putting on display. For

we grew up with the idea that, true enough, we are Jews, but we should not be Jewish. He is a Jew by God's mercy; we are condemned to eternal Jewishness.[28]

One might compare this with his experience passing through Bialystok during the 1906 pogrom. At the time, he wondered whether he could pass as a Russian to save his life. One can hear an echo of Ahad-Ha'am's "Slavery in Freedom," the idea that, despite all his freedom, the Western Jew was enslaved by his embarrassment of his origins, whereas the ghetto Jew, enslaved externally, was free internally.[29]

* * *

Despite, or perhaps because of, Jabotinsky's sharp criticism, Pyotr Struve invited him to air his views in *Russkaia Mysl'* (*Russian Thought*), the prestigious journal that Struve edited. Jabotinsky's essay appeared in the first issue of 1911, with the title "Letters on Nationalities and Districts: Jews and their Attitudes."[30] After an introductory section, Jabotinsky got to his main argument: Struve was wrong to identify Russian as the exclusive nationality of the empire because in fact Great Russians did not even make a majority. According to the 1897 census, only 43 percent of the population identified Russian as its native language, from which Jabotinsky concluded that 57 percent likely belonged to other nationalities.[31] Jabotinsky pointed out, for example, that most Jews live in areas whose majority is Lithuanian, Belorussian, Polish, or Ukrainian. If Jews are asked to, they can assimilate into those nations. Furthermore, some nations are themselves engaged in a struggle with Russians for recognition of their own national identity, and some Jews have joined them—Ukrainians, for example.[32] Therefore, Russians risk alienating Jews, and not only Jews, if they follow a chauvinistic line.

Jabotinsky portrayed Jewish nationalism as entirely dependent on the sufference of people such as Struve. Jabotinsky wrote, "The question, whether Russian Jewry is destined to assimilate or to develop as a separate nationality hangs mainly on the general question: which direction is Russia heading, will it become a nation-state or a 'state of nationalities'?"[33] He continued: "We 'people of the other nationalities' (*inorodtsy*) predict one of two possibilities. Either there will be freedom and rights or each of us will consciously use his freedom and rights for the creation of an independent national identity in Russia . . . . Either Russia will follow the path of decentralization or not a single element of democracy will be conceivable, beginning with general suffrage. For Russia, progress and *Nationalitätenstaat* are synonyms and any attempt to skip over this truth, affirm a conservative order against the will and consciousness of three-fifths of the population will end in disaster."[34]

Jabotinsky's warning—that Russia could not form a national state because the numbers did not tally—was countered by several groups. Liberals believed in the voluntary assimilation of other nations into Russian society. Russian nationalists maintained that Russia should dominate and ultimately subsume other peoples. Nonetheless, according to Jabotinsky, Russian nationalists pretended not to grasp the demographic reality that they were a minority in their own state.

Polish politics also drew Jabotinsky's attention as Poles began to test the possibility of throwing off Russian occupation (Russia, weakened by revolution, was vulnerable). The Polish question had always been thorny for Jews. For over a century, Russian liberals had supported Polish independence as a natural response to their criticism of the Russian government. Yet many Jews felt ambivalence. Some identified with Polish national ambitions, but others felt that there was more to gain by backing Russia.[35] Polish antisemitism repulsed Jabotinsky. He gave voice to his fears in an article published in a volume titled *Poles and Jews*, which appeared in Russian in 1910 and included essays by Polish nationalists Dmowski, N. Dubrovsky, Wladislaw Grabsky, and others.[36] Antisemitism intensified in 1910 as the Duma deliberated a bill, promoted by Stolypin's government, that would have restricted Jewish representation to 10–20 percent in Polish cities. Polish Duma representatives favored the restrictions.[37]

Jabotinsky announced that the only way Jews could support Polish political ambitions would be if Poles were to reject a nation-state and embrace an alliance with national minorities living on Polish soil.[38] Reacting to Dmowski and other Endeks, Jabotinsky claimed that Poles must revise their view that all Jews were russifiers. He claimed that most Jews identified with the Jewish national movement and therefore did not side with Russia.[39] To gain Jewish support for Polish independence, Jabotinsky urged Poles to recognize democratic principles because democracy lent the Polish cause moral legitimacy.[40] In fact, he cautioned that antisemitism would cause Poland's demise: if Poles turned into oppressors, who would support Polish national aspirations? He added, pointedly, that only a degenerate people would victimize another nation that had been victimized. He wrote, "In particular the hands-on treatment by the representatives of one oppressed nation in relation to another oppressed nation deepens the extraordinarily immoral, demoralized character of the nation and forces all of Russia's Jews to fight it with more strength than they ever had before."⁴¹

A coda to his reproach of Polish chauvinism is an article he wrote in 1910, "Homo Homini Lupus" ["Man Is Wolf to Man"]. The way the Poles, an oppressed people, treated the Jews, another oppressed nation, led Jabotinsky to consider the meaning of suffering. "It is nice to believe that anyone who has suffered for a long time under the yoke of the strong will not come to oppress the weak. We often build the most optimistic hopes on the very idea that when such-and-such a nation has itself endured so much, it will sympathize and understand, and its conscience will not permit it to harm the weak with the same humiliations under which it groaned so recently itself."⁴² In reproaching Poles, one Jabotinsky—the realist hard-nosed nationalist—meets the humanist Jabotinsky, a believer in universal truths and goodness of humanity. He explains further:

> Wise was the philosopher who said, "Homo homini lupus [est]." Man is a wolf to man, and it will be a long time before we do anything about it, by means of governmental reform or culture or the bitter lessons of life. Stupid is he who believes his neighbor, even the kindest and most sympathetic neighbor. Stupid is he who relies on justice; it exists only for those who are able to get it with their fists or their persistence. When you're reproached for preaching about alienation, distrust and other tough subjects, sometimes you feel like saying: Yes, guilty. I preach and will continue to preach, because in the midst of alienation, distrust, eternal "vigilance"—eternally holding a stick behind your back—this is the only way to remain standing in this wolf's den.⁴³

The future author of "The Iron Wall" had drawn a line in the sand more than a decade earlier, contending that sympathy for the other does not exist. One can rely only on oneself, he wrote. Be ready and able to defend oneself, through armed force if necessary.

Here Jabotinsky expressed an ambivalence with ethno-nationalism. It was one thing to criticize Russian nationalism, to criticize antisemitism in Russia; these phenomena could be utilized to win over Jews for Zionism. But the situation in Poland was dire. There ethno-nationalists were capable of monopolizing political power and denying power to non-Poles. In such a case, rhetoric—shaming, complaining, eloquence—would not work. Here Jabotinsky had to use the harshest, most forceful accusations. At the same time, he admired the power of ethno-nationalism, although he calculated its culpability in the court of universal morality. How could there be a community of nations in a world marked by intolerant eliminationist nationalism? Could the circle be squared somehow?

* * *

Around 1910, many Jewish intellectuals—Maxim Vinaver, Semyon Dubnov, and others—tried to explain why the Revolution of 1905 had failed. Jabotinsky joined the debate. He believed that the spiritual energy fueling the Revolution had not been channeled into practical politics. While their intentions were laudable, the opponents of tsarism were weak, and it was easy for the government to recover and retain full power. Jabotinsky wrote, "From this perspective one has to acknowledge that the path between October 17, 1905 and July 12, 1906 was a solid, unbroken line of enormous political errors, leaps from pothole to pothole, that the ruling institutions of the movement regularly arriving on the scene turned out to be completely unfit for political leadership, bereft of the necessary feeling of proportion, the necessary understanding of their true strength. And each of their tiny, but significant, actions undermined their own authority and brought disorganization and demoralization into the ranks of the liberation movement."[44]

Jabotinsky placed a good deal of blame on the inexperienced leaders. In becoming famous, they turned arrogant, foolishly expecting heroism from the people. As a result, they were unable to see the situation, and the true extent of their power, clearly, and they were easily undermined. Regarding the tsar's success in dispersing the first Duma, Jabotinsky blamed the Kadet leaders. "The first Duma exposed many strong virtues—only the main thing that is needed for leading the masses, the ability to correctly gauge one's cash resources, was unavailable to the majority of the opposition. . . . And when they dispersed [the Duma], no one made a move."[45] The defiant act at Vyborg by the Duma's representatives who opposed the dispersal showed heroism but had no real effect. "The failure was decisive proof to the government that there was no longer any strong, principled authority in the country, that society was in moral disarray and one could seize individuals and eliminate them. . . . The fate of the Vyborg Appeal destroyed belief at the end, and from this day the rise of political pessimism and apathy began."[46]

Jabotinsky maintained that the initial suppression of the Revolution had weighty consequences. Once the government realized how weak the opposition was, they understood that they could enact laws limiting the right of suffrage and configure the Duma according to their will. Jabotinsky's analysis is similar to that of Vinaver, Dubnov, and other critics.[47] The main difference is the emphasis. Jabotinsky puts the blame for 1905 not on the left, the revolutionaries, or the government, but primarily on the liberals. Everyone acknowledged that the liberals in the first Duma were inexperienced and therefore error prone, but the other critics offered pity rather than condemnation.[48] One cannot escape the feeling that Jabotinsky is settling old scores, taking revenge for the liberals' refusal to reach an agreement with Zionists in those heady days. This analysis once again exaggerates Zionist strength, giving the mistaken impression that Zionists somehow held an important lever in the success of democratic politics in 1905.

* * *

Jabotinsky's condemnation of antisemitism had its antipode in a new heroic tonality. Jabotinsky embodied this view in his 1911 volume of translations of Hayim Nachman Bialik's poems, in which he embedded an introduction exploring the idea of Jewish heroism.[49] He writes, for example: "Then Bialik threw 'The Tale of the Pogrom' ['The City of Slaughter'] in the face of his dishonored brothers and revealed to them a feeling that they did not know how to name. The name was shame. More than a day of grief, it was a day of shame: the basic idea of this strike with a hammer was the form of the poem." But, he continues, "Kishinev's shame was the last shame. [The Homel pogrom] occurred in 1904, and several hundred pogroms broke out across Russia in 1905: Jewish grief was repeated even more mercilessly than previously, but shame did not return."[50]

Pride in the ability to defend oneself physically became for Jabotinsky the sine qua non of Jewish national consciousness. It connected Jabotinsky to the pogrom in Kishinev, to Jewish self-defense, and to Bialik, the author of "City of Slaughter." Although people often associated Bialik with the image of the Jewish man cowering in fear behind a wall while his wife or daughter is violated, Jabotinsky drew another image: Kishinev led directly to the Jewish fighter, the physically strong Jew, proud and vigorous.[51] Jabotinsky cultivated and then utilized these images for his own self-fashioning.

The translation of Bialik into Russian meant not only that "Bialik had more readers through Jabotinsky than in the original Hebrew," as some liked to joke. It also permitted Jabotinsky to enhance his own reputation, his own self-image, through his introduction and translations, which underscored Bialik's symbolic role. "Bialik is a national poet in the full and highest meaning of this term—national even when he sings about the sun and love. For he wrote only about things he experienced, and his life, in all its works and days, was a reflection and replication of the collective life of the Jewish street in the last quarter of the nineteenth century and the beginning of the twentieth."[52] Jabotinsky tried to fashion his self-portrait to emphasize his struggles on behalf of Russian Jewry, his observations about the strong Jew, and his calls for military preparedness. People began to associate the name Jabotinsky with physical strength, dignity, and pride.

Having seen Jews denied equal rights in Russia, and having been the victim of arbitrary mistreatment, Jabotinsky likely was not surprised by the Beilis Affair of 1911–13. Nonetheless, the trial shocked much of the "civilized world."[53] Although people think Jabotinsky focused on the affair, in fact he only wrote about the early period in 1911. Unlike many journalists, he did not cover the trial, nor did he write to express exultation or relief at the outcome. Additionally, he did not use the affair to vent his venom at the government; rather, he faulted Jews for letting themselves be trapped in an untenable situation. In his article, however, he did inveigh against the antisemitic attitudes of at least two Russian philosophers, Vasily Rozanov and Pavel Florensky. The Beilis Affair convinced Jabotinsky—if he needed any more proof—that Jews could rely only on themselves and that there was no alternative to political Zionism.

The trial of Mendel Beilis (1911–1913) on the charge of killing a child in order to use his blood to make matzos made little sense. The most recent trial in Hungary in 1882, the Tiszlaeszlár affair, had brought that country a good deal of public opprobrium and condemnation. What could the tsarist government gain even if it proved and won its case? Certainly the government could argue and win support for the view that Jews were dangerous and should be kept separate from Christians.[54] However, just by prosecuting the case it risked alienating many governments and world public opinion, never mind Jewish financiers in the United States and Western Europe.

Jabotinsky reacted to the Beilis trial as a Zionist. He published "Instead of an Apology" in 1911, pointing out the difficulty of convincing non-Jews that Jews do not employ Christian blood to make matzot.[55] A defense based on empirical evidence—that throughout history, Jews have been exonerated of this accusation and their persecutors punished—may not persuade the average Russian, who is either a *muzhik* (peasant) or a recent arrival to the city, he argued. He noted that the Russian educated elite was hardly better disposed, and warned that only in fairytales does morality always win.

Leonid Katsis has compellingly argued that Jabotinsky attacked the antisemitic Russian writer Vladimir Rozanov, and parried a number of Rozanov's arguments, including his fantasy of a secret Jewish sect that engages in ritual murder.[56] Rozanov compared Jewish sectarians to *Khlysty* (flagellants), an underground Russian Orthodox sect.[57] In "In Place of an Apology," Jabotinsky wrote, "We do not have ritual murder and never have had it. If they absolutely want to believe that 'there is such a sect,' be my guest, let them believe as much as they want. What do we care, why should it worry us?"[58]

His reaction to Rozanov was not apologetic. Just like Bialik in his response to the Kishinev Pogrom, Jabotinsky addressed Jews exclusively. He implored Jews to refrain from answering their accusers. "Should we be happy to crawl onto the defendant's seat, we, who heard these lies long ago before the cultured nations of today even existed; we who know the value of [the accusation], of ourselves and them? We don't owe anyone an accounting, we don't have to take an exam, and no one is old enough to call us to obedience. We arrived before them and we will leave after them. We are who we are, we are good for ourselves, and we will not become something else, nor do we want to become something else."[59]

Jabotinsky's credo is characteristically Zionist in the spirit of Leo Pinsker: the non-Jewish world is hostile; one has to stay clear of non-Jews, lest one lose one's self-regard as a result of viewing oneself through a distorted lens. Like Pinsker, Jabotinsky is markedly pessimistic. His advice—to ignore the inquisition—nonetheless acknowledges the dangers confronting the Jewish community in Russia.

Jabotinsky's response during the Beilis libel trial betrays the distance he traveled between 1905 and 1911. His optimistic vision of a democratic Russia, where Jews might gain civic and national rights, had disintegrated. Now he advocated isolation and self-preservation. Although the trial offered an opportunity for Jews to thank the defenders—Maklakov, Miliukov and Gruzenberg, liberals who defended Beilis in court and in the press—Jabotinsky was silent regarding the collaboration. One suspects one knows why. His goal was not to make Russia more hospitable for Jews. It was to push them to seek a maximalist solution: emigration to Palestine.

* * *

Internal and inherent contradictions bedeviled Jabotinsky after 1905, especially the question of what Zionist political goals should be. He wanted to secure the Jewish community and arrange for its relocation to the Jewish homeland. He also wanted to engage politically with like-minded allies in order to change the framework of Russia. In this context, he articulated a vision that would assure national cultural rights in multicultural national empires (e.g., Russian, Austro-Hungarian, and Ottoman). But if Palestine was the answer, one wonders why he expended energy toward realizing autonomy. Additionally, how could one deal honestly with non-Zionists if the goal truly was Palestine? Finally, if you engage in Diaspora politics under the Zionist banner, how should you orient yourself with regard to those Jewish politicians who don't share a commitment to Palestine (such as Vinaver) but seek to secure autonomy? In the last years before the war, he was trying to resolve these issues without much success.

An example is his attitude toward radical nationalism and liberalism. He sympathized with liberalism, defending the right of Jews to democratic suffrage, equal rights, and economic opportunity. He seems to have believed that all minorities should have collective national rights in the countries where they live. In fact, for almost a decade, Jabotinsky had been investigating various kinds of alternative democratic and legal means of insuring rights representation for minorities. That is why his article "Reactionary" (1912) provokes bewilderment.

He made a strange confession and spoke of ethno-nationalists with affection. He contrasted those who idealize universal values, such as socialists, liberals, and believers in the unity of all peoples, with ethno-nationalists. "There aren't any profanities they haven't heard. They are proclaimed as haters of man, enemies of human brotherhood. They are reactionaries, opponents of culture. They are betrayers, they lead the dark masses by the nose and give them rocks instead of bread. They say to the masses 'Germans out!' instead of saying, 'All people are brothers.' They say to them, 'Create a state!' instead of saying, 'Democratize the state.' They say to them, 'There is no difference between poor and rich until we realize the national ideal,' instead of saying, 'The proletariat of all countries, unite.'"[60]

Jabotinsky acknowledged his closeness to nationalists. He continued, "They are reactionaries, similar in spirit to [Nikolai] Markov and Purishkevich [Russian nationalists from the extreme right], they should be chased and strangled. But then let's be consistent, let us take another step and put Garibaldi in the same parenthesis. Wasn't he, his supporters, and his entire epoch vulnerable to exactly the same accusations that we have formulated? And if we were honest, if the struggle for Italy were occurring now before our eyes, wouldn't we repeat the same accusations from every public tribune? What's the deal? What's the difference?"[61]

Jabotinsky pointed to the paradox inherent in condemning Russian and Polish nationalists while lauding an Italian patriot, Garibaldi. He understood the effectiveness in winning over the majority nation by excluding others, including Jews. Thus, although he was wounded by antisemitism, he acknowledged that an antiforeign position can be effective in the struggle for national liberation. Therefore, although he identified with reactionaries, he was also repulsed by them. Nonetheless, he understood that in a different situation, if he were the leader of the majority nation, he might be hated in exactly the same way that he hated Markov and Purishkevich. In fact, if he were successful, he would be hated exactly as they were.

It is impossible not to view "Reactionary" as a harbinger of the future militarist who a decade later would write "The Iron Wall." The article in 1912 showed a distinct change; Jabotinsky imagined the role of oppressor of other nations. This is strange because he had complained about antisemitism for over a decade, and, indeed, had railed against Dmowski and Polish nationalists for invoking an exclusionary nationalism toward Jews, though the Poles themselves had experienced Russian oppression. He condemned the leap from victim to aggressor on the part of the Poles.[62] Yet he acknowledged that ethno-nationalists had an effective strategy, and he too was willing to pursue it.

How are we supposed to reconcile Jabotinsky's 1913 article about extraterritorial rights for national minorities with "Reactionary," published in 1912? The two positions are contradictory. How can one reconcile the goal of minority rights with the goal of a nation-state?

At the minimum one can say that Jabotinsky evolved intellectually. He had arrived at a distinctly more ambiguous position in which two contradictory routes appeared. One route led to the deepening of liberalism, with extraterritorial personal rights for national minorities. The other route questioned the idea of tolerance and equality for all national minorities. One route deepened the ideals of 1905 and the principles articulated in 1906 at the Helsingfors Conference; whereas the other claimed the right of the nation to occupy territory exclusively for its own benefit. Perhaps most interesting of all is the realization that, if Jabotinsky became a reactionary, he might oppress minorities and therefore become a target of the same moral complaint that he made against the Poles: how can the victim of oppression become the oppressor?

At this point, Jabotinsky was not sure which path to choose. But he gradually realized that a choice had to be made. In his 1913 article regarding national rights, Jabotinsky added a few paragraphs from the perspective of the majority. He wrote: "Actually, since there are minorities in the world, it is impossible to forget about the interests of majority nations. These interests are multifarious, but precisely the synthesis of them includes territory—the fundamental natural and operational base of all the functions of national life. Of all the responsibilities of the nation quanation, the preservation and development of its values—language, faith, rituals, law, etc., the responsibility for the control of national territory is the most sacred."[63] Such a passage gives one the feeling that Jabotinsky was wondering what would happen if Jews became a majority people. His thoughts were gradually shifting from the situation of a Jewish minority in Russia to the possibility of a Jewish majority somewhere else. He would soon expend a good deal of energy planning for a future Jewish majority in Palestine and Transjordan. He imagined a Jewish nation-state with an Arab minority. In contrast to Markov and Pruishkevich, this minority would have guaranteed civil equality and perhaps under the right circumstances, full national rights as well.

The nationality question continued to bother him, especially as it became tangled with the new discourse about race. He tried to untangle race from nationality in a 1913 article, entitled "Race."[64] To understand the article, one must realize that "race" and "nation" were used indistinguishably at the time, especially by nationalists to help legitimize their subject.[65] Clearly Jabotinsky felt the need to adapt his ideas on nations to the latest science. "So-called 'race' is always a product of the mixture of certain elements in various proportions. But the selection and quantity of these elements and the proportions in which they are mixed are far from identical, and the difference between the races consists in this difference in the racial spectrum or, if one can express it this way, the racial recipe."[66]

The article contains two interesting insights, although neither concerns race directly. The first is that the interaction of a race with others actually strengthens feelings of difference and advances cultural chauvinism. "The Russian people began to produce great poets, i.e., they created a national literature precisely after they had been exposed to two centuries of Europeanization."[67] The other insight concerns migration; here Jabotinsky speaks as a Zionist who regrets two thousand years of Jewish movement. "Migration is the disease of a social organism, the result of social disorganization, a pathological phenomenon. It follows, when the social structure heals, when there is an organization of economic life in which each citizen will have the concrete right to work, no one will have to move to the ends of the earth to make his living. At the very moment when we remove the reasons that inhibit nations from living in peace, migration will cease."[68]

This article, which appeared to argue against migration, actually defended it, since Jabotinsky knew that struggles between nations would not cease. The piece was also an underhanded means of using racial science to defend Jewish nationhood. If not for the misfortune of history, Jews would still be in Palestine, their national home, and would never have left, and would never need to return. In this way Jabotinsky turned Jewish diversity in Diaspora against itself. The imperative to racial purity was inviting Jews back to Palestine.

In the year before World War I, Jabotinsky appeared to conceive of Zionism in a new way. According to Shlomo Zal'tsman, new thoughts were boiling up in Jabotinsky: "In 1913, after the congress in Vienna, he said to me, 'A master of necessity, I am forced to create a new party because I see that the Zionist Union is barren regarding Zionism, we will disappear and will cease to exist. Only the foundation will remain to collect money, without the spirit of life close to it. This does not interest me, although it is painful for me to break from the general Zionists."[69] Among the points of contention were the construction of a university in Jerusalem and the use of Hebrew in the Diaspora. Jabotinsky favored building an institution for undergraduates rather than an elite research institute (Weizmann's suggestion) and he actively promoted the study of modern Hebrew in the Diaspora.[70]

The examples from his life reveal that Jabotinsky moved inside and outside the World Zionist Organization. At times, he held official positions in the organization and received a salary. At other times, he acted as a gadfly, criticizing the leaders and their presumptions. In the battles over a Jewish university and Hebrew in schools, he wanted to implement his whole program without compromise. He made far-reaching arguments that encapsulated utopian thinking that pragmatists were unwilling to embrace. The image of a passionate fighter who nonetheless burned bridges with colleagues would repeat itself in the next period of his life, during World War I.

During these pre–War years, he hardened in his belief that Jews could rely only on themselves. The hope of a union of Zionism and liberalism was betrayed, and the vision of Synthetic Zionism was crushed. The positive concept that Zionism promoted, the paradigm of rights and cultural accomplishment, succumbed to the negative impetus of antisemitism. A new path would have to emerge from the options now available. But before he could formulate the new path, war broke out.

Jabotinsky's Russian years, from 1907 to 1914, reflect his struggle to realize the ideals of 1905. The failed attempts to build coalitions with Russians and Poles, the government's use of antisemitism for political ends, and the hostility toward Jews in Russian and Polish society forced him to modify his positions. But these modifications led to paradox. He was unsure how to unite the goals of Helsingfors—minority rights in the Diaspora—and exclusionary nationalism. Luckily for him, the flawed democracy in Russia prevented him from facing his contradictions. But the confusion could not last forever.

Notes

1. Alfred Levin, *Third Duma: Election and Profile* (New York: Gazelle Book Services, 1973).
2. Georgii Adamovich, *Vasilii Alekseevich Maklakov, politik, iurist, chelovek* (Paris, 1959), 157–58.
3. Petr Struve, "Intelligentsiia i national'noe litso," in *Patriotica: Politika, kul'tura, religiia, sotsializm* (Moscow: Respublika, 1997), 208; originally appeared in *Slovo* (March 10, 1909), 207.
4. Brian Horowitz, *Russian Idea—Jewish Presence* (Boston: Academic Studies, 2013), 47–48.
5. D. Zaslavskii and St. Ivanovich, *Kadety i evrei* (Petrograd, 1916), 8–9.
6. Christof Gassenschmidt, *Jewish Liberal Politics in Tsarist Russia, 1900–1914: The Modernization of Russian Jewry* (New York: New York University Press, 1995), 68–69.
7. Vladimir Levin, *Mi-mahapeha le-milhama: Ha-politika ha-yehudit be-rusya, 1907–1914*. Jerusalem: Zalman Shazar Center for Jewish History, 2016, 75–90. In the fourth Duma, the Kadets wanted to put to a vote their bill for civil equality for all; ibid.,122.
8. Aleksandr Mindlin, *Gosudarstvennaia Duma Rossiiskoi Imperii i evreiskii vopros* (St. Petersburg: Alteleiia, 2014), 249.
9. Semyon Goldin, "Liberalizm, nacjonalizm i 'kwestia żydowska' w Imperium Rosyjskim (koniec XIX - początek XX wieku)," *Kwartalnik Historii Żydów* 2, no. 258 (Czerwiec, 2016): 258.
10. Ibid., 261–62.
11. Vladimir Jabotinsky, *Fel'etony*, 2nd ed. (Berlin, 1922), 118.
12. Jabotinsky, "Asemitizm," *Fel'etony* (1922), 115.
13. Attacks on the Kadets during the third Duma was the main line of *Rassvet*, the newspaper edited by Abram Idel'son. See Levin, *Mi-mahapeha le-milhama*, 75–90.
14. David Vital, *Zionism, The Crucial Phase* (Oxford: Clarendon, 1987), 39–40.

15. Vladimir Jabotinsky, "Chetyre stat'i o 'chirikovskom insidente,'": 1. "Dezertiry i khoziaeva"; 2. "Asemitizm"; 3. "Medved' iz berlogi"; 4. "Russkaia laska." All the articles were republished in both volumes of *Fel'etony* (1913 and 1922).

16. Zionist attacks on Vinaver and other "assimilationists" in the Jewish People's Group were published with frequency in *Rassvet*. Jabotinsky was one of many in this regard, especially Idel'son. See Viktor Kel'ner, *Shchit': M. M. Vinaver i evreiskii vopros v Rossii v kontse XIX – nahale XX veka* (St. Petersburg: Evreiskii Universitet v St. Peterburge, 2018), 175–177.

17. Jabotinsky, *Fel'etony* (1922), 120.

18. Ibid.

19. Pyotr Struve, "Intelligentsiia i natsional'noe litso," *Slovo*, March 10 and 12, 1909.

20. Vladimir Jabotinsky, *Evidence Submitted to the Palestine Royal Commission, Jabotinsky, on Behalf of the New Zionist Organization, House of Lords* (Tel Aviv, New Zionist Organization in Palestine, 1937), 7.

21. Jabotinsky, *Fel'etony* (1922), 78.

22. Ibid.

23. Shaul Gintsburg, *Meshumodim in Tsarishen Rusland: forshungen un zikhroynes vegn Yidishn lebn in amolikn Rusland* (New York: Tsiko Bikher Verlag, 1946).

24. Jabotinsky, *Fel'etony* (1922), 74.

25. Ibid., 39.

26. Ibid., 48.

27. Vladimir Jabotinsky, *Fel'etony* (St. Petersburg, 1913), 10.

28. Ibid., 11.

29. Ahad-Ha'am, "Avdut be toch herut," *Al parashat derakhim*. (Berlin: Yudisher Farlag, 1921).

30. Vladimir Jabotinsky, "Pis'ma o natsional'nostiakh i oblastiakh: evreistvo i ego nastroeniia," *Russkaia Mysl'* 1 (January 1, 1911). Svetlana Natkovich interprets the article as criticism of Zionist Socialism. *Ben aneney zohar: Yetsirato shel Vladimir (Ze'ev) Z'abotinski ba-heksher ha-hevrati.* (Jerusalem: Magnes, 2015), 104.

31. Jabotinsky, "Pis'ma o natsional'nostiakh," 113.

32. Jabotinsky continues this line of reasoning in his article "Urok iubileia Shevchenko (1911)," *Fel'etony*, 2nd ed. (Berlin, 1922), 186–194.

33. Ibid., 112.

34. Ibid., 113

35. This was the subject of Lev Levanda's novel, *In Heated Times (Goriachee vremia)* (1873).

36. *Poliaki i evrei: Materialy o pol'sko-evreiskom spore po povodu zakonoproekta o gorodskom samoupravlenii v Pol'she. Iz statei i zaiavlenii deputata Grabskogo, R. Dmovskogo, N. Dubrovskogo, V. Ahabotinskogo, deput. I. Petrunkevicha i A. Sventokhovskogo* (Odessa: M. S. Kozmana, 1910).

37. Theodore Weeks, *National and State in Late Imperial Russia: Nationalism and Russification on the Western Frontier, 1863–1914* (DeKalb: Northern Illinois University Press, 1996), 172–192; Levin, *Mi-mehapeha le-milhama*, 73–75.

38. Roman Dmowski in particular saw no place for Jews in modern Poland. Gregorz Krzywiec describes his attitude toward Jews: "Dmowski specifically excluded Jews from this world-order. Jews alone were the radical opposite of the legendary Aryans (among whom he included Poles), and they posed an ongoing threat. This early worldview linked three

leitmotifs of eliminatory racist antisemitism: nationalist Judeophobia; the Aryan myth; and a sort of European imperialism, connected with the presupposition that superfluous ethnic groups, as worthless to 'civilization,' could be subjected to elimination. Such processes, according to Dmowski, were signs of progress." Krzywiec, "Eliminationist Anti-Semitism at Home and Abroad: Polish Nationalism, the Jewish Question and Easter European Right-Wing Mass Politics," in *The New Nationalism and the First World War*, ed. Lawrence Rosenthal and Vesna Rodic (New York: Palgrave, 2015), 66.

39. Vladimir Jabotinsky, "Poliaki i evrei," in *Poliaki i evrei: Materialy o pol'sko-evreiskom spore po povodu zakonoproekta o gorodskom samoupravlenii v Pol'she. Iz statei i zaiavlenii deputata Grabskogo, R. Dmovskogo, N. Dubrovskogo, V. Ahabotinskogo, deput. I. Petrunkevicha i A. Sventokhovskogo* (Odessa: M. S. Kozmana, 1910), 23.

40. Ibid., 28. This was a conventional distinction of the time in the political literature; Vladimir Solov'ev and Semyon Dubnov made a similar distinction between harmful and benevolent nationalism. See Horowitz, *Russian Idea*, 26–28.

41. Jabotinsky, "Poliaki i evrei," 29.

42. Jabotinsky, *Fel'etony* (1922), 220.

43. Ibid., 223.

44. Jabotinsky, *Fel'etony* (1913), 59.

45. Ibid., 58.

46. Ibid., 58–59.

47. In his memoir of the period, Pavel Miliukov attributes the failure of this generation of liberals to the absence of any preparation. They had little experience as politicians, and their allegiance to the intelligentsia's credo of uncompromising commitment to truth actually undermined them because it created a set of expected outcomes that could not be attained without deep concessions. Pavel Miliukov, "Vinaver kak politik," *M. M. Vinaver i russkaia obshchestvennost' nachala XX veka* (Paris: 1937), 19.

48. Vasilii Maklakov, "1905–1906 gody," in *M. M. Vinaver i russkaia obshchestvennost' nachala XX veka* (Paris: 1937), 60. See also V. Maklakov, *Pervaia Gosudarstvennaia Duma, 27 aprelia-8 iiulia 1906 goda* (Moscow: Tsentrpoligraf, 2006).

49. Kh. N. Bialik, *Pesni i poemy: Avtorizovannyi perevod s evreiskogo i vvedenie Vl. Zhabotinskogo*, 2nd ed. (Berlin: S. D. Zal'tsman, 1922). See also Miron, "Trumato shel Ze'ev Z'abotinski le-shira ha-ivrit ha-modernit," in *Ish be-sa'ar: Masot u'mekhkarim 'al Ze'ev Z'abotinski*, ed. Avi Bareli and Pinhas Ginossar (Ber-Sheva: Universitat Ben-Guryon ba'Negev, 2004), 187.

50. Vladimir Jabotinsky, "Vvedenie," in Kh. N. Bialik, *Pesni i poemy*, 43–44.

51. See Bialik's poem, "Ir ha-harega" ("In the City of Slaughter"). Also note the discussion of the image in Avner Holtzman, *Hayim Nahman Bialik: Poet of Hebrew*, trans. Orr Scharf (New Haven, CT: Yale University Press, 2017), 92–96.

52. Jabotinsky, "Vvedenie," 19.

53. A. Tager, *Delo Beilisa: Tsarskaia Rossiia i Delo Beilisa, Issledovaniia i materialy* (Moscow: Gesharim, 1995); (first edition, 1934).

54. Hans Rogger, *Jewish Policies and Right-Wing Politics in Imperial Russia* (Berkeley: University of California Press, 1986), 40–55; Heinz Dietrich-Lowe, *The Tsars and the Jews: Reform, Reaction and Anti-Semitism in Imperial Russia, 1772–1917* (Chur: Routledge, 1993), 284–290; Levin, *Mi-mehapeha le-milhama*, 44.

55. Jabotinsky, *Fel'etony* (1922), 16

56. Leonid Katsis, "V. Zhabotinskii i V. Rozanov: Ob odnoi nezamechennoi polemike (1911–1913–1918), *Russkaia eskhatologiia i russkaia literatura* (Moscow: OGI, 2000).

57. See the testimony of Aron Shteinberg in the chapter of memoirs entitled "Na peterburgskom perekrestke. Vstrecha s V. V. Rozanovym," in *Druz'ia moikh rannikh let (1911–1928)* (Fontenay-aux-Roses: Syntaxis, 1991), 165–66.

58. Jabotinsky, *Fel'etony* (1922), 17. About the essay, Katsis writes, "In 1911, V. Jabotinsky wrote an article entitled, "Instead of an Apology." This article was dedicated only to the very start of the Beilis Affair—in fact, it was intended as a reaction to Beilis' arrest on the charge of ritual murder, although in the article the name of the man arrested was not mentioned." Katsis, "V. Zhabotinskii i V. Rozanov," 65.

59. Jabotinsky, *Fel'etony* (1922), 17.

60. Ibid., 181.

61. Ibid., 183.

62. Jabotinsky, *Poliaki i evrei*, 29.

63. Vladimir Jabotinsky, "Samoupravlenie natsional'nogo men'shinstva," *Vestnik Evropy* 9 (September 1913): 125.

64. Jabotinsky, *Fel'etony* (1922), 167–176.

65. John M. Efron, *Defenders of the Race: Jewish Doctors and Race Science in Fin-De-Siècle Europe* (New Haven, CT: Yale University Press, 1994).

66. Jabotinsky, *Fel'etony* (1922), 167.

67. Ibid., 174.

68. Ibid., 174.

69. Shlomo Zal'tsman, *Min he-avar: Zichronot u'reshumot* (Tel Aviv: Sh. Zal'tsman, 1943), 251.

70. For more on these controversies, see Shlomo Haramati, "Zeev Jabotinsky—yozem beit ha-sefer ha-ivri-leumi be-tfutsot," in *Ish be-sa'ar*, 299–324. The quarrel was over language. The other writers maintained that one should not mandate Hebrew in schools in the Diaspora, but realized that certain subjects required one's native language, Yiddish. Also Slutzky, *Ha-itonut ha-yehudit-rusit ba-mea ha-esrim (1900–1918)* (Tel Aviv: Ha-aguda le-haker toldot ha-yihudim, 1978), 243–44; Zoya Kopelman. "Zhabotinskii: Ot romanticheskogo chteniia k postupku," *Judaica Petropolitana* 8 (2017).

Figure 1. Vladimir (Zeev) Jabotinsky, portrait (1935). Courtesy of the Jabotinsky Institute in Israel.

Figure 2. Vladimir (Zeev) Jabotinsky with son Eri, Eretz Israel (1929). Courtesy of the Jabotinsky Institute in Israel.

Figure 3. Vladimir (Zeev) Jabotinsky, portrait, wearing officer's uniform of the 38th Battalion (1918). Courtesy of the Jabotinsky Institute in Israel.

Figure 4. Delegates to the HaTzoHar Founding Conference (Zionist Revisionists), Paris. First row from left: Meir Grossman, Zinovy Tiomken, Asher Ginzburg, Vladimir Tiomken, Yaakov Cohen, and A. Gurevich. Second row from left: Merle Nehama, Yazibor Frenkel, Norbert Hoffman, Schulman, unknown, Vladimir (Zeev) Jabotinsky, Aharon Propes, unknown, Jack Segal, Michael Harbein, and Israel Trivus. Third row from left: Albert Starra, Boris Czeskis, Yehoshua Yeivin, Leo Czeskis, and unknown. (April 20, 1925). Courtesy of the Jabotinsky Institute in Israel.

Figure 5. Vladimir (Zeev) Jabotinsky as a student in Odessa, portrait (01/01/1899). Courtesy of the Jabotinsky Institute in Israel.

Figure 6. Editorial board of weekly *Rassvet* (*HaShahar*), Petersburg. Seated from left: Vladimir (Zeev) Jabotinsky, Avram Idelson, and Max Soloveichik. Standing from left: Shlomo Gepstein, Avraham Goldstein, and A. Zeidman. Courtesy of the Jabotinsky Institute in Israel.

6

THE JEWISH LEGION'S RUSSIAN INSPIRATION, 1915–1917

* * *

Statistics about Zionism in Russia on the eve of the war were not encouraging. The scholar David Vital weighs successes and failures:

> The weekly printing of *Ha-Olam*, edited in Vilna and very much the organ of Zionism's Russian wing (and therefore as good an indicator as any of the size of the ranks of the fully dedicated) was at most 6,000 (in 1911); postal subscriptions numbered 3–4,000. Subscription to the pro-Zionist Russian-language *Rassvet* may have reached 10,000. All told, throughout the Empire, there were at least one thousand local Zionist associations of various sizes, and in a country in which all such associations and activity were illegal and liable, as we shall see, to police repression, this was an achievement. But, again, measured against the five to six million Jewish subjects of the Tsar and the general restlessness among them so well indicated by the continual migration out of Russia to the west, it cannot be described as a truly powerful showing.[1]

Needless to say, all independent political organizations in Russia were in disorder after 1907.

It is symbolic that, in the years before the outbreak of World War I, Jabotinsky earned his keep giving lectures throughout the Pale of Settlement. He was, literally and metaphorically, making endless circles. But where was he heading? Where was Russian Zionism heading? Or even Zionism generally? In 1914, he would write about his situation,

> Here ends the first part of the story of my life, because the thread became interrupted on its own; it was a period that had no continuation. If I wanted to live, I had to be reborn anew. But I was thirty-four, long past my youth and half into middle age, and I had wasted both. I do not know what I would have done if the whole world had not turned upside down and thrown me

into unforeseen paths. Perhaps I would have gone to Eretz Yisrael, perhaps to Rome; maybe I would have created a political party, but that summer the world war broke out.²

We don't need to believe that Jabotinsky actually had many options. But one can plausibly imagine his desire to build a life with more purpose.

The war opened up new worlds for Jabotinsky. It seems that serendipity played its part. The Legion bridged his original motivation to join the Zionists—self-defense in Odessa—with the present moment. Jabotinsky's memory was not entirely correct: he says in *Story of the Jewish Legion* (1927) that he realized the need for a Jewish armed force in 1915, when Turkey entered the war.³ In fact, Turkey joined the war on October 28, 1914. Gradually the possibilities of an Ottoman defeat dawned on Jabotinsky. His account in *Story of the Jewish Legion* vividly dramatizes the moment, albeit anachronistically.

> I must confess: until that morning, in Bordeaux as elsewhere, I had been a mere observer, without any particular reasons for wishing full triumph to one side and crushing disaster to the other. My desire at that time was a stalemate, and peace as soon as possible. Turkey's move transformed me in one short morning into a fanatical believer in war until victory; Turkey's move made this war "my war." . . . As I saw it, the matter was crystal clear: the fate of Jews in Russia, Poland, Galicia—very important, undoubtedly—was, if viewed from the historical perspective, only something temporary as compared to the revolution in Jewish national life that the dismemberment of Turkey would bring us. I never doubted that once Turkey entered the war, she would be defeated and sliced to pieces: here again I am at a loss to understand how anyone could ever have had any doubts on this subject. It was no guesswork, but a matter of cold statistical calculation. I am glad of the opportunity to mention it here, as I have been accused of gambling on a winner in those years. . . . That Germany would be beaten into unconditional surrender, of course not even a journalist could have foreseen at that time. But that Turkey more than anyone else would have to pay for this war, I did not and could not doubt for one moment. Stone and iron can endure a fire; a wooden hut must burn, and no miracle will save it.⁴

This statement reflects an awareness of Turkey's situation at the beginning of World War I.⁵ Jabotinsky's calculations turned out to be relatively accurate. However, most Zionists had a different view, and instead of seeking advantage in Turkey's destruction, they obeyed the Zionist leadership and took an oath of neutrality in the war.⁶ By contrast, Jabotinsky pursued an alliance with Great Britain. Although he may not deserve full credit for the Balfour Declaration (as he claimed in 1927), Jabotinsky's actions likely abetted the strenuous diplomatic work that Chaim Weizmann, Nahum Sokoloff, and others had begun.[7] The proof is that several British leaders and military officers—Colonel John Henry Patterson (the Legion's commander), C. P. Scott, Leopold Amery, Charles Mastermann, and General Sir Ian Hamilton—became lifelong friends of Zionism and worked on behalf of Zionist goals during, and in some cases after, the war.[8]

Everything else aside, there was little of the militarist or soldier in Jabotinsky before the outbreak of World War I. As an aging journalist-intellectual in his midthirties, he shunned the army. The tsarist government was perceived as mistreating Jewish recruits.[9] Nonetheless, he was not a pacifist. Like many Jewish intellectuals in Russia, he took pride in Jewish self-defense and Jewish guards (Ha-Shomrim) in Palestine. But the war—events, people, relationships, and political opportunities—made him dream of bigger things and changed him profoundly.

* * *

Jabotinsky had predicted the outbreak of war, but guessed that it would come in 1913, instead of August 1914. In "Horoscope," an article from 1912, he shows that people knew the potential costs of war: "Above all, a great war stands first among events in Europe—the war that the world fears so much, and at the same time awaits with such morbid, painful curiosity. War in the center of Europe, between two (or more) first-class cultural powers, fully armed with the grandiose madness of the latest technology, with the participation of land, sea, submarine and air forces, with an unbelievable quantity of human sacrifices and with such financial losses, direct, indirect, and peripheral, for which, it seems, there aren't enough numbers in arithmetic. This war should break out between England and Germany."[10]

In the years before the war, Jabotinsky had acquired a good sense of what was happening in the world. He had been in Turkey, Palestine, and Europe. He closely followed the imperial appetites of the Europeans who nibbled at the Turkish Empire in the Balkans and in the Arab lands too. Not fooled by diplomatic niceties, Jabotinsky understood that the big states acted solely in their own interests and had no compunction about taking what belonged to others. In "Right and Force" (1912), Jabotinsky writes, "It's either one or the other: either you shouldn't steal or you should steal at the most propitious moment. Even from the point of view of humanity (if you can presume, for a moment, that such a viewpoint is appropriate in questions of this kind) it is much better that the war should take place now, because it would end more quickly, fewer would be killed and drowned, and less of the national wealth on both sides would drop to the bottom of the sea."[11]

Predicting that the war should start soon, he clearly understood that nations did not follow moral dictates. The biggest powers, France and Britain, expressed their imperial will by swooping down and gobbling up weaker nations, no matter that they were located on the other side of the globe. Jabotinsky wrote, "Honestly, I do not know why there are such scruples on this beautiful planet. Why the appearances? It would be much simpler to point to our neighbors—to England that captured Egypt, Aden, Persia, and Cyprus; to France, which gulped down Algiers, Tunisia and Morocco; to Austria-Hungary, which ate up Bosnia, and so on, and so forth—and respond with the Italian proverb: '*Così fan tutti.*' Everybody does it."[12]

Although he sarcastically feigned indifference to imperialism, Jabotinsky opposed the immorality practiced by great nations and strongly condemned the timidity of the world press. By ignoring massive crimes, journalists proved themselves irrelevant and reduced their own standing before important leaders. If that cowardice continues, he maintained, the fourth estate won't be capable of influencing policy. Jabotinsky believed in the value of journalists as watchdogs.

Jabotinsky attributed at least part of his knowledge of world affairs to his early associations with the grain merchants of Ukraine, of whom his father was one. In his autobiography, he describes how the merchants' stories exposed the subtle relations between Ukraine and other places, and revealed the interconnectedness of the personal and private with international politics and economics. He describes conversations he heard as a young man: "Once, in Alexandrovsk, a dozen old men from among the veterans of the grain trade gathered around me and tried until midnight to explain to me the essence of my father's charm. I did not understand, but I took away a powerful impression of the intricate combination of connections, relations, and networks of influence uniting Argentina with Ukraine, the Black Sea with the three oceans, the Ballhausplatz in Vienna, seat of the foreign office of Austria-Hungary, with the Café Robinat, where the grain dealers in Odessa used to meet."[13]

This passage, published in 1936, is one of the rare instances where Jabotinsky speaks about his father. He attributes many of his talents to his father, a timber merchant who managed a large Russian boat company. He injects some local patriotism into the narrative. Although Russian intellectuals often viewed Ukraine as an economic backwater, Jabotinsky showed that Ukraine was connected to various parts of the world and to an intricate economic web reaching beyond Europe. This encomium for a single world, linked through communication and money, appears at odds with the ethno-nationalist portrayed earlier.

The historian is led into a conundrum. Jabotinsky depicted himself two different ways: as a politician who sympathized with ethno-nationalists; and as a journalist who opposed imperialism and valorized universal morality. But which one did he choose? He seems to have cultivated both in order to keep all doors open and leave himself room to maneuver in the most advantageous direction. In a sense, his life, as he lived it up to that moment, was still subject to change; he could choose political activism as a Zionist, but he could also choose journalism.

When war broke out, Jabotinsky found himself jobless. In the years before the war, he had decided to write less and devote more time to Zionism. His income came primarily from lectures, and now the war disrupted his livelihood. He explained in *Story of My Life*:

> My steady participation in the Russian press had ceased some two years earlier, as I had refrained from interesting myself in almost any of the things that interested the editor and reader. *Rassvet* was not a source of income. There was a newspaper in Yiddish, *Der Fraynd,* in St. Petersburg, but it did not even occur to me that a fellow like me could produce articles in the language we then called "jargon," and in which I did not know how to express even simple terms (so it seemed to me). For about two years I was living mostly by giving lectures: a solid and wide field of activity in a country with a Jewish population of six million. Lectures all year round; but this income source was destroyed in the world catastrophe, or so it seemed to me. What to do?[14]

In early fall of 1914, Jabotinsky visited Moscow, where he made an agreement with the liberal Moscow newspaper *Russkie Vedomosti* to travel around Europe and report how war affected the home front. Jabotinsky's description of his visit to the newspaper offices in *Story of My Life* offers a vivid impression of Russia of the time.

> The newspaper *Russkie Vedomosti* was something like the great-great-grandfather of the entire Russian press, the temple of the progressive liberal tradition, a supreme court of good and evil. Nowadays there are no longer any papers like it in the whole world; only the *Manchester Guardian* in England, before the war, had a moral prestige similar to this. Why I went there, I do not know. I knew next to no one in the editorial office, but I was well aware that they were all very scrupulous with regard to progressive purity, whereas the

status of a Zionist as a progressive was still dubious in those days. However, I received quite a cordial welcome, and they also accepted my proposal to be the newspaper's special correspondent "on the Western Front and around it."

I asked, "For how long is the agreement?"

"Until you come back."

This way of doing business was called the "depth of the Russian soul," a quality which even in business is frequently more advantageous than any minute calculation. My salary was also measured according to that same "depth." I hope, and that is what I heard also from competent persons, that they did not regret the arrangement. As for me, I certainly did not; it is not an exaggeration if I say that my whole fight for a Jewish Legion, or almost—about three years in a row—I fought at the expense of the Moscow newspaper.[15]

Jabotinsky left Russia for Europe in late 1914; he visited Odessa once again in 1915. A portrait of him at this time can be found in the memoirs of his son, Eri, who describes his father taking his leave of the family. Eri, five years old at the time, would not see his father again until 1917, when Jabotinsky's wife, Jeanne, and Eri were able to reach London.[16] In the story, Eri Jabotinsky describes how he was raised speaking only Hebrew, but by 1915, had not seen his father in a year. The son bids his father farewell in Russian, "*S bogom*" ("May God watch over you"), in the accent of his nurse, a woman from the Kaluga region.[17] Eri's language signals that, despite his father's attempts to cultivate Hebrew as a native language among Jews in the Diaspora, it is easy to fall back on the dominant language. Additionally, one sees how little time Jabotinsky had for his son in the key years of Eri's development.

* * *

Jabotinsky's experiences during the first years of war were diverse and exotic. Indeed, it can be difficult to find order and coherence in the different accounts of those years. The biographer has an insatiable appetite for facts, but discounting all the dubious stories about Jabotinsky would leave his book largely unwritten, because the stories that Jabotinsky told about himself round out the portrait.

As a correspondent, Jabotinsky had the opportunity to travel first in Europe and then to North Africa, Egypt, Lebanon, and Syria. He also spent time in Scandinavia, Belgium, Portugal, Austria, Hungary, and Great Britain. Even today, his war reportage possesses a certain freshness because it captures the intellectual and emotional atmosphere of the time. Jabotinsky possessed enormous literary talent.

Jabotinsky offered his own understanding of the reasons for war, placing emphasis on national psychology—the pretensions of small and large nations and their desire for respect. Each country wanted to enter the fight, he wrote, although few had much to gain from it. In a word, the whole world "had gone crazy." In Stockholm, he met with Sven Hedin, the famous explorer, who expressed the bizarre notion that Russia was about to invade, and Sweden would defend itself.[18] Soon after, Jabotinsky found himself in Lisbon, where he discerned the same yearning for battle, despite the fact that Portugal at the time was a relatively small country, albeit with an illustrious past. In *Story of My Life*, Jabotinsky describes the demise of civilization by way of an anecdote concerning a conversation he had with Colonel Patterson, the commanding officer of the Jewish Legion.

> But a strange impression remained in my mind after these conversations: as if fear was not the most important thing but some other psychological phenomenon—let me call it an itch for a fight. On the Transjordan front, Colonel Patterson (he was Irish-born) told me the story of a countryman of his, a wanderer who came to a foreign city and saw a riot in the marketplace, about a dozen hard young men battering each other with lethal blows. He stopped to look, and his face expressed envy, nostalgia, and longing; and finally he turned to one of the onlookers and asked politely: "Pardon me, sir: is this a private fight, or may a stranger also take part?" Sweden was a peaceful country, and so was Norway; however both of them had a romantic past, and apparently, to countries such as these, the thunder of the cannon in the distance and the polishing of swords echo a hidden and exciting appeal.[19]

Jabotinsky raved about the "itch for a fight": "The magnetic power of war was one of the fundamental and dominant forces of the world. If I were allowed the time and had the talent to write a story of the history of the mysteries within the heart of the individual and society, I would speak a lot about the depth, the meaning, and the scope of this factor, and I would also analyze its moral nature: was it for good or evil that the Creator planted it in our soul?"[20]

Jabotinsky's psychological explanation for World War I fits well with his earlier discussions of imperial appetites. The only difference is that here rapaciousness belongs to the individual instead of the collective. However, Jabotinsky clearly lacked the historian's ability to analyze the motives of empires.[21] Instead, he has the habit of projecting individual traits onto nations. Thus, he discovered that passion motivated politics. In this instance, Jabotinsky was influenced by Vitalism, as articulated by Nietzsche, Henri Bergson, and Gorges Sorel's theory of violence.[22]

Jabotinsky understood some things—such as the rally to patriotism—but his overall analysis of the war was shortsighted. In large part his perspective depended on his professional work, which focused on the home front—widows, the elderly, children, the wounded, and the multitudes of noncombatants who made the war machine run. Embedded in Paris in October 1914, he wrote: "We must travel throughout France in order to understand what universal military service means. All types of people, those we used to meet on the street endlessly, who at times composed the very essence of the street: the dandy, the apprentice, the student, the legal assistant, the sales-clerk, the journalist—in a word, the male civilian from the age of 20 to almost 50—has disappeared completely. He appears only as a rare exception and attracts a disapproving curiosity."[23]

Although his newspaper writing is interesting on many levels, we should focus on subjects related to his future: his travels to Arab lands in 1915, his visit to the camp of Jewish exiles in Alexandria, Egypt, and his sojourns in Britain. In 1915, Jabotinsky wrote to his editor asking permission to change his route and report from North Africa and the Middle East because rumors abounded that Turkey was planning a holy war, a jihad, against Britain and France. Since Russia allied itself with Britain and France, and since Turkey had a long history of complicated relations with Russia, it appeared a propitious moment to visit North Africa to see for oneself whether jihad was likely or merely a bluff.

Jabotinsky arrived in Morocco in late December 1914 and quickly oriented himself to political life in the Maghreb. As he saw it, the situation in North Africa involved a division of the country into two incompatible ideologies: the Muslim brotherhoods that, according to Jabotinsky, had local and religious roots; and the Caliphate, a pan-Islamic political organization. Regarding the brotherhoods, Jabotinsky perceived their animosity toward any foreigner. "The European is not liked and they would be happy to get rid of him. But they feel almost the same degree of dislike, for example, for the Turk, whose life differs so sharply from theirs; and not only for the distant Turk, but also for the Arab from neighboring countries, who has different customs, and, finally, simply for the person from another brotherhood. This is the ideal of conservatism for conservatism's sake."[24] Jabotinsky continued:

> At the same time the Caliphate appeared as something artificial to the majority of Arabs. Of course they acknowledged the Caliph, but purely theoretically, and even doubly theoretically: first of all, for them he is only the pope and not the emperor; secondly, the majority of the brotherhoods do not consider the

Turkish Sultan to be the Caliph: that belongs to the Moroccan Sultan because he is a "Sharif"—from Mohammed's family; and since Rahm and Avipon are on site, it means in essence that the Caliph does not occupy the throne. Therefore the real, authentic leader for these brotherhoods is not the Caliph, but the so-called "Mahdi" [the messiah]. This, in its original meaning, [the Mahdi] is simply the spiritual leader, a person with a holy life, an "elder": if he possesses, in addition, the talents of an administrator and military officer, even better—and then his influence can be extremely serious and threatening for Europe; but this influence has, in essence, a local character and ideas of "Pan-Islamism" are alien to him.[25]

Jabotinsky realized that jihad was unlikely. His investigations led him to conclude that Arab attitudes toward the Ottomans were, if not openly hostile, at least oppositional. "It is clear that the idea of a united Islam, especially of political unity, was organically alien."[26] Unity was impossible. The countries were different; considered themselves different; and were divided on the role of religion in political life. The Arabs were divided over religious belief and practice; they were jostling for position, thinking, as Jabotinsky was, about the postwar map and where the power of determination would reside.

Everywhere he went, he heard the same refrain. In Tunisia, people were skeptical, in Morocco the same. Speculating about the relative strength of Pan-Arabism in alignment with Turkey, Jabotinsky wrote, "The closer you get to the East, the more popular the idea, but there beneath it lies hidden what are essentially separatist national tendencies for which neither the Sultan nor Istanbul has adopted the green banner. 'Démodé,' that same Tunisian merchant said to me, whistled and waved his hand dismissively."[27]

Jabotinsky maintained that pan-Islamism was unlikely to form. Among the chief reasons was the disunity among the countries involved. They spoke different languages—in fact, many Moroccans use French in their education, the language of the enemy. In a moment of what we today would call "orientalizing," Jabotinsky attributes to the Arabs an insignificance, or irrelevance, due to "indolence." Airing views he would expand on in the 1920s, he wrote: "Concerning the psychology of the Arab, certain words have long been in common use: fanaticism, Caliphate, infidel, holy war and so on. All these, perhaps, are even true; but in addition there would be one other common word that should not be forgotten: fatalism. This psychological peculiarity has manifested itself as an ordinary character trait for them. It has, it seems, no Russian name; Romance language-speakers call it 'indolence.' For the last thirty years it has gotten stronger and fuller; it has grown fat under the influence of the satiety and peace imported from the European administration."[28]

Clearly, Jabotinsky repeated a conventional dichotomy, European and non-European, in which the European is modern and therefore quick, smart, advanced, and secular, while the non-European, a subaltern, embodies the opposite qualities. Jabotinsky imposed his own superiority as the knowledge-maker, the journalist, the expert who comes from a materially superior place to examine the religious, ethnic, and racial "other." Here he shows his own conventionality by reflecting the dominant epistemologies of his time.

Jabotinsky's travels in North Africa provided him with knowledge that would be key to his involvement in the Legion. First, he understood that jihad was a farce: there was nothing to fear from Ottoman threats of holy war. Second, he gained insight into Muslim brotherhoods, which he viewed as an example of Arab nationalism formed with the help of religious claims. A local leadership bound up with xenophobia and coercion could prove a difficult rival to Jewish nationalism. But Jabotinsky consoled himself by imagining the Arab opponent as paralyzed by "indolence."[29] Their indolence might just aid Zionists in the quest to occupy Palestine on the coattails of a British victory. In this sense, Jabotinsky was optimistic that the disorder within the Ottoman Empire might change the face of the Middle East and bring unexpected opportunities.

* * *

The path to establishing a Jewish Legion in the British Army was complex, and its success depended on Jabotinsky's vision and Britain's willingness to implement it. It also depended on serendipity and luck. Ottoman losses initially motivated Jabotinsky because a potential dismemberment of the Empire implied that there would be a postwar reconfiguration in Palestine. Jabotinsky sensed that whoever helped to conquer Palestine would receive a share. Therefore, he envisioned a cohesive fighting force consisting of Jewish soldiers contributing to that effort. His realization that jihad was not going to happen was an essential element of the puzzle, because, without Arab support, the Ottoman Empire would disintegrate, and the pieces would become the property of those who bet on the winner. That much was clear to Jabotinsky.

Jabotinsky was not alone in his prediction. England and France had drawn up contingent plans and negotiated a treaty in 1916, the Sykes-Picot

Agreement, which stipulated that parts of the Middle East would be split into spheres of influence.[30] Earlier, in 1915, Sir Henry McMahon had promised Hussein Ibn Ali, the Sharif of Mecca, the restoration of the Caliphate.[31] However, as we know, when the invasion of Palestine turned into a rout, Great Britain decided to rescind the agreement to share Palestine with France and looked to the Balfour Declaration (November 1917) and the subsequent postwar mandate from the League of Nations for legitimacy.

To realize the Jewish Legion idea, various elements had to come together. First, someone had to propose a separate Jewish armed force. At the time, the presence of Jewish servicemen in the armies of Europe was an ordinary occurrence.[32] What was not ordinary, however, was the idea of creating a Jewish armed force that would further Jewish national goals—for example, an invasion in Palestine. Although Jabotinsky awoke to Zionism in 1903, during his participation in the self-defense effort in Odessa, the Legion was, naturally, a project of greater complexity. Self-defense was about protecting a community from physical harm. Simple. The Legion aimed to promote a political agenda, one that world powers did not necessarily share. Hence, the difficulty and complexity.

According to Jabotinsky, the idea emerged in Alexandria, in the camp of Jewish evacuees from Palestine. In his reportage from 1915, Jabotinsky describes the diverse "refugee camp," all Jews and non-Ottoman citizens, who had been exiled from Palestine by the Turks and interned in the British-run camp. According to Jabotinsky, these people had come to Palestine from all corners of the earth, and their clothes, languages, and food habits created the atmosphere of an "Arab bazaar," an uncontrollable motley of colors, smells, sounds, and people.

In his articles about the camp, Jabotinsky didn't describe so much as *prescribe*. He endorsed diversity over unity, Diaspora over homeland, multiplicity over oneness: Jews from everywhere had become a united people in Palestine. He gave as his example the Hebrew language: "I counted twelve languages there: Arabic, Russian, Yiddish, Ladino, Italian, Bukharin, Georgian, Tat (Dagestan), Polish, German, English and French. I haven't counted among these the various Arab dialects that strongly differentiate the Syrian, Yemeni and Moroccan from one another. One could go crazy in such a mess if not for the thirteenth language—Hebrew. Almost all the children and young people who grew up in the country speak only Hebrew; most of the adults also speak it fluently."[33] He added:

> It seems to me that I am not getting carried away or exaggerating if I say: what has happened with this language in Palestine in the last 25 years is one of the most amazing events in the history of languages, and one of the most incredible in the history of education. I have been digging in the documents of different national movements for nearly ten years now; I have examined the so-called 'rebirth of languages.' [. . .] All of these [other] tribes have an argot, and they spoke this language even before the 'rebirth.' The rebirth essentially consisted of vocabulary enrichment alone. Here in Palestine, the task was incomparably harder: to bring into living use a language that no one had spoken anywhere for more than two thousand years.[34]

To make his points, Jabotinsky claimed that Palestine brings moral health to the degenerate European:

> The characteristic appearance of the school-age dandy and coquette that we in Russia expect is entirely opposite here. Sometimes a boy arrives from Odessa or Kiev, a dandy and cavalier; he enters the fifth class and after six months you cannot recognize him. Excursions, gymnastics, soccer, and the environment turn him into a sort of man, an awkward irregular in the Turkish army [*bashibuzuk*] with a hole in his elbow, just like you'd expect in a fifteen-year old. In the gymnasium there are many girls—around a third; they study together, they sit side by side, but outside of class, as often happens in mixed schools, the boys and girls go off into different groups and live separate lives.[35]

The overall impression that one comes away with is of a community that is fundamentally healthy and morally sound.

The actual origins of the Legion are somewhat murky. According to most historians, Jabotinsky met Yosef Trumpeldor in Alexandria and shared the idea of a Jewish unit under British command.[36] However, Pinhas Rutenberg, the former Russian revolutionary and later an engineer and industrialist in Palestine, rejected that version, taking full credit for the original idea. In a letter to Viscount Allenby, dated April 27, 1933, Rutenberg wrote, "I am proud to state now the fact, known to few, that I am the author of the idea of the Jewish Battalions to fight with the Entente Powers in the Great War. To redeem with Jewish blood Jewish Palestine. That was in August 1914. . . . It was the privilege of Jabotinsky to make that dream a reality."[37]

Although both Rutenberg and Jabotinsky make a good case, it is nonetheless important to recall that Jews in Palestine were already preparing and implementing ideas for armed conflict. In 1907, the Shomer movement was formed, and Jewish guards took over the security of settlements from Circassians and Arabs.[38] During World War I, the Aronsons, Aron and Sarah, spied on Turkish positions and passed the information to Great Britain.[39] They were caught, tortured, and hanged. Before the war, Palestine Jews were motivated to protect themselves and further their social, political, or economic interests. The Jews in the Alexandrian camp volunteered to win back "their country."

In *Story of the Jewish Legion*, Jabotinsky described how, in Alexandria, the Russian attaché tried to invoke a clause in a Russo-British treaty to the effect that, in times of war, the citizens of one country might be returned to the other to serve in its military. The exiles decided to write a letter asking Britain to permit them to serve as a special "Jewish detachment" under British aegis. Over one hundred people signed it. Jabotinsky described the scene: "Next day, as I was coming into the camp courtyard, I saw a complete parade. Three groups of young men were learning to march, having chosen their own instructors from among Russian ex-soldiers; several girls were stitching a flag in a corner, and a committee of schoolboys was engaged in translating military terminology into Hebrew. Then Trumpeldor arrived. The three groups formed a column of files and marched past him in a kind of ceremonial procession. He watched with a satisfied smile. 'Good heavens,' I whispered to him, 'they march like geese.' '*En davar*,' he replied. ('No matter.')"[40]

According to Trumpeldor's biographer, Alexander Shul'man, a meeting with General John Maxwell in March 1915 won no concessions. However, Maxwell encouraged the evacuees to organize themselves as volunteers for a transport unit that would be integrated into the British Army.[41] This nucleus became the basis of the "Zionist Mule Corps," a transport unit that was sent to Gallipoli. The unit's official name, Assyrian Jewish Refugee Mule Corps, and its shorter name, "Mule Corps," infuriated Jabotinsky, who resigned from the project. Apparently he was offended that, after two thousand years, the first Jewish soldiers in a specifically Jewish detachment would be associated with mules. It was undignified, demeaning. Trumpeldor disagreed, claiming that in war there is no difference between a front soldier and a transport unit: both are essential and wind up risking their lives.

Colonel John Henry Patterson, a Protestant Irishman and Zionist sympathizer, was appointed commander, with Trumpeldor serving as his assistant.[42] Just a few weeks after it was formed, the Corps men, accompanied by about 750 mules, were sent to the Gallipoli front, joining numerous other non-British troops who were added to the massive Mediterranean Expeditionary Force—"a veritable Tower of Babel," as it was dubbed by a contemporary historian.⁴³ Jabotinsky admitted later that Trumpeldor was right. During the failed Gallipoli campaign in 1916, Jews served heroically; 8 men were killed and 55 wounded, and 3 members received honors. The service of the 650 men gained them respect everywhere, especially among British military personnel.⁴⁴ The "Mule Corps" were disbanded in May 1916, less than fourteen months after it was created. Nonetheless, Gallipoli effectively prepared the ground for the establishment of a full-fledged Jewish Legion.⁴⁵

After Trumpeldor went to Gallipoli, Pinhas Rutenberg and Jabotinsky traveled to build support for the Jewish Legion.⁴⁶ In mid-May 1915, Jabotinsky went to Stockholm, Copenhagen, Petrograd, Moscow, Odessa, and Kiev. "Everywhere his idea of a Jewish fighting force met with hostility," writes the historian Yehuda Reinharz.⁴⁷ The Zionist leadership, consisting primarily of German, Russian, and Polish Jews, had moved its central bureau to Copenhagen and declared neutrality in the war. Therefore, the leadership rejected Jabotinsky's plan to establish a Jewish Legion for Britain. However, Jabotinsky refused to back down, promising to pursue the Legion idea as a "private citizen." That suggestion was not appreciated.

Yehuda Reinharz describes the meeting with the Greater Actions Committee in July 1915:

> Leon Simon rejected the idea as Jabotinsky's 'wildest scheme . . . a scheme quite impossible of realization and fraught with great danger to our people.' [Moses] Gaster thought Jabotinsky's scheme the work of an adventurous journalist. Menachem Ussishkin, who had been Jabotinsky's opponent since the early congresses [sic], felt confirmed in his dislike of the man. It was only natural that the pro-German Shmarya Levin belittled Jabotinsky's "unfortunate Legion," but so did Jabotinsky's good friend Victor Jacobson, who was firmly opposed. The Po'alei Zion in the United States also chimed in, warning against any action that would place the Jewish nation firmly in the camp of one of the belligerents.⁴⁸

It is important to remember that Zionism's leaders had an entirely different conception of how things would turn out. The majority of Jabotinsky's colleagues opposed the Legion idea as a "crazy scheme," a "dangerous" plan that would "ruin the Jewish people." Complaints came from the Russian Zionist leadership, which feared that a special alliance with Britain would put the Yishuv at risk because Germany might win. Many of the leading Russian Zionists felt sympathy toward Germany, having spent years studying in German-speaking cities (Leib Jaffe and Joseph Klausner had studied in Heidelberg). Furthermore, Ussishkin, Chlenov, and Klausner were eager to see Russia lose the war; they hoped a defeat would stimulate political reforms in Russia. Therefore, they considered Jabotinsky's support for Britain, Russia's ally, as a betrayal. In this context, Jabotinsky describes a collision between his mother and Ussishkin on a street in Odessa in 1915, in which Ussishkin vented his frustration, saying, "Your son should be hanged."[49]

Jabotinsky met with Chlenov and Jacobson in May 1915 for three hours. He related that his two "senior colleagues"

> aided by the brave Dr. Hantke from Berlin, argued that [not only the Legion project, but] the Mule Corps too was a criminal offence, [and] that if I continued to conduct this propaganda—why, I would be burying the Zionist enterprise for all eternity. Jacobson and Hantke particularly distinguished themselves.... Dr. Hantke proved to me, on the basis of political economy, history, and statistics, that Turkey would never give up its rights to Erez-Israel. The man demonstrated to me, with the clarity of the multiplication tables in the noon sunlight, that the victory of Germany was assured on all the fronts. And both together revealed to me the awful secret that rebellions would soon be breaking out in Egypt, Algeria, and Morocco.[50]

Although he poured on the sarcasm, one might consider the risks in Jabotinsky's program. The Zionist organization had decided on neutrality in order to hedge its bets. The leaders did not want to see Zionist interests in Palestine diminished, whoever ultimately won. Additionally, Jews were serving in all armies, and it seemed unfair that a few Jews would get special dispensation for serving in a British unit in Palestine. The news of such a unit might draw jealousy or hostility to Jews everywhere. Another objection to the Legion, especially among "the Russians" (Zionists), was that by aiding Britain, the Legion gave support to Britain's ally, Russia—that is, the tsar and his government of oppression and antisemitism.[51] Furthermore, Jabotinsky endangered the many Jewish immigrants in England who had escaped Russia to avoid the draft, only to find themselves subject to recruitment in Britain.

To align Zionist hopes so closely with Britain, as Chaim Weizmann was doing, and to reject the will of the official Zionist leadership took courage.[52] In *Story of the Jewish Legion*, Jabotinsky discusses Weizmann, noting that he offered private support but was unable or unwilling to risk his public authority for this speculative project. He explained further:

> Dr. Weizmann was in favor of my plans, but he admitted to me honestly that he could not and did not care to make his own political work more complicated

and difficult by openly supporting a project formally condemned by the Zionist "Actions Committee" and extremely unpopular with the Jewish population of London.

Once he told me, and it was very typical of him: "I cannot work like you in an atmosphere where everybody is angry with me and can hardly stand me. This everyday friction would poison my life and kill in me all desire to work. Better let me act in my own way; a time will come when I shall find the means to help you as best I can."[53]

Jabotinsky recounts this conversation in order to discredit Weizmann and expose him as a coward. Although the contents are accurate, Weizmann had good reason not to yoke himself to Jabotinsky. First of all, Jabotinsky had a reputation for being a hothead, and that image was the antithesis of the one that Weizmann was trying to cultivate, that of a level-headed realist who headed an organization with reasonable and moderate goals. Secondly, Weizmann had greater experience in England and knew that pro-Zionist sources lay not in the British military or Foreign Office, but in the political elite. Finally, Weizmann was slowly building a consensus among different people and groups in England. He was afraid of showing his hand too early and empowering opponents.

The Weizmann–Jabotinsky tensions revealed the differences of opinion among the Russians in Britain. Trumpeldor, for example, considered himself a Russian patriot. He could have taken Ottoman citizenship as "the price of permission to remain in the country, a price which many of his comrades among the wholly committed settlers and most of his friends in the Deganiya collective thought a modest one to pay."[54] The Zionist organization had advised taking Ottoman citizenship too. Nonetheless, David Vital writes that "Trumpeldor thought otherwise. He seems to have regarded it as impermissible for a former Russian officer (still in receipt of a modest pension) to join Russia's enemies and perhaps be forced to fight with them against her.... He was strongly anti-German; he loathed what he saw as Prussian militarism. He hoped and probably believed that the alliance with the Anglo-French *entente* would end by softening the Russian Autocracy."[55] In contrast to Trumpeldor, Jabotinsky's thinking appears to have been guided less by personal principles and more by his reaction to the scenes of upheaval he witnessed in Europe, North Africa, and now Egypt. There was a profound logic in offering military service in exchange for a potential homeland in Palestine.

Another player, Meir Grossman, a Russian-Jewish journalist with the liberal newspaper *Birzhevye Vedomosti (Stock Market News)*, joined

Jabotinsky's cause. Grossman lived in Copenhagen from 1915 to 1916 and published *Yudishe Folks-Tsaytung*, which "was formally owned by a limited company, but was to a certain degree controlled by WZO's Copenhagen office."[56] Grossman edited 233 issues of the paper, but he tripped up when he published an interview with Jabotinsky regarding the Legion idea. Fired from his job, he joined with Jabotinsky in publishing *Di Tribune (The Platform)*, a Yiddish newspaper in which he and Jabotinsky demanded that Zionists side with Britain and engage in armed struggle for a future Palestine.[57] The newspaper became a soapbox for the Legion.[58]

* * *

Jabotinsky announced his Legion goals as early as November 1915 in *Di Tribune*. In "Turkey and Us," he wrote about acquiring Palestine for Jewish immigration. "A colossal majority of Zionists is not pleased with Turkey and dreams about an intervention. The large majority from the Zionist world would be happy if Palestine would leave Turkey's authority and they hope moreover that it will happen. If it does not happen, all the friends . . . would be happy if at least we got support thanks to guarantees from the European governments against Turkish absolutism."[59]

Many of *Di Tribune*'s articles focused on the Legion and its purpose. But perhaps its main subject was the struggle with the official Zionist organization.[60] By not taking sides, official Zionism announced its irrelevancy and missed opportunities to promote the cause. As the editor of *Di Tribune*, Meir Grossman, wrote, "Now one turns toward action in the organization. One considers that everything is not in order. In Switzerland and the Scandinavian countries one begins to get acquainted with internal disorder in certain initiatives and resolutions, searching to find the secret of our political impotence."[61]

Di Tribune had a small circulation and reached few of the readers it might have served. Since it was written in a foreign language (Yiddish), it could not be sold in Russia, where the government banned all material published in a non-Cyrillic alphabet; at the same time, Great Britain mistakenly banned it as "anti-alliance." The periodical lost money. Often Grossman used his own money to pay the typesetters and printers. Still, the paper served as a billboard for the "activist" position that Jabotinsky pursued: argument with the official organization, support for Britain, enthusiasm for a Legion.

Grossman's role in helping Jabotinsky propagandize his ideas has been acknowledged; why he got involved with Jabotinsky is less settled. His activities as a Zionist representative to the Ukrainian Central Rada in

1917, and later as a leader of HaTzoHar (Revisionist Zionism) and the Jewish State Party, reflect his militancy. His book from 1920, *The Case Against the "Mixed" Jewish Agency*, closely cleaves to Jabotinsky's position opposing non-Zionist donors in the Jewish Agency.[62] From 1916 Grossman was inspired by the idea of a Legion and threw his resources and talents behind Jabotinsky. Grossman's full support reflected the power of the Legion idea, but perhaps also Jabotinsky's personal charisma.

* * *

Would the Legion ever be created? It was entirely up to Britain. Why would the British government want to do what no other army on the continent had done—give Jews their own unit? Lord Kitchener, head of the British armed forces, absolutely refused. Until his death in 1916, he opposed "fancy regiments," and the idea gained little momentum. After that, there was potential, but conditions still needed to come together.

During the early part of the war, Jabotinsky had visited Great Britain often. He observed anxiety and anger over the army's recruitment policy. Britain had a volunteer army, and the lower classes joined to express patriotism but also out of economic desperation. At the same time, it was considered bad manners and antipatriotic for men to avoid service, especially when so many were dying on the western front. The public displayed anger at service-dodgers, including the "Jewish tailors," immigrants from Russia who had exploited British generosity toward immigrants but refused to fulfill their civic duty to their adopted homeland.[63]

Jabotinsky described the English attitude toward conscription in an article from October 1915. He quoted a Mrs. Pock, the average English housewife. "'We have compulsion,' she said, 'only not for everyone. And we have forced service only for two categories of people: for very moral people and for those in great need. Honor forces the first type and necessity forces the second. Nothing forces the others and they sit at home. *Compulsory service* means that the others are forced too, isn't it so? Oh, in that case I am for it, I'm for it all the way.'"[64]

Writing in December 1915, Jabotinsky noted the change from 1915 to 1916:

> So far, the English soldier, Tommy Atkins, never had real roots in his country. Even in October of last year, when I met some English soldiers near Soissons, I had the same impression and, I seem to recall, I wrote about him: in general these are not the core organic elements of the nation—not the bread-winners, not the farmers, not the workers, but Tommy Atkins, for whom no one cries.

At the time there were only contingents of old hunters at the front. But now everything had changed radically.... The new contingent, "Kitchener's army," is a huge piece of the living meat of the nation. At every step you see ruined family nests: the husband joined the army, his wife joined the Sisters of Charity, the children were left with their grandmother. Five or ten people grieve for every casualty; every casualty leaves several orphans and homeless dependents behind. For Russia and France this is the order of things, but England has never experienced anything like this.[65]

The British were becoming irritated at the Jewish immigrants. Newspapers were writing about it; British officials wanted to see more Jewish service volunteers as a sign of gratitude. England's Jews were becoming aware of the pressure, too. They worried that the "reluctance of Russian Jews to serve their adopted country would have a bad effect on their own good name as loyal subjects. Moves were made in high places by Leopold de Rothschild, Sir Joseph Sebag-Montefiore and other influential figures, with Lucien Wolf, a journalist-cum-lobbyist acting as an intermediary."[66]

In mid-1916, the government started threatening to return immigrants to Russia or impose a draft on the community, forcing Jews to serve. Jabotinsky was ready to help, but he felt that Britain also had to yield. He maintained that the "Jewish tailors," as he called them, would volunteer, but only to defend something they really cared about, such as Palestine or the British Isles. Thus, Jabotinsky wanted a promise from the British army that the immigrants would be organized as a closed detachment and used only for the invasion of Eretz Israel. A letter to Herbert Samuel, a British army officer of Jewish descent and a Zionist sympathizer (and later the first high commissioner for Palestine), from September 16, 1916, reveals Jabotinsky's self-assigned role as leader of the Russian-Jewish immigrants in Britain:

I propose to lead the campaign on the following lines:

1. Immigrants must enlist.
2. They must be posed in distinct groups, sufficiently large to be welded afterwards in a legion, should the necessity arise.
3. They must be reserved for home-defense, including dominions, i.e., Egypt.
4. They will be considered as fighting units, not labor or transport companies, and will undergo regular military training.
5. If Palestine should come within the scope of British operations, they will form a sort of legion and will be deployed there.

Of course, the whole campaign will have a nationalistic and 'legionistic' character, with the option of participation in the conquest of Palestine as one of the principal motives. Apart from my own opinions, this is the only way to raise some enthusiasm at this hour of general and Jewish disappointment; and I do not believe in the success of propaganda, where the only argument for voluntary enlistment would be the frightfulness of the alternatives.[67]

The idea of a Jewish military unit had evolved from the Zionist Mule Corps to a full-scale Legion. The credit belonged to Jabotinsky (which does not preclude the role of others too). In a letter of October 31, 1915, to Major P. H. Cosgrain in the War Office, Jabotinsky expressed his hopes: "I propose: a) to transform the Zion Mule Corps into a fighting unit, with a suitable change in the second part of its name; b) to create a central office in London in order to organize the recruiting of foreign Jews for the Zion Corps in all the areas and countries concerned."[68] The army was very interested in reaching a compromise, and Jabotinsky, along with Trumpeldor, was invited to the War Office for discussions.

We now view the Legion from the perspective of history. It's easy to forget the enormous uphill battle that Jabotinsky fought on its behalf. The army put up many obstacles, and there was opposition in the High Command. Until the last minute, it was not certain the Legion would actually come into being. Jabotinsky's letter to Edward Derby, the general director of recruitment, gives a clear indication that, as late as August 1917, all was not well with the Legion's organization:

> When I submitted my proposal I asked for two essential conditions: 1) The immediate formation of a nucleus, and 2) a well-worded official appeal to the ideals of Jewish manhood. Neither has been done yet. There are already hundreds of applications for transfer from officers and men, but the nucleus has not yet been formed. In official papers I saw the Jewish Regiment is styled "for service in Palestine," but their destination has not been confirmed publicly and officially. A Committee has been formed to assist in raising the unit, with Lord Rothschild, Sir Stuart Samuel, Israel Zangwill and many other leaders of Jewry, but the activity is not being encouraged—indeed, it is rather actually discouraged. All this lends credit to mischievous rumors spread by willful people: that the unit is not meant as a complement to Jews, but simply as a body of aliens *qua* aliens, singled out to be used in case of hopeless danger instead of English troops.[69]

It is important also to realize that the Jews of the East End despised Jabotinsky. Yehuda Reinharz explains,

> His harsh and uncompromising language on the duties of the Russian immigrants to their national pride and their adoptive country failed to arouse sympathy for his ideas. . . . Unlike Weizmann and his colleagues, who attempted

to encourage voluntary, rather than coerced enlistment—an approach urged simultaneously by radicals and liberals for citizens as well [as immigrants]—Jabotinsky retained the option of pursuing his own line.... In September 1916 he was able, with aid from public funds secured by [Herbert] Samuel, in addition to the regular contributions supplied by Joseph Cowen, to widen and intensify his campaign.[70]

Jabotinsky intended to satisfy both sides with this argument. The British wanted the immigrants to serve, but Jewish immigrants from Russia could not be expected to volunteer after learning of the carnage in Flanders and elsewhere. They had come to Britain seeking refuge, not to sacrifice their lives for little benefit. Jabotinsky explained in a conversation with Joseph King, a liberal MP,

> There is a vast difference between your boys and those East-End boys. Your boys are British; if Britain wins their people is saved. Ours are Jews; if Britain wins, millions of our brothers will still remain in purgatory. You cannot demand equal sacrifices where the hope is not an equal one.... A compromise. In order to be just, you can demand only two things from the foreign Jew: first, "Home defense," to protect Britain itself, because he lives here; second, to fight for the liberation of Palestine, for that is to be the Heim of his people. "Home and Heim"—that is my war motto for your Whitechapel friends.[71]

In his memoirs, Chaim Weizmann strongly criticized Jabotinsky, but he enthusiastically praised the Legion work. Weizmann wrote, "It is almost impossible to describe the difficulties and disappointments which Jabotinsky had to face. I know of few people who could have stood up to them, but his pertinacity, which flowed from his devotion, was simply fabulous. He was discouraged and derided on every hand."[72] Although in *Story of My Life* Jabotinsky mocked Weizmann (no surprise, given their political rivalry later on), the documents of the time show that Weizmann offered and performed behind-the-scenes services for Jabotinsky, including interceding with Lloyd George, who became prime minister in December 1916. Martin Watts describes the help: "Of fundamental importance was his relationship with Chaim Weizmann, through whom Jabotinsky began to develop a network of important contacts and supporters, both Jewish and Gentile, such as Joseph Cowen, Montague Eder and C. P. Scott, the editor of the *Manchester Guardian*. Cowen, who had become the owner of the *Jewish Chronicle* in 1907, had been introduced to Zionism by his relative, Israel Zangwill, and was a founder of the British Zionist Federation."[73] Weizmann also allowed Jabotinsky to lodge at his home for several weeks in 1916, during which time

Jabotinsky became especially close with Weizmann's wife, Vera Weizmann, and with Chaim himself.

After many unsuccessful meetings with British military officials, Jabotinsky volunteered as a private in the British army. He may have hoped to find more success working within the establishment. But he often had to meet with top brass about the Legion, about propaganda, logistics, and leadership, and these meetings between a lowly private and high officials were awkward, if altogether unique.[74] Although he was in his mid-thirties, he volunteered and went through boot camp; in the army, he had to eat and sleep with ordinary conscripts, not officers.[75]

After seemingly endless opposition from the Foreign Office and the War Office, the final go—ahead occurred only at the end of July 1917. A leading role in the ultimate success of the project belonged to Leo Amery, a British Conservative Party politician, whose "imperial ambitions" and "pro-Zionist attitudes" helped keep the idea of a Legion alive. The image of Jabotinsky in these days came from his colleagues, especially Colonel Patterson, the commanding officer of the Legion.[76] Jabotinsky worked hard to raise awareness of the Legion, publishing articles in the press and giving speeches in the East End, spreading the word.

On August 8, 1917, in the headquarters of the War Office, "and in the presence of Weizmann, Jabotinsky, Lord Rothschild, James de Rothschild, Mark Sykes, and other prominent Zionists and government officials, Colonel John Henry Patterson reiterated this announcement and explained the purpose of the newly established Jewish Legion."[77] Then the struggle to recruit soldiers began. Years later, Jabotinsky recalled the Legion's many opponents who came to meetings in London's East End and threw eggs and shouted down the speakers. In *Story of the Jewish Legion*, he describes his regret at refusing the offer of British security for these meetings, at which pacifists, anarchists, socialists, and others disrupted his efforts.[78]

Ultimately, around ten thousand individuals volunteered for the Legion. Many came from as far away as the United States and Australia.[79] Commonly referred to as the Jewish Battalion (or the Judean Regiment or the "First to Judah"), the Legion's soldiers were permitted to display Jewish insignia: the uniforms bore Jewish stars. They made up a part of the 39th and 40th Royal Fusiliers Battalions.

Under Patterson and Trumpeldor, the soldiers learned to march and fire their rifles in response to Hebrew commands. Although the war was almost over, the unit was shipped off to Egypt to help shore up General

Allenby's forces in Palestine.[80] Jabotinsky described his experiences at the end of the offensive and subsequent guard duty in the boiling heat of summer in the Judean Hills.[81] "Perhaps he imagined himself a Jewish Garibaldi liberating Palestine at the head of a Jewish army."[82] He ended the war as an honorary lieutenant in the battalion.[83]

Although historians have cautiously evaluated the Legion's value as a fighting force, the Legion deserves recognition as a symbol. For the first time in nearly two thousand years, Jews were fighting in a Jewish military unit for Jewish national interests. The force had limited military value, and no direct link between the Legion and the postwar peace talks can be established. Thus, it is difficult to assess the Legion's role in bringing about the Balfour Declaration.

Jabotinsky did not agree. In 1927, when he published *Story of the Jewish Legion*, he made a bold proclamation: the Jewish Legion was responsible for the Balfour Declaration.

> I say with the deep and cold conviction of an observer—speaking only of the short war period: half the Balfour Declaration belongs to the Legion. For the world is not an irresponsible organism; Balfour Declarations are not given to individuals. They can be given only to movements. And how could the Zionist Movement express itself in those war years? It was broken and paralyzed, and was, by its nature, completely outside the narrow horizons of a warring world with its war governments. Only one manifestation of the Zionist will was able to break through onto this horizon, to show that Zionism was alive and prepared for sacrifice; to compel ministers, ambassadors and—most important of all—journalists, to treat the striving of the Jewish people for its country as a matter of urgent reality, as something which could not be postponed, which had to be given an immediate yes or no—and that was the Legion Movement.[84]

Jabotinsky's phrase, "Balfour Declarations are not given to individuals," is a barb directed at Chaim Weizmann and the view that Weizmann promoted, that he alone was responsible for the Balfour Declaration. Weizmann, for his part, acknowledged Jabotinsky's work during the war, but he emphasized his own actions as far more consequential.[85] Jabotinsky's attempt to edit history should be viewed in the context of his personal struggle for leadership in the 1920s. He was angry at Weizmann and objected to the decision to compromise with Britain on core points, such as immigration limits and support for land use. That other Zionists had a role in the Balfour Declaration has always been known, and in recent years scholars have attempted to revise Weizmann's self-portrayal by showing that others, such as Nahum Sokoloff, had important roles too.[86]

Jabotinsky recounted his war experiences in his memoir about the Legion. When he arrived with the Legion, in autumn 1917, Allenby had already liberated Jerusalem. But there were still skirmishes between Turkish and British forces. In September, the Legion's men were among the first units to cross into Transjordan. They proved useful in the final battles and then in guarding POW's.[87] The descriptions in Jabotinsky's memoir underscore his personal sufferings, but also his enthusiasm at witnessing moments of victory. Writing about service in the Judean Hills, he says, "In summer, it is a purgatory. In a town like Jericho, the heat may be endured, for you can shut yourself up in a windowless and almost doorless Arab house. But outside—Gehenna! Even the Bedouins usually absent themselves for two months between mid-July and September, just at the time that our men were stationed in the Mellaha, close to Jericho and the Dead Sea—not far, if you like, from Sodom and Gomorrah."[88] Jabotinsky recalls marching a group of Turkish, German, and Austrian prisoners to Jericho. Describing the stragglers who could not march on, he asks: Should one kill them or leave them for the jackals? Jabotinsky gives no answer but waxes philosophical: "Awesome is the life of a nation, hard the march through the desert. You can't take it? Then lie down and die. Mankind is a regiment, too, only without a kind *padre*, and no one will carry you to Jericho. Go on and drag yourself as far as you can, hard toward yourself and your neighbor; or lie down and go down with your hope unfulfilled."[89]

As one can see, *Story of the Jewish Legion* is not just a memoir, but a proclamation, announcing the author's political aspirations. Jabotinsky blamed the decommissioning of the Legion for the Arab violence that broke out in 1920 and 1921: "The third period of our service—the Armistice period—I consider the most important. Moreover, the main purpose of the creation of the Legion was not so much its participation in the war, although we naturally desired this, as its remaining as the garrison of Palestine after the war."[90] Jabotinsky links peace with the Legion's prominence and visibility. "As long as the Legion was a visible force in Palestine not a single clash occurred, despite what was happening in Egypt. Only when there remained from our Legion of five thousand only four hundred—only then were Trumpeldor and his comrades killed at Tel Hai, only then did the pogrom break out in Jerusalem. But these tragedies are not part of my story. I tell of the Legion, and just so long as the Legion existed all was quiet and peaceful—and the military chronicler had nothing to write about."[91]

In Jabotinsky's interpretation, the British had diminished their great achievement by stepping back from their promise in the Balfour Declaration. Although British and Zionist interests could coincide, Britain had taken a different path, but Jabotinsky still saw some hope; Britain was not monolithic, and the Colonial Office clearly held stronger anti-Jewish attitudes than the government. He would try to bring order to a disorderly situation.

* * *

Jabotinsky's war experiences in the Middle East led him to make some unusual and exaggerated claims. He asserted, for example, that the real reason for World War I was dividing the spoils of a dismembered Ottoman Empire. Sure, other causes were offered to inspire the population to fight. But these were false, illusory. He explained, using a parable:

> Imagine an old town in which an epidemic disease suddenly breaks out. People are naturally anxious to discover the source of the scourge and to remove it. Some think that the cause lies in the absence of vegetation; others say that the streets of the town are too narrow and the houses too dark. Others again insist on the necessity of improving the underground drainage. Thus a complete scheme of reconstruction of the old town is formed, which attracts sympathies and excites enthusiasms. It works its own way further: Mr. Somebody is suddenly reminded of his own old feud with his neighbor, a field-boundary dispute unjustly decided by the court, and he goes around saying that there can be no health where there is no justice, and that a radical struggle against the disease implies a reform of the tribunals—and the revision of some old quarrels. But the Doctor knows that the real cause of the epidemic is the bad quality of the potable water, because the source from which it comes is infected; and to disinfect it the picturesque beauty of the river-margin must be deformed by a plain but hygienic embankment. That is the difficulty, because many of his fellow citizens love the romantic river-side in its wildness. So the Doctor says: "Your scheme is very good. I grant you, green spaces are necessary, wide streets and bright houses are healthy, a more perfect drainage is of the greatest importance. I even agree with the desirability of a reform of the courts. Try it all if you can. I shall be glad if you succeed. But don't forget that even if you succeed in all this you don't destroy the root of our plague, and it will persist. If you want to get rid of it you must embank the river. That is the main thing—that is the thing to be done. I know you don't like it; but I can't count on your feelings on this question. Drop the whole scheme if necessary, but remember the river."[92]

Jabotinsky remarks further that we mustn't forget the war's secondary goals—the protection of smaller nations, the re-annexation of Alsace-Lorraine, and the taming of the German *Junkerdom*. At the same time, he writes, the "root of the present plague is Asia Minor, and the first and last aim of the war is the solution of the Eastern question."[93]

According to Jabotinsky, everyone had a hand in the pot. Britain wanted Mesopotamia, Egypt, and Palestine; France wanted Lebanon, Syria, and the holy places; Russia wanted Istanbul, the Dardanelles, Armenia, and a warm (ice-free) seaport. In contrast to the other nations, whose success depended on Turkey's fragmentation, Germany wanted to swallow Turkey and its possessions whole, and in this way satisfy its need for foreign colonies—that is, foreign markets.[94]

History could have turned out differently, writes Jabotinsky, but the Turkish government made a serious mistake when the Young Turks demanded that all the national minorities assimilate into Turkish culture. Although centralization made sense in France, where French culture was superior to those of its colonies, for the Ottomans the opposite was true: Turkish culture was weaker. It was useful only for the bureaucracy and the military. Therefore, in order to save Turkey, the Ottomans had to curtail all progress. Jabotinsky claims that "They abhor every idea of real political progress, not because they like inertia, but because under current conditions in Turkey, progress means the liquidation of Ottoman rule."[95] He continues, "This natural fear of progress is not only felt in political matters. It can be said without exaggeration that it became the mainspring of the whole Young Turkish system, applied even to problems of a purely economic character. The absence of a Turkish commercial, industrial or intellectual middle class means that any step forward in the economic development of the country must inevitably result in enriching the non-Turks and consequently in weakening the Turkish element."[96] The reason for this attitude is that fate made them gardeners in a too-large garden. "So it inevitably became their only concern to prevent grass from growing, buds from flowering—if possible, the sun from shining. This was their only way to keep the colossal household from somehow overgrowing, throttling, and ejecting its masters."[97]

Jabotinsky had already expressed this view of Turkey, claiming, in 1909, that the Ottomans had a choice between growth and control, and their self-preservation forced them to choose control. This, of course, simplifies a much more complex situation in which the Ottomans were developing on many levels, through the modernization of the army and diplomatic initiatives with the European powers.[98] However, Jabotinsky's paradigm served to tell his story of a Turkey that would inevitably self-destruct because, among other things, it could not enable the kind of change required to bring about a successful Jewish colonization of Palestine. According to Jabotinsky, the Ottoman loss of power brought new opportunities. He predicted that the Arab nations would be unable to create a unified kingdom because of European opposition. "The Great Powers do not want to be turned out of the northern coasts of Africa, and if they succeed now in establishing their rule on some parts of Asia Minor, they will not want to be turned out from there either."[99]

Jabotinsky ended his book with a recommendation: Britain should conquer the Middle East. He acknowledged the legitimacy of Germany's claims, and noted its character as a culturally rich and economically vibrant country whose needs for expansion should not be thwarted completely. But he also believed that Britain's victory in the Middle East could stop the war by removing Germany's primary motivation: "Turkey is the *ultima spes* of the German businessman; in the notorious scheme of a self-contented *Mitteleuropa*, which represents to German minds the only alternative to overseas expansion, Turkey is the vital link, the spring of the clockwork. If you strike at it the whole system collapses."[100] Jabotinsky admitted that few saw the geopolitical situation in these terms. It was a shame, because war would continue precisely because true motives are shrouded.

The reader of *Turkey and the War* is likely to feel that Jabotinsky had overstated the case that the heart of the war lies not in Europe, but in the Middle East.[101] For Jabotinsky, however, Palestine was the real goal, even if people spoke about markets, imperialism, and national expansion. Nonetheless, it is also possible that too little attention had been given to the Ottomans as a lynchpin of power, and to the German need for extended markets in the Turkish sphere. As we all know from history, the war's big winner in the Middle East was Britain: it divvied up the land and minted new countries. However, Jabotinsky made the same argument that John Maynard Keynes would make soon enough: that one needed to treat Germany with care and not ignore its demands, because the consequences of weakening Germany excessively could be worse for Britain and France than yielding to its growing power.[102]

The book came out soon after World War I, by which time many of the claims and issues it raised were no longer relevant. The postwar situation focused not on Germany and Turkey, but on the fall of three empires: Russia, Ottoman, and Austro-Hungary. In the Middle East, Britain was now the master, and it won a mandate to govern Palestine. For Jabotinsky, life changed quickly once again. He was demobilized against his will. He decided to stay in Palestine and play a part in the building of the Jewish community under the British Mandate.

In the realm of an armed Zionism, the comparison of Jabotinsky with Herzl, which Jabotinsky repeated, was unconvincing. While it is true that both affirmed the primacy of politics and the political struggle, Herzl couldn't conceive the need for a Jewish armed force. He was ready to rely on the great powers for security. Jabotinsky, in contrast, insisted on loyalty to the Legion, even if his followers did not understand the reason. Herzl had a very different view of the colonization effort, maintaining that Jews would contribute to the efforts of a Western power. Jabotinsky thought similarly, but he imagined something like autonomy as he had described it in the years before the war.[103] Both looked to the great states for support, but Jabotinsky argued that those states would only regard Jews with respect if they could fight for themselves. In fact, Jabotinsky was the first Zionist to see the essential need for an army. In this way, he understood the value of Jewish armed forces for the sake of politics rather than merely to protect belongings and life and limb. He might later deny his relationship to Jewish terrorists, to Brit ha-Biryonim (Band of Hoodlums), and other enthusiasts for militarism, but in fact a direct line could be drawn between him and them. The line from them to Herzl was indirect, broken in places, and forced.

Notes

1. David Vital, *Zionism: The Crucial Phase* (Oxford: Clarendon, 1987), 44.
2. Vladimir Jabotinsky, *Story of My Life*, eds. Brian Horowitz and Leonid Katsis (Detroit: Wayne State University Press, 2017), 106. This marks the end of the first part of the Hebrew version of *Story of My Life*, which was published in the 1946–47 edition of Jabotinsky's collected works, *Ketavim*.
3. Vladimir Jabotinsky, *Story of the Jewish Legion*, trans. Shmuel Katz (New York: B. Ackerman, 1945), 29.
4. Ibid., 30.
5. William Hale, *Turkish Foreign Policy Since 1774*, 3rd ed. (New York: Routledge, 2012), 9.
6. Morton H. Narrowe. "Jabotinsky and the Zionists in Stockholm (1915)," *Jewish Social Studies* 46, no. 1 (1984): 9–10.
7. Jehuda Reinharz, *Chaim Weizmann: The Making of a Statesman* (New York: Oxford University Press, 1993), 172–212.
8. David Cronin, *Balfour's Shadow: A Century of British Support for Zionism and Israel* (London: Pluto Press, 2017).

9. Yochanan Petrovsky-Shtern, *Jews in the Russian Army, 1827–1917: Drafted into Modernity* (Cambridge: Cambridge University Press, 2009), 17.
10. Vladimir Jabotinsky, "Goroskop (1 Ianvaria 1912)," *Fel'etony* (Berlin: S. Zal'tsman, 1922), 262–263.
11. Vladimir Jabotinsky, *Fel'etony* (St. Petersburg, 1913), 128.
12. Ibid., 138.
13. Jabotinsky, *Story of My Life*, 38.
14. Ibid., 109.
15. Ibid., 109–110.
16. Eri Jabotinsky, *Avi, Ze'ev Jabotinsky* (Jerusalem: Stimatzky, 1980), 34.
17. Jabotinsky, *Story of My Life*, 110.
18. Ibid., 112–113.
19. Ibid., 115.
20. Ibid., 118.
21. Murray Frame, ed., *Russian Culture in War and Revolution, 1914–1922*, 2 vols. (Bloomington, IN: Slavica, 2014); Yigit Akin, *When the War Came Home: The Ottoman's Great War and the Devastation of an Empire* (Palo Alto: Stanford University Press, 1918).
22. Jacob Golomb, *Nietzsche and Zion* (Ithaca, NY: Cornell University Press, 2004), 60–62.
23. Vladimir Jabotinsky, "Vo Frantsii," *Russkie Vedomosti* (October 1, 1914): 2.
24. Vladimir Jabotinsky, "Ot Morokko do Tunisa," *Russkie Vedomosti* (December 28, 1914): 3.
25. Ibid. I consulted Professor Susan Gilson Miller, an expert on Moroccan history. Her impression of this passage is as follows: "The information he imparts is a bit of a mish-mash. The Moroccan Sultan was indeed equivalent to the Ottoman Caliph in his claim to be the religious head of state—the 'Commander of the Faithful.' It is also correct that he was a 'Sharif,' or direct descendent of the Prophet, and in that regard, even superior to the Turkish ruler, who could not claim that distinction.... I could not identify Rahm and Avipon; this is likely a reference to lower ranking French officers who indeed were 'on site.'" Professor Miller adds, "By 1915, the French had occupied all of North Africa with the exception of Libya. Before the French arrived in Morocco in 1912, the Moroccan head of state was both a religious and political leader, holding both spiritual and temporal authority. After 1912, temporal authority was seized by the French, who left the Sultan's religious authority intact." Private communication, September 18, 2017.
26. Jabotinsky, "Ot Morokko do Tunisa," 3.
27. Ibid. To understand the "green banner," I consulted Professor Yigit Akin, who communicated that "the Ottoman flag at the time of the war was very similar to modern Turkish flag (red background with white crescent and star). The green flag reference here is probably to an overarching, pan-Islamic symbol that would supersede all national identities to bring all Muslims together under one flag. (The color green in Islam is generally associated with Heaven.)" Private communication, September 20, 2017.
28. Vladimir Jabotinsky, "Na severe Afriki, Tuzemtsy," *Russkie Vedomosti* (January 6, 1915): 3.
29. Jabotinsky, *Story of the Jewish Legion*, 32–33. The original Russian, *Slovo o polku; Istoriia evreiskogo legiona po vospominaniiam ego initsiatora* appeared in 1928. Significantly the title of the original book contains a pun: "polk" means regiment in English, so the title

reads, "A Word about the Regiment." But it is also an allusion to the famous epic poem of the fourteenth century that has the same title at least in part, "Slovo o polku Igorove" ("The Lay of Igor" or colloquially known as "The Igor Tale.")

30. See British and French Governments: The Sykes-Picot Agreement (May 15–16, 1916), in *The Israeli-Arab Reader: A Documentary History of the Middle East Conflict*, ed. Walter Laqueur and Barry Rubin, 7th ed. (New York: Penguin Books, 2008), 16.

31. Ibid., 11–12.

32. Derek Penslar, *Jews and the Military: A History* (Princeton, NJ: Princeton University Press, 2013).

33. Vladimir Jabotinsky, "Gabbaro (ot nashego korrespondenta)," *Russkie Vedomosti* (April 10, 1915): 5.

34. Ibid.

35. Ibid.

36. Alexander Shul'man, "Biographiia," in Iosif Trumpel'dor, *Gekholuts, novyi put': Biografiia, vospominaniia, stat'i* (Moscow: Koktebel', 2012), 52. See also Ahron Propes, *Dos Legen fun Yosef Trumpeldor* (Warsaw: Tel-Chai, 1930), 14.

37. Quoted in Martin Watts, *The Jewish Legion and the First World War* (London: Palgrave Macmillan, 2004), 4.

38. Eliyahu Golomb, *The History of Jewish Self-Defense in Palestine (1878–1921)* (Tel Aviv: Lion the Printer, for the Zionist Youth Department, 1947), 13–15. Incidentally, in 1934, David Ben-Gurion wrote an article on the Shomer group as a response to Jabotinsky's assertion that a Jewish armed force in Palestine had its origins in the Legion. In Ben-Gurion's perspective, the Shomer played the larger role and stands at the head of a new tradition. David Ben-Gurion, *Chaluzischer Zionismus oder Revisionismus* (Berlin: Hehalutz, 1934), 26.

39. David Niv, *Ma'arakhot ha-irgun ha-tsevai ha-leumi ("ha-hagana ha-leumit")* (Tel Aviv: Mosad Klausner, 1965–1980), 1:50–51.

40. Jabotinsky, *The Story of the Jewish Legion*, 41.

41. Shul'man, "Biografiia," 53.

42. John H. Patterson, *With the Zionists in Gallipoli* (London: Hutchinson, 1916).

43. Eugene L. Rogan, *The Fall of the Ottomans: The Great War in the Middle East* (New York: Basic Books, 2015), 143.

44. Ari Dubnow and Brian Horowitz, "Jabotinsky, Vladimir (Ze'ev)," *1914–1918 on-line, International Encyclopedia of the First World War* (Freie Universität Berlin: Friedrich-Meinecke-Institut, 2018), www.1914-1918-online.net.

45. Trumpeldor's description of his life in Gallipoli can be found in Joseph Trumpeldor, *Tagebücher und Briefe* (Berlin: Jüdischer Verlag, 1925), 286–305.

46. Reinharz, *Chaim Weizmann*, 81.

47. Ibid.

48. Ibid.

49. Joseph Schechtman, *The Life and Times of Vladimir Jabotinsky: Rebel and Statesman, The Early Years* (Silver Spring, MD: Eshel Books, 1986), 216.

50. This is Jabotinsky's description of events. Quoted in Vital, *Zionism*, 149.

51. Jabotinsky describes the outburst of patriotism among Petersburg's Jews at the start of World War I. *Story of My Life*, 108. Viktor Kel'ner has also written about Jewish attitudes at this time. Viktor Kel'ner, "The Jewish Question and Russian Social Life During World War I," *Russian Studies in History*, 43/1 (Summer 2004): 28.

52. Kel'ner, "The Jewish Question," 32.
53. Jabotinsky, *The Story of the Jewish Legion*, 59–60.
54. Vital, *Zionism*, 139.
55. Ibid.
56. "Sorach Skorochod (1878–1957) and Josef Nachemsohn (1865–1936), two leading members of the small Danish Zionist movement, were the responsible editors, but in reality Meir Grossman was editor." Mortin Thing, "Yiddish in Denmark," *Mendele Review* 11, no. 6 (May 25, 2007), http://yiddish.haifa.ac.il/tmr/tmr11/tmr11006.htm.
57. In 1916, Grossman and the paper moved to London, where Jabotinsky and Trumpeldor were already located.
58. Twenty-one issues of *Di Tribune* appeared before Grossman went to London to publish a paper with Jabotinsky. When this project failed, he went to independent Ukraine, where he published a paper and was a member of parliament. After the Bolshevik takeover, he went back to Denmark and to London to appeal for help." Thing, "Yiddish in Denmark."
59. Vladimir Jabotinsky, "Mir un die Terkay," *Di Tribune* 4 (December 1, 1915): 10.
60. Watts, *The Jewish Legion*, 49.
61. Meir Grossman, "Der anheyb," *Di Tribune* 2 (November 1, 1915): 18.
62. Meer [Meir] Grossman, *The Case against the Mixed Jewish Agency* (London: Union of Zionist Revisionists, n.d.).
63. The full story on recruitment and the Legion can be found in Harold Shukman, *War or Revolution: Russian Jews and Conscription in Britain, 1917* (London: Vallentine Mitchell, 2006); Watts, *The Jewish Legion*; Anne Patricia Lloyd, "Jews under Fire: the Jewish Community and Military Service in World War I Britain" (PhD diss., University of Southampton, 2009).
64. Vladimir Jabotinsky, "O konskriptsii," *Russkie Vedomosti* (October 24, 1915): 5.
65. Vladimir Jabotinsky, "Angliia i 'mir v nich'iu'," *Russkie Vedomosti* (May 12, 1915): 5.
66. Shukman, *War or Revolution*, 8.
67. Letter of Vladimir Jabotinsky to Hebert Samuel, September 16, 1916. In Jabotinsky Institute Archive.
68. Letter of Vladimir Jabotinsky to Major Cosgrain, October 31, 1915. In Jabotinsky Institute Archive.
69. Letter of Vladimir Jabotinsky to Edward Derby, August 19, 1917. In Jabotinsky Institute Archive.
70. Reinharz, *Chaim Weizmann*, 85.
71. Jabotinsky, *Story of the Jewish Legion*, 67.
72. Chaim Weizmann, *Trial and Error: The Autobiography of Chaim Weizmann* (New York: Harper, 1949), 167.
73. Watts, *The Jewish Legion*, 54.
74. Jabotinsky, *Story of the Jewish Legion*, 40.
75. Martin Watts describes the military experience of the Legion's officers: "With the exception of Patterson and Trumpeldor, neither the British nor Jewish officers had any previous military service, which had severe implications for the conduct of the unit in combat particularly in view of the brief period of training—less than one month—that was afforded to the corps." Watts, *The Jewish Legion*, 28.
76. Brian Dennis, *The Seven Lives of Colonel Patterson* (Syracuse, NY: Syracuse University Press, 2008), 106–107. See also John H. Patterson's autobiographical accounts, *With the Judeans in the Palestine Campaign* (New York: Macmillan, 1922).
77. Reinharz, *Chaim Weizmann*, 168.

78. Jabotinsky, *Story of the Jewish Legion*, 61.

79. Eliyahu Golomb, "Ve-tnuat ha-gdudim ha-ivriim," *Ma'arahot: Yarho le-she'elot mediniyot, kalkaliot ve-tsva'iyot* (Heshvan-Tevet, 1941): 6–12.

80. Keren describes the fighting experience of the Legion. "The first Legion, the 38th Legion of the Royal Fusiliers, whose recruits were Jewish immigrants to England, was established too late to allow participation in the main battles of the Palestine campaign, which was launched on 31 October 1917 under the command of a General Edmond Allenby. However, the 38th and the 39th Legions (which included a large component of volunteers recruited in the United States and Canada) of the Royal Fusiliers fought in Allenby's battles over the Jordan Valley in the spring of 1918." Michael Keren and Shlomit Keren, *We Are Coming, Unafraid: The Jewish Legions and the Promised Land in the First World War* (Lanham, MD: Rowman & Littlefield, 2010), 71.

81. Jabotinsky, *Story of the Jewish Legion*, 130.

82. Walter Laqueur, *History of Zionism* (London, 1972), 342.

83. Svetlana Natkovich, "The Rise and Downfall of Cassandra: World War I and Vladimir (Ze'ev) Jabotinsky's Self-Perception," *Medaon-Magazin für jüdisches Leben in Forschung und Bildung* 10 (2016): 5.

84. Ibid., 182.

85. Weizmann, *Trial and Error*, 206–208.

86. See Martin Kramer, "The Forgotten Truth about the Balfour Declaration," *Mosaic* (an on-line magazine), June 5, 2017, https://mosaicmagazine.com/essay/2017/06/the-forgotten-truth-about-the-balfour-declaration/.

87. Dubnow and Horowitz, "Jabotinsky, Vladimir (Ze'ev)."

88. Jabotinsky, *Story of the Jewish Legion*, 130.

89. Ibid., 143.

90. Ibid., 144.

91. Ibid., 147.

92. Vladimir Jabotinsky, *Turkey and the War* (London: T. Fisher Unwin, 1917), 17–19.

93. Ibid., 21.

94. Ibid., 257.

95. Ibid., 131.

96. Ibid., 135.

97. Ibid., 139.

98. Sean McMeekin, *The Ottoman Endgame: War, Revolution, and the Making of the Modern Middle East, 1908–1923* (New York: Penguin Books, 2015), 33–58.

99. Jabotinsky, *Turkey and the War*, 224.

100. Ibid., 260.

101. One of Jabotinsky's followers continued to view Turkey as the central axis of twentieth-century history. Eliahu Ben-Horin, *The Middle-East, Crossroads of History* (New York: Norton, 1943).

102. Amartya Sen, "The Economic Consequences of Austerity," *The New Statesman*, June 4, 2015.

103. Dmitry Shumsky, *Beyond the Nation-State: The Zionist Political Imagination from Pinsker to Ben-Gurion* (New Haven, CT: Yale University Press, 2018), 170–171.

7

POSTWAR DISAPPOINTMENTS, PALESTINE 1918–1922

* * *

IN THE POST–WORLD WAR I PERIOD, JABOTINSKY FACED challenges and opportunities that pushed him further to the political right. Among the challenges were the struggle to preserve the Legion and, when it was decommissioned, to fulfill its tasks by other means (illegal militias); Britain's alleged retreat from the Balfour Declaration; and Weizmann's inevitable compromises with a reluctant Britain. It was hardly lost on Jabotinsky that the political left and center were well represented in Zionism; only the right was unrepresented. Additionally, Jabotinsky was growing more committed to a tough line on the Arabs; a defense of private property (versus socialism); and demands for an expanded Jewish Palestine, including Jewish settlements on both sides of the Jordan River.

The period 1918–1923 must have seemed like the crown to Jabotinsky's career: his dream of reaching the top of the Zionist leadership was at hand. His stubborn certainty in forging ahead with the Legion, despite bitter opposition, had paid off. In fact, his confrontation with the Zionist leadership had redounded to his advantage since he had correctly predicted that Britain would win and Palestine's future belonged to the Zionists. Svetlana Natkovich observes that there was never again a time in his life when Jabotinsky was so acclaimed, admired, and appreciated.[1] However, once the war was over, the Zionist leadership returned to the status quo ante, and Jabotinsky again found himself in relative obscurity. He would use his position on the ground in Palestine to advance his cause and boost his status.

Chaim Weizmann had risen to the leading position in Zionism thanks to his scientific work in Manchester; his role in coordinating people and opinions in Britain; and his position as an intercessor with British officials. He seemed to have something to offer: the support of Britain's interests in the Middle East on behalf of world Jewry. As president of the World Zionist Organization, he invited Jabotinsky to visit the United States as a representative of Keren Kayemet, and also gave him a seat on the Zionist Organization's Executive Committee. When Britain refined its role as an even-handed broker in Palestine—examples of which included the White Paper of 1922—reactions were varied: Weizmann, for one, led the World Zionist Organization along a cautious path of compromise. Jabotinsky reacted with public demonstrations of disappointment and anger.

Jabotinsky used his emotions as a political weapon, bringing attention to himself by resigning from the Zionist Executive and ranting at his colleagues. At the same time, he began to conceive of an alternative path that led to the radical right. His move must have seemed curious: Why would he stray from the public's adoration and return to being a figure of opprobrium? Why, when he was finally close to the center of power?

There are various explanations for Jabotinsky's metamorphosis into a clearly recognizable right-wing politician. Jabotinsky believed that right-leaning policies aided the Zionist effort better than left or center policies. He was also aware that a strongman image could distinguish him from Weizmann and Ben-Gurion. In fact, he saw the successful rise to power of the strongman in the Soviet Union (Lenin) and then Italy (Mussolini) and realized he could attain his goals by mimicking their political style.[2]

* * *

At the time, politics in Palestine centered on the British perception of Arab-Jewish relations; how would Arabs and Jews coexist, solve problems, and engage in compromise? For many Jews, the issue of morality was connected to the health of the Yishuv, the Jewish settlement in Palestine. Was Zionism a worthy endeavor if it harmed another people? If its acquisition of land meant a loss to others? If, at its core, Zionism justified coercion and violence? Such considerations stimulated inquiry and debate among Zionists, but did not shake Jabotinsky. He was fully and irreversibly convinced of Zionism's legitimacy, and he based his certainty less on the Bible than on universally accepted moral principles: Palestine was largely underpopulated and therefore available to save the Jewish nation, which was mistreated, poor, hungry, and landless.

Did Jabotinsky have a position on the Palestinian Arabs, a single coherent view of the Arab-Jewish conflict? To unpack the question, we should note that some Zionists thought Jews should acculturate to their new environment and dress, act, and talk "like the natives" (that is, the Arabs).[3] Jabotinsky rejected this position. Like Herzl and others before him, he was convinced that Palestine's destiny depended entirely on consistent and effective governance by a large imperial power, such as Britain. Politically, this meant rhetorical appeals to governments—"the world's conscience"— and to Jews around the world. In particular, it meant cultivating similar views and ideas: a vision of Palestine as a refuge and a site for the development of Jewish self-consciousness.

On the question of Arabs' rights, he was implacable. Their rights were understandably curtailed in comparison with those of culturally more advanced peoples. The Europeans had the right to dictate rules and exploit the resources of the less advanced, but not due to strength alone. Colonialism and its byproduct, the subjugation of subalterns, was justified because of cultural superiority. Jabotinsky explained in 1921 that

> There is one and only one power in the world and its name is culture—the arrangement through which society has evolved in the course of generations. Cultured people have ruled and shall continue to rule. France shall remain France, and Morocco shall remain Morocco. The native land of the Tel-Hai marauders shall share the fate of Morocco, for culture subdues and rules while desert tribes must perforce submit and learn. Europe will not take its orders from Damascus. Damascus will take orders from Paris and London and will carry them out as she carried out only recently the orders from Constantinople.[4]

To modern ears, such language is discomfiting, as it reflects the arrogance of colonial power. However, at that time (or perhaps a generation earlier) such views were widespread. In Jabotinsky's case, the goal wasn't to insult Morocco, but, rather, to straighten the back of Zionists who were losing confidence in the Palestine project because of Arab resistance. He wrote, "And don't consider the Englishman a liar. He is not a liar. Don't regard the Englishman as weakened. He is not weakened. And don't think of the marauder of Tel Hai and his secret envoys in Damascus as a power. They are not a power."[5] Jabotinsky refers here to the false claim that Arab nationalists with connections to Communists in Damascus were responsible for the attack at Tel Hai in 1920.

Here Jabotinsky made an unusual rhetorical move and spoke from the Arab point of view, describing their hostility to Zionism. In contrast to many Zionists who saw the Arabs as good natives (by analogy with the myth of the "good Indians" in America), he acknowledged that, as a proud, dignified, smart people, they would not voluntarily surrender their land.[6] One might think that this realization would lead him to consider compromise. However, his goal was to turn optimists away from compromise, and convince them instead to condone the use of force against a stubborn enemy.

According to Yosef Gorny, Jabotinsky had an "Arab theory"; he was a separationist and belonged "among those who rejected the possibility of Jewish-Arab integration and co-operation." Gorny also cites the historian Joseph Klausner, who "called attention to the danger of assimilation of the Jewish settlers into Arab culture." Gorny explains that "Revisionism was not the sole mouthpiece of the separatist outlook. These views were shared by others, remote from the Revisionists in social origin and cultural background. The scholar and writer Avraham Elmaleh, for example, formerly a member of the Herut group, was advocating similar views in the late twenties." Gorny also includes Yosef Meyuhas, a Sephardi intellectual.[7] One should add to the list Jabotinsky's followers Abba Achimeir, Yehoshua Yievin, and Uri Zvi Greenberg, the members of the Brit ha-Biryonim; as well as Menachem Begin, Joseph Schechtman, and others. Schechtman in particular advocated transferring Arabs in Palestine as a means of solving the Arab-Israeli conflict.[8] People who felt that the two populations needed to be separated, who wanted to fight Arabs, or who sought radical solutions found a representative in Jabotinsky.

* * *

In 1920, the League of Nations gave Britain a mandate over Palestine. The mandate was a political contract that offered privileges and obligations. Britain could use the resources of Palestine for its own profit but was obligated to provide government services and institutions, from a police force to a political structure that would benefit everyone in the country.[9] The British government appointed Herbert Samuel, a Jew and a Zionist, to be the first high commissioner.[10] From the start, Britain wanted to appear evenhanded with both Jews and Arabs; the latter made up close to 85 percent of the population.[11] Britain demobilized the Jewish Legion, while enlisting Arabs to serve as policemen.[12] Additionally, British officials hired Arabs in greater numbers than Jews for the British administration and civil service in Palestine. If that were not worrisome enough for Zionists, Britain's first White Paper, the Churchill White Paper, in 1922, threatened to curtail Jewish immigration.[13]

Zionist fortunes continued to slide. In 1922, Britain sliced Transjordan off the Palestine region and make it a separate state for Abdullah son of Hussein ibn Ali to rule. Admittedly, the borders of Palestine had not been clearly defined earlier in November 1917. Within Palestine, Zionists complained that Britain did not contribute state money for Jewish schools and withheld access to state lands. Even more disastrous for Zionists, Jews weren't coming to Palestine, despite the invitation to revive their ancient homeland. The massive Jewish immigration that would transform Palestine did not occur. Jews were still a small minority in the country. Britain used this fact to justify its response to Zionists, though in truth, it was swayed more by Palestinian Arab opposition to Jewish immigration. It had other reasons, too. Both the British government and Colonial Office were protecting British interests in the Middle East. Supporting Zionism, they feared, would put those interests in jeopardy.[14]

Britain's attention to the Arabs in Palestine, whom it invited to establish an Arab Agency (an Arab version of the Jewish Agency), made sense from the British perspective. Arab leaders declined the offer, believing that cooperation would give legitimacy to Zionist claims.[15] Britain wanted to create a parliament of sorts, in which the majority of delegates would represent the overwhelming Arab majority. But this attempt to provide political legitimacy for the mandate failed. The Jews opposed the project, as did Arab leaders.

Looking at Palestine from the British viewpoint, we can acknowledge the impossible challenges faced by a mandatory power pursuing a policy of "trying to be all things to all people." The Zionists were convinced that British and Zionist interests could run in parallel and believed that when interests clashed, it was because of a misunderstanding or antisemitism. Bernard Wasserstein has written that "The conflicting engagements left many British officials in Palestine with an uneasy conscience, leading some to sympathize with the idea that the British Government's pro-Zionist policy involved an injustice to the Arabs of Palestine. . . . This feeling, which was widespread among British officials in Palestine throughout the mandatory period, especially during its earliest and latest years, was reinforced by traditional attitudes of the British officer class towards Jews and Arabs—unspoken or half-spoken assumptions which conditioned their thinking about the Palestine problem."[16]

Wasserstein explains that although the British government would not disavow Balfour in full, "the wide discretionary powers accorded to British officials by Allenby enabled the military administration to contain Zionist activity within the narrowest possible limits by means of administrative fiat ... The result was a series of official decisions whose cumulative effect was to provoke Zionist fury."[17] These included banning "Hatikvah" (the Jewish national anthem); postponing the creation of the Hebrew University; refusing to recognize Hebrew as one of the official languages; and limiting Jewish immigration. Furthermore, land transfers were withheld. Although these discriminations were enacted under military administration and did not continue under Samuel, during the formal mandate, they were nonetheless insulting. Wasserstein writes that "as a result, by mid-1919 the feeling of disillusion and betrayal was almost universal among the Yishuv (apart, of course, from anti-Zionist elements)."[18]

* * *

From 1918 to 1920, Jabotinsky made Jerusalem his home. He arrived in Palestine with the Legion and stayed after demobilization. He moved into an apartment outside the old city, off Jaffa Road. Memoirs portray a youthful atmosphere of optimism and even celebration as people from Jabotinsky's past, such as Bialik and Zal'tsman, came to visit.[19] His home served as a salon where politicians, intellectuals, Jews and non-Jews, British friends, and others met to discuss issues. The apartment also had a Russian atmosphere, as his son Eri describes in his memoirs:

> Our home was an open house. Among the visitors was the agronomist Akiva Ettinger, Zvi Nadav, the judge Nofef and others. Pinhus Rutenberg was a noted visitor. I arranged his first contacts with the British authorities in which he approached them about his idea for the electrification of the country by using the Jordan River. My mother, who after this became Rutenberg's friend, liked him very much, although at first she was afraid of him because she knew that he had "eliminated" Gapon, Russia's priest. Azef, the well-known spy had put a hit out for Rutenberg at the time because he had murdered the "friend of the workers" Gapon.[20]

Gapon was the famous priest who led the march to the Winter Palace in St. Petersburg on January 22, 1905, known as "Bloody Sunday," because tsarist soldiers fired on the people. It turned out that Gapon had been a double agent, and it was a point of honor among Socialist Revolutionaries—the party to which Rutenberg belonged then—to "eliminate" Gapon.

British policies aggrieved Jabotinsky, but none angered him as much as the dissolution of the Jewish Legion. In 1918, Allenby refused to permit the Legion's fighters to engage in the Galilee, which frustrated those who wanted to liberate "their homeland."[21] This proved a harbinger. About a third of the legionnaires in the United Kingdom were not allowed to travel to Palestine at all. Those who did serve were targets of catcalls by soldiers and officers alike.

In September 1919, Jabotinsky clashed with British officials when he objected to his "involuntary" demobilization. British military officers, citing Arab objections to an armed Jewish group, decided to disband the Legion. Jabotinsky regarded his demobilization as a personal attack. He wrote to his commanding officer:

> I consider myself wronged by the conditions under which I am being demobilized. I consider it unfair that, being so closely connected with the unit, I am ordered to leave it against my will. I consider it especially bad when the Jewish contingent—as I am informed officially—is going to be granted a special name (The Judeans) and a badge representing a national Jewish emblem (the Menorah). In this way, after 2000 years, the nucleus of a National Jewish Force is being created, and I, who was the initiator of the idea, officially recognized and consulted as such by the British Authority—I am now denied the privilege of wearing my uniform. With this deepest reluctance and regret I must say that I consider this action as ingratitude. I do not deserve it at the hands of the British Authorities. From the first days of this War I have worked and struggled for British interests. I am neither a British subject nor immigrant. I had never been in the United Kingdom, or in any British dominion, before this War. My compulsory demobilization under these conditions will throw a slur on my name. I consider it unjust. I demand that it be annulled and that I be reinstated in my well-earned position as an officer of the Judeans.[22]

Besides the personal affront, he was convinced that Britain was making a terrible mistake: the Legion, in his view, was essential to maintaining order in the country. His attitude can be gleaned from his many letters to Meir Grossman, his collaborator. On September 16, 1919 he wrote: "In London you will meet many delinquents who will tell you crap, but you know that the Legion brought a lot of good, brings it now and (even including the upheavals [there were small riots among the legionnaires]), generally speaking, is the sole political institution in Palestine..."²³

* * *

Jabotinsky felt his fears were justified when violence broke out on April 4, 1920, during the Nebi Musa procession in Jerusalem. There was also violence up north in Tel Hai, where Trumpeldor was part of an agricultural commune. Although Jabotinsky had advised Trumpeldor to move to a safer outpost, Trumpeldor and his buddies refused. The outpost was overwhelmed, and a number of Jews were killed, including Trumpeldor. Labor Zionists and Revisionists would memorialize Tel Hai, and Jabotinsky in particular cast his death as a martyrdom that should inspire commitment and contributions.²⁴

When the violence began in Jerusalem, Jabotinsky and Rutenberg went to see the military governor, Ronald Storrs.²⁵ They asked for permission to defend the Jewish quarter in Jerusalem and were refused. British troops were not permitted to enter the old city. When violence ensued, old men, women, and children were the main victims.²⁶ The Jewish defenders came out anyway, and were arrested; Jabotinsky "had organized a desperate and rudimentary defense; he was arrested as well."²⁷

Jabotinsky had created a self-defense unit several weeks before with the name "Haganah" (Defense).²⁸ Although his group had probably saved Jerusalem's Jews from greater casualties, the British interned Jabotinsky in the famous Acre (Akko) prison and sentenced him to three years of hard labor. Prison wasn't the misery one would expect: He was well treated; was fed decent food; and had friends among the British officers, who permitted him books and writing paper. Jabotinsky wrote a memoir about the experience called "The Acre Fortress."²⁹ He was released after only three months thanks to a media blitzkrieg that generated worldwide sympathy.³⁰

Now that Jabotinsky's star shined as the "hero of Jerusalem," Chaim Weizmann, head of the World Zionist Organization, enlisted him on behalf of Keren Hayesod (the Land Fund) to visit North America, spread the Zionist message, and woo wealthy donors who could provide financial support for the Yishuv.³¹

* * *

In America, Jabotinsky gave speeches explaining his theory of history. He projected an image of the national hero, that allegorically portrayed his own complex situation mirrored Jabotinsky's own. Apparently influenced by Leo Tolstoy's view that history is made by ordinary people—a theme of *War and Peace*—Jabotinsky praised the tramp, the beggar, who appears to have no function. The transcript of his speeches appeared in Zionist information bulletins:

> There is a Russian legend about a great northern hero whose name was Elias Murometz. That was seven or eight hundred years ago; Russia was invaded by the Tartars, and the Tartar yoke was oppressive and tyrannical. The legend says that Murometz freed the country from Tartar yoke. He was brave and strong and chivalrous. Many beautiful songs are dedicated to his exploits and victories. But for me, the most interesting in the whole legend is just one very short page, whose hero is perhaps not Murometz himself but another man. In his youth Murometz was a cripple. He was paralyzed, he could not lift a hand, and he used to spend all his days sitting on a wooden bench in front of his father's cabin. So he reached the age of 33, and everybody in town was sure that he would live and die a useless cripple. But once, when he was sitting on that bench all alone, a tramp, coming from nowhere, accosted him and said: "Young man, I am thirsty, bring me a mug of water." "I cannot move," said Murometz, "I am paralyzed." But the tramp said: "Nonsense, get up and do it." Murometz tried to lift his hand, and it moved; and he got up and brought the tramp some water; the tramp drank, and went his way. No one knows his name, or whence he came or whither he went. But Elias Murometz became a great hero and liberated Russia.

Jabotinsky then repeated a similar story about Garibaldi, who as a young sailor was approached by a tramp who read some patriotic ditties to the future leader from a soiled piece of paper. Once again, "nobody knows the name of that sailor tramp, or whence he came, or whither he went." But Giuseppe Garibaldi became a great hero and restored Italy.

Jabotinsky continued:

> I sometimes wonder, who it was that freed Russia and Italy and every country and every people that were ever restored to freedom. Was it the hero whose name we revere, or was it the tramp who remained nameless forever? I believe it is always the tramp. . . . Do not shrink from the word "tramp." It is simply a slang translation of the same idea which my clever friend expressed in the [Yiddish] words *Zionisten mit die fiss* ["Zionism with feet"]. It is the one that goes and who gets things done. It is the one that carries the seed to scatter it in every corner of this ground of a nation.[32]

This speech is fascinating: it illuminates Jabotinsky. The tramp fertilizes the waiting egg, so to speak. The man of history whom Jabotinsky portrays twiddles his thumbs until history strikes. Then he gets up, overcoming his paralysis (literally), and assumes his monumental role. Jabotinsky, the man of history, waited in Russia without a task, but when war broke out, he arose and created the Legion. Then again he rested, but history (the tramp) called upon him to defend Jerusalem.

But now he faced a different challenge. He was again sitting and waiting. He had become a Zionist bureaucrat who served on the Zionist Executive and in Keren Hayesod. He was like Murometz or Garibaldi; he had nothing to do but wait until the tramp arrived. Jabotinsky aired his doubts about joining the organization's bureaucracy, even in a leading position, in contrast with the true makers of history.

Maxim Gorky, a writer Jabotinsky admired, described such a figure in his novel *Mother*, contrasting action to inertia.[33] Gorky painted a down-and-out young man who is called in the historical moment to lead the people during the Revolution of 1905. In Gorky, as in Jabotinsky, iron will, indifference to the crowd, and stoic perseverance matter most.

Fund-raising in America, however, did not go well. Americans were bewildered about Russia and the recent Bolshevik takeover; and so a story about the Russian Murometz was not the ideal subject for a Zionist fund-raiser. Indeed, Jabotinsky did not raise much money on his trip.[34]

* * *

The security situation in Palestine troubled Jabotinsky, and he began to attack Britain's policies, which, he maintained, contributed to a breakdown of order. On May 14, 1921, he published an article in the *Times of London* regarding the security situation. "In the atmosphere of the East the natural drift of any Arab troops raised at the present moment would be to use them to follow the general trend of the pan-Arab movement. Only the blind could fail to see that in this movement anti-Zionism is a mere insignificant detail, the real issue being the whole tremendous question of Europe's right to pacify, reconstruct and educate the Middle East."[35]

It is hard to prove Jabotinsky's thesis: that violence was born exclusively out of an anticolonial feeling. In any case, Britain could not keep order, as the anti-Jewish riots of May 1–7, 1921 showed. The latest violence, as Bernard Wasserstein correctly writes, "Did nothing to advance the political aims of the Arab nationalists. But it boded ill for the Zionists' sanguine expectation of achieving their ends peacefully."[36]

For Jabotinsky the core problem was not the violence. That was merely a symbol to be used to frighten potential immigrants. Jabotinsky fumed at Diaspora Jews who refused to grasp the meaning of this moment: finally, Palestine was open to Jewish immigration. Although Palestine's Jews numbered 83,790, it was a far cry from the mass immigration that Jabotinsky and others had envisioned. In 1922, Jabotinsky tried to put a good spin on the fact that Arab growth had equaled or surpassed Jewish increase in population: "But if you ask me 'are you satisfied with the progress?'—My reply and the reply of every Zionist, especially of a member of the Zionist Executive, will be 'No!' Had our progress been even twenty times as great, we should still be most emphatically dissatisfied. All that is really 'nothing' in comparison with what we want."[37]

Jabotinsky prized the elusive goals of political stability, investment, and security. The development of the Jewish sector—what Britain called "absorptive capacity"—depended most critically on these factors. As Jabotinsky explained to Weizmann in October 1920:

> My object in insisting on certain conditions was to secure our main need—the immediate large-scale immigration of Jews into Palestine on a sound economic basis. This aim, in my opinion, cannot be achieved, nor can adequate financial means be provided, without the following essential guarantees:
>
> a) Stability of a benevolent administration in Palestine;
> b) Safety, guaranteed by the presence of Jewish troops;
> c) An efficient Zionist Agency in Palestine enjoying the confidence of both the Yishuv and the Diaspora;
> d) An efficient Zionist Executive.[38]

Jewish immigration suffered because of a crisis of confidence, Jabotinsky believed. If essential problems were solved, Jews would come with their businesses. But who could invest in a future without guarantees about who, Jews or Arabs, would gain control of the country?[39]

Jabotinsky insisted on the need for radical change in the mandate, especially "with a view to securing—among other guarantees—some legal and effective channels to influence the choice of candidates for the highest administrative appointments in Palestine, above all in the choice of candidates for the High Commissioner's post." Changes were needed "to prevent the repetition of the sad experiences of the past, when anti-Zionists and even antisemites were given high offices in Palestine, bringing to naught Mr. Balfour's declaration and even direct instructions issued by the Foreign Office."[40]

Jabotinsky rejected the idea of "absorptive capacity," the British government's argument that Palestine had a certain optimal or maximum population depending on water supplies, agricultural land, and productive enterprises.[41] Jabotinsky considered "absorptive capacity" a coded expression for limiting the number of Jews so they couldn't become a majority. Jabotinsky was hardly alone in opposing immigration quotas. With the exception of the later Brit Shalom group, nearly all the Zionist political groups in Palestine insisted on unlimited Jewish immigration.

In 1922, Jabotinsky rejected any argument that denied Zionism full right to settle in the land. Jabotinsky saw the issue in moral terms:

> The essential facts of the Zionist problem are two. First, Jews have no country where they constitute a majority, and this circumstance leads, almost always and almost everywhere, to moral or material suffering. Second, the Allied and Associated Powers have recently won a war for the liberation of all suffering peoples. As a result of these two factors, in 1917, Great Britain offered the Balfour Declaration, pledging to help establish a Jewish national home in Palestine; the other allied powers confirmed this pledge at San Remo in 1920, and two American Presidents, Mr. Wilson and Mr. Harding, expressed their sympathy with this decision.[42]

According to Eri Jabotinsky, his father considered "the work to be morally just"—end of discussion.[43]

Jabotinsky met opposition in many quarters.[44] Some officials in Britain's Foreign Office rejected Zionist claims. Lord Northcliff (Alfred Charles Harmsworth), the owner of *The Times* and *The Daily Mail*, argued that Jews in Palestine abused the principle of self-determination because the Arab majority opposed Jewish immigration. Jabotinsky responded by holding up a mirror. "What would have become of America, Australia, or South Africa, if this point of view had prevailed at the time when English settlers, Lord Northcliff's forefathers, began to colonize those countries in obvious disagreement with the majority of the inhabitants on the spot? The inference is that the colonization of America, etc., was a moral crime; and that the right and proper thing to do would have been to leave these continents in their undisturbed possession of their former occupants."[45]

A master of polemics, Jabotinsky did not yield the high ground. In fact, he always maintained that Zionism could only succeed if the cause was moral, both its means and ends, to the degree that anyone anywhere would recognize the Jews' right to settle in Palestine and create a colony where they were the majority. Instead of conceding the principle of self-determination,

Jabotinsky claimed that he alone respected it. His definition of the term, however, was idiosyncratic. In contrast to the usual definition—the will of a people in a specific geographic area—Jabotinsky claimed that it applied "to peoples as entities" and "not to every square mile of the world's populated surface." He continued: "And if your statistics show you one people possessing five times more land than it is able to cultivate, while another has no land at all, then it is only just that the former should be requested to concede a fraction of its surplus so that the latter may have a homestead."[46]

This was the case with the Arab-speaking populations of Asia and Africa, which numbered thirty-eight million and occupied an area "twenty times as large as Britain" and offered forty acres per person. "Colonization by Jews, while giving a homeland to the only homeless people in the whole world, leaves the Arab race still one of the richest in land among the nations, with the same forty acres per head practically untouched for their own self-determination."[47] There is more to moral right than historical precedent: historical necessity should play a role, too.

These arguments appear logical, although in fact they rest on uncertain premises, such as the assumption that the Arabs are a single community and that the Middle-East land mass can be divided by size and population without considerations of culture, history, and political interests. Jabotinsky's mathematical system discounts the will of the Arab people, their right as the present masters to oppose a colonial effort imposed on them.

Jabotinsky was aware that many Zionists and non-Zionists opposed violence as a means of attaining a Jewish stronghold in Palestine. It would backfire, and be morally indefensible, if it violated somebody else's rights. These views, gaining traction as political Zionism began, would be adopted by the Brit Shalom group in the late 1920s.[48] Meanwhile, the vast majority of Jewish settlers were neither pacifists nor the opposite. They saw the need for self-defense, but wanted also to avoid the label "overly aggressive."[49]

Jabotinsky acknowledged the tension between Arabs and Jews, but he didn't believe that it disqualified Zionism's goals. He refused to accept any justification for Arab violence. "Is this the first instance in the world's history in which a just claim is opposed and has to be defended? Was any country in the world ever colonized without friction with the indigenous population? We do not demand that Zionism as such should be 'enforced.' Zionism will pave its way by peaceful, constructive effort, by creative work from which the Arabs, too, will benefit. But there is one thing which, if broken, must be 'enforced,' in Palestine as well as in Europe and everywhere, and that is public order, protection against violence, murder, pillage, arson, and rape."⁵⁰

This claim—that nongovernmental violence in any form represents criminal activity and its perpetrators deserve prosecution—makes full sense in a rule-of-law state. But one can argue that violence had a different meaning in Mandate Palestine, where the political order was shaky and parts of the population rose in opposition. In such places, violence was sometimes used as a political weapon, especially where the ruling power was perceived as illegitimate and there did not exist peaceful and practical means to change the political order.

In his private correspondence, Jabotinsky described Jews and Arabs as diametrically opposed to one another. In a letter to Oscar Gruzenberg, the Russian-Jewish lawyer and Zionist sympathizer, he explained his view further, and more crudely:

> We are Europe, and not only the pupils, but creators of European culture. What do we have in common with the "East"? And really, everything "Eastern" is doomed to death; look at how Kemal-Pasha cuts off beards just as Peter the Great did. As long as the Arabs do not renounce their ways, they cannot be our friends. And when it does happen—in fifty years—a federation with Syria and Egypt will hardly be necessary. I strongly hope that by that time the civilized world will have become a federation generally, where even a small state can live in security between Syria and Egypt.⁵¹

Here Jabotinsky was clearly asserting that he and his people were historically more advanced than the Arabs. He viewed the Russian Jews as real Europeans, not "Ost-Juden"—sub-Europeans. At the same time, his position might be interpreted as a reaction to Britain's latest proposed solution to the conflict: shared governance.⁵² He finished with his bottom line: "I am not a supporter of an Arab-Jewish state."⁵³

* * *

The years 1921–23 may be regarded as an unstable, contradictory, or even incoherent period in Jabotinsky's life. Jabotinsky made three important decisions in that span: he approved Britain's 1922 White Paper; he rejected the so-called Nordau Plan; and he participated in the scandalous Slavinsky Affair. When we unpack these decisions, we see that they stem from Jabotinsky's mood after his release from the Acre prison in 1920. Jabotinsky was at a crossroads, unsure what to do with his life. He had recently gained renown after being imprisoned for the defense of Jerusalem, but his future was uncertain. Where should he invest his talents? What would catapult him to the leadership? Chaim Weizmann now ran the movement, and he was a friend. How could his friendship be used to further personal goals and the goals of Zionism?

Britain had acquired the mandate on the basis of its military victory in Palestine as well as the Balfour Declaration.[54] As the official representative of the Jewish community in Eretz Yisrael, the Zionist movement had become tighter, more disciplined; it needed to speak with one voice, or at least fewer voices, in its dealings with the British government. Jabotinsky's Legion period was over, but he hadn't really considered what came next. He hoped to remain in Palestine and engage in building the Yishuv, but in several ways he was at odds with local politics. The growing labor movement, the politics of the kibbutz movement, and the socialist-leaning leaders Tabenkin, Katzenelson, and Ben-Gurion, were foreign to him. He had little in common with the Second Aliyah in terms of education, experience, and political visions, with the exception of his enthusiasm for Hebrew.

Of all the people in the Zionist movement, paradoxically he was closest to Chaim Weizmann. They were both "russified," educated in high culture—literature and science—and understood Zionism as a politics of diplomacy (negotiations with the imperial power) and international party politics. In fact, Jabotinsky owed Weizmann a debt of gratitude: becoming a Zionist functionary had brought Jabotinsky a regular salary and helped his reputation among wealthy businessmen, British officials, and American politicians, who had doubts about him, but now saw him as a reliable associate. Indeed, the Weizmann-Jabotinsky relationship seemed to benefit both men. Weizmann had favored Jabotinsky as early as 1918, although the association was riskier for Weizmann, whose British friends disliked Jabotinsky.[55] They complained that "Jab[otinsky] is the tail that wags C[haim] W[eizmann]."[56] Already in 1920, however, "Jabotinsky was agitating in prison against Weizmann for his compromising attitude toward the British, neglect of the Jewish Legion, and abandonment of a comrade."[57] After 1922, Jabotinsky would begin to ravage Weizmann as the symbol of everything wrong with Zionism.

Jabotinsky's three decisions (mentioned above) show him mulling his fate. He agreed to work within the organization, but he also remembered the "tramp," the call to history. Which is why, when Maxim Slavinsky suggested creating a Jewish detachment in the Ukrainian army to prevent pogroms, he was excited. Jabotinsky thought history had summoned him. Slavinsky, the foreign minister of the newly independent Ukrainian Republic, agreed to allow Jewish military detachments to serve with the Ukrainian forces during the 1921 counterattack against the Bolsheviks. These Jewish detachments would stand ready to protect Jewish communities from pogroms by the Ukrainians. And if the offensive succeeded, the White and Ukrainian forces might overthrow the Bolsheviks and rescue millions of Jews who remained in Soviet Russia in 1917, allowing them potentially to make Aliyah. However, failures on the battlefield quickly revealed to Jabotinsky that Slavinsky was not the call from history. But he also realized that service on the Zionist Executive was futility of a similar sort.

Already in early 1923, Jabotinsky regretted affirming Britain's White Paper as a member of the Executive. He tried to put a positive spin on it, but he knew that the White Paper amounted to a "watering down" of the Balfour Declaration.[58] In fact, many Zionists were reluctant to sign, but as Walter Laqueur explains, the British government threatened that if it was not ratified, the government would seek to "revise the draft of the Mandate and in particular paragraph four which recognized the Jewish Agency."[59] There was also the hope that a scaling-back of Balfour would lead to the acceptance of the declaration by the Palestinian Arabs. However, as the Zionists interpreted things, "since the Arabs had refused to recognize the declaration, the 1922 White Paper was no longer valid."[60] According to Joseph Schechtman, Jabotinsky also justified his actions by blaming fatigue and stress: he had arrived in London from America nearly the same day; the twenty-four-hour deadline and his feeling of responsibility to the group had clouded his judgment.[61] It is relevant that only a few months earlier, Jabotinsky had opposed the so-called Nordau Plan, a proposal by the former Zionist leader, Max Nordau, to promote rapid and mass emigration of Jews to Palestine.[62] Therefore, one must observe an ambiguity here: was he for or against rapid, massive, and unlimited Jewish immigration?[63]

Jabotinsky's behavior is difficult to parse in terms of timing and intention. In June 1922, he not only resigned from the Zionist Executive, but also from the entire organization. "I hereby announce my resignation from the Executive: and it's clear that, naturally, since I do not acknowledge the authority of this Executive, I consider myself divorced from the Zionist organization."[64] Although he later claimed to have resigned from the Executive because of the White Paper, in fact the resignation occurred one day after "the leaders from the Zionist Organization voted to open an official investigation into his pact with Ukrainian political leaders"—that is, the Slavinsky Affair.[65]

Although these explanations make sense, Geoffrey Wheatcroft has offered a completely different viewpoint. In his opinion, Jabotinsky left the Executive not over the White Paper or the Slavinsky Affair, but over the Executive's acquiescence in the bifurcation of Palestine (that is, the creation of a separate state in Transjordan).[66] This assertion is also valid because, having left the Executive, Jabotinsky reverted to his earlier endorsement of unlimited and massive emigration to create a Jewish majority in the land. In fact, Jabotinsky was dismayed by the "amputation" and inserted in the Revisionist Party program a demand for Jewish settlement on both sides of the Jordan River.[67] This plank led to a ditty that was jokingly recited by Revisionists: "Both sides of the Jordan are ours, this side and the other too."

The Slavinsky Affair haunted Jabotinsky to the end of his life because many used it as a weapon to attack and discredit him. Daniel Heller has written about the response from the Zionist leadership: "They feared that Soviet officials would use the agreement between Zionists and anti-Bolshevik Ukrainian forces as an excuse to further persecute Russian Zionist activists within the Soviet Union. They also saw Jabotinsky's decision to enter into the agreement without their approval as a blatant challenge to their own authority. They quickly seized upon the event as a chance to brand him as a reckless dreamer, willing to endanger and betray his own people in the name of his political ambitions."[68] The vilification of Jabotinsky in subsequent years was relentless.[69] According to his enemies, the Slavinsky Agreement showed that Jabotinsky was a friend of pogromists, a militarist, someone who was deluded, unhinged, immoral, and capable of any savagery to attain his goals. Initially, Jabotinsky tried to defend his actions, but with time he saw that the Affair was merely bait for ad hominem attacks.[70]

Nonetheless, it is interesting to observe that during the trial in Paris in 1927 of Shlomo Schwarzbard, who was accused of assassinating Symon Petliura, Jabotinsky did try to exonerate Petliura, to his own detriment.[71] However, as David Engel shows, on the eve of the trial "[Jabotinsky] tried to make himself look better, by declaring no less emphatically that 'the responsibility for the pogroms [in Ukraine between 1918-1921] fell upon [Petliura].'"[72]

As Laqueur noted, Jabotinsky damaged himself by pursuing political action for its own sake; certainly the storm that exploded over Jabotinsky because of the Slavinsky Agreement would seem to affirm this. However, in 1922, Jabotinsky felt the need to act outside of the Executive in order to change history. The Slavinsky Agreement was an error, but it seemed to offer an opportunity to bring millions of Jews to Eretz Yisrael. Supporting it, therefore, was totally in character with Jabotinsky's political instincts and tactical methods.

Assessing Jabotinsky's contradictions from 1921 to 1923, the historian does have to select one or another truth. Jabotinsky had twice shown his gratitude to Weizmann for giving him a position. He had opposed the Nordau Plan and signed the White Paper. But his heart was elsewhere, and soon his head would follow. He wanted unlimited mass immigration; he wanted a Jewish majority on both sides of the Jordan River; and, as the Slavinsky Affair showed, he wanted to make history in a dramatic way outside the framework of the Zionist organization and even in opposition to it. Jabotinsky's resignation from the Zionist organization, and his resignation from the Executive, meant that he could now pursue his goals unobstructed by the constraints of party membership.

His friends, however, did not condone his resignation. Joseph Schechtman responded angrily, "We do not accept this step. We regret it and condemn it. We see in it a threatening symptom." Schechtman continued:

> Jabotinsky left the organization. Moreover, he set himself against it. And he did this without trying to check whether that fatal step was truly necessary. He was defeated in the A[ctions] C[omité], he divorced himself from the Executive—a cause justifying that he resign from the Executive (*Leitung*). But from the organization? Is the A. C. really the decisive institution? In 6 or 8 months the Congress will take place; it is the supreme body of the movement. Was the path of appeal to the Zionist masses, to the broad Zionist public, closed to Jabotinsky? A talented writer and orator, he could wage a struggle for his principles and demands. He would have found supporters in this struggle. Perhaps he would have lost the campaign and the congress would reject his demands. But then he would have fulfilled his obligations before the organization. He would have done his duty and the congress could act as its sovereign will dictates.[73]

In the same article, Schechtman sang the praises of the World Zionist Organization, calling it "the most valuable inheritance that we have." His closest colleagues clearly felt that Jabotinsky had erred in breaking irrevocably with the official institutions of the movement.

Schechtman could not grasp his friend's motives. What was the advantage of quitting? Did Schechtman not realize that Jabotinsky liked to be the gadfly who tells it like it is, while being uninterested in working for change from within? Jabotinsky had behaved similarly in 1910 in his conflict with

David Wolffsohn, and in 1915 with the Zionist leadership over the Legion. Jabotinsky sensed that histrionics, disagreements, and sharp breaks can energize supporters. Jonathan Frankel has described this behavior as characteristic of Russian intellectuals.[74] Because ideological purity was prized over compromise and nothing was really at stake (the participants did not hold any real power), it was easy to choose principle over pragmatism, theatrics over compromise.

* * *

After his resignation, Jabotinsky quickly displayed his independence, especially on the Arab issue. In 1923, he published "About the Iron Wall (We and the Arabs)" and "The Ethics of the Iron Wall," two articles asserting his militarist vision of Zionism.[75] Although people interpret them as a philosophical statement on the Arabs, they were in fact written at a specific moment, to a particular reader, for a specific reason.[76]

By 1923, the Arab question had become the central problem in Zionism, and one's position on the question encapsulated one's overall orientation. Schechtman writes, "One needs to realize clearly: the Arab problem is now the single, almost all-encompassing external political problem of our movement. Linked to it and exhausted by it in the narrow understanding of the word are the political difficulties and obstacles that Zionism experiences in the present."[77] Any solution offered on the Arab issue would have the greatest consequences for the movement.

Therefore, Jabotinsky approached the Arab issue as he treated Zionism generally: he expressed his future vision pugnaciously, befitting his trust in militarism and Britain's good will. Jabotinsky's first and main point was that Britain must pursue a policy devoted exclusively to Zionist success in Palestine. Secondly, Britain must deliver this message with sufficient force so that Arabs would see that there is no option but submission. Since no nation has ever willingly accepted colonization, and the Palestinian Arabs were no exception, they would only submit under one condition: that they realized resistance was futile. Jabotinsky wrote, "We cannot offer compensation for Palestine either to Palestinians or other Arabs, therefore voluntary agreement is inconceivable. People who consider such agreement the *conditio sine qua non*, can now already say no and reject Zionism. Our colonization either has to stop or continue against the will of the local population. And therefore it can continue and develop only under the defense of a force [that is] independent of the local population; an Iron Wall that the local population is not strong enough to puncture."[78]

According to Jabotinsky, it was absurd to argue that the two sides did not understand each other or that their viewpoints hadn't been presented clearly enough. Each side was painfully clear, he claimed, about the other's motives and goals. Moreover, he chided Chaim Weizmann and his associates, who pursued a path of obfuscation and made it seem as though there was some miscommunication between the two sides. Jabotinsky claimed that on the main issue—open immigration for Jews with the goal of a Jewish majority in Palestine—there was no difference between the so-called "carnivores" and "vegetarians," militarists and pacifists. Actually, he was wrong about that—Weizmann, among others, would have compromised with the British government to accept a Jewish minority status, although that would likely have been merely a tactic to gain time to increase Jewish numbers.[79]

Jabotinsky continued by arguing (against logic) that he respected Arabs, citing his blunt talk about Zionist demands. He claimed that it was useless to lie about Zionist goals because Arabs understood what was at stake. And anyway, lying would not work; no native would be fooled. Only honesty was morally justifiable, since by giving fair warning of what was to come, Jews could minimize Arab suffering. He had a ready answer to the accusation that his assertions were heartless and unethical. "We should have answered this question before we took the first shekel. And we did answer it positively. If Zionism is moral, i.e., [legitimately] just, then justice should be realized independent of anyone's agreement or disagreement. And if A, B or C want to interfere by means of force in our realization of justice because they find it profitable, then we can interfere with them again with force. This is ethics, there is no other ethics to speak of."[80]

This is almost convincing except that it ignores the opposing arguments. In Jabotinsky's conception, ethics inheres in, and only in, Zionism. The other political parties or players are obligated to back down. In his demand for exclusive justice, however, a universal standard is rejected.

The initial purpose of the articles was to respond to the Arab violence of 1920 and 1921, which had successfully turned British and world opinion against the Zionist cause. The violence had to stop, but how? Jabotinsky proposed an "Iron Wall." The wall can be viewed literally as a barrier, but also as a metaphor, a preponderance of might that neutralized any threat from the Arabs. Behind this protective barrier, Zionists could slowly and methodically complete the national project.

Jabotinsky's intended audience consisted of Chaim Weizmann and other Zionists, the British government, American Jews, and the Arabs of Palestine. In particular, his proposal for an Iron Wall against Palestinian Arabs was meant first and foremost as a rebuttal of the White Paper of 1922. It was also a comment on Britain's construction of the Hashemite Kingdom in Transjordan in 1921, land that Jabotinsky had always viewed as part of Zionism's patrimony and appropriate for Jewish settlement.[81]

The Iron Wall articles were also aimed at Weizmann, whom Jabotinsky accused of cowardice. He felt that Weizmann's unmerited caution would ruin the Yishuv. In fact, Jabotinsky's provocative declaration was meant to force the articulation of ultimate goals, which embarrassed Weizmann, who was trying to present Zionism as a peaceful ideology. The articles were also addressed to Arabs, if less directly, because for one thing, they appeared in Russian. However, soon they could be read in different languages and "About the Iron Wall" purposely played into the hands of Zionism's opponents, and not only Arab critics, who argued that Zionism's goals could not be attained without harming the native population.

His other addressee was Britain, its government and public. Jabotinsky asked the British people to remember morality: the rights of the hungry versus the satiated, the life of a dog versus a human. Britain might feel inclined to abandon its commitment temporarily, but Jewish suffering legitimized the Iron Wall because only with a wall (or a preponderance of might) could Jews suppress Arab opposition. The articles were a response also to potential immigrants. Jabotinsky was aware that immigration had stalled. Despite the British acquisition of the Mandate, fewer Jews had arrived than had been hoped. Jabotinsky had to face the reality that either Zionism was not the solution for world Jewry or something was hindering Jews from coming. What should be done to change things?

For Yosef Gorny, the innovation in Jabotinsky's Iron Wall was that it changed Zionism's time-line. Instead of gaining the land through creative endeavor, it made military conflict the primary strategy. Gorny writes, "They reversed the order of Zionist priorities by arguing that military force took precedence over the constructive effort, rather than growing organically out of the building of the society. Jabotinsky also called on Great

Britain to demonstrate its support for Zionism and its respect for the Balfour Declaration by establishing a Jewish Legion to guard the Yishuv. This extreme demand was intended to exert pressure on British politicians to arrive at positive decisions regarding Zionism."[82]

In his own camp, some of his collaborators thought he had gone too far. Fellow émigré Alexander Kulisher considered the entire thesis a misjudgment. In Kulisher's view, the most effective method for colonizing a region was the voluntary assent of the natives: "Actually a successful colonization effort is only possible with the agreement and cooperation of a certain part of the local population. The most brilliant example is the colonization of America in the eighteenth century."[83] According to Kulisher, Britain won because it pursued assent, winning over native peoples. In contrast, the French followed Jabotinsky's method. "If anyone pursued such policies in America, it was the French in Canada. As a result they were defeated in the war with Britain, i.e., France had extensive military preparations, 'garrisons,' and 'commanders.'"[84]

Kulisher also argued that Jabotinsky's recourse to violence imitated the violent acts of Jews' enemies throughout Jewish history. That alone disqualified it from serving Jewish interests. "With a large demagogic voice V. E. Jabotinsky's group pursues propaganda, the purpose of which is a general revision of the ideology without which there would never have been a question regarding a Jewish Palestine. The solution of the situation is found in the recourse to militaristic nationalism that has been our vilest enemy throughout our entire history."[85]

It is interesting to note that the Jewish historian Mikhail Gershenzon made exactly the same argument at this time. Although he had cooperated on a number of Zionist literary projects in Moscow, in 1922 he released a bombshell, publishing *Fates of the Jewish People*.[86] In that book, Gershenzon aired his disagreement with Zionism, arguing that nationalism, the bane of existence of the Jewish people for centuries, should not guide Zionism. The Jewish people, he claimed, had a more elevated purpose than politics, and although he could not describe it now, it would emerge in the course of history.

Despite feeling alone, Jabotinsky knew that the Zionist leadership was aware of the Arab problem and was equally disappointed with Britain's response. In a private letter, Weizmann wrote to Herbert Samuel, "It seems that everything in Palestinian life is now revolving round one central problem—how to satisfy and 'pacify' the Arabs. Zionism is being gradually, systematically, and relentlessly 'reduced'.... A great depression, almost despair, prevails in Palestine and is almost universal.... It pains me deeply to have to write all this.... We are all anxious to help you in your difficult task, but we must be given a fair chance."[87] It was Jabotinsky's trademark to say publicly what others would say only in private.[88]

*　*　*

The question that is usually asked about Jabotinsky is how to connect his provocative statements of 1923 with his definition of himself as a liberal. Because the arguments show him ignoring the rights of others, one would like to understand his contradictions. Why did Jabotinsky respond to the political configuration of 1923 with the Iron Wall? To answer this, we need to turn to Jabotinsky's evaluation of Zionism in 1923.

Because of the high Arab birthrate, and the higher rate of Arab immigration than Jewish immigration, Jews did not appear capable of becoming the majority population. It is important to note that Jabotinsky conceived of a Jewish majority as affirming political legitimacy. Statehood as a word meant very little because, as Jabotinsky quipped, Illinois was a state, as was New Jersey. According to Jabotinsky, Zionist theorists had from the beginning sought sovereignty based on a Jewish majority. The vague language of Herzl, a "Heimstätte," or in Britain's terminology, a "national home codified in law," were euphemisms used to calm the native population, he argued. However, everyone understood that Zionism's goal was a majority in the land.[89]

But would Jews ever reach a majority? Jabotinsky understood that even if they should find themselves in the majority someday, Jews would likely hold only a marginal advantage since the region would remain overwhelmingly Arab. Surely it was on his mind that if Zionism were to succeed, Jews would need to rule over Arab citizens in order to avoid permanent debilitation by British opposition.

Here it is worthwhile to compare the Iron Wall with the Helsingfors Conference that Jabotinsky invoked again in his article (he promised to respect minority rights). The 1906 Zionist conference had the goal of protecting minority groups in a multinational, multiethnic, and multiconfessional empire. It is hard to see how such protections could be enacted under an Iron Wall policy.

A much better example would be the British Empire in its dominion over India or Ireland, where British subjects were in the minority. Over several centuries, the British had colonized other nations by dividing and conquering, co-opting elites, promoting integration, and the use of force, among other methods.

However, the history of another empire much closer to Jabotinsky's experience might have served him as a cautionary warning. I am speaking of Russia's dominion over the other nations within its historical borders and on its peripheries. The most important of Russia's imperial possessions was Poland, a proud nation with a rich literary history. Poland had a large Jewish population. Although in many ways Poland does not look like Palestine, a closer examination shows some important parallels, and offers lessons about ruling other nations against their will.

Although for the most part Russia ruled over its subject peoples, especially those less familiar with Western cultural norms, it had violent clashes with Poland during the nineteenth century. The Russians had to suppress two major insurrections, in 1830 and 1863. Attempts at integrating or russifying the elites had not pacified the Poles. It was not until the Russians made it entirely clear that opposition to Russian rule was absolutely futile, and costly, that the Poles yielded to greater force. The expropriation of the land of rebellious nobles, the exile of many thousands of Poles to Siberia, the banning of the Polish language by state schools and government services, and the retention of a large army in the country convinced Poles that they had no choice but to submit. The Poles named the nonconfrontational approach "Positivism," and it was characterized by a rejection of revolution in favor of small deeds and economic pursuits. Until 1905, and even thereafter, the Russians ruled Poland in relative peace. The Iron Wall policy looks very similar to what Russia strived to achieve in Poland.

It may be possible to label as immoral the minority rule of a majority. But immorality was just one problem with the Iron Wall. Practical issues were also involved. Repression of populations by force rarely works, and there are many examples to prove this point, as Kulisher had noted. Although Jabotinsky could not have predicted Britain's painful experience of decolonization after World War II, he was certainly aware of the outcome of the Polish drama. Poland had not remained quiet. In 1918, Jòsef Pilsudsky waited for the appropriate moment to organize forces to gain the country's freedom. Earlier, Roman Dmowski had prepared his Endek party for an anti-Russian revolt. In 1919, Poland attacked Russia. That conflagration ended in a stalemate, at a terrible cost to both countries. History shows that it's hardly simple for one people, especially a minority, to rule others by force.

But that is not all. The situation of the Jews in the history of Polish-Russian fighting should also have worried Jabotinsky. At one time or another, Jewish allegiance had been pursued by both sides, although neither had kept its promises. Jews had suffered, no matter who won. Why was Jabotinsky so certain that Britain, even if it adopted an anti-Arab policy, would meet its promises to the Jews, who were once again a kind of third wheel?

In light of Jabotinsky's experiences as a Russian subject, it is difficult to understand the certainty with which he expressed the Jewish right to rule over Palestinians. It is equally hard to understand how Jabotinsky could portray Jewish rights in moral terms, while giving no legitimacy to Palestinian Arab political claims. Although one can acknowledge that Jabotinsky discriminated against Arabs a little—as when, during his wartime travels, he made prejudicial observations about the "indolence" of Arabs—he did not use the abusive language of racial prejudice or seek to rid the country of them.

He did not conceive of Arabs as noble savages or project onto them unmasked prejudice. He thought they were backward by Western standards, but he viewed them as having the same political desires as Jews: prosperity, dignity, and especially sovereignty. Nonetheless, his recognition of their humanity did not lead him to acknowledge their right to political equality. He claimed that their fate as a minority would be better than that of the Jews in Eastern Europe, who had been objects of discrimination and victims of pogroms. However, it is hard to account for his certainty on this score; living under an Iron Wall policy might be more painful than Jabotinsky would admit.

Although Jabotinsky viewed morality as the justification for a Jewish majority, it is impossible to see liberal Zionism as a model for Jabotinsky's Iron Wall. The Helsingfors ideal speaks of autonomous nations pursuing their own culture in peace and security with full democratic rights, while the Iron Wall implies political and cultural repression. Here one sees a direct link to the ethno-nationalism, chauvinism, and political repression that Jabotinsky witnessed earlier. It appears that, between two kinds of nationalism, he had chosen the radical rightist version.

One should not forget, however, that many of the evils that people accuse Jabotinsky of were actually implemented, though not by him or his party. It was labor Zionists who promulgated many of the laws, rulings, and policies that dispossessed Arabs of their land during and after 1948. One could say that Jabotinsky's rhetoric contributed to an atmosphere of intolerance. One could also say that the logic of events led to the political and legal divisions that remain in today's Israel, and that Jabotinsky merely predicted accurately.

Although Jabotinsky was an early right-wing politician in the Zionist camp, he was no political innovator. In fact, iron walls (that is, militarist solutions to political problems) were beginning to pop up here and there, in South Africa, Ethiopia, India, and elsewhere. Jabotinsky thought one would work well in Palestine, too. But one might recall the historical consequences of using force to rule over others. Jabotinsky was more than a little optimistic that Jews could attach their interests to Britain's colonial apparatus and form a majority on the land without a cataclysm arising from Arab opposition. His vision might have been clearer if he had recalled Russian rule in Poland and also the experience of the Jews between two larger powers. In addition, his case for Jewish legitimacy—based on the morality of Jewish suffering—loses its potency before Arab suffering and the Jewish role in inflicting that suffering. Recall that in 1911, Jabotinsky had chastised Poles for their aggressive imperial attitude toward the national minorities in Poland, noting that it was despicable to become an oppressor after one had been oppressed oneself. Now he himself was vulnerable to same accusation, a proponent of the "morality of cannibals," as he had called it.

Notes

1. Svetlana Natkovich, "The Rise and Downfall of Cassandra: World War I and Vladimir (Ze'ev) Jabotinsky's Self-Perception," *Medaon-Magazin für jüdisches Leben in Forschung und Bildung* 10 (2016): 5.

2. Vladimir Jabotinsky, "Wegen Avanturizm," *Haynt*, February 26, 1932.

3. Oz Almog, *The Sabra: The Creation of the New Jew*, trans. Hai Watzman (Berkeley: University of California Press, 2000), 198–201; Abigail Jacobson and Moshe Naor, *Oriental Neighbors: Middle Eastern Jews and Arabs in Mandatory Palestine* (Waltham: Brandeis University Press, 2016), 65.

4. Vladimir Jabotinsky, "The Crisis" (unpublished document in the Jabotinsky Institute Archive, 1920).

5. Jabotinsky, "The Crisis."

6. S. G. Gwynne, *Empire of the Summer Moon: Quanah Parker and the Rise and Fall of the Comanches, the Most Powerful Indian Tribe in American History* (New York: Scribner, 2010), 44.

7. Yosef Gorny, *Zionism and the Arabs, 1882–1948* (Oxford: Clarendon, 1987), 53, 49, 173.

8. Joseph B. Schechtman, *The Arab Refugee Problem* (New York: Philosophical Library, 1952).

9. A. J. Sherman, *Mandate Days: British Lives in Palestine, 1914–1948* (London: Thames and Hudson, 1998), 15.

10. Rory Miller, introduction to *Britain, Palestine and Empire: The Mandate Years*, ed. R. Miller (Surrey, UK: Ashgate, 2010), 2–3.

11. Even according to a revised Israeli estimate for 1922, there were only 11.1 percent Jews among the total population of Mandatory Palestine. See R. Bachi, *The Population of Israel*, (Paris: CICRED, 1974), 5.

12. Michael Keren and Shlomit Keren, *We Are Coming, Unafraid: The Jewish Legions and the Promised Land in the First World War* (Lanham, MD: Rowman & Littlefield, 2010), 49–50.

13. Ben Halpern and Jehuda Reinharz, *Zionism and the Creation of a New Society* (Hanover, NH: University Press of New Britain-Brandeis University Press, 2000), 209.

14. Mark Makovsky, *Churchill's Promised Land: Zionism and Statecraft* (New Haven, CT: Yalen University Press, 2007), 7.

15. Ilan Pappe, *A History of Modern Palestine: One Land, Two Peoples* (Cambridge: Cambridge University Press, 2006), 87–88.

16. Bernard Wasserstein, *The British in Palestine: The Mandatory Government and the Arab-Jewish Conflict, 1917–1929*, 2nd ed. (London: Blackwell, 1991), 10–11.

17. Ibid., 42.

18. Ibid.

19. Eri Jabotinsky, *Avi, Ze'ev Jabotinsky* (Jerusalem: Stimatzky, 1980), 58–59.

20. Ibid., 59. On Rutenberg, see Vladimir Khazan, *Pinkhas Rutenberg: Ot terrorista k sionistu*, 2 vols. (Moscow: Mosty Kul'tury-Gersharim, 2008).

21. Wasserstein, *The British in Palestine*, 44–45.

22. Vladimir Jabotinsky to Bir Salem from September 1, 1919, Jabotinsky Institute Archive. The menorah badge was indeed given to soldiers. "At the end of 1919, the shrinking legions received some recognition with the granting of the title of the 'First Judean Battalion,' whose badge was the Jewish symbol of the Menorah." Keren and Keren, *We Are Coming*, 71.

23. V. Jabotinsky to M. Grossman, September 16, 1919, Jabotinsky Institute Archives.

24. Joseph B. Schechtman and Yehuda Benari, *History of the Revisionist Movement, 1925–1930* (Tel Aviv: Hadar, 1970), 166–167.

25. This paragraph is based on the research of Wasserstein, *The British in Palestine*, 64–65. See also Rory Miller, "Sir Ronald Storrs: The Dream that Turned into a Nightmare," *Middle Eastern Studies* 36, no. 3 (2000): 114–144.

26. Gur Alroey, "The Hebrew Hero and the Jewish Victim: Pogroms in the Ukraine in the Years 1918–1920 and the Riots of 1920 and 1921 in Palestine," *Zion* 4 (2015): 551–81.

27. Wasserstein, *The British in Palestine*, 65.

28. Daniel Heller, *Jabotinsky's Children: Polish Jews and the Rise of Right-Wing Zionism* (Princeton, NJ: Princeton University Press, 2017), 32.

29. Vladimir Jabotinsky, "Mivtsar Akko (keta)," in Vladimir Jabotinsky, *Katvim, Avtobiograiya* (Jerusalem: Ari Jabotinsky, 1946–47), 307–313.

30. Joseph B. Schechtman, *The Life and Times of Vladimir Jabotinsky: Rebel and Statesman, The Early Years*. Silver Spring: Eshel Books, 1986, 347–352.

31. See Jehuda Reinharz, *Chaim Weizmann: The Making of a Statesman* (New York: Oxford University Press, 1993), 367. Michael Berkowitz has a chapter on the Jewish National Fund and the role of culture and philanthropy in the official Zionist institutions. Michael Berkowitz, *Zionist Culture and West European Jewry Before the First World War* (Chapel Hill: North Carolina Press, 1996), 164–187.

32. Vladimir Jabotinsky, "From Door to Door: Propaganda Speech at a Keren Hayesod Drive Meeting in New York, Publicity Dept., May 1922." Found in the Jabotinsky Institute Archive.

33. George Sorel, *On Violence* (New York: Dover, 2004).

34. Yehuda Reinharz writes, "The efforts of Sokolow and Jabotinsky to raise money were only partially successful, while their absence was keenly felt in London." Reinharz, *Chaim Weizmann*, 367.

35. Vladimir Jabotinsky, "Peace in Palestine: Hostility of Arab Troops, To the Editor of the *Times*," London *Times*, May 14, 1921. (English slightly modified for clarity).

36. Wasserstein, *The British in Palestine*, 72.

37. Vladimir Jabotinsky, "Zionist Administration in Palestine: Some Facts and Results," *Jewish Chronicle*, April 14, 1922.

38. Letter of Vladimir Jabotinsky to Chaim Weizmann, October 7, 1920. Jabotinsky Institute Archive.

39. Vladimir Jabotinsky, "My burzhui," *Rassvet*, 23, no. 15–16 (April 17, 1927): 5–7.

40. Ibid.

41. Anita Shapira, *Land and Power: The Zionist Resort to Force, 1881–1948* (Stanford, CA: Stanford University Press, 1999), 109.

42. Vladimir Jabotinsky, "The Zionist Case of the Justice of the Jewish Claim," *New Palestine* (April 28, 1922): 256. Jabotinsky would have a diplomatic success in America with these arguments. Yehuda Reinharz writes, "The one diplomatic victory of the Zionists during Weizmann's sojourn in Italy was scored not on the Continent but in the United States, thanks to the intensive lobbying of Nahum Sokolow and Vladimir Jabotinsky in collaboration with Louis Lipsky. On April 12, 1922, Senator Henry Cabot Lodge, ironically a leader of American isolationism, introduced a resolution in the Senate Foreign Relations Committee affirming support for the establishment of the Jewish national home in Palestine. On May 3, the Committee recommended adoption of the resolution." Reinharz, *Chaim Weizmann*, 386.

43. Jabotinsky, *Avi*, 21.

44. See Lord Northcliff's articles in the *London Times* and *Daily Mail* from 1921–22. Chaim Weizmann has a similar opinion of Lord Northcliff. "Apart from the attacks which have been leveled at us within the Organization . . . we have had to bear the onslaught of Northcliff—and naturally this has given the Arab Delegation, which was dying a natural death, a new lease on life." Quoted in Reinharz, *Chaim Weizmann*, 370.

45. Jabotinsky, "The Zionist Case," 255.

46. Ibid., 256.

47. Ibid.

48. Shalom Ratzabi, *Between Zionism and Judaism: The Radical Circle in Brith Shalom, 1925–1933* (Leiden, Boston, Köln: Brill, 2002), 62.

49. Many Zionists in England, for example, walked the tightrope of support for the Jewish leadership in Palestine but also worried about hostility to Britain. Gorny, *Zionism and the Arabs*, 211.

50. Jabotinsky, "The Zionist Case," 257.

51. Jabotinsky to Oscar Gruzenberg May 6, 1925; Vladimir Zhabotinskii, "Pis'ma Oskaru Gruzenbergu," *Vestnik Evreiskogo Universiteta v Moskve* 2, no. 6 (1994): 226–227.

52. Shapira, *Land and Power*, 190.

53. Jabotinsky, "Pis'ma Oskaru Gruzenbergu," 226.

54. William L. Cleveland and Martin Bunton, *A History of the Modern Middle East*, 6th ed. (Boulder, CO: Westview, 2016), 231–233.

55. Weizmann appointed Jabotinsky to the Political Committee, the central group of Zionists in Britain. In 1918, Weizmann and Jabotinsky were apparently still friends, as Jabotinsky corrected Weizmann's speech for the stone-laying ceremony for the future Hebrew University in July 1918. Reinharz, *Chaim Weizmann*, 1:215 and 1:259 respectively. Reinharz, *Chaim Weizmann*, 1:215.

56. Ibid., 1:199.

57. Ibid., 1:319.

58. Redaktor, "Beseda s V. Zhabotinskim." *Rassvet* 4, no. 41 (January 28, 1923): 10.

59. Laqueur, *A History of Zionism*, 347.

60. Colin Shindler, *The Triumph of Military Zionism: Nationalism and the Origins of the Israeli Right* (London: I. B. Tauris, 2009), 33.

61. Schechtman, *Rebel and Statesman*, 416–424.

62. Shapira, *Land and Power*, 118. Israel Kolatt maintains that Jabotinsky did not belong at this time to the group that advocated a nation-state. "Makomo shel Ze'ev Z'abotinski be-pitaron leumi," in *Ish be-sa'ar: Masot u'mekhkarim 'al Ze'ev Z'abotinski*, ed. Avi Bareli and Pinhas Ginossar (Ber-Sheva: Universitat Ben-Guryon ba'Negev, 2004), 10.

63. Later in life, Jabotinsky displayed his regret regarding the Nordau Plan. In his autobiography, he appealed for a similar plan of rapid and mass immigration of Jews to Palestine. In *Story of the Jewish Legion*, he exonerates himself by making it appear that he had supported Nordau in 1915. Jabotinsky describes how they met during the war: Nordau was living in Spain after having been kicked out of France as a noncombatant enemy. Jabotinsky tells him about the Legion idea. Nordau counters with an adage about Jewish logic: A Jew hesitates to buy an umbrella until he's soaking wet. The joke mocks the Jewish people as being blind to their own interests. The story reflects self-criticism for rejecting the Nordau Plan, which potentially could have brought about the rapid transformation of a Jewish Palestine. Jabotinsky, *Story of The Jewish Legion*, 31–32.

64. "Beseda s V. Zhabotinskim," 10.

65. Heller, *Jabotinsky's Children*, 33.

66. Geoffrey Wheatcroft, "The Finchley Factor," *London Review of Books*, 40, no. 17 (September 13, 2018): 15–18.

67. *Die Neue Zionistische Organisation* (Paris: 1935), 1.

68. Daniel Heller, "The Rise of the Zionist Right: Polish Jews and the Betar Youth Movement, 1922–1935" (PhD diss., Stanford University, 2012), 42.

69. Joseph B. Schechtman describes this in his biography, *The Life and Times of Vladimir Jabotinsky: Rebel and Statesman*, 406–415.

70. Joseph B. Schechtman, "The Jabotinsky-Slavinsky Agreement: A Chapter in Ukrainian-Jewish Relations," *Jewish Social Studies* 17 (1955): 294–296.

71. Vladimir Jabotinsky, "Di 'Krim'-kolonizatsye," *Morgen Zhurnal* 4 (June 1926). See also "Vopros o Petliure," *Rassvet* 10 (March 8, 1925): 4–8; and David Engel, "The Elite and the Street: The Schwarzbard Affair (1926–1927) as a Turning Point in Jewish Diplomacy," in *Jahrbuch des Simon-Dubnow-Instituts* 15 (2016): 157–166; also David Engel, ed., introduction to *The Assassination of Symon Petliura and the Trial of Scholem Schwarzbard 1926–1927: A Selection of Documents* (Göttingen, 2016), 7–94.

72. Vladimir Jabotinsky, "Petliura i pogrom," *Poslednie novosti* (October 11, 1927). See David Engel, introduction to *The Assassination of Symon Petliura*, 91.

73. Joseph B. Schechtman, "Ukhod V. E. Zhabotinskogo," *Rassvet* 5 (February 4, 1923): 11–12.

74. Jonathan Frankel, *Crisis, Revolution, and Russian Jews* (Cambridge: Cambridge University Press, 2009), 99–100.

75. Vladimir Jabotinsky, "O zheleznoi stene. My i araby," *Rassvet* 19, nos. 42/43 (November 4, 1923): 1–3; "Etika zheleznoi steny," *Rassvet* 19, no. 44/45 (November 11, 1923): 2–4. All quotations Vladimir Jabotinsky, *Rechi, stat'i, vospominaniia* (Minsk, 2004). The next pages use my own previously published work. See Brian Horowitz, "Principle or Expediency: Violence and Vladimir Jabotinsky's Struggle to Dominate the Zionist Movement," *Jahrbuch des Simon-Dubnow-Instituts* 15 (2017): 15–32.

76. Eran Kaplan analyzes the articles as Jabotinsky's philosophical statement on the Arab Question. See *The Jewish Radical Right: Revisionist Zionism and its Ideological Legacy* (Madison: University of Wisconsin Press, 2005), 48–49.

77. Joseph B. Schechtman, "Nasha arabskaia politika," *Rassvet* 31 (August 5, 1923): 4.

78. Jabotinsky, "O zheleznoi stene," 268.

79. Yosef Gorny corrects the common misconception that Weizmann trusted in the British. In fact, it was Jabotinsky who could be characterized as the die-hard loyalist.

> Weizmann and his supporters, unlike Jabotinsky, never deluded themselves that a Jewish society could be achieved in Palestine with the active aid of Great Britain. They were, from the first, suspicious of Britain's political intentions, and their political instincts sharpened as they observed British stratagems. The question they faced was whether it was possible to achieve their goal against the wishes of the British. British opposition would spell the end of Zionist aspirations. Did acceptance of this fact imply that Weizmann was resigned to the anti-Zionist trends in British policy? The reverse is true. It advocated total exploitation of the democratic parliamentary framework, and strove ceaselessly to gain access to policy-making circles in the ruling party and within the opposition. Weizmann was a skilled politician and won unparalleled gains, displaying considerable self-confidence and an amazing aptitude for impressing all those with whom he came into contact. Gorny, *Zionism and the Arabs*, 108.

80. V. Jabotinsky, "O zheleznoi stene," 268. Jabotinsky expressed this same argument in 1937 at his appearance in London before the Royal Commission.

81. On the issue of Jabotinsky and Transjordan, it is interesting that Herbert Samuel first proposed the attachment of Transjordan to the Palestine patrimony in his pamphlet, *Zionism: Its Ideals and Practical Hopes* (London, 1919). Bernard Wasserstein points this out, as does Walter Laqueur. See Wasserstein, *The British in Palestine*, 76; also Walter Laqueur, *A History of Zionism*, 347.

82. Gorny, *Zionism and the Arabs*, 176–177.

83. Thanks to Mark Tolts for bringing this article to my attention and for his help in understanding Alexander Kulisher's role in *Rassvet*.

84. Alexander Kulisher, "Voennyi Sionizm," *Svershenie* 1 (1925): 96. For more on Kulisher, see Mark Tolts and Anatoly Vishnevsky, "Nezamechennyi vklad v teoriiu demograficheskogo perekhoda: k 125-letiiu so dnia rozhdeniia Aleksandra Kulishera," *Demograficheskoe obozrenie* 2, no. 4 (2015): 6–34.

85. Kulisher, "Voennyi Sionizm," 92.

86. Mikhail Gershenzon, *Sud'by evreiskogo naroda* (Moscow, 1922).

87. Wasserstein, *The British in Palestine*, 112.

88. Yosef Gorny views the Iron Wall article as

> the ideological link between two periods in Jabotinsky's public life. In the first period, after the death of Herzl, he was one of the rising stars of Zionism and won renown as a brilliant writer and tireless man of action. In the later period, from 1925, when he founded the Revisionist movement, he was the leader of a political movement and party. The earlier article clearly delineated two parallel paths of thought—his faith in the Helsinki platform, which he helped to compose and to which he adhered to the day of his death, and the concept of "Legionism," whose author he was. These ideas appeared to be in conflict, but would be reconciled in the future. Gorny, *Zionism and the Arabs*, 168.

89. There were many others who also defined Zionist success as becoming the majority population. "To be fair, one also has to stress that the Revisionists were not the only Zionist faction determined to reduce the Palestine Arabs to a minority population in Palestine. The notion was very popular among all the activist factions, particularly activist sections of the Labor movement, i.e., the 'Ahdut ha'avoda party.' Its approach, characteristic of the 1920s, was crystallized at the fourth 'Ahdut ha'avoda conference (12–19 May 1924) in Ein Harod." Jan Zouplna, "Revisionist Zionism: Image, Reality and the Quest for Historical Narrative," *Middle Eastern Studies* 44, no. 1 (2008): 8.

8

RUSSIAN-JEWISH EMIGRATION AND THE PATH TO ZIONIST REVISIONISM, 1923–1925

* * *

IN 1923, FINDING HIMSELF WITHOUT A JOB OR prospects, Jabotinsky was now as far from the Zionist leadership as he had been in 1919, when he was demobilized from the Legion, or in 1912, when he could not find collaborators for his plans for Hebrew in the Diaspora. In 1922, he left Palestine for lack of work and because his wife was unhappy there, and moved first to Berlin and then to Paris.[1] After 1917, Russian émigrés formed communities in a number of European cities—Prague, Belgrade, and Berlin. Berlin was especially attractive because of the city's tolerance, economic opportunities, and "cheap" currency, but the German mark's stabilization in 1924 caused prices to precipitously rise and drove many émigrés to Paris.[2] Jabotinsky's trajectory paralleled the Russian emigration because for all intents and purposes, he was an émigré with a Nansen passport; he relied on his contacts—the people, services, and institutions of the Russian emigration.

After the Bolshevik takeover in October 1917, nearly two million people left Russia.[3] Regarding the Jewish element, Hebrew University demographer Mark Tolts writes, "The first sizable wave of post–World War I Jewish international migration from Eastern Europe occurred in 1918–1921, when more than 200,000 Jews emigrated from Soviet Russia to different European countries, mostly through neighboring Poland and Romania; they settled chiefly in Germany, and later in France. In the first years of the 1920s, however, many of these refugees joined the general Jewish migration movement to the United States and Palestine."[4] Jewish immigrants had diverse employment profiles. Some were workers, professionals, doctors, and lawyers; others were journalists and intellectuals of various kinds—religious and non-religious. In terms of Jewish politics, one can observe integrationists, such as Maxim Vinaver and Mikhail Vishniak, who were associated with the Parisian newspaper *Evreiskaia Tribuna* (*Jewish Tribune*), as well as individuals more committed to socialism, who gathered around Yiddish newspapers such as *Der Emes* and *Haynt*. In the center and center-right, some émigrés wrote for *Rassvet*, the Russian-language weekly that first appeared in Berlin in 1922 and moved to Paris in December 1924.[5]

Paris was not the most obvious home for a leading Zionist organization, owing to its relative geographical isolation. A more obvious choice would have been London, the capital of the Mandate power, or Jerusalem. However, Paris was the leading center of the Russian emigration. Jabotinsky's decision to create a base in Paris would have consequences for Revisionist Zionism.

There was certainly a tension in Jabotinsky's overall situation. He felt nostalgia for the Russian language and was on friendly terms with non-Jewish émigrés—Pavel Miliukov, Boris Savinkov, and Viktor Chernov. In fact, he had not given up his status as a Russian writer: in 1926, he published a novel in Russian, *Samson–Nazarei* (*Samson the Nazarite*); in 1930, he published *Razskazy* (*Stories*), a volume of short fictional works that had appeared in prerevolutionary Russia.[6] It was common for émigrés to republish earlier works after settling into their new countries.

"Russian Zionists" who lived in Europe made up a specific group. Schechtman attempted to define them this way: "That which is called Russian Zionism is now only an idiosyncratic mixture brought out of Russia of the former views and attitudes of Russian Zionists with new European impressions. I would say that it is a new Zionist type: Russian-émigré Zionism. It does not appear to be similar to the Western model, but it differs significantly from Russian Zionism. It is a synthesis between the two, some say. It is an uncreative mixture of differing elements, others stipulate."[7] Admittedly, it had been five years since the Bolshevik takeover, and the émigrés had shifted their focus from the immediate fall of the Soviet Union to improving their lives outside Russia. The result was a new orientation for Russian Zionists, who realized that emigration might be permanent or at least last for a long time.

Zionist émigrés from Russia, like émigrés generally, were inconsolable on the Bolshevik issue. They found it especially painful to recall that, before the October Revolution and in the first two years after it, Zionism enjoyed mass popularity.[8] Many of the émigrés were liberals who rejected the tsarist government and also shared the Kadets' allegiance to a rule-of-law state; they, too, despised communism and what they saw as "thuggery"—the expropriation of private property, suppression of religion, and political opposition. Moshe Kleinman expresses the general view when he writes, "With a single swing of the axe, Russian anarchism cut down powerful, centuries-old trees; is it surprising that under these blows our young seedlings would fall? And let them not lie: it was not a 'conquest' by another people, but the real genuine black-earth *Rus'* that one day in an ecstatic frenzy raised its wild axe and with a single swing cut down its own centuries-old trees of culture and civilization."[9] Making clear that Jews should not be blamed for Bolshevism—despite the number of Jewish persons in the original Bolshevik leadership (many worried that Jews would be blamed for the Judeo-Kommuna)—Kleinman argues that Bolshevism was a purely Russian phenomenon that emerged from an anarchistic, destructive psychology.

The Russian-Jewish émigrés in Europe shared much the same fate as the ethnic Russian émigrés in terms of financial opportunities and cultural life. However, the Zionists among them tended to focus their political energies less on liberating Russia from the Bolsheviks than on the Jewish situation in Palestine. A central question for Jabotinsky and his Revisionist colleagues was collaboration: was it possible to join former members of the White Army and fight for mutual interests, knowing that pro-monarchy groups harbored antisemitic attitudes and cooperated with murderers? Between 1918 and 1921, tens of thousands of Jews in Ukraine were violently killed. Joseph Schechtman, for example, favored maintaining a distance from Russian groups, whereas Alexander Kulisher and Nikolai Sorin thought collaboration was possible.[10] Kulisher and Sorin felt that since *Rassvet* appeared in the Russian language, and in Berlin rather than Palestine, that both they and their contributors gave their implicit support to the "free Russia" movement.[11] They hoped that Jews would be involved in Russia's liberation: "The very fact that *Rassvet* has been reestablished in Berlin, in Russian, effectively bears witness that its directors took into consideration the future of Russia and the configuration in Russia of the Jewish population. In accord with the view that 'very soon the Russian intelligentsia will again make Russia democratic,' we assume that Russian Jewry will also make this Russia democratic."[12] Sorin and Kulisher, like so many liberal Russian émigrés, dreamed of retaking Russia from the Bolsheviks and establishing a democratic state.

A good deal of Jabotinsky's turn to the radical right should be viewed in historical context—that is, the generation from 1905 to the Bolshevik takeover. This means, first of all, accepting of the role of violence in politics. Schechtman comments poetically: "All of us who lived through that terrible fifteen-year period, 1905–1920—Jabotinsky's generation, which at the same time is 'our generation'—have adopted the severe and merciless truth that the highest ideals need forceful armor and a strong sword, and the noble metal only becomes a viable coin with which one can buy the right to life and a place under the sun, when it is fortified by a bronze dash of power."[13]

This reflects a visceral attitude toward power. People who experienced revolution, who were ejected from their homes at the edge of a bayonet, had fewer scruples about the use of power. For them, violence was part of life. Jabotinsky's reputation as a militarist and fighter attracted supporters and followers among the émigrés, but not only them. The war, with its myriad casualties, prompted new thinking about violence. People internalized violence as necessary and ordinary.

When he resigned from the Zionist Executive, Jabotinsky lost his steady salary. He continued earning income by lecturing to individual groups, but that was hardly an effective means of reaching a mass audience. To create a political party, he needed acquire a platform, a means of disseminating his message. That meant operating a newspaper.

It was a challenge for Russian émigrés in Europe to establish newspapers or political parties without a reliable financial stream. Jabotinsky had capable and loyal cadres: Meir Grossman; his partner, the Viennese Zionist Richard Lichtheim; and a group of Russian-Jewish intellectuals, Shlomo Gepstein, Moshe Kleinman, Joseph Schechtman, and Julius Brutzkus. This partnership allowed Jabotinsky to organize centers in three cities: Grossman in London; Jabotinsky and Mikhail Gindin in Paris; and Lichtheim in Vienna. Admittedly, representation in Palestine was weak. Jabotinsky had a short list of donors who promised support, but even so, his financial problems were serious. Perhaps looseness of organization could be a virtue, however. Everyone could fend for themselves financially, and a party of ideas could emerge as an alternative to the established institutions, the Zionist left in Palestine and Weizmann's General Zionists.

Although Jabotinsky might have preferred a newspaper in German, English, French, or Yiddish—the leading languages of Europe—he sensed an opportunity when the editorial board of the Russian-language *Rassvet* approached him and asked him to take charge. The newspaper came to serve as the voice of Revisionist Zionism.[14] Jabotinsky published his articles, including polemics, and broadcast Revisionism's manifestos on its pages. *Rassvet*'s importance in Jabotinsky's biography in the 1920s cannot be overstated.[15] According to one source, its readership more than doubled in 1924, from 1,000 to 2,500 by the end of the year.[16] Though the intellectual quality was high, the journal struggled financially. Nevertheless, it managed to run from 1922 to 1934—no small achievement for a newspaper in Russian published far from Russian soil.[17]

The first issue appeared in Berlin on April 16, 1922, before Jabotinsky was officially associated with the newspaper. The editors—Mikhail Gindin, Mikhail Aleinikov, and Joseph Schechtman—defined the paper's mission as bringing a cultural renaissance to the Russian-Jewish emigration. "We strongly believe in this explosive awakening of our powers. We believe and know that, both in the old land of ashes and here too, our energies are alive and vigorous in the large Russian-Jewish emigration."[18] As Zionists who had emigrated to Western Europe, not Palestine, they acknowledged their estrangement. "We sharply feel the whole tragic strangeness of the rebirth of the old tribunal of Russian Zionist thought [*Rassvet*] right here in the German capital. But still another 'grimace of the Galut' does not stop us. Long ago we recognized and pondered the depth and strength of the old curse: 'to be a shipwreck on the waves of foreign seas.' For a long time we have been living with and breathing in hatred for the curse."[19] Presumably most of the writers could have emigrated to Palestine. Perhaps, as intellectuals, they saw more opportunities for gainful employment in Europe.

Because the paper was published in Berlin, the writers spoke first and foremost to émigrés, the large Russian-speaking population living in that city. To get a sense of what Jewish political life was like, one might turn to Joseph Schechtman's analysis in the January 1923 issue. "What is a blessing 'there' in Russia has become a curse in the emigration. Because 'there' they were leaders who had disciplined cadres, they were responsible for real things; the Zionist masses backed their decisions, and, elected or non-elected, they enjoyed general acclaim. Here in the emigration they, leaders without an army, an elite without the masses, represent merely themselves and a group of people whose voice has no public resonance. . . . Try to find the guilty one—and the typical sick immigrant atmosphere grows."[20]

This description of the Russian-Jewish Zionists within Germany obviously mirrors the conventional description of White Army officers, who famously sat in the cafés of Europe and drove taxis for a living. Given the poverty, displacement, and hopelessness among Russian Jews in Germany, Schechtman asked, "What motivates Russian Zionism in the emigration? What is its specific character, its moods, physiognomy, its daily life, and future perspective?"[21] The Russian émigrés were themselves a motley; they came from different parts of the former Russian Empire and had different experiences. Could this diverse cohort be united and shaped into a political force under Jabotinsky's leadership?[22]

Making *Rassvet* his primary journalistic outlet was dangerous for Jabotinsky. On the positive side, Russian was a language with millions of readers outside Soviet borders. It could be possible to smuggle issues into the Soviet Union. And it was hardly expensive, since there were no editors and translators to hire. But the fact that few non-Russians in Western Europe knew the language—and the newspaper's inability to reach an influential public (British readers, for example)—counted against it. The language issue was solved when Revisionist journals began to appear in different languages in 1925.[23]

However, questions regarding *Rassvet*'s mission surfaced immediately. If Jabotinsky tried to transform *Rassvet* from an informational bulletin for Jewish émigrés into a political vehicle, what should be done about those writers who didn't share Jabotinsky's politics? Should the paper stop functioning as a general source of information? Indeed, a number of writers, including Viktor Jacobson and Mikhail Aleinikov, opposed Jabotinsky and left the paper.[24] The faction that invited Jabotinsky—Schechtman, Shlomo Gepstein, Julius Brutzkus, Moshe Kleinman, Israel Trivus, and M. Schwarzman—was composed overwhelmingly of contributors to the earlier newspaper of the same name, *Rassvet* (also known as *Evreiskaia Zhizn'*), which existed from 1904 to 1917 in St. Petersburg.

The individuals who gave the émigré paper the name *Rassvet* knew that they were making a statement by linking themselves to a tradition that began in 1860, when another *Rassvet*, the first Jewish newspaper in the Russian language, appeared in Odessa.[25] Probably one reason for taking the name was to honor the paper that the Bolsheviks had recently closed.[26]

Before Jabotinsky arrived, *Rassvet* lacked an ideological focus. On the paper's masthead stood two pro-Zionist messages: "The newspaper was founded by Avram Idel'son in 1904," and "Zionism strives to create a legally-recognized Jewish home in Palestine"—the statement from the First Zionist Congress in Basel. However, on the same masthead, the editors also wrote that *Rassvet* was a "political and literary newspaper devoted to Jewish interests." In other words, the paper was charged with reflecting Jewish life generally, in Europe, the Soviet Union, and Palestine, and promised "not to be the newspaper of any party, fraction or tendency in Zionism. It would be the organ of Russian Zionist thought in its creative dynamics."[27] The editors explained: "We turn not only to Zionists, but to Russian-Jewish society as a whole. The destruction of the half-century work of Russian Jewry, on the one side, and the new character of the problem in Palestine that before our eyes has turned from a Zionist into a general Jewish problem, on the other—gives us a common language with all national-minded people."[28]

Jabotinsky modified the ideology of *Rassvet* when he took control in mid-1923. It became a forum for what he called "activist Zionism," in which he emphasized his own and Revisionist colleagues' activities. But he rejected proposals to deliver only propaganda and chose to retain its broad perspective and openness to a variety of thoughts and opinions. The paper, for example, had a large cultural section that provided information about events in the Jewish world in Paris and other European cities. Furthermore, the editor offered individuals the chance to disagree with him. There was intellectual vitality in the paper because of Jabotinsky's willingness to debate ideas. Preserving *Rassvet*'s independence may have been strategically wise because it signified that Revisionism was not narrow or sectarian, but a political movement with roots in European culture.

Jabotinsky's fame was one reason he was invited to edit *Rassvet*. Equally important, the paper found new readers who were attracted to his politics. His passionate supporters lived in far-flung cities of the emigration: Vienna, Paris, Berlin, Prague, Wilna, Warsaw, and Kharbin. Among Jews from the former Russian Empire, he was in his element; he, too, was an émigré who shared their past experiences and future dreams.

Julius (Yuly) Brutzkus offers a concrete example of some émigré attitudes toward Jabotinsky. In an article about Jabotinsky's place in history, Brutzkus argued that Pinsker and Herzl had effectively created an organization and awakened the public, but little in reality was accomplished. Then came Avram Idel'son, the editor of *Rassvet* in St. Petersburg. He knew the ghetto and could articulate its problems, talents, and flaws, but he was too close to the ghetto to understand how to escape it. As he saw it, Jabotinsky had the objective distance to view Jews as just another minority nation, like

Poles, Ukrainians, and Estonians, and could prescribe a common path to national liberation. Brutzkus writes:

> He acquainted the Jewish reader with the struggle for survival experienced by other nationalities and with the European methods of this struggle for real interests. Zionism is not a miracle that gave birth to itself from the fog; nor did it fall from the sky. It can and should be the result of a national renaissance that is achieved by [certain] methods of struggle for interests that are not romantic, but real. This struggle should be carried out by means that have already been developed in contemporary European political life. So the establishment and self-organization of Jewish nationhood [will take place] among future major revolutions in Eastern Europe. This is an organic part and premise for the realization of Zionism.[29]

It is unclear whether Brutskus thought the revolution was the idea of the nation-state, which was becoming the norm in Eastern Europe, or whether another revolution had to take place that would change political life worldwide and contribute to the final realization of Jewish national dreams in Palestine. In any case, one can feel the world-shattering ambitions of Jabotinsky's collaborators.

* * *

Jabotinsky established his own party, HaTzoHar, in 1925. It is hard to tell from Jabotinsky himself how it occurred since he was an inveterate mythmaker, self-promoter, and storyteller. By his own account, the motivation for the Revisionist movement arose in 1923, after he spoke to a group of young Zionists in Riga. "The next day Hasmonaea [the group's name] invited me to a meeting at its club, and squarely put to [me] the question: 'And what now? You have no right to preach such views and stir up young people if you don't intend to call them to action. You either keep quiet, or organize a party.' . . . Later, after midnight, the guest and Hasmonaea rose and gave each other a solemn pledge to roll up their sleeves and straighten out the Zionist movement."[30]

Needless to say, the tale simplifies a much more complicated trajectory for Jabotinsky. Yet it provides interesting details that deserve notice. For example, Jabotinsky portrays himself as an unwilling leader drawn in by a special request. Furthermore, the job he accepts is not merely to return to politics, but to "straighten out the Zionist movement"—that is, battle the existing Zionist leadership. Furthermore, what is this Hasmonaea youth group in Riga? As one might guess, they were actually "Russian Jews," who until 1917 were located within Russia's borders. Now, although the borders had shifted, they remained Russian; they had never really been integrated into the Latvian culture. They spoke Russian, and their political, social, and cultural orientation came from Russia.[31] One of the future Revisionist leaders, Aharon Zvi Propes, was a member of the group. In fact, Propes had invited Jabotinsky to give a talk, "Jews and Militarism," at a Riga Tarbut Hebrew-language school.[32]

The origins of Revisionism as a political party were shaped in large part by Jabotinsky's relationship with the Russian-Jewish emigration. Few know about it because the history of the party has not yet been adequately researched. Jan Zouplna writes about the distortions of real facts in Revisionist history, locating them especially in later Israeli politics: "Indeed, the ongoing debate about Revisionist Zionism frequently tends to be ahistorical, the most important questions of 'who,' 'when' and 'what' seldom being answered with any precision."[33]

Several points need immediate clarification. For example, HaTzoHar did not aim to be a political party in the narrow sense of having exclusively political goals. Jabotinsky conceived of a broad movement of people who shared particular values, such as hostility to Bolshevism, interest in military power, and knowledge of Russian culture and language. The party emerged from conversations and social interaction. Its first pamphlet, *What Do Revisionists Want?*, "presented the party as a nonpartisan group united in its opposition to the Zionist Organization's leadership."[34] Zouplna insightfully comments: "Unlike the commonly held belief regarding the Revisionists, the original leadership resembled more of a political discussion club than a disciplined party gathered around its leader, with each prominent member freely voicing his opinions regardless of his colleagues' views."[35] This fact explains the ideological heterodoxy of the movement and its lack of hierarchy. Because of the absence of a fixed organizational structure, the movement was in fact focused on Jabotinsky himself, but it also tolerated diverse opinions.

Among the Revisionist movement's weaknesses, perhaps the most serious was Jabotinsky's status. He had attained a modicum of fame, but he was still merely an émigré from Russia, and, like most émigrés, he had no money or deep connections in Western Europe. This fact had serious ramifications. A passage from Jabotinsky's letter to Abraham Recanati from

September 1924 depicts Jabotinsky's (and his colleagues') financial condition, with some added pathos as a fund-raising tool:

> There are now some fifty groups of adherents, from Canada to Harbin in Manchuria, but there is no center. The center we established in Berlin disintegrated for the sad and simple reason that those who headed it were Russian refugees, poor, tired, never sure of how they were going to feed their children tomorrow, or where they were going to be in a fortnight. I am myself after all nothing but a refugee. Since I resigned from the Zionist Executive, I haven't spent a whole month in any one city.... If I succeed in arranging my affairs in such a way as to be able to live somewhere for one year steadily, I will establish a central bureau, try to revive *Rassvet* and organize a movement. If not, I will send a circular letter to all our friends stating plainly and bluntly that life has beaten me, that I am renouncing all Jewish political activity. All this will be decided during the month of October; please have patience until then, and believe me that I am not a man to arouse an enthusiasm that I do not intend to bring to fulfillment; I will go to the very end, or I will not move at all.[36]

* * *

Between 1923 and 1925, Jabotinsky was busy lashing his opponents and formulating a program that would get him elected to the Zionist leadership. In *Rassvet* he published weekly tirades against official Zionism, especially Chaim Weizmann, and he began criticizing Ben-Gurion and the political left in Palestine. Soon after promising to use his freedom from the constraints of the Zionist Executive to tell the truth, Jabotinsky started a campaign against Weizmann's proposal to invite wealthy philanthropists to join the Zionist Executive in exchange for economic aid. Jabotinsky claimed that the idea was antidemocratic (which it was) and had the potential to corrupt the movement by giving preference to the wealthy. Jabotinsky spewed his ire: "It is difficult to write about it calmly. Three generations of Zionism kept the movement clean of sleazy bait. In our time we did not permit arguments from antisemitism to be heard in order not to debase the movement, to destroy its pure idealistic pathos. Now it's all swept away; the ideology of the bribe as the main political method is gradually being reestablished."[37]

Jabotinsky's favorite rhetorical devices are present in his criticism of Weizmann. He portrayed Weizmann's compromises with Britain less as an intentional betrayal than the mistake of a callow negotiator. In negotiating, he explained, the one who is less generous emerges as the winner. Say we are dealing with a piece of land. The one who concedes from the start that both sides have reasonable claims would support a 50/50 division. The other party rejects the first side's claims fully. The judge then conducts a compromise. Each is asked to give up part of his claim. The first party gets 25 percent and the second party 75 percent. This is the case with Palestine and the Arabs, Jabotinsky insisted. Weizmann could only get 25 percent of what he wanted because he started out too conciliatory.

Walter Laqueur debunks Jabotinsky's argument that Zionist leaders merely needed to have a frank talk with Britain; that they never tried hard enough, or weren't honest enough. In fact, Weizmann did register complaints and tried to cajole and trade favors, but he was unable to coax Britain's government into giving more than it was offering. To a large degree, Jabotinsky's assertion that Britain would give more if only it were asked—which he repeated often—was a red herring. It provoked indignation but had no basis in reality.[38] Laqueur writes,

> His [Jabotinsky's] analysis of the weaknesses of the line his colleagues were taking, especially in the foreign political field, was forceful if usually somewhat exaggerated. But he had no alternative to offer, other than the promise that if given the opportunity he would achieve better results. At the Fourteenth Zionist Congress he was challenged by his critics to say what he would use to bring pressure to bear on Britain. He replied that he was neither a friend nor an enemy of Britain but that he knew that force was not needed to persuade a civilized people like the British. He could not tell them in advance how he would convince them; nor would Herzl have been able to give such information to confess. The main things were that the demands of the Zionists were logical and consistent and should be pressed forcefully.[39]

Jabotinsky's dissatisfaction with Weizmann extended to the British high commissioner, Herbert Samuel. Like many others, Jabotinsky placed his confidence in Samuel because he was a Jew and a Zionist, but Samuel was first and foremost a British official and was pulled in many directions at once.[40] Jabotinsky felt rage toward Samuel: "The project of establishing an Arab Agency in contrast to the Jewish Agency was proposed to the Arabs by Mr. Samuel and rejected by them; a project that contains elements that in its anti-Zionist tendency exceeds all the earlier plans of this administrator."[41] Although Jabotinsky criticized Herbert Samuel in print, he said that he wanted to resist "personalizing the debate."[42] What he was doing, he claimed, was helpfully correcting Britain's mistaken policies.[43]

During this time, Jabotinsky began attacking Ben-Gurion and the Zionist political left. Disdain for radicalism generally, and the Soviet Union in particular, prompted a rightward shift. He believed that antagonism between economic classes was dangerous for the Yishuv. At this point in its development, the Yishuv's primary goal was to stimulate immigration; any activity that hurt the economy and frightened away investment had to be curbed. Thus, Jabotinsky favored arbitration over strikes. If workers had grievances or wanted higher pay, their case should go to arbitration, where the interests of each side would be respected and neither side could destroy the other. Because Revisionists were often willing to work during strikes, they were seen as "toadying" to the bosses. Fist fighting between supporters of Revisionism and Labor Zionism occurred with some frequency in Palestine in the mid-1920s.[44]

Jabotinsky railed against collectivism in the Yishuv in such articles as "Leftists" and "The Enemy of the Workers."[45] He claimed that the socialist movement in the country had been infected with Soviet ideology. Such rot, he argued, found its first expression in the Yishuv's hostility to the Fourth Aliyah, the shopkeepers and clerks from Poland and elsewhere who disdained socialism. "This is not the viewpoint of a colonist, this is the hostility of a storeowner to a 'competitor.' So they write me from Palestine. 'They hate the competitor because he eclipsed yesterday's Ben-Yehuda, and it threatens to end with the reallocation of the budget.' One doubts that any of the workers' leaders would dare argue with the accuracy of this observation."[46]

Jabotinsky was concerned that the Zionist leadership in Palestine was moving further to the left. He wrote,

> Already in 1922 Mr. Ben-Gurion said at one congress that the socialism of Palestinian workers emerges only from their Zionism: they think that it is unthinkable to create a Jewish Palestine any other way. "Accelerate immigration," he said. "That is the only concern that defines our activity. Our task is not to build this or that form of society in the name of abstract ideals of justice, but to find a real solution to the Zionist problem. . . . In this sense we are not socialists and not communists, but Zionists." For a leader of the workers to repeat these words now would be hypocrisy.[47]

What had changed? Achdut ha-Avoda, with its control of the Histadrut, gave preference to its own workers over the agricultural workers from Yemen and non-Histadrut workers from Poland. Jabotinsky opined, "I call these tactics political degeneracy, and this psychology—collective corruption. If this is the true, once-and-for-all-time, the objectively inevitable physiognomy of the workers' movement in Palestine, then I am really its enemy and am proud of the name."[48]

Jabotinsky's attitude toward the Zionist left did not differ demonstrably from his criticism of Weizmann. Jabotinsky maintained that Ben-Gurion had his heart in the right place, but was too timid. He predicted that Zionism's success under "leftist" leadership would be minimal, just as under Weizmann, because neither was prepared to fight tooth and nail for Zionism. All the slogans about "building the land and being built by it" were nothing but a smokescreen for inactivity. Jabotinsky gave mocking appreciation in his article "Leftists":

> Those we call "leftists" could be the best among Zionists. It's not Zionism that is being replaced now; in its place we have what was called in the old days love for Palestine, but what it is now common to call "construction of the land": a dangerous term, because, after all, our task does not lie in "building the land," but in turning the land into a land with a Jewish majority. We forgot about this and so, in the period 1920–1923, the joy that accompanied the growth of Tel Aviv and the Jezreel Valley eclipsed, in our eyes, the basic fact that the percentage of the Jewish population did not grow at all at this time. This aberration of the "leftists" is expressed particularly clearly. Therefore, it is impossible to call them the best of the Zionists. But unarguably, they are the best of the Choveve-Tsion of the latest slogan.[49]

Jabotinsky worried that Socialism would mean the end of Zionism. The current policies would cause stagnation; only individual self-interest could motive people to relocate to Palestine. Socialism might inspire a few idealists, but it wouldn't make a real difference. Therefore, while Jabotinsky was in agreement that the Zionist collective funds (Keren Kayemet and Keren Hayesod) served a salutary function, they alone could not bring about a Jewish Palestine. Only the opportunity for private investment and profit, and the safety and security of person and property, would achieve that goal. Although Jabotinsky staunchly defended capitalism, he was not, in fact, a fan of the system, which created huge disparities in wealth. In the early 1920s, he described his appreciation for a kind of beneficent syndicalism that guaranteed a minimum income.[50] Nevertheless, he strongly supported private initiative, profit, and property.[51]

Although Jabotinsky was perhaps unfair in comparing Achdut ha-Avoda to the Bund, circa 1905, he was not wrong to conclude that the political left in the Yishuv was hostile to private initiative. According to Anita Shapira, members of the Yishuv had a pejorative term for such a person, "nepman," which connoted a type of "speculator in Russia that was readily used to criticize the newcomers of the Fourth Aliyah in Palestine."[52] Whereas groups that united Zionism and Socialism, such as Achdut ha-Avoda, emphasized class conflict and favored the Jewish working class, one needs to remember the context of the time and the perception that many Jewish socialists sympathized with Bolshevism. Shapira writes, "Ahdut Ha-Avodah, the major labor party in the Yishuv, considered itself—as did specifically Third Aliyah groups such as the Labor Brigade—to be closer to the revolutionary than the reformist wing of socialism. Impatience with, and disbelief in, evolutionary processes came to characterize both the leadership and the rank and file and were, to a certain extent, substitutes for any ordered body of dogma—something neither was prepared to accept. Their revolutionary impulse was expressed in their belief in 'Zionism on a grand scale' (*Tsiyonut gedolah*), in socialism here and now."[53] These beliefs found expression in the establishment of the Histadrut in 1921, which was viewed by Ben-Gurion, among others, as a general "commune."[54] The Histadrut, referred to as a labor exchange, was an institution that distributed work among Jews in Palestine and also provided health insurance, personal loans, and other benefits.

For Ben-Gurion, the Soviet model offered a powerful example of effective leadership. The chairman made decisions; the institutions executed them; thus were goals accomplished. In this way, society's forces could be unleashed and, in "Soviet-speak," time could be accelerated, a new dynamism released, and nature harnessed.

Jabotinsky connected Achdut ha-Avoda with Bolshevism and the lamentable fate of Soviet Jewry. Jabotinsky railed against the forced collectivization of the Soviet population and the repression of Jews and traditional Jewish life. On the other side, Jabotinsky was already being criticized for his supposed hostility to "the worker." He suspected that some of the animosity came from his opponents within Zionism, but perhaps also Soviet sympathizers, who remembered the Slavinsky Affair, in which Jabotinsky had sided with the Ukrainians against the Red Army. In any case, battle lines were drawn, and the ideologies of the Zionist right and left were now well defined. Each side questioned the other's motives. Compromise between the two became more difficult.

* * *

Before establishing his new political party, Jabotinsky unveiled Revisionism's program. In "Political Offensive," an article from 1924, he announced his plan:

> This program is not complicated, but the logical thread can get twisted in a lengthy exposition. Therefore, it is useful to review:

> The aim of Zionism is a Jewish state.
> The territory is on both sides of the Jordan.
> The method is mass colonization.
> The financial system is a national loan.

These four points cannot be realized without the sanction of the international community, and therefore the task of the moment is as follows:

> First, a new political offensive.
> Second, the full capitalization of the Jewish Colonization Bank.
> Third, the militarization of Jewish youth in Palestine and the diaspora.[55]

The program embodied several political principles: the Legion idea, private enterprise, and a rejection of socialism. The sine qua non of his political program was the Legion; Jews needed to form it, at their own expense, to study military strategy, march like soldiers, and practice shooting. Jabotinsky believed that security was essential to a Jewish future in Palestine. In *Revisionist Principles* (1929), he wrote: "The Jews shall have their share in the defense of the country. The Jewish Regiment, which existed in 1917–1921, shall be reestablished as an integral and permanent part of the Palestine Garrison."[56]

In "Legion," an article from 1924, he describes the consequences of a weak Jewish military presence:

> Finally, in a moral context, the status of the *Schutzjuden* humiliates us and lowers our prestige in the eyes of the English and the Arabs. The English, knowing from their own history that real colonizers never use a foreign army, are accustomed to look upon Jews as an element that is not entirely suitable for real colonization, and therefore view our entire work as an artificial, hothouse project. The Arabs, on the other hand, have formed an impression that is even more humiliating for us. And since our main political strength lies in our moral potential, the respect for ourselves and our ideal that we can instill in the outside [non-Jewish] world, then that position of being the "defendants" must in the final analysis inevitably lead to a weakening of our political positions.[57]

To ensure the Legion's success, Jabotinsky insisted on five conditions that distinguished a professional force from mere amateurs:

1. An entirely legal status, excluding any danger of war on two fronts.
2. The full possibility of perfecting security technology.
3. Equipment so advanced that no secret enemy-organization [*kontr'-organizatsiia*] would be able to keep up with it.

4. An imposing appearance that would affect the whole population "prophylactically."
5. A system of discipline and control that would guarantee both us and our neighbors protection from possible impropriety or nervous action by individual people.[58]

His vision of political Zionism contained one central idea—a Jewish majority in the land:

> Above all, it is necessary to recall the main truth: the aim of Zionism is the creation of a Jewish state. Of course, the term "state," as has already been explained on our pages, does not imply absolute external sovereignty. Newfoundland is also a state. And the concept "Jewish state" of course does not permit the displacement or oppression of other ethnic groups. But the term "Jewish state" necessarily posits two conditions: first, a Jewish majority in Palestine, and second, sovereignty of the population in all the internal affairs of the country. In this context the old Herzlian term is the only precise and only possible definition of Zionism's aim.[59]

During the 1920s, Jabotinsky gained support only slowly.[60] However, he continued to fulminate against Weizmann and Ben-Gurion, blaming them for Zionism's stagnation. Although some disagreed with his criticisms, many Russian-Jewish émigrés approved of his program, which connected political activism, military preparedness, and pride in oneself, to the struggle for a Jewish homeland.

In addition to Russian émigrés, Jabotinsky was able to attract a sizeable group from Salonica, Greece, because his proreligious attitude, his positions on mass immigration, and his appreciation for craftsmen appealed to the conservative Jews. Esther Benbassa and Aron Rodrigue write:

> It was also within the Mizrahi organization that the core of Salonika Revisionist Zionism was formed. At the beginning of the twenties, disagreements emerged between supporters of the Mizrahi movement and the General Zionists.... All these factors favored the creation of the Revisionist movement in Salonika, which emerged in 1924. Abraham Recanati, head of the Mizrahi, was one of the founders and its president. He had already published articles by Vladimir Jabotinsky, spiritual father of the Revisionist movement, in the French-language paper *Pro-Israël*, founded in 1917, which subsequently became a pillar of this new tendency. This paper had also intervened with the Greek and British authorities in 1918 with a view to enrolling 300 volunteers in the Jewish Legion founded by Jabotinsky.[61]

One can discern Jabotinsky's attitude toward Sephardic Jewry from his letter to Recanati. The Sephardic world, unlike the Ashkenazi world, does not try to "make things more complicated." The Sephardic Jew understands reality:

> Sephardic Jews have made the impression on me of good reason and clear vision. Permit me therefore to hope that today your readers do not need a book of eloquence in order to understand that two times two is four; that when we perish in the old ghettos and when we have again acknowledged Palestine as being the right of our national home, we must now demand from the powers the realization of this project and must demand it loudly if we want it. They understand from us that, if we want to be defended against attacks from our enemies, we must provide our own defenders and not ask a Christian nation to take charge of our defense.[62]

In his autobiography, Jabotinsky makes clear his admiration for Sephardic Jewry:

> If reincarnation does exist, and if I were reborn again, and were I to be granted from above permission to choose for myself a nation and race, I would say: "All right, let it be Israel, but please, Sephardi." I fell in love with the Sephardim, perhaps precisely due to those qualities that are ridiculed by their Ashkenazi brothers: their superficiality, which I prefer a thousand times to our cheap deep-mindedness; their inertia, which holds for me a greater appeal than our tendency to pursue every passing fancy; their generations of intellectual passivity, which have preserved their spiritual purity. And regarding cultural vigor, I doubt that a liter of French and Italian education or a ton of Russian mysticism really brings a man closer to the threshold of Western civilization (in my view there exists no other—civilization and Occident are the same thing). In Salonica, Alexandria, and Cairo, you will find a Jewish intelligentsia of the same level as in Warsaw and Riga; and in Italy they surpass that of Paris or Vienna. I am prepared to admit they have one great defect as far as Zionist activity is concerned (although the national idea is more widespread among them, relatively speaking, than it is among us): they have no appetite for conquest in their hearts, no ambition. But these too will awaken in due course.[63]

Although not entirely enthusiastic, Jabotinsky was slowly realizing that Sephardic Jews, not Ashkenazi Jews, were his natural constituency. His Sephardi supporters, with whom he admittedly had only a cursory experience, would develop a complex relationship with him: while they appreciated his ideology, they did not want to remain a permanent opposition. Rather, they wanted to use politics in a more practical way to gain concrete benefits through political alliances. The same cannot be said about Jabotinsky.

* * *

On April 26, 1925, Jabotinsky convened the first conference of the Party of Revisionist Zionists (HaTzoHar) at the Taverne du Panthéon in the Latin Quarter in Paris. His colleagues included other émigrés: Meir Grossman, Joseph Schechtman, and Alexander Kulisher, but also Richard Lichtheim, Abraham Recanati, Abraham Propes, Israel Cohen, Dr. N. Hoffman, Charles Nehama, and many others. Around two hundred people attended. Walter Laqueur describes the new party: "It was not intended as a radical new departure. Not Zionism was to be revised, only its current policies. Revisionism saw itself as the only true heir of the Herzl-Nordau tradition of political Zionism, in contrast to the official Zionist leadership, which, by making concession after concession, had deviated from it. Jabotinsky and his followers were maximalists, claiming not only Palestine for the Jews but 'the gradual transformation of Palestine (including Transjordan) into a self-governing commonwealth under the auspices of an established majority.'"[64]

In his opening speech, Jabotinsky described himself as a "black guest," who appeared at the feast (official Zionist functions) as though he were at a funeral:

> It would be difficult to find a more "inappropriate" moment for such a gathering. Founding congresses are usually organized by dissenters after some kind of big crisis, when the flaws of the system that are causing the discontent suddenly appear, exposed and prominent. We now have an entirely different generation. The Jerusalem celebrations have just ended, and Jews throughout the entire diaspora have responded to them with an extraordinary outburst of joy. The economic situation in Palestine is a good deal better than before. Immigration is holding at a high number. There haven't been any serious attacks on Jews for a long time. Mr. Samuel has become the public darling. The Geneva failure has not had any fundamental ill effects. The American millionaires have agreed to rule over us. The largest federations in Zionism unanimously expressed their delight that the Zionist organization will soon be silenced. Everyone is happy. Under these conditions, you have to feel very sure you are right in order to call for a gathering of dissenters at precisely this point. It is like going to a wedding while dressed in mourning. Mourning dress signifies that the guest in black has no faith in the marriage: the groom is sick, the dowry of the bride exists only in the imagination, they're not in love, the whole celebration is built on an illusion, and it will not end well. . . . All this is true, but the problem is that the guest in black is right.[65]

According to Jabotinsky, a catastrophe was imminent. Zionism in Palestine was nothing other than "a great architectural achievement on the slope of a smoldering volcano; there is the mass illusion that reminds one at times of mass insanity; and, above all, there is the backward, ignorant frivolity of the leaders of the movement and the Yishuv, and around them, shameless flattery, unprecedented sycophancy, and pathetic cowardliness."[66] This assertion reflects Jabotinsky's arrogant certainty (which we have seen before) that he was right, and everyone else was mistaken and foolhardy. Only Jabotinsky was privy to the truth, and only he could be trusted to fix things. His grim predictions inevitably worked to his advantage, since they could be adapted to any situation in Palestine that did not go as well as planned. This proved an effective way to boost his reputation as a leader without achieving anything at all.

Running a political party without assured funding, trying to win support on three continents, trying to elect candidates in local elections—these were daunting tasks. It was far from certain that Jabotinsky was capable of organizing a team and creating a structure that could meet the challenges. The results in initial elections were disappointing, as were the small donations and dues.[67] The establishment of the Revisionist Union did not signify a breakthrough either organizationally or financially. In the elections to the Fourteenth Zionist Congress, in August 1925, the Revisionists gained a single seat (held by Jabotinsky) and that due to an election alliance with the radical Zionists in Palestine. Only after Jabotinsky had been joined by three independent congressmen were the Revisionists able to form a club. The vision of "taking the Zionist movement by storm or establishing an entire movement" would have to be postponed.[68]

Historians have by and large given Jabotinsky low marks as party leader.[69] His strengths lay in rhetoric, agitation, and sparking enthusiasm—not in the prosaic business of running a political party, especially one as geographically diffuse as Revisionism. But geography was only one problem. Another involved Jabotinsky's propensity for sharing power, giving others responsibility over practical affairs so that he could devote himself to intellectual pursuits. That would not necessarily hurt the party, but few of Jabotinsky's allies understood how to run a party organization. Jabotinsky was also naïve (or irresponsible) about fundraising. In fact, he never identified a stable funding source for Revisionism, despite having criticized Weizmann for inviting unelected plutocrats to the Zionist Executive. If the World Zionist Organization lacked the funding to function properly without courting non-Zionists, why did Jabotinsky believe that a renegade group would do better? Revisionism never had sufficient resources to fulfill all, or even most, of the goals that Jabotinsky formulated for it.

Still, his message had an audience: others were dissatisfied with the pace of immigration, economic development, security in Palestine, and the leftist ideology that Zionists in the Yishuv often spouted. But money, or lack of it, was again an issue. Many of Revisionism's leaders were penniless émigrés. Jabotinsky wrote to Oscar Gruzenberg, the famed defender of Beilis, describing an early organizational meeting: "There were few of us. Ten people came. Another six could not come because of visas or money. Besides Riga, Paris, and Tel Aviv, in my view there were only one or two [representatives]. If only we could send people to travel, we could create an organization of thousands. But we are penniless. But rarely did we feel as good internally. The *niveau* [level] was good, the meeting—intelligent and honest, a serious ascent. There was interest among the non-Zionists, a good public—it was the best of our meetings."[70] Although the Revisionist party began slowly, it would gradually gain support beyond émigrés from Russia. Its new constituencies included Jews in Palestine from Yemen; members of the Fourth Aliyah from Poland; religious Jews who despised labor Zionism's hostility to religion; and certain youth groups that vaunted militarism.[71]

In the mid-1920s, as he shifted rightward, Jabotinsky realized that several countries in Europe had popular right-wing movements whose ideology had been shaped in response to a resurgent left.[72] In previous years, leftist revolutions (the Spartacus League and Communists [Béla Kun]) had been suppressed in Germany and Hungary. Right-wing groups justified their actions by citing fear of the Soviet Communist "menace," which they labeled "Judeo-Kommuna" or "Judeo-Marxism."[73]

One hallmark of the radical right was the idolization, even the apotheosis, of the leader. Adherents conceived of the leader as the embodiment of the hopes, yearnings, virtues, and expectations of the group. He was a kind of father figure who told difficult truths, acted toughly, and punished enemies. He should embody the general will of society, but he need not be popular among all sections of society. Often, supporters believed that some parts of society were corrupt or perfidious, and therefore democracy was not the most effective means of selecting the leader or creating political legitimacy. Jabotinsky was viewed as a representative of the radical right primarily because of his emphasis on militarism and his consistent hostility to socialism and leftist politics.[74] On the military question, he insisted that Jews should have the legal right to an armed force, and he believed that an officially sanctioned army would be intimidating, and thus prevent wars. At the same time, he encouraged average people—individuals, everyone—to learn to shoot guns and be prepared to defend themselves if necessary.[75]

Jabotinsky modeled himself in part on Józef Piłsudski, the leader of Poland. Piłsudski was a socialist-turned-nationalist who embodied the principle that the nation's will was expressed through its leader. He took power in a coup d'état in 1925. He inspired all age groups and economic classes in Poland, and won the people's allegiance by standing above day-to-day bickering and quotidian politics. He was relatively moderate, opposed to extreme nationalists and antisemites. He had come to power as a military leader who led the country in its war with Russia; his rise continued, in the early 1920s, when he united with the political right to consolidate power and keep radicals in check.[76] Jabotinsky admired his military origins and his transformation from the head of a party into the representative of a united Poland.

There is evidence that Jabotinsky knew about Mussolini's nascent regime.[77] He saw both positive and negative in fascist Italy.[78] The same, of course, cannot be said about Hitler and fascism in Germany, which Jabotinsky abhorred and fought tirelessly.[79] However, to understand Jabotinsky's position vis-à-vis the radical right, it is vital to distinguish between how the radical right of the 1920s was perceived, and how we perceive fascism today. It is vital to remember that fascism was a "normal" political philosophy in the first quarter of the twentieth century, even if people find themselves unable to evaluate it objectively today. Zeev Sternhell, for example, has written, "Indeed, to think of fascism as a phenomenon that is inseparable from the mainstream of European history and to consider the fascist ideology as a European ideology that took root and developed not only in Italy and, in a very violent and extreme form, in Germany but also elsewhere can lead to parallels and comparisons that, for many people, are still difficult to accept."[80]

For Jabotinsky, the radical right offered solutions to a number of seemingly intractable problems in the 1920s. As nation-states emerged out of the collapse of the major empires of Europe, the newly formed governments could rely on rightists to win over the population, support "national interests," and oppose socialism and communism. Fascism, with its leadership principle, hostility to democracy and leftism, admiration of violence, and valorization of nationalism, became quite popular in Eastern European states like Romania and Poland. Already in the 1920s, sizeable groups of Europeans were turning away from the nineteenth-century ideals of democracy, progress, and tolerance.

One cannot easily discern whether Jabotinsky arrived at his positions by an unconscious path or whether he was intentionally imitating models that he had encountered. One would have trouble believing (and there is no evidence for it) that Jabotinsky admired the *Freikorps* in Germany, for example, or that he based his militaristic youth movement, Betar, on that group.[81] The *Freikorps* were antidemocratic, antiliberal, anti-Semitic, and did not hesitate to use murder to further its goals.[82] At the same time, politicians throughout Europe saw that decommissioned former soldiers, veterans groups, and unemployed young men could be inspired by a nationalist message and spurred into action. This was right-wing politics from the bottom up, anarchistic and only partially controlled.

Like right-wing organizers everywhere, Jabotinsky brought together veterans of the Legion, and he spread his ideas at anniversary gatherings. Among paramilitary groups, he proclaimed his admiration for the Sokol youth movement in Czechoslovakia, a civic and sports club typical of its day in Central Europe, in which organizers emphasized hiking, marching, and marksmanship as well as discipline and camaraderie.[83] Although Sokol youth were identified with right-leaning politics, enthusiasm for nationalism, and the struggle against Communism, they did not share the *Freikorps*' tendency for violence, antidemocratic struggle, and fierce antisemitism. Rather, a typical Sokol member was often of school age and viewed himself as a representative of law and order rather than its opponent. Jabotinsky imitated the Sokol group when he designed the Betar youth movement.[84]

In the late 1920s, he began to wear a military uniform, and the Betar youth were dressed in brown shirts. They claimed that their attire was not modeled on the Italian fascists; nonetheless, their general attitudes, behavior, and appearances had origins in the radical right. The young men and women were imbued with the ideal of "*hadar*" (roughly, "gentlemanly behavior"), a word Jabotinsky invested with special meaning. For boys, *hadar* meant military training and respect for discipline, but also chivalry, good manners, and personal hygiene. Betar girls were given the traditional (but still important) tasks of cooking, bearing children, and raising a family.

One important aspect of *hadar* was displaying Jewish honor to the non-Jewish world. Anita Shapira explains, "In his endeavor to act with total and complete candor and always say what he actually meant without any concern about expediency, one can discern something of that legacy of that deep aspiration to restore lost Jewish dignity. . . . The element of *hadar* in his educational thinking was a direct continuation of the approaches calling for Jewish action that would engender respect, so that Gentiles would no longer accuse Jews of shameful shrewdness and cunning."[85]

* * *

Jabotinsky was viewed as contradictory. While he appeared to adopt ideas of the radical right, he also condemned those ideas in his statements. In 1926, he wrote:

> For it is not hostility to Jews that lies at the base of fascist and quasi-fascist attitudes (it does not play a role in Spain, Italy, or Greece), but precisely the attempt to conceive a new political ethics. The old political ethics bequeathed by the nineteenth century was based on freedom of opinion, the equality of all people, and the primacy of universal suffrage; in particular, it was based on the fact that state power is simply a function of the elected representatives of the people, only as long as they are elected and not a minute longer, not the prerogative of the divinely chosen, as if "leaders" could be distinguished by a special sign. This system has its flaws, and sometimes the flaws are even irritating. Therefore impatient people proclaimed that "democracy is bankrupt." Of course, in a certain sense democracy has become bankrupt—just like all great doctrines in this imperfect world. Science has also become bankrupt, as it still hasn't liberated humanity from as much as a toothache; philosophy has become bankrupt, as it still doesn't know what space is; religion is also bankrupt, as it has never educated a truly moral person. All civilization consists of bankruptcy; humanity and history are bankrupt, and so on and so forth. One can continue this rhetoric for another three pages and even for three hundred, and it will nonetheless remain rhetoric.[86]

In contrast to this critique that fascism equals nihilism, Jabotinsky offered as his credo the old virtues of the nineteenth century: individualism, equality, democracy, and freedom. These principles comprised the only true panacea, the building blocks of a prosperous, happy society. "We admit our adherence to the old beliefs: we prefer the long, well-traveled roads. We believe in the equality of all people, that in an election both the fool and the wise man should have the same vote, that the prime minister is an elected official, not a 'leader,' that freedom of speech and assembly are superior to the salvation of the fatherland because—with the exception of catastrophic times of war, earthquakes or pestilence—in this freedom is the duty to save the fatherland."[87]

However, Jabotinsky's shift to the right—if that is the appropriate expression—occurred earlier, as early as World War I, in fact, when he and Meir Grossman decided to pursue an "activist" program. His shift intensified in 1923, with his endorsement of militarism in the Iron Wall articles. The Legion experience and his resignation from the Executive demonstrated that extreme political actions and gestures could forge a path to leadership, whereas following the pack could not. Jabotinsky realized that the Zionist political landscape was already occupied by labor Zionists from the Second Aliyah—Ben-Gurion and Berl Katznelson—and general Zionists—Chaim Weizmann, Chaim Sokoloff, and Menachem Ussishkin. If Jabotinsky wanted a following, he had to claim his own political territory. The political right offered an open space.

Since Jabotinsky's *confession de foi*—love for liberalism—belied his actions, one should regard his statements with skepticism. They might be empty, mere rhetoric, part of his strategy to appear liberal and therefore retain the loyalty of older Russian émigrés and centrists, while support grew among young rightists and sympathizers of fascism. The group of activists around Abba Achimeir in Palestine can serve as an example. Jabotinsky genuinely viewed himself as a liberal who was misdiagnosed by enemies and friends. Some neophytes wanted him to play the role of Mussolini, abrogating democracy in the party and serving as Revisionism's supreme leader.

The jury is still out as to whether Jabotinsky should be labeled a fascist. He was not a fascist like Hitler—that's for sure. And he never had real power in a government. In his writings, he resembled Pilsudski or Admiral Miklòs Horthy—he appeared comfortable emphasizing militarism, nationalism, and discipline. Nonetheless, one should remember not to view Revisionism, at least in its early period, as a break with the general Zionist movement. Such a break occurred much later, in 1935. Nonetheless, as an irony of fate, Jabotinsky initially wielded the term fascist against his enemies; he used it to describe Weizmann's antidemocratic proposal to increase the size of the Executive by inviting wealthy donors into its membership. By fascist, he meant Mussolini's Italy and the negative kind of discipline, populism, and indifference to humanist values. He thought of himself as concerned with humanist values, and to an extent he was; however, his concern did not extend to the Arabs, enemies of the Zionist enterprise.

* * *

Notes

1. A number of Russian Zionist factions were established at the same time. "Sympathizers of Zionism, emigrants from the former Russian Empire, created in Germany an organization of Russian Zionists, a Federation of Russian-Ukrainian Zionists, the Herzl Jewish-Zionist Club, and Union 'Beit-Vaad' (Group). Tarbut (Culture) published *Rassvet*, edited by Sh. Gepshtein, and V. E. Jabotinsky after him." Oleg Budnitsky and Aleksandra Polan, *Russko-evreiskii Berlin, 1920–1941* (Moscow: Novoe Literaturnoe Obozrenie, 2013), 172.
2. Marc Raeff, *Russia Abroad: A Cultural History of the Russian Emigration, 1919–1939* (Oxford: Oxford University Press, 1990), 37.
3. Evgenii Kulischer [Kulisher], *Europe on the Move: War and Population Changes, 1917–1947* (New York: Columbia University Press, 1948), 56.
4. Mark Tolts, "Migration since World War I," in *The YIVO Encyclopedia of Jews in Eastern Europe*, ed. Gershom D. Hundert, 2 vols. (New Haven, CT: Yale University Press, 2008), 1435.
5. Budnitsky and Polan, *Russko-evreiskii Berlin*, 172, 175.
6. Vladimir Jabotinsky, *Samson Nazarei* (Paris, 1926).
7. Iosif [Joseph] Schechtman, "Emigrantskii sionizm, part III," *Rassvet* 2 (January 14, 1923): 9.
8. Ibid.
9. Moshe Kleinman, "Ot 'Rassveta' do 'Rassveta'," *Rassvet* 1 (April 16, 1922): 5.
10. Alexander Kulisher and Nikolai Sorin, "Russkaia demokratiia i natsional'nyi vopros," *Rassvet* 5 (1922): 6–7.
11. Oleg Budnitsky, "Berlin Debates: The Jews and the Russian Revolution," *Jewish Thought, Utopia, and Revolution*, ed. Elena Namli et al. (Amsterdam: Rodopi, 2014), 25.
12. Kulisher and Sorin, "Russkaia demokratiia," 7.
13. Iosif [Joseph] Schechtman, "Sovetskaia Rossiia, Sionizm i Izrael," in *Kniga o russkom evreistve, 1917–1967*. Jerusalem: Gesharim, 2002, 325.
14. Budnitsky and Polian, *Russko-evreiskii Berlin*, 25.
15. Ibid., 172–175.
16. Shimon Markish, "Quand Vladimir Jabotinsky était parisien: *Le rassviet*, revue sioniste-révisioniste en langue russe," trans. Boris Czerny and Catherine Nicault, *Les Belles lettres: Archives Juives* 1, no. 36 (2003): 72.
17. Daniel Heller has a point nonetheless: "Bearing the name of the Zionist Organization's flagship newspaper in Russia prior to the First World War, *Rassvet* was able to gain a following among Russian Jewish émigrés in Paris and Berlin. The newspaper was, however, merely a shadow of its former self. It never achieved the status, circulation or financial success that Jabotinsky had envisioned for it. Ultimately, he was forced to earn his living by writing articles in Yiddish for newspapers elsewhere." Daniel Heller, "The Rise of the Zionist Right: Polish Jews and the Betar Youth Movement, 1922-1935" (PhD diss., Stanford University, 2012), 46.
18. Mikhail Gindin, Mikhail Aleinikov, and Joseph Schechtman, eds., "16 aprelia 1922," *Rassvet* 1 (April 16, 1922): 1.
19. Ibid.
20. Iosif Schechtman, "Emigrantskii sionizm," *Rassvet* 1 (Jan. 14, 1923), 10.
21. Iosif Schechtman, "Emigrantskii sionizm: part II," *Rassvet* 2 (January 7, 1923): 7.
22. Tolts, "Migration," 1435.

23. See Mina Grauer, ed., *Ha-itonut shel ha-tenua ha-revizionistit ba-shanim 1925–1948* (Tel Aviv: Machon Jabotinsky, 2000), 7.

24. Joseph B. Schechtman and Yehuda Benari, *History of the Revisionist Movement, 1925–1930* (Tel Aviv: Hadar, 1970), 15–16.

25. Shimon Markish describes the four Jewish newspapers with the name *Rassvet* as linked into a longer tradition.

> In the history of Russian-Jewish journalism this name is the most popular one used most often. The first [newspaper] in the history was called it (Odessa, 1860–1861) and so did a weekly that came out in Petersburg and lasted a bit longer than its Odessa namesake—1879–1883. The third *Rassvet*, also a weekly and also in the capital, was a resoundingly Zionist instrument and survived even longer than the second, 1907–1915, when tsarist censors closed it; then there was another year, 1917–1918, when the new Soviet power finally finished it off. And finally, the fourth *Rassvet*, the émigré one which is mentioned in our title. At first it appeared in Berlin for two full years (1922–1924), and from December 1924 to December 1934 it was published in Paris. "Zhabotinskii v parizhskom *Rassvete*," *Lechaim* 10, no. 114 (October 2001), accessed June 4, 2016, https://lechaim.ru/ARHIV/114/markish.htm.

26. M. Kleinman, "Ot 'Rassveta' do 'Rassveta'," 2 (April 16, 1923): 4. "The Petersburg *Rassvet* shared the fate of its Jewish brothers and the entire Russian non-Communist press. After the general destruction of the press, Russian publications still appeared, now and then, having attempted to buy their right to existence through the hypocritical acknowledgement of 'the Soviet program.' There was not a single Jewish publication that did not pay this price."

27. "Berlin," Rassvet (16 April 1922): 2.

28. Ibid.

29. Iu. Brutzkus, "V. Zhabotinskii v russkom sionizme," *Rassvet* 42 (October 19, 1930): 9.

30. Joseph Schechtman, *The Life and Times of Vladimir Jabotinsky: Fighter and Prophet, The Last Years.* Silver Spring: Eshel Books, 1956, 31.

31. Daniel Heller, *Jabotinsky's Children: Polish Jews and the Rise of Right-Wing Zionism* (Princeton, NJ: Princeton University Press, 2017), 34.

32. Ibid. Jabotinsky was a big supporter of Hebrew-language study in the Diaspora. Furthering knowledge of Hebrew was part of a large project and one should regard his work on a world atlas in Hebrew in this context. The atlas was published in 1925. See Adam Rovner, "Jewish Geographies: Jabotinsky and Modernism," *Partial Answers* 15, no. 2 (2017).

33. Jan Zouplna, "Revisionist Zionism: Image, Reality and the Quest for Historical Narrative," *Middle Eastern Studies* 44, no. 1 (2008).

34. Heller, *Jabotinsky's Children*, 39.

35. Zouplna, "Revisionist Zionism," 5.

36. Quoted in Schechtman and Benari, *History of the Revisionist Movement*, 26.

37. Vladimir Jabotinsky, "De Profundis," *Rassvet* 27 (July 8, 1923): 3.

38. Walter Laqueur, *A History of Zionism* (London, 1972), 347.

39. Ibid., 346.

40. Bernard Wasserstein, *The British in Palestine: The Mandatory Government and the Arab-Jewish Conflict, 1917–1929*, 2nd ed. (London: Blackwell, 1991), 110.

41. Vladimir Jabotinsky, "V. Zh.," *Rassvet* 38–39 (October 21, 1923): 4.

42. Vladimir Jabotinsky, "Oppozitsiia i voina," *Rassvet* 5 (March 2, 1924): 2.

43. Ibid.

44. Anita Shapira, *Ha-Maavak ha-nikhzav: 'Avoda ivrit,' 1929–1939* (Tel Aviv: Univeristat-Tel Aviv, 1977), 193–197.
45. Vladimir Jabotinsky, "Levye," *Rassvet* 4 (January 25, 1925), 2–3; Vladimir Jabotinsky, "Vrag rabochikh," *Rassvet* 31 (February 8, 1925), 2–6.
46. Jabotinsky, "Vrag rabochikh," 4. "Ben-Yehuda" here refers to the street in Jerusalem, which is even today a central artery of commerce.
47. Ibid., 3.
48. Ibid., 5.
49. Jabotinsky, "Levye," 2.
50. He admired Popper-Lynkeus's economic theories. See Stanislawski, *Zionism and the Fin de Siècle: Cosmopolitanism and Nationalism from Nordau to Jabotinsky* (Berkeley: University of California Press, 2001), 214–215.
51. Joseph Heller, "Zeev Jabotinsky and the Revisionist Revolt against Materialism: In Search of a Worldview," *Jewish History* 12, no. 2 (Fall 1998): 64.
52. Anita Shapira, "Black Night–White Snow: Attitudes of the Palestinian Labor Movement to the Russian Revolution, 1917–29," in *Studies in Contemporary Jewry* 4 (1988): 158.
53. Ibid., 145.
54. Ibid., 152.
55. Vladimir Jabotinsky, "Politicheskaia offentsiva," *Rassvet* 8–9 (March 2, 1924): 3.
56. *Basic Principles of Revisionism: Compiled from the Resolutions of the First, Second, and Third World Conferences of the Union of Zionists-Revisionists* (London: Union of Zionists-Revisionists, 1929), 7.
57. Vladimir Jabotinsky, "Legion, stat'ia pervaia," *Rassvet* 10 (June 6, 1924), 3. "Schutzjuden" (German) refers to the Jewish intercessor with the government.
58. Ibid.
59. Jabotinsky, "Oppozitsiia i voina," 1.
60. Schechtman and Benari, *History of the Revisionist Movement*, 82–83.
61. Esther Benbassa and Aron Rodrigue, *Sephardi Jewry: A History of the Judeo-Spanish Community, 14th–20th Centuries* (Berkeley: University of California Press, 1995), 140–141.
62. Vladimir Jabotinsky to Abraham Recanati, April 14, 1924, Jabotinsky Institute Archives.
63. Vladimir Jabotinsky, *Story of My Life*, eds. Brian Horowitz and Leonid Katsis (Detroit: Wayne State University Press, 2017), 99.
64. Laqueur, *History of Zionism*, 347. Incidentally, Yitzhak Tabenkin also claimed Transjordan for Zionism.
65. Vladimir Jabotinsky, "Chernyi gost' (iz rechi, proiznesennoi pri otkrytii konferentsii Sionistov-Revizionistov," *Rassvet* 18 (May 3, 1925): 4.
66. Ibid., 5.
67. Schechtman and Benari, *History of the Revisionist Movement*, 74.
68. Ibid., 16.
69. Heller, *Jabotinsky's Children*, 11.
70. Jabotinsky to Oscar Gruzenberg, May 6, 1925; Vladimir Zhabotinskii, "Pis'ma Oskaru Gruzenbergu," publication of Kh. Firin (Viktor Kel'ner), *Vestnik Evreiskogo Universiteta v Moskve* 2, no. 6 (1994): 222–223.
71. Colin Shindler, *The Rise of the Israeli Right: From Odessa to Hebron* (Cambridge: Cambridge University Press, 2015), 79–87, 154.

72. For one example, that of France, see Zeev Sternhell, *Neither Right nor Left: Fascist Ideology in France* (Berkeley: University of California Press, 1986), 90–118.

73. Henry Abramson, "Two Jews, Three Opinions: Politics in the Shtetl at the Turn of the Twentieth Century," in *The Shtetl: New Evaluations*, ed. Steven T. Katz (New York: New York University Press, 2007), 94.

74. Vladimir Jabotinsky, "Militarism," *Haynt* (January 25, 1929). See Shindler, *The Rise of the Israeli Right*, 88–96.

75. Vladimir Jabotinsky, "Aufn pripichek . . . " *Haynt* (October 15, 1931): 9–10.

76. Wacław Jędrzejewicz, *Pilsudski: A Life for Poland* (New York: Hippocrene Books, 1995), 95.

77. Yosef Nedava, "Be-sa'ar ha-yamim," in *Ha-ish sh'haita et ha-zarem*, ed. Abba Achimeir (Tel Aviv, 1987), 10.

78. Vladimir Jabotinsky, "Wegen Avanturizm," *Haynt*, February 26, 1932, 5.

79. *Blue-White Papers: Survey of the Revisionist Program* (London: London Offices of the Union of Zionist Revisionists, 1935), 6.

80. Zeev Sternhell, *The Birth of Fascist Ideology. From Cultural Rebellion to Political Revolution* (Princeton, NJ: Princeton University Press, 1994), ix.

81. Betar would be established only in 1927.

82. Robert G. Waite, *Vanguard of Nazism: The Free Corps Movement in Postwar Germany, 1919–1923* (New York: Norton, 1969).

83. Stanislav Holubec, "'We Bring Order, Discipline, Western European Democracy, and Culture to this Land of Former Oriental Chaos and Disorder.' Czech Perceptions of Sub-Carpathian Rus' and its Modernization in the 1920s," in *Mastery and Lost Illusions: Space and Time in the Modernization of Eastern and Central Europe*, ed. Wlodzimierz Borodziej et al. (Oldenbourg: De Gruyter, 2014), 235.

84. Heller, *Jabotinsky's Children*, 44.

85. Anita Shapira, *Land and Power: The Zionist Resort to Force, 1881–1948* (Stanford, CA: Stanford University Press, 1999), 160.

86. Vladimir Jabotinsky, "Dnevnik," *Rassvet* 3 (January 17, 1926): 1.

87. Ibid.

9

RUSSIA IN THE LIFE AND WORK OF JABOTINSKY AFTER 1925

* * *

AFTER 1925, JABOTINSKY DEVOTED HIMSELF TO PARTY WORK, organization, negotiation, fundraising, and the formation of policy. He entered a protracted period that was characterized by intraparty and internecine struggles. In the decade from 1925 to 1935, the Russian aspects of his career diminished and became obscured by other elements. He interacted with different kinds of people who now constituted a majority in the Revisionist movement: young Jews from Poland, Palestine, and the Arab lands—Jews with religious commitment (in contrast to secular Russians of his own generation).

By the mid-1920s, Jabotinsky was associated with the political right. His exclamations about the need for an Iron Wall to crush Palestinian Arabs, his consistent attacks on the Zionist left, and his praise for Betar, the Revisionist youth group devoted to military training, led many to link Jabotinsky with Benito Mussolini and Józef Pilsudski, individuals who had emerged from the war as heroes and who took the reins of power to abolish political corruption and national decay. In 1935, Jabotinsky took his Revisionists out of the World Zionist Organization and established his own alternative, the New Zionist Organization. It was an act of unmitigated hubris, with some desperation thrown in, because it was clear that his Revisionist Party would never gain enough votes within the movement to be anything but a permanent opposition.

During these years, Jabotinsky fought unflattering images; he especially did not like to be called a dictator. In 1926, his novel (written in Russian) *Samson Nazarite* appeared; in 1936, he published a novel in Russian entitled *The Five* and an autobiography in Hebrew, *Story of My Life*, in which he offered a more flattering image of himself than the press, which often mocked and derided him.[1] Political rivals accused him of being a hothead, a rabble rouser, and a fascist.[2] These charges helped earn him the reputation as a right-wing extremist. Some of his own supporters—Abba Achimeir, for example—demanded that he embrace the position of supreme, uncontested, and unchecked leader.[3]

Although he had finally created his own political party, Jabotinsky devoted considerable energy to portraying a vanished past: A Russia that had ceased to exist (it was now the Soviet Union, a Communist country), and his previous life there. The manipulation of memory and intentional ideological distortion were involved in his reconstruction. Jabotinsky advanced the image of a liberal, a democrat, a defender of minorities. For anyone who thought otherwise, he explained his life credo in *Story of My Life* (1936):

> It is my unshakable belief that between these two [humanity and the nation] the nation comes first, just as the individual has priority over the nation. And the individual also should subordinate his whole life to the service of the nation. I do not see any contradiction if that is his desire and free will and not obligation. In my short play *Ladno* [*All Right*], produced at the Odessa Theater in 1901, I devoted a long monologue to this idea. Briefly, its contents: A person is born free—free of obligations toward Heaven and Earth; do not make sacrifices—the blessings of achievement do not spring from sacrifice. You shall build an altar to Will; that is your leader, go wherever it will lead you—whether its road be up the mountain or down to Hell; majesty or crime, frivolity or servitude—or even the yoke of service to the people—this yoke too you should accept not as a slave submitting to an order, but as a free man fulfilling his sovereign will.[4]

Although a reader might regard this as an unintentional admission of authoritarianism—giving up freedom for a higher purpose—Jabotinsky offered his confession to show that he stood up for freedom. He appears to be saying, "How can I be a fascist if in my youth I heralded the philosophy of freedom and defend it still?" Certainly his readers were likely confused by obvious paradoxes, but he tried to explain, "One of my friends who read this manuscript already reminded me that he also heard from me another refrain: 'In the beginning God created the nation'—there is no contradiction. The second formula I used against those who assert, 'In the beginning "humanity" was created.'"[5] In other words, Jabotinsky rejected the accusations that he was an uncompromising ethno-nationalist, partial to leader worship, and a militarist. However, the image of the liberal Jabotinsky is countered by examples of the opposite—Jabotinsky proclaimed Jewish rights over Arabs, he emphasized the need for military strength, and as a leader he resorted to arbitrary (nondemocratic) decisions when it suited him. For Jabotinsky, self-fashioning meant manipulating his memories of his Russian past.

Jabotinsky turned to Russia for another reason: memories were easier to control than the present. Jewish political struggles in Europe and Palestine were contentious and complicated. Antisemitism was rising; squabbles between the Revisionists and the other parties were intense; and Revisionists fought among themselves. For example, in the late 1920s Jabotinsky's vision was at odds with that of the Brit ha—Biryonim in Palestine. He also fought with his former colleagues among the Russian émigrés. In 1933, Meir Grossman, his close friend and Revisionist Executive member, attempted a coup d'état to overthrow Jabotinsky as head of the party. He failed when Jabotinsky summarily took control and expelled the Executive Committee, ending its role as the supreme organ of the movement (called the Łódz Declaration) on March 22, 1933.[6] Although Jabotinsky's position as head was secure, his power over the Revisionist institutions (HaTzoHar, Betar, Aliyah Bet, and Etzel) was weakening, and would continue to weaken over the decade. In his final years, he relied on assistants who often had their own agendas and power bases. He spent a good deal of the late 1930s engaged in consultations with the Polish government to negotiate an evacuation of Jews from Poland.[7] Put another way, he collaborated with antisemites to get rid of Poland's Jews. Little came of all these efforts.

From the mid-1920s to the end of his life, Jabotinsky dwelled on Russia, remembering his Russian past, transmuting those memories into fiction and fictional autobiography. However, because his fictional treatment of the past was so different from the politics of the present, readers have been confused. What is the relationship between fiction and politics? Why does the author appear so different from the Revisionist leader? What is Jabotinsky trying to say with these idealized versions of his past? This chapter attempts to offer new interpretations.

* * *

In 1926, Jabotinsky published *Samson the Nazarite*, a major piece of fiction set in the biblical period and featuring the figure of Samson as Jabotinsky reimagined him. The book deserves inclusion here because it can be read as a roman à clef of the preceding years when Jabotinsky was in Palestine with the Legion and later with the Russian emigration in Berlin and Paris. One critic agrees, writing, "Even in those works that seem far from his own place and time, such as the novel *Samson the Nazarite,* an insightful reader can locate ideas that parallel Jabotinsky's own views."[8] In fact, the author makes use of the bildungsroman, the novel of personal development, to stimulate such discoveries: How did Samson become the man that he became, the head of the Dan tribe among the ancient Hebrews—a judge, warrior, and lover? Similarly, how did Jabotinsky become the head of the Revisionists?

A central theme in *Samson the Nazarite* is the image of the writer/hero who renounces high culture to serve the Jewish nation, although that nation is inferior culturally. This rejection of cosmopolitanism, higher culture, and civilization is a leitmotif in Jabotinsky's self-fashioning. In fact, Jabotinsky drew attention to this paradigm in his life and in the novel—the struggle to make a modern Jewish culture (nearly) from scratch was necessary in order to legitimate Zionism. As Jabotinsky saw it, modern Hebrew culture was as critical for Jews (even Jews who knew no Hebrew) as English culture was for the British and French literature was for the French. Jabotinsky couldn't accept that Jews, even British Jews, would take pride in British culture, when, he claimed, it was foreign to them and they did not belong to it.

His rejection of his own ideals in favor of politically expedient principles is closely related to issues of authority and the legitimacy of his leadership. The story of Samson takes place at the time of the biblical judges, but Jabotinsky places modern-day issues of national identity and leadership front and center. Loyalty is the book's central motif. To whom will Samson extend his loyalty: the people of Dan or the Philistines?

The hero, Samson, half-Philistine and half-Jew, acknowledges an undeniable attraction to Philistine culture and life. He enjoys the wine and parties, the skills of the Philistine men in fighting, and the beauty and erotic attractions of the women. His loyalty to the tribe of Dan or the Philistines is uncertain, and his split personality is represented in his two names, Samson and Taish. In the end, Samson rejects the Philistines and embraces Dan, a decision that preoccupies Jabotinsky. Why did Samson side with the less developed group? At one point, a Philistine taxman tells Samson that when a man loves one tribe, he hates the other. Samson answers ambiguously:

> "To Love." . . . Really is one's own and not one's own perceived through love? Do you really love the work of a Saran (accountant), you love to count taxes

and judge crooks? I have heard a lot about you: you love scrolls from papyrus, the stars in the heavens, and sailor stories. Nevertheless you are a Saran.
—My father was a Saran, and all my grandfathers,—his voice from the darkness registered.
In Samson's answer anger already appeared.
—I understand your hint. Let's leave it. Even if what came down to you from your journey to Tsorait were the truth, what of it? Let's say that one of my two ancestors played the lute and wore a multi-colored cap. But the other like an ant scrawled through slavery, through the desert, like an ant bore a path in the dry earth of this damned region; and everything he met he gnawed to the bone and swallowed. Maybe they met face to face at the hour of my conception; but, if that is so, then the ant in me would long ago have eaten your colorful cap. Your blood is a goblet of wine; that blood is a cup of poison; if they mix—what will remain of the wine? I am not yours. Call me to your drinking parties, Philistine, I will come and entertain you . . . even if the drinking will take place around my execution. I love to drink and joke with you. But build? You said, "Build"? With you? From you? I do not trust you.[9]

This is, of course, romanticism incarnate. One can drink with members of the other nation, but building a community, society, or country is another thing completely. That can only be done with one's own nation. In this passage the author (through Samson) explains that identification does not depend, as most would believe, on heritage or genealogy, or even on one's preference based on pleasure. At other points in the story, Jabotinsky seems to say that a central component in identity building is need: both sides should feel a need for one another. "Judge . . . does the tribe of Dan need his judgment and rule? The people of Dan do not like him because they do not understand his way, they keep their distance, squint at him as at a foreigner. But now they say to boot that he is dangerous. Perhaps, of course, he is no longer needed by them?"[10]

Throughout most of the book, Jabotinsky explores Samson's feeling of uncertainty. He feels alien to both peoples and cannot locate his proper place. The psychological division is depicted as an irresolvable paradox. Even though the tribe of Dan trusts him, they never forget that he does not belong to them entirely. "With tremendous effort he strained the muscles around his eyes and glanced at the hundreds of lost and oppressed faces; and despite the fog and chaos, the old wild instinct momentarily imprinted in his head their common thought. He clearly read it: they believed immediately, without hesitation: now they were quiet and remembered. Everyone remembered, everything that separated him from them from early childhood, everything that they could understand in him, the whole mystery of Samson and Taish."[11]

In *Samson the Nazarite*, the hero's loyalty and choice cannot be easily deciphered or explained by logic, tradition, or standard practice. The choice itself is portrayed as a problem for the hero and the community, and the reasons behind the hero's choice are never clarified. But one thing is certain: this is an example of romanticism—loyalty to the group no matter what. Romanticism and modern nationalism work well together because, fundamentally, modern nationalism has its origins in romanticism, in the feeling of one's national identity as a rejection of choice, logic, universalism, and the Enlightenment.[12]

The focus on Samson's loyalty justifies an allegorical reading of the book. Samson is the embodiment of Jabotinsky's dreams, ideals, and desires, although the reader is not invited to see a pro-Zionist or pro-Revisionist Zionist message except in perhaps the most general way: Jabotinsky lauds physical strength among the ancient Jewish tribes. Of course one could say much more about the novel, including the theme of sexuality, Jewish nationhood, the figure of Samson, and the formal elements of storytelling and its relation to Russian literature.[13]

The loyalty paradigm is loaded with political meaning. Through his act of self-sacrifice, Jabotinsky gained political authority among Zionists and the right to lead the Jewish nation. A Nietzschean thematics is behind this posturing too, although the roots of such a political move go back much further. Politically legitimacy, especially in mythic stories (and sometimes in real life), is produced through the election to the throne of an unwilling leader who must be drafted, coaxed, and implored multiple times by the people. David of ancient Israel renounced the throne and waited to be called to power; Boris Godunov did the same; and Nietzsche's Zarathustra also ran from the crowd to take an even more important role as a prophet and philosopher. In these and many other cases, the leader's rejection of a role increases his political authority and legitimacy later on. In 1926, Jabotinsky wanted to create a Revisionist Zionist culture; *Samson the Nazarite* was part of the effort.

One notices a pattern in Jabotinsky's life: although crowned a future titan of Russian culture by the high priest Maxim Gorky, one of Russia's leading writers, Jabotinsky publicly rejected the honor, preferring to serve the Jewish nation and Jewish culture.[14] In expressing his preference,

Jabotinsky emphasized that he was rejecting a higher culture for a lower culture. Shimon Markish explains Jabotinsky's psychological reversal:

> Jabotinsky selected another loyalty, and it was totally exclusive—loyalty to the Jewish people. A rare almost imitable quality is found precisely in his loyalty. A Russian-Jewish author belongs to two cultures equally. Jabotinsky belonged to the Jews fully, although to the end of his life he kept his intimate connection with Russian, his native language, expressed in Russian the most important, deep and personal thoughts. And therefore this extraordinary master—no exaggeration here!—of Russian literature could cry out in 1908 to Jews who left for "great" literatures: "You joined your rich neighbor—we turn our back on their beauty and kindness. You genuflect before their values and have abandoned our chapel—we grit our teeth and shout to the entire world from the depths of our heart that one baby babbling in Hebrew is worth more to us than the achievements of your masters from Athens to Moscow." And 32 years later, he repeated [those same sentiments]: although I know half of Pushkin by heart, I would give away all of contemporary Russian poetry for seven letters in the square Hebrew alphabet.[15]

Samson the Nazarite offers a blueprint for Jabotinsky's legitimacy at the birth of HaTzoHar, his new party. Thus, although the novel might seem foreign to Jabotinsky's own life, in fact it reveals a great deal about Jabotinsky's attitude toward Russian culture, culture in general, politics, political legitimacy, and loyalty to Zionism.

* * *

Story of My Life describes Jabotinsky's early childhood years until 1914, recounting the death of his father, his school years, his travels to Italy, and his return to Odessa.[16] Jabotinsky also recalls his Zionist work in St. Petersburg, Vienna, and Istanbul, and his return to Russia. The book is fascinating because precisely in 1936, and in Hebrew, Jabotinsky felt the need to tell the story of how he became a Zionist. He acknowledged 1905 and especially the Helsingfors Conference as key moments in his life. Most others would focus on the Kishinev pogrom in 1903 or the Jewish Legion during World War I. But Jabotinsky focused on 1905.

Jabotinsky depicted the 1905 Revolution as a banner of hope. Comparing 1905 to 1848—political reactionaries dashed both revolutions—Jabotinsky offered a retrospective vision of himself as young man who believed in freedom and happiness. At the same time, he gave the impression that nationalism and individual freedom, which are thought of as contradictory in the twentieth century, could be united as they once were in the nineteenth century (in Garibaldi's Italy, for example).

Although the autobiography reads like an objective recounting of events, Jabotinsky carefully organized *Story of My Life* with a polemical aim. He offered a different version of the development of Zionism from that of labor Zionism. In the Mapai perspective, Zionism was catapulted forward in the post-Herzl era, thanks to the political left in general and the members of the Second Aliyah in particular. Jabotinsky, however, tells Zionism's story differently, focusing on Russia around 1905 and the struggle for national identity by his fellow journalists Avram Idel'son, Israel Trivus, Arnold Seidenman, Nikolai Sorin, Julius Brutzkus, Isaac Naiditsch, and Vladimir Tiomkin. All wrote for *Rassvet*, the Zionist newspaper produced in Russian.[17]

That same year (1936), Jabotinsky published *The Five*, a novel-memoir set in Odessa during the Revolution of 1905.[18] The title is of course a double entendre; it refers to the five Milgrom children, the book's protagonists, but also the revolution of 1905. We may ask: Why did Jabotinsky harken back to Russia circa 1905? The present was busy and interesting enough: Jabotinsky was the head of Revisionism, and the center of Zionist activity had shifted from Europe to Palestine. Why did he often refer to the 1906 Helsingfors Conference in the final decades of his life, the peak of his political activity?[19] Why publish *The Five* at a time when the Nazi threat and the critical situation in Palestine occupied Zionists everywhere? What explains Jabotinsky's appreciation of the breadth and depth of the so-called First Russian Revolution?

The answer lies in the multifunctionality of 1905 for Jabotinsky's image making.[20] He used 1905 to confer political legitimacy on HaTzoHar, and proudly linked Revisionism with Synthetic Zionism, the political approach that emerged at the Helsingfors Conference, which envisioned full political and national rights for Russia's ethnic minorities. He used 1905 to defend himself as a liberal, having been slandered as a dictator, a militarist, and an extremist. He countered by describing himself as a child of 1905, one who desired freedom, youth, love, cosmopolitanism, and individuality. Altogether, these themes and functions involve complicated and inconsistent attitudes that depart from the conventional evaluation of 1905 as a signpost of the evolution toward 1917.[21]

We have the author's personal comment about the book's construction, as relayed by his secretary and biographer Joseph Schechtman, who writes that "Jabotinsky simply drew on the precious treasure house of personal memories of the happy 'Altalena' years spent in this lively Black Sea harbor city, which he adored, yearned for, and was haunted by all his life."[22] Then he transmits Jabotinsky's own words: "I feel that I have once again recaptured all the nonsense, all the hopes and the entire 'swing' of that period."[23]

Although this statement implies that the book had no deeper meaning, one is not certain. The book has bedeviled critics because, although based on autobiography and written in the 1930s, there is no sign in it of Jabotinsky the Zionist militarist or dictator-like leader of the Revisionist movement.[24] In *The Five* the protagonist, named Jabotinsky, is portrayed as a smart-aleck journalist, a self-conscious young man who is both a pretentious bon vivant and a down-to-earth friend of the Milgroms. Alice Stone-Nachimovsky sees the novel as a Zionist parable: the Milgrom family falls apart, disaster befalls the children, and therefore the author wants to punish them. What is their crime? Indifference to Zionism.[25]

Perhaps this interpretation is flawed because assimilation as an ideology is not attacked. In fact, it is the only perspective that gets a full hearing.[26] The problem of perspective begins with the narrator. There are at least two Jabotinskys in the novel, the young man of the story, and the narrator, who is clearly older and closely resembles (the reader is likely to consider) the author. The narrator, like the Milgroms, is an acculturated Jew, a russified intellectual, and his criticisms of the Milgroms are muted; he loves the entire family, especially Marusya, precisely for her personal flair, feminine beauty, dreams, and ideals. In the book, each of the five children is engaged in an internal struggle between Jewish identity and universalism; pleasure and a desire for purpose; politics and lofty art. However, they all reject Jewish nationalism; one sides with Communism, another with Nietzschean immorality, and another adopts an aesthetic approach to life. Only Marusya believes in Jewish continuity; she marries a bland Jewish pharmacist and has two children with him.

To understand the novel, one should acquaint oneself with "polyphony," the interpretive concept that Mikhail Bakhtin describes in his *Problems of Dostoevsky's Poetics* (1929).[27] Bakhtin noticed that in Dostoevsky's novels, the author inserted characters whose voices seem independent from the narrator and contradict the author. Bakhtin maintained that these voices could not be reduced or resolved at the end but remained distinct and separate worlds within the novel.

Clearly, polyphony is present in *The Five*. Here the third-person narrator does not have a final say or resolve all the threads. The five children take five separate paths. For Sergei (Serezha) Milgrom, the revolution is a kind of plaything; his ménage à trois with a girl and her mother serves as a test case of whether morality exists or "everything is possible." Lika Milgrom becomes a professional revolutionary thanks to an attraction to conspiracy, wearing masks, and gaining power through the obfuscation of her identity. Torik has some interest in Zionism, but he's uncertain about national distinctions and sectarianism. Marko is perhaps the least formed character. His role centers on his ambiguous accident/suicide when he jumps into a canal to save a woman he thought was drowning. His kindness is mocked by his senseless death.

The central figures of the novel are Marusya and the narrator. Marusya, the Milgroms' eldest, is a redhead, a fiery young woman in her early twenties who represents beauty, depth of soul, and deep kindness. She has many friends and hosts a salon in her home. She also has two serious suitors, Aleksei Runitsky, a Russian sailor, who loves her passionately, and Samoilo Kozodoi, a pharmacist who is boring but who promises to give her Jewish children. Marusya's mother is worried that Marusya will marry Runitsky and join the Russian nation. In fact, the highpoint of the book is the scene in which Marusya is at the church, about to marry Aleksei, but runs away at the last moment when she realizes that the marriage would destroy her personality. She ends up marrying Kozodoi and leads a quiet life in seemingly happy domesticity. Several years later she is killed in an accident; a fire in the kitchen spreads to her highly fashionable but also highly flammable clothing, but she manages to save her two children. This scene underscores Marusya's inner virtues: she is a perfect mother who saves her children from death at the cost of her own life. Of course the reader wants to know why Jabotinsky killed off his protagonist. The meaning emerges from an overall analysis of the theme of assimilation.[28]

The narrator, whose name is Vladimir Jabotinsky, but who should be identified only partially with the author, questions his own life. In this context, we encounter Odessa, a city whose people enjoyed a rare harmony unattainable elsewhere. It was a place, Jabotinsky writes, where "people learned to laugh at themselves and everything in the world, even at their pains and things they love."[29] The singular virtue of Odessa, we learn, is tolerance. "Gradually one's customs disappear, one stops taking one's own sanctuaries seriously, gradually understanding the single most important secret in the world: what is sacred to you is stupidity to your neighbor, and your neighbor is not a thief or vagrant."[30]

We need not be surprised at Jabotinsky's praise of tolerance. However, he even lauds assimilation.[31] In the context of the Odessa of 1905, assimilation appears to the narrator as a road leading to a higher level of reality. Towards the novel's end, the narrator muses, "Torik said 'Disintegration.' Maybe he is right. The lawyer . . . spoke about decadence but he added that epochs of decadence are sometimes the most fascinating times. Who knows? Perhaps not only fascinating, but also superior in their own way? Of course I am in the camp that struggles against disintegration, I do not want neighbors, I want all people to live on their own islands. But who knows?"[32]

That metaphysical question—"Who knows?"—shows Jabotinsky examining his own views. Against our expectations, he describes assimilation as the start of something beautiful and ideal. Attracted to the dreams of universal brotherhood, the narrator announces a utopian vision.

> One thing is already a proven historical truth: one has to pass through disintegration to reach renewal. This means that disintegration is like a fog before the birth of the sun or like a predawn dream. Marusya said that the most wonderful dreams are predawn ones. Whose poem is this? "The prophesy of dawn is still imperceptible, emerald and cornelian, lilac and azure: the unsung words drift into my mind, perhaps of an unborn poet, the singer of a country still not created by the creator, where invisible visions are silent like music and whose shroud for a moment, the moment before awakening, lifts up predawn dreams to us." I am afraid that these verses are my own. Getting old, I quote myself more and more often. I quote (for the second time) the following: "I am a child of my time, I love all its stains, love its full poison."[33]

The last part of his speech—"I am a child of my time"—is entirely comprehensible, as is his confession of love for the poison of his culture. But what are we to make of the predawn dreams, the reaching beyond to a better world? What is the higher stage that should emerge from assimilation?

Certainly the allusion to dreams, the use of synesthesia—silent music— and such paradoxical language as "unborn poets" and "a country not yet created by the creator" recall concepts of Russia's Silver Age, with its emphasis on the intangible, ideal, and spiritual aspects of being. The last quote, a confession of sorts, serves as a perfect example of the complicated and contradictory quality of Jabotinsky's "emotional essence."[34] For the author, assimilation appears wonderful, dangerous, ideal, and unattainable.

Zionism comes into question especially in discussions with Torik, the youngest Milgrom, who had taken an interest in Jewish nationalism but decides to convert to Lutheranism. His fate saddens the narrator. Despite the conversion, the author does not depict him as morally bankrupt. Torik's arguments have an impeccable logic that the narrator acknowledges. When the narrator counters with the Bund or Zionism as a possible path, Torik responds:

> The Bund and Zionism, if you reason clinically, are really the same. The Bund is a preparatory class or, let's say, a public school; it readies you for Zionism. It seems that Plekhanov said about the Bund that they're "Zionists who fear seasickness." And Zionism is like a high school. But the university, where everyone is unconsciously heading, is called assimilation. Gradually, without desire, joyless, for the majority it will even be disadvantageous, but still it is unavoidable and irreversible, with baptism, mixed marriages and the full liquidation of the race. There is no other way. The Bund clings to Yiddish. They say it's the most amazing language in the world. I only know a little, but my tutors, unable to get into the university, quote the word "Boychik," i.e., simple fellow, Whitechapel, and they say it is a *tour de force*. Elements of three languages in one little word and it sounds natural, it's an ideal amalgam. But in twenty-five years there won't be any Yiddish. And there won't be any Zion. Only one thing will remain: the desire "to be the same as other nations."[35]

The narrator does not reject this viewpoint; he expresses it loud and clear.

Through his examination of Odessa, Jabotinsky created a snapshot of decadence, an attitude that dominated intellectual life in the city. Characters hostile to Zionism are given free space for expression. Admittedly, the Milgrom children find tragic ends that correspond to the decadent mood of the novel. Perhaps, as some critics have argued, the fates of the Milgroms imply the author's condemnation of universalism, but perhaps not. The use of polyphony distorts the projection of the author's consistent and clear attitude. The only thing certain is that, by offering others a chance to contradict Zionism, Jabotinsky presented an intellectual portrait that is fuller and, one might argue, closer to the tenor of the age.

It is something of a conundrum that the narrator expresses mixed feelings about assimilation and speaks so positively about tolerance. In the 1930s, Jabotinsky was entirely hostile to assimilation; the message that he carried throughout Europe, America, and South Africa was emigration to Palestine. Why write a novel about cosmopolitanism and decadence in Odessa in 1905 at a time when the Jews of Europe were endangered by a terrifying antisemitism? Although the documents do not provide a single answer, some educated guesses emerge from the study of his oeuvre and the historical context.

To explain how the novel reveals the author's evolution, one might turn to Jabotinsky's overall self-projection in the late 1930s. He was reeling from the attacks against him and his party following the murder of Hayim Arlosorov, for which the Revisionists were blamed.[36] That event stoked fires already burning; earlier, his political opponents accused him of sympathy for fascism and attempted to impugn his reputation by linking Revisionism with street thuggery. Jabotinsky was portrayed as a Jewish Nazi, not a hero struggling to liberate the Jewish people.[37]

Jabotinsky wanted to improve his image, and *The Five* is certainly part of his campaign to reassert Revisionism's link with liberalism. During the same period, Jabotinsky published another text in which he applauded freedom and individualism, while criticizing discipline and blind obedience. In "The Revolt of the Old Men" (1930) he wrote, "[I] find the spiritual edifice of the first third of the twentieth century quite disgusting, and I think that we should rise in revolt against it. For such a revolt there is a particularly suitable age group—'old men.'"[38] He added:

> I mean firstly, those whose minds were formed in the nineteenth century, and secondly, those who are proud of this anachronism. Spiritually speaking, the nineteenth century came to its close around 1905, and my generation was then around thirty-five, thirty, or twenty-five years old; that is, of an age when all the convolutions of the brain and all emotional habits had already become fixed.... The nineteenth century had a vividly characterized personality. From its beginning to its end, born in Europe and America, and in South Africa too, it really did develop round one main axis. They say that among White Russian émigrés there are some who can be moved to tears by the mere enumeration of the railway stations between Moscow and St. Petersburg; the very names make them remember everything—the landscape, the taste of cabbage pies, the droshky drivers' baggy coats, the covers of the thick Liberal monthlies, and their first love. In the same way it is enough for my generation, instead of attempting to describe the face of our century, just to recite a list of names, in any haphazard order, with no respect for chronology or geography or completeness: Garibaldi, Gladstone, Lincoln, Mickiewicz, Heine, Hugo, Leopardi, Ibsen, Bjørnson, Nietzsche, Walt Whitman, Lassalle and Jaurès, and even Marx—as he then seemed to us. One could mention many more such names, all unlike each other, but all the same in one respect—and in that similarity is found the spirit of the nineteenth century. They were all firebrands of ego, liberators and releasers of personality. They all, in different ways, fought to ensure that the dirtiest of tramps stumbling on his own reflection in a mirror should never forget to spring to attention and yell: "Hail, Your Majesty!"[39]

Once again the tramp appears as an symbol of the sanctity of the individual. With his inherent dignity, he is equal to the other heroes—an extremely diverse list—who embodied Jabotinsky's ideals. Despite the differences among them, the old men and the tramp were united by confidence in their own judgments and pride in their individuality. These men were therefore inoculated against fascism, mass politics, and collectivism. They believed in the individual, self-respect, freedom, and self-determination, and fought for authority based on morality, not aggression. Jabotinsky implicitly includes himself and his Revisionists among them, "old men" who would cry at the recitation of the names of the stops on the train from Moscow to St. Petersburg.

Certainly Jabotinsky's conception of liberalism, while not formulated in full, appears idiosyncratic. The original ideas from 1848 (and thereafter) were never meant as total anarchy for the individual. Liberal nationalism enabled individuals to gain rights from a hardened aristocracy, but the rights were supposed to elevate an entire class—the bourgeoisie—and promote the reemergence of old nations, and assist their revolt against their oppressors. It is true that the liberal heritage came to Russia through revolutionary thought—Alexander Herzen, and Nikolai Ogarev—and minimized the national struggle, while emphasizing the idea of social and personal liberation. However, here Jabotinsky's narrow definition of liberalism—as personal liberation exclusively—amounted to a truncated version of the liberal doctrine. He removed from the admixture the social dimension that was so important to him elsewhere.

But he recovered his balance in 1937, in his testimony before the Palestine Royal (Peel) Commission in London, where he answered questions about a British plan to partition Palestine. The Revisionists rejected the partition plan. Jabotinsky's testimony explains his position, which is not liberalism, but might be called rescue. "I do hope the day may come when some Jewish representative may be allowed to appear at the Bar of one of these two Houses [of Parliament] just to tell them what it really is, and to ask the English people: What are you going to advise us? Where is the way out? Or, standing up and facing God, say that there is no way out and that we Jews have just to go under."[40] He adds, "Our demand for a Jewish majority is not our maximum—it is our minimum, it is just an inevitable stage if only we are allowed to go on salvaging our people."[41]

His testimony articulates the major principles of Revisionist Zionism, including the idea of Jewish self-defense, Jewish settlement on both sides of the Jordan River, and the need for British help in colonizing the region. On the Arab Issue, he repeats his opinion that humanitarian considerations justify giving Palestine to the Jews. "One fraction, one branch of that race, and not a big one, will have to live in someone else's State: well, that is the case with all the mightiest nations of the world. . . . I fully understand that any minority would prefer to be a majority, it is quite understandable that the Arabs of Palestine would also prefer Palestine to be the Arab State No. 4, No. 5, or No. 6—that I quite understand; but when the Arab claim is confronted with our Jewish demand to be saved, it is like the claims of appetite versus the claims of starvation." But he adds, "What I do not deny is that in that process the Arabs of Palestine will necessarily become a minority in the country of Palestine. What I do deny is that *that* is a hardship."[42]

In the years before World War II, Jabotinsky soured on Britain and began to speak of replacing Britain and having the League of Nations appoint another country that could better advance the goals of the Mandate (as Jabotinsky conceived of them).[43] That represented a major change in his point of view. However, one should realize that Jabotinsky was largely bluffing, since no one wanted this task, and Britain was not prepared to give up Palestine, a vital strategic asset, at such an important historical moment. With war on the horizon, Britain wanted to satisfy, if only in a minimal way, Arab demands to halt Jewish immigration. Although the British government voted in favor of partition in 1937, the plan never went forward because of the exigencies of the war, among other things. Nonetheless, the 1939 British proclamation of a new White Paper restricting emigration to seventy-five thousand, which thereafter made immigration contingent on the granting of Arab consent, revealed Britain's divided intentions.[44]

Regarding Jabotinsky's liberalism, one cannot ignore an obvious contradiction: he was well known exactly for the qualities that he condemns. Both his enemies and his friends maintained that he advanced the cult of leadership in Revisionism, that he looked to Betar volunteers to subordinate their individuality and march in strict lines in military parades. Given Jabotinsky's outsized role as Revisionism's figurehead, what are we to make of his veneration of nineteenth-century individualism? Was this a ruse to confuse his rivals and regale his followers, or was he serious that Revisionism and liberalism were one and the same?

I find it difficult to entirely dismiss his statements. Jabotinsky seemed to believe that Revisionism was morally justifiable given present-day antisemitism in Europe and the long history of Jewish suffering around the world. He believed that Zionism had moral authority, as we can see from his testimony in London before the members of the Royal (Peel) Commission.[45]

At the same time, we can't exclude the possibility that the liberation theme satisfied in Jabotinsky some kind of psychological need. There is a good deal of evidence to support such a hypothesis. In the second half of the 1930s, at a desperate time for Jews worldwide, Jabotinsky turned to the past. The many texts he wrote about his youth circa 1905 reflect nostalgia for a time when hope, rather than despair, filled the Jewish world; when respect for morality was alive rather than jettisoned before the power of coercion and violence.

It is worthwhile to recall that few Zionists romanticize 1905. In fact, most Zionists of the 1920s and '30s see the Balfour Declaration in November 1917 and the First Zionist Congress in 1897 as dates to cherish. Similarly, many historians recognize 1914 as a key year. Here one may recall Lenin's argument that 1905 was only a rehearsal for 1917. The year 1917 looms large in world history, 1905 much less. Russian liberals such as Pavel Miliukov and Maxim Vinaver idealized the 1905 Revolution and especially the First Duma, although they acknowledged them as moments of unrealized potential.[46]

Jabotinsky's interpretation of 1905 nonetheless gives us clues to his worldview. For Jabotinsky, 1905 is central because, more than 1914 or 1917, it gave him a utopian vision that he carried throughout his life. Helsingfors offered a blueprint of a liberal kind: a Jewish nation renewed spiritually, with its political vision of sovereignty acknowledged as morally legitimate. Furthermore, he seemed to genuinely believe that a political solution for Jews and Arabs could be attained on the basis of Helsingfors. Admittedly, he realized that the Arabs disagreed, and therefore advocated the Legion Principle, advising Jews everywhere to learn to use a gun.[47]

In 1936 the liberal vision was as far from reality as it was in 1905. The Arabs of Palestine had just begun a three-year-long revolt. Britain responded by lowering immigration quotas for Jews. Jabotinsky opposed the proposal by the Peel Commission in 1938 to partition Palestine by giving the Yishuv a small area of Western Palestine. Although Ben-Gurion accepted the partition, Jabotinsky doubted that a viable, defensible Jewish state could be constructed within such truncated borders.[48] In most of Europe, Jews were under threat from Nazism, local violence, and political, social, and economic exclusion.

In 1936, Jabotinsky's liberal dreams must have seemed valuable only as subjects for autobiography and fiction. To his credit, he didn't become lost in his dreams; instead, he initiated his Ten-Year Plan for evacuating eight million European Jews, and soon called for the immediate evacuation of one million and then ten million Jews.[49] Those goals didn't signal a solid grasp of reality, but they were certainly not mere figments of the imagination.

He tried to connect his memories of 1905 with these last-ditch efforts to save European Jewry. In a sense, these memories betrayed him because they rekindled a vision of nineteenth-century values—humanism, liberalism, progress—that had run out of energy. Reality didn't care about his heroes or values; reality spoke of antisemitism and eliminationist nationalism and the right to citizenship being stolen from European Jewry. Palestine and Zionism, considered a utopian vision, became a life-and-death hope.

One is tempted to apply to Jabotinsky the quotation that he had applied to Herzl and Lomonosov: it was easier to take Jabotinsky from Russia than Russia from Jabotinsky. Russia as a concept remained inside him and continued to resonate in various ways, in his journalism and political writings, fiction, and memoirs, and in the writings of others about him. One would think that once he left, Russia as a concept would cease to develop and change; that his memory would grow ossified. But that didn't happen. Instead, he adapted his memory to changing needs, to describe his present, even as that present was unraveling before his very eyes.

Notes

1. Vladimir Jabotinsky, *Samson Nazarei* (Paris, 1926); *Piatero* (Paris, 1936); *Sippur yamai*, appeared in *Golah ve-hitbolelut* (Tel Aviv: Sh. Zal'tsman, 1936).
2. Daniel Heller, *Jabotinsky's Children: Polish Jews and the Rise of Right-Wing Zionism* (Princeton, NJ: Princeton University Press, 2017), 9.
3. Colin Shindler, *The Rise of the Israeli Right: From Odessa to Hebron* (New York: Cambridge University Press, 2015), 96.
4. Vladimir Jabotinsky, *Story of My Life*, eds. Brian Horowitz and Leonid Katsis (Detroit: Wayne State University Press, 2017), 59.
5. Ibid.
6. Jan Zoupla, "Vladimir Jabotinsky and the Split within the Revisionist Union: From the Boulogne Agreement to the Katowice Putsch, 1931–33," *Journal of Israeli History: Politics, Society, Culture* 24, no. 1 (2005): 55.
7. Laurence Weinbaum, *A Marriage of Convenience: The New Zionist Organization and the Polish Government, 1936–1939* (Boulder, CO: East European Monographs, 1993), 211–212.
8. I. Orena, "Predislovie," in Vladimir Jabotinsky, *Samson Nazorei* (Tel Aviv: Aliya, 1990), ix.
9. Vladimir Jabotinsky, *Samson Nazarei* (Tel Aviv: Aliya, 1990), 307–08.
10. Ibid., 171.

11. Ibid., 256.
12. Nicholas V. Riasanovsky, *The Emergence of Romanticism* (Oxford: Oxford University Press, 1995).
13. Mikhail Veiskopf, "Liubov' k dal'nemu: literaturnoe tvorchestvo Vladimira Zhabotinskogo," *Vestnik Evreiskogo universiteta v Moskve*, 29: 11 (2006): 196.
14. Maxim Gorky, *Literaturnoe nasledstvo* (Moscow: Nauka, 1988).
15. Shimon Markish, "Zhabotinskii: 50 let posle konchiny: ob''iasnenie v liubvi," *Evreiskii Zhurnal* 1 (1991): 65.
16. Vladimir Jabotinsky, *Story of My Life* (*Sippur yamai*), in *Golah ve-hitbolelut* (Tel Aviv: Sh. Zal'tsman, 1936). It was republished in V. Jabotinsky, *Avtobiografia* (Jerusalem: Eri Jabotinsky, 1946–47), 9–187.
17. For a discussion of the importance of the Second Aliyah in the development of Zionism in Palestine, see Anita Shapira's many works, for example *Berl: The Biography of a Socialist Zionist, Berl Katznelson, 1887–1944* (Cambridge: Cambridge University Press, 1984).
18. I am using this edition of *Piatero* (Tel Aviv: Biblioteka Aliia, 1990).
19. For the meaning of 1905 in Russian-Jewish consciousness, see Ezra Mendelsohn and Stefani Hoffman, eds., *The Revolution of 1905 and Russia's Jews* (Philadelphia: University of Pennsylvania Press, 2008).
20. The next pages are based on my article in the Hebrew journal *Zion*: "Vladimir Jabotinsky and the Mystique of 1905," *Zion* 80, no. 4 (2015): 503–520.
21. Abe Ascher has also taken issue with the conventional view of the 1905 Revolution. See *The Revolution of 1905: Russia in Disarray* (Palo Alto, CA: Stanford University Press, 1998), 1–2.
22. Altalena was Jabotinsky's favorite pseudonym. In Italian it means "seesaw."
23. Joseph Schechtman, *The Vladimir Jabotinsky Story: Fighter and Prophet,, The Last Years* (New York: Thomas Yoseloff, 1961), 534.
24. The book was serialized in *Rassvet* starting in 1932. The secondary literature on the novel is large and growing. For a select bibliography, see Barry Scherr, "An Odessa Odyssey: Vladimir Jabotinsky's *The Five*," *Slavic Review* 70 (2011): 94–115.
25. Alice Stone Nakhimovsky, *Russian-Jewish Literature and Identity: Jabotinsky, Babel, Grossman, Galich, Roziner, Markish* (Baltimore, MD: Johns Hopkins University Press, 1992), 63.
26. Brian Horowitz, "Hail to Assimilation: Vladimir 'Ze'ev' Jabotinsky's Ambivalence about Odessa's *Fin de Siècle*," *Novoe Literaturnoe Obozrenie* 73 (2005): 109–116. We are aware of the distinction between "assimilation" and "acculturation" that Ezra Mendelsohn has clarified, although here we are speaking about the ultimate disappearance of Jews as a separate ethnos. Ezra Mendelsohn, *On Modern Jewish Politics* (Oxford: Oxford University Press, 1993), 16.
27. Mikhail Bakhtin, *Problemy tvorchestva Dostoevskogo* (Leningrad: Priboi, 1929).
28. Svetlana Natkovich has written well about Marusya in the context of Odessa and *The Five*. See "Odessa as 'Point de Capital': Economic, History and Time in Odessa Fiction," *Slavic Review* 75, no. 4 (Winter 2016): 847–871, esp. 864.
29. Jabotinsky, *Piatero*, 228–229.
30. Ibid., 229.
31. Mirja Lecke, "Odessa without Dogma: Jabotinsky's *The Five*," *Ab Imperio* 1 (2012).
32. Jabotinsky, *Piatero*, 229.
33. Ibid.

34. That expression, "emotional essence," belongs to Alice Stone Nakhimovsky, *Russian-Jewish Literature and Identity*, 67.

35. Jabotinsky, *Piatero*, 224.

36. V. Jabotinsky, "Delo Stavskogo," *Rassvet* 29 (October 22, 1933): 2–3.

37. See Jabotinsky's article, "Jews and Fascism," *Jewish Daily Bulletin* (April 11, 1935). Vladimir Khazan, "Eshche raz o 'fashizme' Zhabotinskogo," *Zhabotinskii i Rossiia: sbornik trudov mezhdunarodnoi konferentsii, posviashchennoi 130-letiiu V. E. Zhabotinskogo (Evreiskii Universitet v Ierusalime, iiul' 2010)*, ed. E. Tolstaya and L. Katsis (Palo Alto, CA: Stanford Slavic Studies, 2014), 68.

38. Vladimir Jabotinsky, "Revolt of the Old Men," *Nation and Society: Selected Articles* (Tel Aviv: Shilton Betar, 1961), 57; trans. from the original "Bunt starcòw," *Nasz Przegląd* (February 12, 1936).

39. Ibid.

40. Vladimir Jabotinsky, *Evidence Submitted to the Palestine Royal Commission On Behalf of the New Zionist Organization, House of Lords* (Tel Aviv, New Zionist Organization in Palestine, 1937), 7.

41. Ibid., 8.

42. Ibid.

43. Ibid., 8–9.

44. Dvora Hacohen, "British Immigration Policy to Palestine in the 1930s: Implications for Youth Aliyah," *Middle Eastern Studies* 37, no. 4 (October 2001): 214–218.

45. Jabotinsky, *Evidence Submitted to the Palestine Royal Commission*, 8–12.

46. See Brian Horowitz, "Maxim Vinaver and the First Russian State Duma," in *Russian Idea-Jewish Presence: Essays on Russian-Jewish Intellectual Life* (Boston: Academic Studies, 2013), 18–36.

47. See Vladimir Jabotinsky, "Aufn pripichek . . . ," *Haynt* (October 15, 1931): 9–10.

48. Shmuel Dothan, *Pulmus ha-halukah bi-tekufat ha-Mandat* (Jerusalem: Yad Itzhak Ben-Zvi, 1979), 131.

49. Vladimir Jabotinsky, "The Evacuation Problem, 'Humanitarian Zionism,'" *Jewish Herald*, no. 2215 (November 3, 1938): 2.

CONCLUSION

* * *

This book shows above all that Jabotinsky was a political player in his time and place. He tried out various options, struggled for attention, and created platforms for himself and institutions to further his goals. At the start, he lacked a set course, his ideology was shaped by different contexts, personal interactions, mistakes, and unexpected events. But he did have models among Russian and Polish nationalists. Despite attempts to separate Jabotinsky from ethno-nationalists, even chauvinists, one cannot overlook the connections. A study of Jabotinsky's roles in the Zionist movement and of his actions and words in real contexts must gather a wide array of evidence and provide background to understand his formation and rise to leadership.

This book emphasizes that the Russian environment and especially Russian Zionism (later the Russian emigration) were the central factors in Jabotinsky's development. Jabotinsky rose to the head of a movement (Revisionist Zionism) as a result of many factors, including the defeat of his rivals as well as his own wily, stubborn, energetic temperament. However, his own development could be described as anything but smooth. He went through many changes before settling down on a career as a Zionist politician. He started out as a young journalist in Rome, and when he returned to Odessa, he wanted to become a Russian writer. Even when he grew interested in Zionism, he did not give up the dream of a writing career. Despite many disappointments, he continued to forge his path as a Zionist, while writing for Russian journals on Jewish and often non-Jewish topics. Journalism was his primary source of income.

It could be said that he failed as a politician more than he succeeded. The party he established in 1925, Revisionist Zionists, never became the largest or most powerful party in the Zionist Organization during his lifetime; it regularly faltered in elections. In 1927, it won only 10,189 votes to the Elected Assembly (Asefat ha-nivharim), the representative body of Jews in Mandate

Palestine.¹ And yet, Jabotinsky helped establish the youth group Betar and was instrumental in the organization of the paramilitary group Etzel, two organizations associated with HaTzoHar. He also spearheaded Aliyah Bet, illegal immigration to Palestine. In these endeavors, his "success" is subject to debate; one could justifiably claim that his activities had greater significance psychologically and ideologically than in the actual world. In fact, if one evaluates Jabotinsky's overall political activity, one has to admit that it was a strange "new politics," characterized by grand gestures, but with few tangible results. He projected a style or psychological atmosphere, but neither in Palestine nor in Eastern Europe did the Revisionists gain enough power to change Zionist policy directly. They were also unable to effectively influence the governments in the states where Jews lived. However, they had strong support among non-Socialists and followers among the so-called "small shopkeepers" of the Fourth Aliyah, militaristic youth in interwar Poland, and religious Sephardim. Revisionism enjoyed its greatest success in the mid- to late 1930s in Eastern Europe, where Betar activists provided camps, schools, and sporting activities for youth.²

Beyond its relatively small numbers, Revisionism had an undeniable psychological effect on Jews worldwide by instilling the idea that they should be proud, strong, and independent, that Jews should prepare themselves mentally and spiritually for difficult challenges ahead. Rejecting despair, Jabotinsky offered his followers pride in their Jewish identity and empowerment as part of a group with a clear mission that placed at its center *hadar*—strength, health, courtesy, and chivalry.

Outside the Revisionist camp, few took his words at face value. Bundists railed against his rejection of class conflict, claiming that Jabotinsky offered empowerment for the upper class, but not for workers. In contrast to the Bund, Zionists on the left criticized Jabotinsky for his militarism, his emphasis on discipline, and his defense of the wealthy. They also disliked his provocative statements, especially in negotiations with England, because he made the Zionist position appear weak and uninspiring. Liberals accused Jabotinsky of unnecessary radicalism and truculence, while individuals within his own circle had little confidence in his proposals for national autonomy. These examples represent a small sample of the many objections to Jabotinsky's politics that he encountered on his path.

Consequently, historians in the aggregate have been tough on Jabotinsky. Bernard Wasserstein asserts that Jabotinsky was "a grandstander rather than a statesman [and] never quite succeeded in translating rhetorical triumphs into real political achievements."³ Jan Zouplna expresses the same idea but in greater detail when he writes, "Jabotinsky never succeeded in creating a viable political power base. Organizations he created showed heterodoxy unique even by Zionist standards, did not produce hardly any significant financial resources for the planned political offensive, and last by not least the Revisionist masses worshipped a somewhat mythical image of Jabotinsky that had very little in common with the actual leader."⁴

After his withdrawal from the Zionist Executive, Jabotinsky gained a small following among Zionists who sympathized with the political right—Russian-Jewish émigrés, Sephardic Jews, and religious Jews who shared an anti-left viewpoint. These individuals did not necessarily share many values, but they united around a rejection of Socialism, collective ownership of property, atheism, and the left's intolerance. Jabotinsky could serve as a potential leader and voice for their interests.

Some scholars have tended to see the similarities between Revisionism, the European radical right, and even fascism as mere coincidences. Gideon Shimoni has observed, "The Revisionists represented, at first, an activist wing of general Zionism, with Jabotinsky being a speaker of the opposition against Weizmann's leadership, rather than an exponent of some new genre of Zionist ideology."⁵

Jan Zouplna tries to spare Jabotinsky's reputation. He remarks that one does not need to seek parallels with the European radical right when there is a tradition of leadership in Zionism and Jewish religious life.⁶ This argument presumes that Zionists were unexposed to European culture. In any case, his examples include the veneration of Herzl and, among Hasidism, subordination to the will of the *rebbe*. "The cult of personality offered an additional scope for the outpouring of traditional (irrational) religious feelings that were not tolerated by themselves in the predominantly secular political culture of the Zionist movement."⁷

A similar viewpoint is offered by Jacob Shavit, who maintains that the inner mechanism of Zionism and its struggles in Palestine and the Diaspora were sui generis and not similar to the radical right as it was understood in Western Europe. It was a utopian movement and ideology that emerged from the particularly Jewish experience in Eastern Europe.⁸ Another account belongs to Svetlana Natkovich, who argues that Jabotinsky's approach was not directly borrowed from the radical right, but mimics it, by coincidence:

Jabotinsky was thus trapped in the paradox of history and myth. On the one hand, ever since the 1920s he believed in and strived to give expression to the ahistorical, irrational foundations of human nature and society; on the other hand he was a pragmatic political leader, ever struggling with conflicting historical challenges and alliances on the personal, organizational, and ideological levels. Moreover, with the rise of fascism in the 1930s, Jabotinsky faced an additional intellectual and ideological challenge. An ardent opponent of fascist totalitarianism, Jabotinsky apparently found it difficult to contend with the fact that his own ideas—primarily his preference for organicism, intuition, irrationality, and ethnicity over materialism, historicism, rationalism, and class—shared some common premises with fascist ideology.[9]

These interpretations acquit Jabotinsky of genetic relations to Europe's radical right, but they do raise doubts: Why is it so unlikely that Jabotinsky looked to the European radical right as his model? Most of the countries of Eastern Europe were leaning rightward; in Germany and France, early fascist leaders sought public office.[10] One essential aspect of right-leaning was an aggressive campaign against socialism, leftism, and collectivism. Jabotinsky certainly shared that with the rightists. While it is true that the Revisionist program may be viewed as similar to the General Zionists's program, one should recall that provocative tactics, as well as scandalous and high-pitched rhetoric, made up an essential part of Jabotinsky's struggle to win support. Jabotinsky tended to personalize debates. His relentless berating of Weizmann provides a vivid example. Leaders vying for leadership on the radical right habitually belittled their rivals and accused them of myriad errors.

As for whether Jabotinsky and the Revisionist party should be labeled rightist, one should note that, despite his expressed antipathy to collectivism, conformism, and even the leader principle, he also admired discipline and apotheosized the leader. Jabotinsky shaped his image and consciously transformed himself and his party into a movement on the political right. His fiery writings and speeches criticized socialism and class politics while stressing the need for a Jewish military force in Palestine and support for the youth group Betar, which embodied his vision for young Jews. The characteristics of a Betarist had similarities with right-wing youth groups in Europe: an emphasis on hygiene, sport, discipline, good manners, and self-sacrifice. That vision was associated with the petite bourgeoisie and the patriarchal family rather than class and revolution.

In chapter six of this book, I assert that the violence in European society from World War I and the Bolshevik Revolution and Civil War (as well as the attacks against Jews in Ukraine) led to a new attitude toward violence in politics. Additionally, the riots against Jews in Palestine could—or perhaps should—be connected as well. It would be naïve to think that these events had no influence at all. Nonetheless, despite Jabotinsky's association with the Legion and "The Iron Wall," he also expressed sympathies for minority rights and even entered into negotiations with members of Brit Shalom in the early 1930s. One historian writes, for example, that "Jabotinsky's seemingly unexpected praise for the Arab national movement moved Kalvarisky of Brit Shalom to congratulate him on his clear-sightedness. Yet, it was not as unexpected as it may seem, stemming as it did from his belief that nationalism was a positive phenomenon, bringing progress in its wake. Anxious as he always was to demonstrate his public integrity, he could not deny to the Arabs that which he sought for the Jews. But when two just causes confronted each other, he favored his own people, without denying the honor of the other side, adopting an attitude of political courtliness."[11]

It will be up to every reader to decide whether political courtliness exonerates Jabotinsky or not. But at least from this book, we know how and from where Jabotinsky became a Zionist and what that designation meant to him.

Notes

1. Ya'akov Shavit, *Jabotinsky and the Revisionist Movement, 1925–1948* (London: F. Cass, 1988), 43.

2. Daniel Heller, *Jabotinsky's Children: Polish Jews and the Rise of Right-Wing Zionism* (Princeton, NJ: Princeton University Press, 2017), 10.

3. Bernard Wasserstein, *On the Eve: The Jews of Europe before the Second World War* (New York: Simon and Schuster, 2012), 59.

4. Jan Zouplna, "'State-Forming Zionism' and the Precedent for Leadership—T. Herzl, V. Jabotinsky, and D. Ben-Gurion," *Asian and African Studies* 13 (2004): 41.

5. Quoted in Jan Zouplna, "Revisionist Zionism: Image Reality and the Quest for Historical Narrative," *Middle Eastern Studies* 44, no. 1 (2008): 5.

6. Zouplna, "'State-Forming Zionism,'" 47.

7. Ibid., 33.

8. Shavit, *Jabotinsky and the Revisionist Movement*, 2–3.

9. Svetlana Natkovich, "The Rise and Downfall of Cassandra: World War I and Vladimir (Ze'ev) Jabotinsky's Self-Perception," *Medaon-Magazin für jüdisches Leben in Forschung und Bildung* 10 (2016): 5.

10. Ernst Nolte, *Three Faces of Fascism: Action Française, Italian Fascism, National Socialism* (New York: Henry Holt, 1966).

11. Yosef Gorny, *Zionism and the Arabs, 1882–1948* (Oxford: Clarendon Press, 1987), 171–172.

BIBLIOGRAPHY

Archives Consulted

Archives of the Vladimir Jabotinsky Institute in Tel Aviv, Israel
Archives of the Jewish Division of the Vernadsky National Library, Kiev, Ukraine
Archives of the Jewish People, Jerusalem, Israel
YIVO Archives, New York, United States

Newspapers Consulted

Betar
Davar
Die Welt
Doar Hayom
Evreiskaia Tribuna
Evreiskaia Zhizn'
Hadagel
Haynt
Jewish Chronicle
The Jewish Herald
Medina Ivrit
Menorah
The New Palestine
Novnyi Voskhod
Odesskie Novosti
Odesskii Listok
Rassvet
Russkie Vedomosti
Vestnik Evropy
Voskhod

Works Consulted

Abramson, Henry. *A Prayer for the Government: Ukrainians and Jews in Revolutionary Times, 1917–1920.* Cambridge, MA: Ukrainian Research Center, 1999.
———. "Two Jews, Three Opinions: Politics in the Shtetl at the Turn of the Twentieth Century." In *The Shtetl: New Evaluations*, edited by Steven T. Katz, 85–101. New York: New York University Press, 2007.
Achimeir, Abba. *Berit ha-Biryonim*. Tel Aviv: Ha-va'ad le-hotsa'at kitve Achimeir, 1972.
———. *Ha-Tsionut ha-mahapkhanit*. Tel Aviv: Ha-va'ad le-hotsa'at kitve Achimeir, 1966.

Adamovich, Georgii. *Vasilii Alekseevich Maklakov, politik, iurist, chelovek.* Paris: Izd. Druzei B. A. Maklakova, 1959.
Ahad Ha'am. *Al parashat derakhim.* Berlin: Jüdischer Verlag, 1921.
——. *Kol Kitve Ahad-Ha'am.* Jerusalem: Dvir, 1947.
Akin, Yigit. *When the War Came Home: The Ottomans' Great War and the Devastation of an Empire.* Palo Alto, CA: Stanford University Press, 2018.
Almog, Oz. *The Sabra: The Creation of the New Jew.* Translated by Haim Watzman. Berkeley: University of California Press, 2000.
Alroey, Gur. "The Hebrew Hero and the Jewish Victim: Pogroms in the Ukraine in the Years 1918–1920 and the Riots of 1920 and 1921 in Palestine." *Zion* 4 (2015): 551–581.
——. *Zionism without Zion: The Jewish Territorial Organization and Its Conflict with the Zionist Organization.* Detroit: Wayne State University Press, 2016.
Alter, Robert. Introduction to *Modern Hebrew Literature*, 1–12. New York: Behrman House, 1975.
Aronson, Grigory. *Rusish-yidishe intelligents (Klal-tuer, shreiber, politiker, tragishe geshtaltn).* Buenos Aires: IDBUJ, 1962.
——, ed. *Russian Jewry (1860–1917).* Translated by Mirra Ginsburg. New York: A. S. Barnes, 1966.
Artsybachev, Mikhail. *Sanin.* Moscow: Zhizn', 1907.
Ascher, Abraham. *The Revolution of 1905: Russia in Disarray.* Palo Alto, CA: Stanford University Press, 1988.
——. *The Revolution of 1905: A Short History.* Palo Alto, CA: Stanford University Press, 2004.
Avineri, Shlomo. *Herzl's Vision: Theodor Herzl and the Foundation of the Jewish State.* New York: BlueBridge, 2017.
——. *The Making of Modern Zionism: The Intellectual Origins of the Jewish State.* New York: Basic Books, 1981.
Bachi, R., *The Population of Israel.* Paris: CICRED, 1974.
Bakhtin, Mikhail. *Problemy tvorchestva Dostoevskogo.* Leningrad: Priboi, 1929.
Baron, Salo W. *The Russian Jew under Tsars and Soviets.* New York: Macmillan, 1964.
Bartal, Israel. *The Jews of Eastern Europe, 1772–1881.* Translated by Chaya Naor. Philadelphia: University of Pennsylvania Press, 2005.
——. *Kahal Israel: Ha-shilton ha-etzmi ha-yehudi le-dorotav.* Jerusalem: Zalman Shazar Center, 2004.
Bartal, Israel and Isaiah Gafni, eds. *Eros, Erusin ve-isurim: Miniut u'mishpakha be-historiya.* Jerusalem: Zalman Shazar Center, 1998.
Bartal, Israel et al., eds. *Ha-Aliya ha-shniya.* Jerusalem: Yad Ben Zvi, 1997.
Basic Principles of Revisionism: Compiled from the Resolutions of the First, Second, and Third World Conferences of the Union of Zionists-Revisionists. London: Union of Zionists-Revisionists, 1929.
Bemporad, Elissa. *Becoming Soviet Jews: The Bolshevik Experiment in Minsk.* Bloomington: Indiana University Press, 2013.
Ben Naeh, Yaron. "The Zionist Struggle as Reflected in the Jewish Press in Istanbul in the Aftermath of the Young Turk Revolution, 1908–18." In *Late Ottoman Palestine: The Period of Young Turk Rule*, edited by Yuval Ben-Basssat and Eyal Ginio, 241–257. London: I. B. Tauris, 2011.

Ben-Bassat, Yuval. "Rethinking the Concept of Ottomanization: The Yishuv in the Aftermath of the Young Turk Revolution of 1908." *Middle Eastern Studies* 45, no. 3 (2009): 461–475.
Ben-Gurion, David. *Chaluzischer Zionismus oder Revisionismus*. Berlin: Hehalutz, 1934.
———. *Mi-Ma'amad le-Am*. Tel Aviv: Am Oved, 1974.
Ben-Horin, Eliahu. *The Middle-East, Crossroads of History*. New York: Norton, 1943.
Benari, I. *Herut, Gahal, Likud: An Analytical Survey and Review of the Evolution of Israel's Main Political Opposition Bloc*. London: Herut Movement, 1974.
Benbassa, Esther, and Aron Rodrigue. *Sephardi Jewry: A History of the Judeo-Spanish Community, 14th–20th Centuries*. Berkeley: University of California Press, 1995.
Bensman, Stephan J. "The Constitutional Ideas of the Russian Liberation Movement: The Struggle for Human Rights during the Revolution of 1905." PhD diss., University of Wisconsin, 1977.
Berkowitz, Michael. *Zionist Culture and West European Jewry before the First World War*. Chapel Hill: North Carolina Press, 1996.
Berlin, Isaiah. *Russian Thinkers*. New York: Penguin Classics, 2008.
Bialik, Kh. N. *Pesni i poemy: Avtorizovannyi perevod s evreiskogo i vvedenie Vl. Zhabotinsky*. St. Petersburg: S. D. Zal'tsman, 1911.
Bickerman, Iosif Menassievich. "O sionizme i po povodu sionizma." *Russkoe Bogatstvo* 7 (1902): 27–69.
Bilski Be-Hr, Rephaella. *Kol yahid hu melech: Ha-machshava he-hevruti ve-ha-medinit shel Ze'ev Z'abotinski*. Tel Aviv: Dvir, 1988.
Bisk, Aleksandr. "Odesskaia literaturka." In *Diaspora*, edited by Vladimir Alloy, 115–126. Paris: Atheneum-Phoenix, 2001.
Blum, Mark E. *The Austro-Marxists, 1890–1918: A Psychobiographical Study*. Lexington: University Press of Kentucky, 1985.
Boele, Otto. *Erotic Nihilism in Late Imperial Russia: The Case of Mikhail Artsybashev's Sanin*. Madison: University of Wisconsin Press, 2009.
Bohon, J. W. "Reactionary Politics in Russia: 1905–1909." PhD diss., University of North Carolina at Chapel Hill, 1967.
Bottomore, Tom, and Patrick Goode, eds. *Austro-Marxism*. Translated by Tom Bottomore and Patrick Goode. Oxford: Clarendon Press, 1978.
Brutskus, Yu. D. et al., eds. *Sbornik pamiati A. D. Idel'sona*. Berlin: Lutse & Bogt, 1925.
Brutskus, Yuly. "V. Zhabotinskii v russkom sionizme." *Rassvet* 42 (October 19, 1930): 9–10.
Budnitskii, Oleg. "Berlin Debates: The Jews and the Russian Revolution." In *Jewish Thought, Utopia, and Revolution*, edited by Elena Namli et al., 111–126. Amsterdam: Rodopi, 2014.
Budnitskii, Oleg, and Aleksandra Polan. *Russko-evreiskii Berlin, 1920–1941*. Moscow: Novoe Literaturnoe Obozrenie, 2013.
Cahan, Natan. *Sefer, sofer, ve-iton: Merkaz ha-tarbut ha-yehudit be-varshe, 1918–1942*. Jerusalem: Hebrew University, 2003.
Chlenov, Yehiel. *Polozhenie sionizma v Rossii: k vii-mu kongresu*. St. Petersburg: Ts. Kraiz, 1905.
———. *Sion i afrika na shestom kongresse*. Moscow: Poplavskii, 1905.
Chukovskii, Kornei. "Evrei i russkaia literatura." *Svobodnye Mysli* (January 14 [27], 1908).
———. "Kak ia stal pisatelem," *Zhizn' i tvorchestvo Korneiia Chukovskogo: Sbornik*. Moscow: Detskaia literatura, 1978.

Cleveland, William L., and Martin Bunton. *A History of the Modern Middle East*, 6th edition. Boulder, CO: Westview, 2016.
Cohen, Hillel. *Year Zero of the Arab-Israeli Conflict: 1929*. Translated by Haim Watzman. Waltham, MA: Brandeis University Press, 2015.
Cohen, Mitchell. *Zion and State: Nation, Class and the Shaping of Modern Israel*. New York: Basil Blackwell, 1987.
Conforti, Yitzhak. "Between Ethnic and Civic: The Realistic Utopia of Zionism," *Israeli Affairs* 17, no. 4 (October 2011), 563–582.
Cronin, David. *Balfour's Shadow: A Century of British Support for Zionism and Israel*. London: Pluto, 2017.
Dekel-Chen, Jonathan et al. *Anti-Jewish Violence: Rethinking the Pogrom in East European History*. Bloomington: Indiana University Press, 2011.
Denis, Brian. *The Seven Lives of Colonel Patterson*. Syracuse, NY: Syracuse University Press, 2008.
Dos Legen fun Yosef Trumpeldor. Warsaw: Tel-Chai, 1930.
Dothan, Shmuel. *Ha-maavak al-Eretz Yisrael*. Jerusalem: Chadkal, 1992.
———. *Pulmus ha-haluka bi-tekufat ha-Mandat*. Jerusalem: Yad Itzhak Ben-Zvi, 1979.
Druyanov, Asher. *Pinsker uzmano*. Jerusalem: Reuven Mass, 1953.
Dubnov, Arie. "'Ha-medina she ba-derko imperiya maka shenit? Imperialism Federativi uLeumiyut Yehudit be-ikvot Milchemet ha-Olam ha-Rishona." *Israel* 24 (Fall 2016): 5–36.
Dubnov, Arie, and Brian Horowitz. "Jabotinsky, Vladimir (Ze'ev)." *1914–1918-onLine—International Encyclopedia of the First World War*. Freie Universität Berlin: Friedrich-Meinecke-Institut, 2018. http//www.1914–1918-online.net.
Dubnov, Semyon. *Pis'ma o starom i novom evreistve*. St. Petersburg: Obshchestvennaia pol'za, 1907.
———. "Uroki strashnykh dnei." *Voskhod* 47–48 (December 1, 1905): 8–12.
Efron, John M. *Defenders of the Race: Jewish Doctors and Race Science in Fin-de-Siècle Europe*. New Haven, CT: Yale University Press, 1994.
Elboim-Dror, Rachel. *Ha-hinukh ha-ivri be-Eretz Yisrael*. 2 vols. Jerusalem: Yad Yitzhak Ben Zvi, 1986.
Emmons, Terrence. "Russia's Banquet Campaign." *California Slavic Studies* 10 (1977): 45–86.
Engel, David. "The Elite and the Street: The Schwarzbard Affair (1926–1927) as a Turning Point in Jewish Diplomacy." *Jahrbuch des Simon-Dubnow-Instituts* 15 (2016): 157–166.
———. Introduction to *The Assassination of Symon Petliura and the Trial of Scholem Schwarzbard, 1926–1927: A Selection of Documents*, 7–94. Göttingen: V&R Academic, 2016.
Erez, Yehuda, ed. *Chalutzim ha'yinu be-rusya*. Tel Aviv: Am Oved, 1990.
Even-Shoshan, Zvi. *Toldot tenuat ha-po'alim be-Eretz Yisrael*. Tel Aviv: Am Oved, 1963.
Fishman, David. *The Rise of Modern Yiddish Culture*. Pittsburgh: University of Pittsburgh Press, 2005.
Frame, Murray, ed. *Russian Culture in War and Revolution, 1914–1922*. 2 vols. Bloomington, IN: Slavica, 2014.
Frankel, Jonathan. *Crisis, Revolution, and Russian Jews*. Cambridge: Cambridge University Press, 2009.
———. *Prophecy and Politics: Socialism, Nationalism and the Russian Jews, 1862–1917*. Cambridge: Cambridge University Press, 1981.
Freeze, Gregory. "A National Liberation Movement and the Shift in Russian Liberalism, 1901–1903." *Slavic Review* 28 (March 1969): 81–91.

Frenkel', Aleksandr. "Falsifikatsiia Zhabotinskogo non-stop." *Narod Knigi v Mire Knig* (August 2014): 1–3.
Friedlander, Yehuda. *"He-arot le-yitsirato ha-sifrutit shel Ze'ev Z'abotinsky."* In *Ish be-sa'ar: Masot u'mekhkarim 'al Ze'ev Z'abotinski*, edited by Avi Bareli and Pinhas Ginossar, 283–298. Ber-Sheva: Universitat Ben-Guryon ba'Negev, 2004.
Fromkin, David. *A Peace to End All Peace: The Fall of the Ottoman Empire and the Creation of the Modern Middle East.* New York: Holt Paperbacks, 2009.
Galai, Shmuel. *The Liberation Movement in Russia, 1900–1905.* Cambridge: Cambridge University Press, 1973.
Galperin, I. "V. E. Zhabotinskii (biograficheskii ocherk)." In *Evreiskii mir: Sbornik* 2, 215–226. New York: Union of Russian Jews, 1944.
Gans, Chaim. *A Just Zionism: On the Morality of the Jewish State.* New York: Oxford University Press, 2008.
Gardzonio, S. "Zhabotinskii ital'ianskogo perioda." In V. (Z.) Zhabotinskii, *Polnoe sobranie sochinenii v 9 tomakh*, 2:6–18. Minsk: Met, 2007–2019.
Gassenschmidt, Christoph. *Jewish Liberal Politics in Tsarist Russia, 1900–1914: The Modernization of Russian Jewry.* New York: New York University Press, 1995.
Gechtman, Roni. "Conceptualizing National-Cultural Autonomy: From the Austro-Marxists to the Jewish Labor Bund." *Jahrbuch des Simon-Dubnow-Instituts* 4 (2005): 17–49.
———. "A 'Museum of Bad Taste'?: The Jewish Labour Bund and the Bolshevik Position Regarding the National Question, 1903–14." *Canadian Journal of History* 43 (Spring-Summer 2008), 31–67.
Gershenzon, Mikhail. *Sud'by evreiskogo naroda.* Moscow, 1922.
Gessen, Iulii. *Istoriia evreiskogo naroda v Rossii.* Moscow: Evreiskii Universitet v Moskve, 1993.
Gessen, V. *V dvukh vekakh: zhiznennyi opyt.* Berlin, 1937.
Gilbert, Martin. *Israel: A History.* New York: Harper, 1998.
Gintsburg, Shaul. *Meshumodim in Tsarishen Rusland: Forshungen un zikhroynes vegn Yidishn lebn in amolikn Rusland.* New York: Tsiko bikher verlag, 1946.
Gol'denveizer, A. A. "Pravovoe polozhenie evreev v Rossii." In *Kniga o russkom evreistve, ot 1860-kh godov do revoliutsii 1917 g.: Sbornik statei*, 115–158. Minsk: Met, 2002.
Goldin, Semyon. "Liberalizm, nacjonalizm i 'kwestia żydowska' w Imperium Rosyjskim (koniec XIX - początek XX wieku)." *Kwartalnik Historii Żydów* 2 (Czerwiec 2016): 253–277.
Goldshtein, Yossi. *Bin tsionut medinit le-tsionut ma'asit: Ha-tenuah ha-tsionit be-rusya ba-reshitah.* Jerusalem: Magnes, 1991.
———. "Jabotinsky and Jewish Autonomy in the Diaspora." *Studies in Zionism* 7, no. 2 (1986): 219–232.
———. *Ussishkin biografiya: ha-tekufa ha-rusit, 1853–1919.* 2 vols. Jerusalem: Magnes, 2000.
Goldstein, Amir. *Derekh rabat-panim: Tsiyonuto shel Ze'ev Z'abotinski le-nokhah ha-antishemiyut.* Kiryat Sedeh-Boker: Jabotinsky Institute, 2015.
Goldstein, Bernard. *Twenty Years with the Jewish Labor Bund: A Memoir of Interwar Poland.* Translated by Bernard Goldstein. West Lafayette, IN: Purdue University Press, 2016.
Golomb, Eliyahu. *Hevyon oz.* 2 vols. Tel Aviv: Mifleget Po'ale Eretz-Israel, 1950–1953.
———. *The History of Jewish Self-Defense in Palestine (1878–1921).* Tel Aviv: Lion the Printer, for the Zionist Youth Department, 1947.
———. "Ve-tnuat ha-gdudim ha-ivriim," *Ma'arahot: Yarhon le-she'elot mediniyot, kalkaliot ve-tsva'iyot.* (Heshvan-Tevet, 1941).

Golomb, Jacob. *Nietzsche and Zion*. Ithaca, NY: Cornell University Press, 2004.
Gordis, Daniel. *Israel: A Concise History of a Nation Reborn*. New York: Harper-Collins, 2016.
Gorky, Maxim. *Literaturnoe nasledstvo*. Moscow: Nauka, 1988.
Gorny, Yosef. *Converging Alternatives: The Bund and the Zionist Labor Movement, 1897–1985*. Albany: State University of New York Press, 2006.
———. "To Understand Oneself: Does It Mean to Understand the Other?" *Israel Studies* 19, no. 2 (Summer 2013): 41–52.
———. *Zionism and the Arabs, 1882–1948: A Study of Ideology*. Translated by Chaya Galai. Oxford: Clarendon, 1987.
Grauer, Mina, ed., *Ha-Itonut shel ha-tenua ha-revizionistit be-shanim 1925–1948*. Tel Aviv: Machon Jabotinsky, 2000.
Greenbaum, Avraham. "Shimon Dubnov ve-'ha-Miflaga ha-Amamit' ('Volkspartei'). In *Safra ve-Saifa—Shimon Dubnov: Historion ve-Ish Tsibur*, edited by Avraham Greenbaum, Israel Bartal, and Dan Haruv, 189–196. Jerusalem: Zalman Shazar Center, 2011.
Greenfeld, Liah. *Nationalism: Five Roads to Modernity*. Cambridge, MA: Harvard University Press, 1992.
Gribetz, Jonathan. *Defining Neighbors: Religion, Race, and the Early Zionist-Arab Encounter*. Princeton, NJ: Princeton University Press, 2014.
Grinbaum, Yitzhak. "Me-Varsha ad Helsingfors (shalosh veidot rishonot shel tsionim be-rusya)," *Katsir: kovets le-korot* 1:33.
———. *Pnei ha-dor*. 2 vols. Jerusalem: Ha-sifriya ha-tsionit, 1957–1960.
Grinberg, Marat. "Was Jabotinsky the Zionist Nabokov?" *Tablet Magazine*, August 4, 2014. http//www.tabletmag.com/jewish-arts-and-culture/books/180735/jabotinsky-the-zionist.
Grossman, Meer. *The Case Against the Mixed Jewish Agency*. London: Union of Zionist Revisionists, 1920.
Gwynne, S. G. *Empire of the Summer Moon: Quanah Parker and the Rise and Fall of the Comanches, the Most Powerful Indian Tribe in American History*. New York: Scribner, 2010.
Hacohen, Dvora. "British Immigration Policy to Palestine in the 1930s: Implications for Youth Aliyah." *Middle Eastern Studies* 37, no. 4 (October 2001): 206–218.
Hagen, Mark von. "The Russian Empire." In *After Empire*, edited by Karen Barkey and Mark von Hagen, 58–72. Boulder, CO: Westview, 1997.
Hale, William. *Turkish Foreign Policy Since 1774*. 3rd ed. New York: Routledge, 2012.
Halkin, Hillel. *Jabotinsky: A Life*. New Haven, CT: Yale University Press, 2014.
Halperin, Liora. *Babel in Zion: Jews, Nationalism, and Language Diversity in Palestine, 1920–1948*. New Haven, CT: Yale University Press, 2014.
Halpern, Ben. *The Idea of the Jewish State*. Cambridge, MA: Harvard University Press, 1961.
Halpern, Ben, and Jenhuda Reinharz. *Zionism and the Creation of a New Society*. Hanover, NH: University Press of New England-Brandeis University Press, 2000.
Haramati, Shlomo. *Ha-hinuch ha-ivri be-mishnato shel Z'abotinski*. Jerusalem: Ha-histadrut ha-zionit ha-olamit, 1981.
Harris, Ya'akov et al., eds. *Idan ha-tsionut*. Jerusalem: Zalman Shazar Center, 2000.
Harshav, Benjamin. *Language in a Time of Revolution*. Berkeley: California University Press, 2003.

Ha-tsionut u'mitnagdcha be-am ha-yehudi: Kovets ma'amarim. Jerusalem: Ha-sifriya ha-tsionit, 1990.
Heller, Daniel. *Jabotinsky's Children: Polish Jews and the Rise of Right-Wing Zionism.* Princeton, NJ: Princeton University Press, 2017.
———. "Obedient Children and Reckless Rebels: Jabotinsky's Youth Politics and the Case for Authoritarian Leadership, 1931–1933." *Journal of Israeli History: Politics, Society, Culture* 34, no.1 (2015): 45–68.
———. "The Rise of the Zionist Right: Polish Jews and the Betar Youth Movement, 1922–1935." PhD diss. Stanford University, 2012.
Heller, Joseph. "Zeev Jabotinsky and the Revisionist Revolt against Materialism: In Search of a Worldview." *Jewish History* 12, no. 2 (Fall 1998): 51–67.
———. *The Zionist Idea.* New York: Schocken, 1949.
Hen-Tov, Jacob. *Communism and Zionism in Palestine: The Comintern and the Political Unrest in the 1920s.* Cambridge, MA: Schenkman, 1974.
Herbert, Samuel. *Zionism: Its Ideals and Practical Hopes.* London, 1919.
Herlihy, Patricia. "Port Jews of Odessa and Trieste: A Tale of Two Cities." *Jahrbuch des Simon-Dubnow Instituts* II (2003): 183–198.
Hertzberg, Arthur. *The Zionist Idea: A Historical Analysis and Reader.* Philadelphia: Jewish Publication Society, 1997.
Hetényi, Zsuzsa. *In a Maelstrom: The History of Russian-Jewish Prose, 1860–1940.* Budapest: Central European University Press, 2008.
Hever, Hanan. *Moledet ha-mavet ha-yafa: Estetika ve-politika be-shirat Uri Zvi Greenberg.* Tel Aviv: Am Oved, 2004.
Heymann, Michael, ed. *The Uganda Controversy: Minutes of the Zionist General Council.* 2 vols. Jerusalem: Hassifriya Haziyonit, 1977.
Hoffman, Stefani and Ezra Mendelsohn, eds. *The Revolution of 1905 and Russia's Jews.* Philadelphia: University of Pennsylvania Press, 2008.
Holtzman, Avner. *Hayim Nahman Bialik: Poet of Hebrew.* Translated by Orr Scharf. New Haven, CT: Yale University Press, 2017.
Holubec, Stanislav. "'We Bring Order, Discipline, Western European Democracy, and Culture to This Land of Former Oriental Chaos and Disorder.' Czech Perceptions of Sub-Carpathian Rus' and its Modernization in the 1920s." In *Mastery and Lost Illusions: Space and Time in the Modernization of Eastern and Central Europe*, edited by Wlodzimierz Borodziej et al., 223–250. Oldenbourg: De Gruyter, 2014.
Horowitz, Brian. "Hail to Assimilation: Vladimir 'Ze'ev' Jabotinsky's Ambivalence about Odessa's *Fin de Siècle*." *Novoe Literaturnoe Obozrenie* 73 (2005): 109–116.
———. *Jewish Philanthropy and Enlightenment in Late-Tsarist Russia.* Seattle: University of Washington Press, 2009.
———. "Maxim Vinaver and the First Russian State Duma." In *Russian Idea–Jewish Presence: Essays on Russian-Jewish Intellectual Life*, 18–36. Boston: Academic Studies, 2013.
———. "Principle or Expediency: Violence and Vladimir Jabotinsky's Struggle to Dominate the Zionist Movement." *Jahrbuch des Simon-Dubnow-Instituts* 15 (2017): 15–32.
———. *Russian Idea–Jewish Presence: Essays on Russian-Jewish Intellectual Life.* Boston: Academic Studies, 2013.
———. *Russian-Jewish Tradition: Intellectuals, Historians, Revolutionaries.* Boston: Academic Studies, 2017.

———. "Vladimir Jabotinsky and the Mystique of 1905." *Zion* 80, no. 4 (2015): 503–520.
———. "Was Vladimir Jabotinsky a 'Good' Politician?" In *Frankel Center Yearbook*. Ann Arbor: Frankel Center, 2012.
———. "What Is Russian in Russian Zionism? Synthetic Zionism and the Fate of Avram Idel'son." In *Russian Idea-Jewish Presence: Essays on Russian-Jewish Intellectual Life*. 54–71. Boston: Academic Studies, 2013.
Hroch, Miroslav. *Comparative Studies in Modern European History: Nation, Nationalism, Social Change*. Aldershot, UK: Ashgate Variorum, 2007.
Ianovskii, Vasilii. *Polia eliseiskie: Istoriia 'nezamechennogo pokoleniia russkogo zarubezh'ia*. Moscow: Astrel', 2012.
Idel'son, Avram. "Marksizm i evreiskii vopros." *Evreiskaia Zhizn'* 8 (August 1905): 86–88.
Ish be-sa'ar: Masot u'mekhkarim 'al Ze'ev Z'abotinski. Edited by Avi Bareli and Pinhas Ginossar. Ber-Sheva: Universitat Ben-Guryon ba-Negev, 2004.
Ivanova, Evgeniia. *Chukovskii i Zhabotinskii: Istoriia vzaimootnoshenii v tekstakh i kommentariiakh*. Moscow: Gesharim, 2005.
Jabotinsky, Eri. *Avi, Ze'ev Jabotinsky*. Jerusalem: Stimatzky, 1980.
Jabotinsky, Vladimir. "Angliia i 'mir v nich'iu'." *Russkie Vedomosti* (May 12, 1915): 5.
———. "Anton Cekhof e Massimo Gorki: L'Impressionismo nella literature russa." *Nuova Antologia* 96, no. 719 (1901): 723–733.
———. "Asemitizm." In *Fel'etony*, 2nd ed., 111–116. Berlin: S. D. Zal'tsman, 1922.
———. "Aufn pripichek. . . ." *Haynt* (October 15, 1931): 9–10.
———. "Bazel'skie vpechatleniia: Kongress sionistov. Ot nashego korrespondenta." *Odesskie Novosti* (August 19, 1903): 2.
———. Bazel'skie vpechatleniia: 'Mizrakhi.' Ot nashego korresp." *Odesskie Novosti* (August 20, 1903): 5.
———. "Bazel'skie vpechatleniia. Gertsl' i Neinsager'y." *Odesskie Novosti* (August 23, 1903): 3.
———. *Bund i Sionizm*. Odessa: Kadima, 1906.
———. "Bunt starcòw." *Nasz Przegląd* (February 12, 1936).
———. "Chernyi gost' (iz rechi, proiznesennoi pri otkrytii konferentsii Sionistov-Revizionistov." *Rassvet* 18 (May 3, 1925): 4–5.
———. (Vladimir Zhabotinskii). *Chuzhbina (P'esa)*. Jerusalem: Gesharim, 2000.
———. "The Crisis" (1920). Unpublished document in the Jabotinsky Institute Archive.
———. "Delo Stavskogo," *Rassvet* 29, no. 29 (October 22, 1933): 2–3; no. 30 (October 29, 1933): 2–3; no. 31 (November 5, 1933): 2; no. 32. (November 12, 1933): 2.
———. *Die Neue Zionistische Organisation*. Paris: 1935.
———. "Dnevnik." *Rassvet* 3 (January 17, 1926): 1.
———. "Etika zheleznoi steny." *Rassvet* 19, no. 44/45 (November 11, 1923): 2–4.
———. "The Evacuation Problem, Humanitarian Zionism." *Jewish Herald* 30, no. 9 (March 11, 1936): 4.
———. *Evidence Submitted to the Palestine Royal Commission on Behalf of the New Zionist Organization, House of Lords*. Tel Aviv, New Zionist Organization in Palestine, 1937.
———. "Evreiskaia revoliutsiia." *Khronika Evreiskoi Zhizni* 3 (January 24, 1906): 4–9.
———. "Evreiskii miting v S.-Peterburge." *Khronika Evreiskoi Zhizni* 46 (November 25, 1905): 10–11.
———. *Fel'etony*. St. Petersburg, 1913.
———. *Fel'etony*. 2nd ed. Berlin: S. D. Zal'tsman, 1922.

———. "From Door to Door." Propaganda Speech at a Keren Hayesod Drive Meeting in New York. Publicity Department. May 1922. Found in the Jabotinsky Institute Archive.
———. "Goroskop (1 Ianvaria 1912)." In *Fel'etony*, 2nd ed., 262–263. Berlin: S. D. Zal'tsman, 1922.
———. "Hêsped." *Evreiskaia Zhizn'* 13 (April 3, 1905): 8–10.
———. *Igrot*. Edited by Daniel Carpi. Jerusalem: Hassifriya Haziyonit, 1995.
———. "Jews and Fascism." *Jewish Daily Bulletin* (April 11, 1935): 2–3.
———. "Legion, stat'ia pervaia." *Rassvet* 10 (June 6, 1924): 4–6.
———. "Levye." *Rassvet* 21, no. 4 (January 25, 1925), 7–9.
———. "Mivtsar Akko." In *Katvim, Avtobiograiya*, by Vladimir Jabotinsky, 307–313. Jerusalem: Ari Jabotinsky, 1947.
———. "My burzhui." *Rassvet* 23, no.15–16 (April 17, 1927): 5–7.
———. "Na severe Afriki, Tuzemtsy." *Russkie Vedomosti* (January 6, 1915): 3.
———. "Nabroski bez zaglaviia." *Khronika Evreiskoi Zhizni* 1 (January 10, 1906): 8–15.
———. "Novaia Turtsiia i nashi perspektivy." *Rassvet* 5 (February 1, 1909): 1–5.
———. "O evreiakh i russkoi literature." In *Fel'etony*, 2nd ed., 62–70. Berlin: S. D. Zal'tsman, 1922.
———. "O iazykakh i prochem." *Odesskie Novosti* (January 25, 1911): 2.
———. "O konskriptsii." *Russkie Vedomosti* (October 24, 1915): 5.
———. "O sionizme." *Odesskie Novosti* (September 8, 1902): 3.
———. "Ot Morokko do Tunisa." *Russkie Vedomosti* (December 28, 1914): 3.
———. "O zheleznoi stene: My i araby." *Rassvet* 19, no. 42/43 (November 4, 1923): 2–4.
———. "Peace in Palestine: Hostility of Arab Troops, To the Editor of the *Times*." *London Times* (May 14, 1921): 6.
———. "Petliura i pogrom:Pis'mo v redaktsiiu." *Poslednie novosti* (October 11, 1927).
———. *Piatero*. Paris, 1936.
———. "Pis'ma o natsional'nostiakh i oblastiakh: evreistvo i ego nastroeniia." *Russkaia Mysl'* 1 (January 1, 1911): 95–114.
———. "Pis'ma Oskaru Gruzenbergu." *Vestnik Evreiskogo Universiteta v Moskve* 2, no. 6 (1994): 215–254.
———. "Pis'ma russkim pisateliam." *Vestnik Evreiskogo Universiteta v Moskve* 1 (1992): 200–21.
———. "Pole brani." *Rassvet* 50 (December 30, 1905): 6–7.
———. "Politicheskaia rol' Sefardov." *Rassvet* (March 22, 1909): 3.
———. *Polnoe sobranie sochinenii v deviati tomakh*. Minsk: Met, 2007.
———. "Predislovie." In *Gosudarstvo i natsiia*, by Karl Renner, 3–7. Odessa: Kadima, 1906.
———. *Razskazy* (sic.). Paris: Voltaire, 1930.
———. *Rechi, stat'i, vospominaniia*. Minsk: Met, 2004.
———. "Revolt of the Old Men." In *Nation and Society: Selected Articles*, 57–60. Tel Aviv: Shilton Betar, 1961.
———. "Russkaia laska." In *Fel'etony*, 2nd ed., 123–126. Berlin: S. D. Zal'tsman, 1922.
———. "Samoupravlenie natsional'nogo men'shinstva." *Vestnik Evropy* 9 (September 1913): 117–138; 10 (October 1913): 131–158.
———. *Samson Nazarei* (Paris, 1926).
———. "Sidia na polu . . . ." *Evreiskaia Zhizn'* 6 (June 1904): 14–21.
———. "Sionizm i Palestina." *Evreiskaia Zhizn'* 2 (February 1904): 203–221.
———. *Sippur Yamai*. In V. Jabotinsky, *Ktavim, Avtobiograiya*, edited by Eri Jabotinsky, 9–187. Jerusalem: 1947.

———. *Sippur yamai*. In *Golah ve-hitbolelut*. Tel Aviv: Sh. Zal'tsman, 1936.
———. *Slovo o polku: Istoriia evreiskogo legiona po vospominaniiam ego initsiatora*. Paris, 1928.
———. *Story of My Life*. Edited by Brian Horowitz and Leonid Katsis. Detroit: Wayne State University Press, 2017.
———. *Story of the Jewish Legion*. Translated by Shmuel Katz. New York: B. Ackerman, 1945.
———. *Taryag Milim: 613 (Hebrew) Words—Introduction into Spoken Hebrew (in Latin Characters)*. New York: Jabotinsky Foundation, 1949.
———. *Turkey and the War*. London: T. Fisher Unwin, 1917.
———. "U kolybeli Gel'singforskoi programmy." In *Sbornik pamiati A. D. Idel'sona*, edited by Iu. D. Brutskus et al., 83–92. Berlin: Lutse & Bogt, 1925.
———. "Urok iubileia Shevchenko (1911)." In *Fel'etony*, 2nd ed., 186–194. Berlin: S. D. Zal'tsman, 1922.
———. "Vegn Militarizm," *Haynt* (January 25, 1929).
———. "Vmesto apologii." In *Fel'etony*, 2nd ed., 9–17. Berlin: S. D. Zal'tsman, 1922.
———. "Vo Frantsii." *Russkie Vedomosti* (October 1, 1914): 2.
———. "Voproso sozyve evreiskogo uchreditel'nogo sobraniia." *Khronika Evreiskoi Zhizni* 46 (November 25, 1905): 36.
———. "Vrag rabochikh." *Rassvet* 31 (February 8, 1925): 2–6.
———. "Vskol'z." In *Polnoe sobranie sochenenii v deviati tomakh*, 2:658. Minsk: Met, 2007.
———. "V traurnye dni (1906)." In *Fel'etony*, 18–23. St. Petersburg, 1913.
———. "Vvedenie k pesniam i poemam Bialika." In *Pesni i poemy Bialika*, 7–55. St. Petersburg: S. D. Zal'tsman, 1911.
———. *Was wollen die Zionisten-Revisionisten?* Paris: Polyglotte, 1926.
———. "Wegen Avanturizm." *Haynt*. (February 26, 1932): 5–9.
———. *Zamelbukh far Beytarisher Yugend*. Munich: Hotsa'at ha-misrad ha-eropai shel shaltun betar, 1947.
Jacobson, Abigail and Moshe Naor. *Oriental Neighbors: Middle Eastern Jews and Arabs in Mandatory Palestine*. Waltham, MA: Brandeis University Press, 2016.
Jędrzejewicz, Wacław. *Pilsudski: A Life for Poland*. New York: Hippocrene Books, 1995.
Kahn, Jacobus. *Erez Israel, das jüdische Land*. Köln: Jüdischer Verlag, 1909.
Kaplan, Eran. *The Jewish Radical Right: Revisionist Zionism and Its Ideological Legacy*. Madison: University of Wisconsin Press, 2005.
———. "A Rebel with a Cause: Hillel Kook, Begin and Jabotinsky's Ideological Legacy." *Israel Studies* 10, no. 3 (Fall 2005): 87–103.
Kaplan, Eran and Derek Penslar, eds. *The Origins of Israel, 1882–1948: A Documentary History*. Madison: University of Wisconsin Press, 2011.
Karlip, Joshua M. *The Tragedy of a Generation: The Rise and Fall of Jewish Nationalism in Eastern Europe*. Cambridge, MA: Harvard University Press, 2013.
Katsis, Leonid F. "N. Ia. Kogan- 'N. Tasin'-V. E. Zhabotinskii v '*Kievskoi Mysli*' 1914–1917." In *Literatura i revoliutsiia, vek dvadtsatyi*, 27–48. Moscow: Liftat, 2019.
———. '*Russkaia vesna*' *Vladimira Zhabotinskogo*. Moscow: Rossiiskii Gosudarstvennyi Gumanitarnyi Universitet, 2019.
———. "V. Zhabotinskii i V. Rozanov: Ob odnoi nezamechennoi polemike (1911–1913–1918)." In *Russkaia eskhatologiia i russkaia literatura*, 62–88. Moscow: OGI, 2000.
Katsis, Leonid and Helen Tolstaya, eds. *Zhabotinskii i Rossiia: sbornik trudov Mezhdunarodnoi konferentsii 'Russian Jabotinsky: Jabotinsky and Russia,' posveshchennoi 130-letiiu*

V. E. Zhabotinskogo (Evreiskii Universitet v Ierusalime, iiul' 2010). Palo Alto, CA: Department of Slavic Languages and Literatures, Stanford University, 2013.

Katz, Shmuel. *Lone Wolf: A Biography of Vladimir (Ze'ev) Jabotinsky*. 2 vols. New York: Barricade Books, 1996.

Katzir: Kovets le-korot ha-tenuah ha-tsionit be-rusya. Edited by Arye-Leib Rafaeli. Tel Aviv: Masada, 1964.

Katznelson, Berl. *Kitvei B. Katznelson*. 12 vols. Tel Aviv: Mifleget Poalei Eretz Israel, 1945–1950.

Kaufman, A. E. *Za kulisami pechati: Iz vospominanii starogo zhurnalista*. St. Petersburg: Rossiiskaia Natsional'naia Biblioteka, 2011.

Kedourie, Elie. *Nationalism*. London: Hutchinson, 1966.

Kel'ner, Viktor. "Dva intsidenta: Iz russko–evreiskikh otnoshenii v nachale XX v." *Vestnik Evreiskogo Universiteta v Moskve* 3, no. 10 (1995): 190–199.

———. "'Ikh tseli mogut byt' vysokim, no oni – ne nashi tseli' (M. M. Vinaver-anti-tsionist)." *Judaica Petropolitana* 1 (2013): 114–133.

———. "The Jewish Question and Russian Social Life During World War I." *Russian Studies in History*, 43, no. 1 (Summer 2004): 11–40.

———. "Nesostoiavshiisia soiuz (Soiuz dostizheniia polnopravikh evreiskogo naroda v Rossii v dokumentakh i memuarakh)." Unpublished manuscript.

———. *Shchit': M. M. Vinaver i evreiskii vopros v Rossii v kontse XIX – nachale XX veka*. St. Petersburg: Evreiskii Universitet v St. Peterburge, 2018.

——— [Kh, Firin]. "Tak govoril Zhabotinskii: iz protokolov S"ezda Soiuza dlia dostizheniia polnopraviia evreiskogo naroda v Rossii." *Vestnik Evreiskogo Universiteta v Moskve* 4 (1993): 180–189.

———. "Vladimir Jabotinsky i russkie pisateli." *Vestnik Evreiskogo Universiteta v Moskve* 1 (1993): 215–255.

Keren, Michael, and Shlomit Keren. *We Are Coming, Unafraid: The Jewish Legions and the Promised Land in the First World War*. Lanham, MD: Rowman & Littlefield, 2010.

Khazan, Vladimir. "Eshche raz o 'fashizme' Zhabotinskogo." In *Zhabotinskii i Rossiia: sbornik trudov mezhdunarodnoi konferentsii, posviashchennoi 130-letiiu V. E. Zhabotinskogo (Evreiskii Universitet v Ierusalime, iiul' 2010)*, edited by E. Tolstaya & L. Katsis, 68–84. Palo Alto, CA: Stanford Slavic Studies, 2014.

———. *Osobennyi evreisko-russkii vozdukh*. Jerusalem: Gesharim, 2001.

———. *Pinkhas Rutenberg: Ot terrorista k sionistu*. 2 vols. Moscow: Mosty Kul'tury-Gesharim, 2008.

Kizevetter, A. *Narubezhe dvukh stoletii, Vospominaniia, 1881–1914*. Prague, 1929.

Klausner, Israel. *Be-darchei tsion: Perakim be-toldot ha-tsionut ve-techiyat ha-dibor ha-ivri*. Jerusalem: Reuven Mass, 1978.

———. *Be-Hit'orer am: ha-aliya ha-rishona me-rusya*. Jerusalem: Ha-sifriya ha-tsionit, 1962.

———. *Opozitsiya le-Herzl*. Jerusalem: Akhiever, 1960.

Klausner, Joseph [Yosef]. *Darki likrat ha-tehiya be-ha-geula: Avtobiograiya (1874–1944)*. Tel Aviv: Masada, 1946.

———. *Yotsrim u'vonim*. 2 vols. Tel Aviv: Dvir, 1929.

Kleinman, Moshe. "Ot 'Rassveta' do 'Rassveta'." *Rassvet* 1 (April 16, 1922): 5.

Klier, John. "Pogroms." In *The YIVO Encyclopedia of Jews in Eastern Europe*, edited by Gershom Hundert, 2:1378–1379. New Haven, CT: Yale University Press, 2008.

Kolatt, Israel. *Ha-tsionut ve-yisrael be-re'i ha-historion*. Jerusalem: Yad Yitzhak Ben Zvi, 2008.

——. "Mekomo shel Ze'ev Z'abotinski be-pitaron ha-leumi." In *Ish be-sa'ar: Masot u'mekhkarim 'al Ze'ev Z'abotinski*, edited by Avi Bareli and Pinhas Ginossar, 7–24. Ber-Sheva: Universitat Ben-Guryon ba'Negev, 2004.
Kopelman, Zoya. "Zhabotinski: Ot romanticheskogo chteniia k postupku." *Judaica Petropolitana* 8 (2017): 117–141.
Kornberg, Jacques. "Theodor Herzl: Zionism as Personal Liberation." In *Theodor Herzl: From Europe to Zion*, edited by Mark Gelber and Vivian Liska, 43–55. Tübingen: Niemayer, 2007.
Kramer, Martin. "The Forgotten Truth about the Balfour Declaration." *Mosaic*, June 5, 2017. https://mosaicmagazine.com/essay/2017/06/the-forgotten-truth-about-the-balfour-declaration/.
Krzywiec, Gregorz. "Eliminationist Anti-Semitism at Home and Abroad: Polish Nationalism, the Jewish Question and Eastern European Right-Wing Mass Politics." In *The New Nationalism and the First World War*, edited by Lawrence Rosenthal and Vesna Rodic, 65–73. New York: Palgrave, 2015.
Kulischer, Evgenii. *Europe on the Move: War and Population Changes, 1917–1947*. New York: Columbia University Press, 1948.
Kulisher, Aleksandr. "Politicheskii vozhd'." *Rassvet* 42 (October 19, 1930): 5.
——. "Voennyi Sionizm." *Svershenie* 1 (1925): 92–96.
Kulisher, Alexander, and Nikolai Sorin. "Russkaia demokratiia i natsional'nyi vopros." *Rassvet* 5 (1922): 6–7.
Laqueur, Walter. *A History of Zionism*. London, 1972.
Laqueur, Walter, and Barry Rubin, eds. *The Israeli-Arab Reader: A Documentary History of the Middle East Conflict*, 7th ed. New York: Penguin Books, 2008.
Lecke, Mirja. "Odessa without Dogma: Jabotinsky's *The Five*." *Ab Imperio* 1 (2012): 325–50.
Levin, Alfred. *Third Duma: Election and Profile*. New York: Gazelle Book Services, 1973.
Levin, Vladimir. "Ha-folks-partey shel Shimon Dubnov—sipur shel kishalon?" *Zion* 77 (2012): 359–68.
——. *Mi-mahapecha le-milhama: Ha-politika ha-yehudit be-rusya, 1907–1914*. Jerusalem: Zalman Shazar Center for Jewish History, 2016.
——. "Politics at the Crossroads—Jewish Parties and the Second Duma Elections, 1907." *Leipziger Beiträge zur jüdischen Geschichte und Kultur* 2 (2004): 129–46.
——. "Russian Jewry and the Duma elections, 1906–1907." *Jews and Slavs* 7 (2000): 233–258.
Lichtheim, Richard. *Toldot ha-tsionut be-germaniya*. Jerusalem: Ha-sifriya ha-tsionit, 1951.
Litvak, Olga. *Haskalah: The Romantic Movement in Judaism*. New Brunswick, NJ: Rutgers University Press, 2012.
Litvina, Viktoriia. "... i evrei, moia krov'": *Evreiskaia drama—russkaia stsena*. Moscow: Vozdushnyi transport, 1991.
Lloyd, Anne Patricia. "Jews under Fire: The Jewish Community and Military Service in World War I Britain." PhD diss, University of Southampton, 2009.
Loeffler, James. "Between Zionism and Liberalism: Oscar Janowsky and Diaspora Nationalism in America." *AJS Review* 34, no. 2 (November 2010): 289–308.
Löwe, Heinz-Dietrich. *The Tsars and the Jews: Reform, Reaction and Anti-Semitism in Imperial Russia, 1772–1917*. Chur: Routledge, 1993.
Maklakov, Vasilii. "1905–1906 gody." In *M. M. Vinaver i russkaia obshchestvennost' nachala XX veka*. Paris: 1937, 53–96.

———. *Pervaia Gosudarstvennaia Duma, 27 aprelia-8 iiulia 1906 goda*. Moscow: Tsentrpoligraf, 2006.
Makovsky, Mark. *Churchill's Promised Land: Zionism and Statecraft*. New Haven, CT: Yale University Press, 2007.
Maor, Yizhak. *Ha-Tenuah ha-tsionit be-rusya*. Jerusalem: Magnes & Hebrew University, 1986.
———. *Sionistskoe dvizhenie v Rossii*. Translated by O. Mints. Jerusalem: Biblioteka Alia, 1977.
Margolin, M. M. *Osnovnye techeniia v istorii evreiskogo naroda: etiud po filosofii istorii evreev*. St. Petersburg: Severnaia Skoropechatnia, 1900.
———. "O zadachakh Evreiskoi Zhizni." *Evreiskaia Zhizn'* 1 (1904): 1–2.
Margolina, Rakhel. *Rakhel Pavlovna Margolina i ee perepiska s Korneem Ivanovichem Chukovskim*. Jerusalem: Stav, 1978.
Markish, Shimon. "Quand Vladimir Jabotinsky était parisien: *Le rassviet*, revue sioniste-révisioniste en langue russe." Translated by Boris Czerny and Catherine Nicault. *Les Belles Lettres: Archives Juives* 1, no. 36 (2003): 70–88.
———. "Russko-evreiskaia literatura: predmet, podkhody, otsenki." *Novoe Literaturnoe Obozrenie* 15 (1995): 217–250.
———. "Zhabotinskii v parizhskom *Rassvete*," *Lechaim* 10, no. 114 (October 2001). https://lechaim.ru/ARHIV/114/markish.htm.
———. "Zhabotinskii: 50 let posle konchiny: ob"iasnenie v liubvi." *Evreiskii Zhurnal* 1 (1991): 61–76.
Marten-Finnis, Susanne, and Marcus Winkler, eds. *Die jüdische Presse im europäischen Kontext, 1686–1900*. Bremen: Edition lumière, 2006.
McMeekin, Sean. *The Ottoman Endgame: War, Revolution, and the Making of the Modern Middle East, 1908–1923*. New York: Penguin Books, 2015.
Mendelsohn, Ezra. *Class Struggle in the Pale: The Formative Years of the Jewish Workers Movement in Tsarist Russia*. Cambridge: Cambridge University Press, 1970.
Merezhkovskii, Dmitry. "O prichinakh upadka i o novykh techeniiakh sovremennoi russkoi literatury." *O prichinakh upadka i o novykh techeniiakh sovremennoi russkoi literatury*. Moscow: Direkt-Media, 2010.
———. *On Modern Jewish Politics*. Oxford: Oxford University Press, 1993.
Miliukov, Pavel. "Vinaver kak politik." In *M. M. Vinaver i russkaia obshchestvennost' nachala XX veka*. Paris: 1937, 19–52.
Miller, Rory, ed. *Britain, Palestine and Empire: The Mandate Years*. Surrey, UK: Ashgate, 2010.
———. "Sir Ronald Storrs: The Dream that Turned into a Nightmare." *Middle Eastern Studies* 36, no. 3 (2000): 114–144.
Mindlin, Viktor. *Gosudarstvennaia Duma Rossiiskoi Imperii i evreiskii vopros*. St. Petersburg: Alteleiia, 2014.
Mintz, Mitiyahu. "Al Shum ma hit'ehakta ha-'ohrana' ha'tsarit al tse'avdav shel Z'abotinski?" In *Ish be-sa'ar: Masot u'mekhkarim 'al Ze'ev Z'abotinski*, edited by Avi Bareli and Pinhas Ginossar, 449–457. Ber-Sheva: Universitat Ben-Guryon ba'Negev, 2004.
Miron, Dan. *Ilan metsel ba-gai: Ze'ev Z'botinski ve-Shirato*. Tel Aviv: Ha-Misdar al shem. Ze'ev Z'abotinski, 2005.
———. "Trumato shel Ze'ev Jabotinsky le'shira ha'evrit ha'modernit." In *Ish be-sa'ar: Masot u'mekhkarim 'al Ze'ev Z'abotinski*, edited by Avi Bareli and Pinhas Ginossar, 187–252. Ber-Sheva: Universitat Ben-Guryon ba'Negev, 2004.
Mogilner, Marina. "Fin de siècle imperii: Ostrovnaia utopia Vladimira Zhabotinskogo." *Novoe Literaturnoe Obozrenie* 1 (2018): 1–11.

Moss, Kenneth B. *Jewish Renaissance in the Russian Revolution*. Cambridge, MA: Harvard University Press, 2009.
Myers, David N. *Between Jew and Arab: The Lost Voice of Simon Rawidowicz*. Waltham, MA: Brandeis University Press, 2008.
Nakhimovsky, Alice. *Russian-Jewish Literature and Identity: Jabotinsky, Babel, Grossman, Galich, Roziner, Markish*. Baltimore, MD: Johns Hopkins University Press, 1992.
Naor, Arye. *David Raziel: Ha-mefaked ha-rashi shel ha-irgun ha-tzvai ha-leumi be-eretz-yisrael, hayav ve-tafkidato*. Jerusalem: Misrad Ha-bitakhon, 1990.
———. *Eretz-yisrael ha-shlema: Amuna u'mediniot*. Haifa: University of Haifa, 2001.
———. "Jabotinsky's New Jew: Concept and Models." *The Journal of Israeli History* 30, no. 2 (September 2011): 141–159.
———. "Mavo." In Ze'ev Z'botinsky, *Leumiut liberalit*, 11–56. Tel Aviv: Machon Jabotinsky be-Yisra'el, 2013.
Narrowe, Morton, H. "Jabotinsky and the Zionists in Stockholm (1915)." *Jewish Social Studies* 46, no. 1 (1984): 9–20.
Nathans, Benjamin. *Beyond the Pale: The Jewish Encounter with Late Imperial Russia*. Berkeley: University of California Press, 2004.
Natkovich, Svetlana. *Ben aneney zohar: Yetsirato shel Vladimir (Zeev) Z'abotinski be-heksher ha-hevrati*. Jerusalem: Magnes, 2015.
———. 'Bezdna' Andreeva v tolkovanii Jabotinskogo." In *Russkii Zhabotinskii. Zhabotinskii i Rossia*, edited by Lazar Fleishman et al., 114–128. Palo Alto: Stanford Slavic Studies, 2013.
———. "The Debate about the Jews and Russian Literature (1908) as a Milestone in the History of Theorization of Jewish Literatures." *Aschkenas. Zeitschrift für Geschichte und Kultur der Juden* 22, no. 1–2 (2014): 471–483.
———. "A Land of Harsh Ways: 'Tristan da Runha' as Jabotinsky's Social Fantasy." *Jewish Social Studies* 19, no. 2 (2013): 24–49.
———. "Odessa as 'Point de Capital': Economic, History and Time in Odessa Fiction." *Slavic Review* 75, no. 4 (Winter 2016): 847–871.
———. "The Rise and Downfall of Cassandra: World War I and Vladimir (Ze'ev) Jabotinsky's Self-Perception." *Medaon-Magazin für jüdisches Leben in Forschung und Bildung* 10 (2016): 1–11.
Nedava, Yosef. "Be-sa'ar ha-yamim." In *Ha-ish sh'haita et ha-zarem*, edited by Abba Achimeir. Tel Aviv, 1987.
———. "Jabotinsky be-Vina." *Gesher* 110 (1984): 56–65.
Netanyahu, Benzion. *The Founding Fathers of Zionism*. Jerusalem: Balfour Books, 2012.
———. "Z'abotinski ki-medinai ve-ki-manhig le-amo: Keitsad haya magiv al be'ayot zmanenu." In *Ish be-sa'ar: Masot ve-mekhkarim al Ze'ev Z'abotinski*. edited by Avi Bareli and Pinhas Ginossar, 25–38. Ber-Sheva: Universitat Ben Gurion, 2004.
Nimni, Ephraim, ed. *National Cultural Autonomy and its Contemporary Critics*. London: Routledge, 2005.
Nisselovich, L. N. *Evreiskii vopros v 3-ei Gosudarstvennoi Dumy: Otchet chlena Gosudarstvennoi Dumy*. St. Petersburg: Ts. Kraiz, 1908.
Niv, David. *Ma'arakhot ha-irgun ha-tsevai ha-leumi ("ha-hagana ha-leumit")*. 6 vols. Tel Aviv: Mosad Klausner, 1965–1980.
———. *A Short History of the Irgun Zevai Leumi*. Translated by D. Shefer. Jerusalem: World Zionist Organization, 1980.

Nolte, Ernst. *Three Faces of Fascism: Action Française, Italian Fascism, National Socialism.* New York: Henry Holt, 1966.
Nowogrodzki, Emanuel. *The Jewish Labor Bund in Poland, 1915–1939: From Its Emergence as an Independent Political Party until the Beginning of World War II.* Rockville, MD: Shengold, 2001.
Orbach, Alexander. "Between Liberal Integrationists and Political Segregationists: The Zionism of Asher Ginsberg (1889–1907)." *Studia Judaica* 6 (1997): 61–70.
———. "The Emergence of Ethnic Politics in 1905: The League for the Attainment of Full Rights for the Jews of Russia." *Russian History* 37 (2011): 412–426.
———. "The Jewish People's Group and Jewish Politics in Tsarist Russia," 1906–1914, *Modern Judaism* 10, no. 1 (February 1990): 1–15.
———. "Zionism and the Russian Revolution of 1905: The Commitment to Participate in Domestic Political Life," *Bar-Ilan University Annual* 24–25, no. 5749 (1989).
Oren, I. "Predislovie." In *Samson Nazarei*, vi–xvii. Tel Aviv: Aliya, 1990.
Oren, I., and Mikhail Zand, eds. "Zhabotinsky, Vladimir." *Kratkaia evreiskaia entskiklopediia.* Jerusalem: Obshestvo po issledovaniiu evreiskikh obshchin, 1992, 2: 486–487.
Orland, Nahum. *Israels Revisionisten: Die geistigen Väter Menachem Begins.* Munich: Tuduv, 1978.
Oz, Amos. *In the Land of Israel: Essays.* Translated by Maurie Goldberg-Bartura. Orlando, FL: Harcourt, 1983.
Pappe, Ilan. *A History of Modern Palestine: One Land, Two Peoples.* Cambridge: Cambridge University Press, 2006.
Pasenko, Natal'ia. "Zhabotinskii i politicheskie partii." *Moriia* 12 (2011): 6–20.
Patterson, John H. *With the Judeans in the Palestine Campaign.* New York: Macmillan, 1922.
———. *With the Zionists in Gallipoli.* London: Hutchinson & Co., 1916.
Pedahzur, Ami. *The Triumph of Israel's Radical Right.* Oxford: Oxford University Press, 2012.
Penslar, Derek. *Israel in History: The Jewish State in Comparative Perspective.* New York: Routledge, 2006.
———. *Jews and the Military: A History.* Princeton, NJ: Princeton University Press, 2013.
Petrovsky-Shtern, Yochanan. *Jews in the Russian Army, 1827–1917: Drafted into Modernity.* Cambridge: Cambridge University Press, 2009.
Pianko, Noam. *Zionism and the Roads Not Taken: Rawidowicz, Kaplan, Kohn.* Bloomington: Indiana University Press, 2010.
Pinsker, Leon. "Auto-Emancipation: An Appeal to His People by a Russian Jew." In *Road to Freedom: Writings and Addresses by Leo Pinsker*, edited by Benzion Netanyahu, 74–106. Translated by David S. Blondheim. New York: Scopus, 1944.
Poliaki i evrei: Materialy o pol'sko-evreiskom spore po povodu zakonoproekta o gorodskom samoupravlenii v Pol'she. Iz statei i zaiavlenii deputata Grabskogo, R. Dmovskogo, N. Dubrovskogo, V. Zhabotinskogo, deput. I. Petrunkevicha i A. Sventokhovskogo. Odessa: M. S. Kozmana, 1910.
Polonsky, Antony, *The Jews in Russia and Poland.* 3 vols. Portland: Littman Library, 1980.
Propes, Ahron. *Dos Legen fun Yosef Trumpeldor.* Warsaw: Tel-Chai, 1930.
Rabinovitch, Simon. *Jewish Rights, National Rites: Nationalism and Autonomy in Late Imperial and Revolutionary Russia.* Stanford: Stanford University Press, 2014.
Raeff, Marc. *Russia Abroad: A Cultural History of the Russian Emigration, 1919–1939.* Oxford: Oxford University Press, 1990.

Ratzabi, Shalom. *Between Zionism and Judaism: The Radical Circle in Brith Shalom, 1925–1933*. Leiden: Brill, 2002.
Rav Tsair (Chaim Tchernowitz). *Perkey haim: Autobiografiya*. New York: Bitzaron, 1964.
Ravitzky, Aviezer. *Messsianism, Zionism, and Jewish Religious Radicalism*. Translated by Michael Swirsky and Jonathan Chipman. Chicago: University of Chicago Press, 1996.
Raz-Krakotzkin, Amnon. "Orientalism, Jewish Studies and Israeli Society: A Few Comments." *Philological Encounters* 2 (2017): 237–269.
Redaktor. "Beseda s V. Zhabotinskim." *Rassvet* 4, no. 41 (January 28, 1923).
Reinharz, Jehuda. *Chaim Weizmann: The Making of a Statesman*. New York: Oxford University Press, 1993.
Reinharz, Jehuda, and Anita Shapira, eds. *Essential Papers on Zionism*. New York: New York University Press, 1996.
Reinharz, Jehuda, and Yaacov Shavit. *The Road to September 1939: Polish Jews, Zionists, and the Yishuv on the Eve of World War II*. Waltham, MA: Brandeis University Press, 2018.
Renner, Karl. *Gosudarstvo i natsiia*. Odessa: Kadima, 1906.
Riasanovsky, Nicholas V. *The Emergence of Romanticism*. Oxford: Oxford University Press, 1995.
Rogan, Eugene L. *The Fall of the Ottomans: The Great War in the Middle East*. New York: Basic Books, 2015.
Rogger, Hans. *Jewish Policies and Right-Wing Politics in Imperial Russia*. Berkeley: University of California Press, 1986.
Roshwald, Aviel. *The Endurance of Nationalism*. Cambridge: Cambridge University Press, 2006.
Rovner, Adam. "Jewish Geographies: Jabotinsky and Modernism." *Partial Answers* 15, no. 2 (2017): 315–339.
Salmon, Yosef. "Tradition and Nationalism." In *Essential Papers on Zionism*, edited by Jehuda Reinharz and Anita Shapira, 94–118. New York: New York University Press, 1996.
Sarid, Levi Ariye, ed. *He-halutz u'tenu'ot ha-noar be-polin, 1917–1939*. Tel Aviv: Am Oved, 1979.
Schechtman, Joseph B [Iosif]. *The Arab Refugee Problem*. New York: Philosophical Library, 1952.
———. "Emigrantskii sionizm." *Rassvet* 1 (January 7, 1923): 7–10.
———. "Emigrantskii sionizm, part II." *Rassvet* 2 (January 14, 1923): 9.
———. "Nasha arabskaia politika." *Rassvet* 31 (August 5, 1923): 4–5.
———. "The Jabotinsky-Slavinsky Agreement: A Chapter in Ukrainian-Jewish Relations." *Jewish Social Studies* 17 (1955): 289–306.
———. *The Life and Times of Vladimir Jabotinsky: Fighter and Prophet, The Last Years*. Silver Spring, MD: Eshel Books, 1986.
———. *The Life and Times of Vladimir Jabotinsky: Rebel and Statesman, The Early Years*. Silver Spring, MD: Eshel Books, 1986.
———. "Sovetskaia Rossiia, Sionizm i Izrael." In *Kniga o russkom evreistve, 1917–1967*, 325–353. Jerusalem: Gesharim, 2002.
———. "Ukhod V. E. Zhabotinskogo," *Rassvet* (February 4, 1923): 11–12.
Schechtman, Joseph B., and Yehuda Benari. *History of the Revisionist Movement, 1925–1930*. Tel Aviv: Hadar, 1970.
Scherr, Barry. "An Odessa Odyssey: Vladimir Jabotinsky's *The Five*." *Slavic Review* 70 (2011): 94–115.

Schwartz, Shalom. *Z'abotinski lokhem ha-umma.* Jerusalem: Dfus Ha-poel Ha-mizrachi, 1943.
Sefer Idelsohn: Divre ha-arakha ve-zikhronot, toldot hayav u'khetavav. Tel Aviv: Omanut, 1946.
Sefer Usisskin: La-yovel ha-shishim. Jerusalem, 1933.
Seltzer, Robert. "Ahad-Ha'am and Dubnow: Friends and Adversaries." In *At the Crossroads: Essays on Ahad-Ha'am,* edited by Jacques Kornberg, 60–73. Albany: State University of New York Press, 1983.
Sen, Amartya. "The Economic Consequences of Austerity." *The New Statesman.* (June 4, 2015).
Shaked, Gershon. *Ha-Sifrut ha-ivrit, 1880–1980.* Jerusalem: Keter, 2000.
Shapira, Anita. *Berl: The Biography of a Socialist Zionist, Berl Katznelson, 1887–1944.* Cambridge: Cambridge University Press, 1984.
———. "The Bible and Israeli Identity." *AJS Review* 28, no. 1 (2004): 11–42.
———. "Black Night–White Snow: Attitudes of the Palestinian Labor Movement to the Russian Revolution, 1917–29." *Studies in Contemporary Jewry* 4 (1988): 144–171.
———. *Ha-Maavak ha-nikhzav: 'Avodah 'ivrit, 1929–1939.* Tel Aviv: Univeristat-Tel Aviv, 1977.
———. *Israel: A History.* Translated by Anthony Berris. Waltham, MA: Brandeis University Press, 2012.
———. *Land and Power: The Zionist Resort to Force, 1881–1948.* Stanford, CA: Stanford University Press, 1999.
Shavit, Ya'akov. *Jabotinsky and the Revisionist Movement, 1925–1948.* London: F. Cass, 1988.
Sherman, A. J. *Mandate Days: British Lives in Palestine, 1914–1948.* London: Thames and Hudson, 1998.
Shilon, Avi. *Menachem Begin: A Life.* Translated by Danielle Zilberberg and Yoram Sharett. New Haven, CT: Yale University Press, 2012.
Shimoni, Gideon. *The Zionist Ideology.* Hanover, NH: Brandeis University Press, 1995.
Shindler, Colin. *The Rise of the Israeli Right: From Odessa to Hebron.* Cambridge: Cambridge University Press, 2015.
———. *The Triumph of Military Zionism: Nationalism and the Origins of the Israeli Right.* London: I. B. Tauris, 2009.
Shivat tsion: Sefer shana le-heker ha-tsionut u'tekumat yisrael. 2 vols. Jerusalem: Ha-sifriya ha-tsionit 1953–1956.
Shore, Marci. *Caviar and Ashes: A Warsaw Generation's Life and Death in Marxism, 1918–1968.* New Haven: Yale University Press, 2006.
Shteinberg, Aron. *Druz'ia moikh rannikh let (1911–1928).* Fontenay-aux-Roses: Syntaxis, 1991.
Shukman, Harold. *War or Revolution: Russian Jews and Conscription in Britain, 1917.* London: Vallentine Mitchell, 2006.
Shul'man, Alexander. "Biographiia." In *Iosif Trumpel'dor, Gekholuts, novyi put': Biografiia, vospominaniia, stat'i,* 14–79. Moscow: Koktebel', 2012.
Shumsky, Dmitry. *Beyond the Nation-State: The Zionist Political Imagination from Pinsker to Ben-Gurion.* New Haven, CT: Yale University Press, 2018.
———. "Tsionut u'medinat ha-leum: Ha'arakha me-hadash." *Zion* 1, no. 2 (January 2012): 223–254.
Silber, Marcos. "S. Dubnow and the Idea of Diaspora Nationalism and its Dissemination." *Iyunim Bitkumat Israel* 15 (2005): 83–101.
Slutzky, Yehuda. *Ha-itonut ha-yehudit rusit be-reshit be-mea ha-esrim (1900–1918).* Tel Aviv: Ha-aguda le-haker toldot ha-yihudim, 1978.

———. *Mavo le-toldot tenua ha-avoda ha-yisraelit.* Tel Aviv: Am Oved, 1973.
Sokolov, Florian. *Avi Nahum Sokolov.* Jerusalem: Daf-Chen, 1970.
Sokolow, Nahum. *History of Zionism.* 2 vols. London, 1919.
Sorel, George. *On Violence.* New York: Dover, 2004.
Stampfer, Shaul. *Families, Rabbis and Education: Traditional Jewish Society in Nineteenth-Century Eastern Europe.* Portland, OR: The Littman Library of Jewish Civilization, 2010.
Stanislawski, Michael. *Autobiographical Jews: Essays in Jewish Self-Fashioning.* Seattle: University of Washington Press, 2004.
———. *Zionism and the Fin de Siècle: Cosmopolitanism and Nationalism from Nordau to Jabotinsky.* Berkeley: University of California Press, 2001.
Stein-Ashkenazi, Esther. *Beitar be-eretz-yisrael, 1925–1947.* Jerusalem: Jabotinsky Institute, 1997.
Sternhell, Zeev. *The Birth of Fascist Ideology: From Cultural Rebellion to Political Revolution.* Princeton, NJ: Princeton University Press, 1994.
———. *The Founding Myths of Israel: Nationalism, Socialism, and the Making of the Jewish State.* Translated by David Maisel. Princeton, NJ: Princeton University Press, 1998.
———. *Neither Right nor Left: Fascist Ideology in France.* Berkeley: University of California Press, 1986.
Struve, Petr. "Intelligentsiia i national'noe litso." In *Patriotica: Politika, kul'tura, religiia, sotsializm,* 208–210. Moscow: Respublika, 1997.
Tager, Aleksandr. *Delo Beilisa: Tsarskaia Rossiia i Delo Beilisa, Issledovaniia i materialy.* Moscow: Gesharim, 1995.
Tcherikover, Elias. "Peter Lavrov and the Jewish Socialist Émigés." *Yivo Annual of Jewish Social Science* 7 (1952): 132–45.
Tessler, Mark. *Islam and Politics in the Middle East: Explaining the View of Ordinary Citizens.* Indianapolis: Indiana University Press, 2015.
Teveth, Shabtai. *Ben-Gurion: The Burning Ground, 1886–1948.* New York: Houghton Mifflin, 1987.
———. *Rettzah Arlossorov.* Jerusalem: Schoken, 1982.
Thing, Mortin. "Yiddish in Denmark," *Mendele Review* 11, no. 6 (May 25, 2007). http://yiddish.haifa.ac.il/tmr/tmr11/tmr11006.htm.
Tobias, Henry. "The Reassessment of the National Question." In *Essential Papers on Jews and the Left,* edited by Ezra Mendelsohn, 101–121. New York: New York University Press, 1997.
Tolstoy, Helen. *Akim Volynsky: A Hidden Russian-Jewish Prophet.* Translated by Simon Cook. Leiden: Brill, 2017.
Tolts, Mark, "Migration since World War I." In *The YIVO Encyclopedia of Jews in Eastern Europe,* edited by Gershom D. Hundert, 1435–1436. New Haven, CT: Yale University Press, 2008.
Tolts, Mark, and Anatoly Vishnevsky. "Nezamechennyi vklad v teoriiu demograficheskogo perekhoda: k 125-letiiu so dnia Rozhdeniia Aleksandra Kulishera." *Demograficheskoe obozrenie* 2, no. 4 (2015): 6–34.
Trivus, Israel. "Pervye shagi." *Rassvet* 42 (October 19, 1930): 17.
Troen, Ilan S. *Imagining Zion: Dreams, Designs, and Realities in a Century of Jewish Settlement.* New Haven, CT: Yale University Press, 2003.

Trumpeldor, Joseph. *Tagebücher und Briefe*. Berlin: Jüdischer Verlag, 1925.
Tsurumi, Taro. "The Russian Origins of Zionism: Interactions with the Empire as the Background of the Zionist Worldview." *Kyoto Bulletin of Islamic Area Studies* 3, no. 1 (July 2009): 261–271.
———. "Sociology as Methodology and Imagination: Analyzing the Emergence of Zionism in the Russian Empire." *International Journal of Japanese Sociology* 24, no. 1 (March 2015): 119–123.
Turgenev, Ivan. "Gamlet i Don-Kikhot." In *Polnoe sobranie sochinenii i pisem v tridtsati tomakh*, 2nd ed., 5:330–348. Moscow: Nauka, 1980.
Ury, Scott. *Barricades and Banners: The Revolution of 1905 and the Transformation of Warsaw Jewry*. Pale Alto: Stanford University Press, 2012.
Ussischkin, M. *Our Program: An Essay*. Translated by D. S. Bondheim. New York: Federation of American Zionists, 1905.
Vainshel, Ya'acov. *Jabo: Sirtutim le-dmuto shel Ze'ev Z'abotinski*. Tel Aviv: Ha-Matmid, 1954.
Veidlinger, Jeffrey. *Jewish Public Culture in the Late Tsarist Empire*. Bloomington: Indiana University Press, 2009.
Veiskopf, Mikhail. "Liubov' k dal'nemu: literaturnoe tvorchestvo Vladimira Zhabotinskogo." *Vestnik Evreiskogo Universiteta v Moskve* 29, no. 11 (2006): 195–250.
———. "Predislovie." In Vladimir Zhabotinskii, *Chuzhbina (P'esa)*, 5–14. Jerusalem: Gesharim, 2000.
Vekhi: Sbornik statei o russkoi intelligentsia. St. Petersburg, 1909.
Vinaver, Maksim. *Istoriia vyborgskogo vozzvaniia (vospominaniia)*. Moscow, 1913.
Vital, David. *The Origins of Zionism*. Oxford: Clarendon Press, 1975.
———. *Zionism: The Crucial Phase*. Oxford: Clarendon, 1987.
Volovici, Mark. "Leon Pinsker's Autoemancipation! and the Emergence of German as a Language of Jewish Nationalism." *Central European History* 50, no.4 (March 2017): 34–58.
"Vtoroe ocherednoe obshchee sobranie odesskogo obshchestva prosvesheniia, 6 marta," *Nedel'naia khronika voskhoda* 16 (1905): 18.
Waite, Zeev. *Vanguard of Nazism: The Free Corps Movement in Postwar Germany, 1919–1923*. New York: Norton, 1969.
Wasserstein, Bernard. *The British in Palestine: The Mandatory Government and the Arab-Jewish Conflict, 1917–1929*. 2nd ed. London: Blackwell, 1991.
———. *On the Eve: The Jews of Europe before the Second World War*. New York: Simon and Schuster, 2012.
Watts, Martin. *The Jewish Legion and the First World War*. London: Palgrave Macmillan, 2004.
Weeks, Theodore. *National and State in Late Imperial Russia: Nationalism and Russification on the Western Frontier, 1863–1914*. DeKalb: Northern Illinois University Press, 1996.
Weinbaum, Laurence. *A Marriage of Convenience: The New Zionist Organization and the Polish Government, 1936–1939*. Boulder, CO: East European Monographs, 1993.
Weitz, Yechiam, ed. *Bin hazon le-reviziya: Me'a shnot historiografiya tsionit*. Jerusalem: Merkaz Zalman Shazar, 1997.
———. *Bein Ze'ev Jabotinsky le-Menachem Begin:Kovets ma'amarim al ha-tenua ha-revizionistit*. Jerusalem: Magnes Press, 2012.
Weizmann, Chaim. *Trial and Error: The Autobiography of Chaim Weizmann*. New York: Harper, 1949.

Wertheimer, Jack. *Unwelcome Strangers: East European Jews in Imperial Germany*. New York: Oxford University Press, 1987.
Wheatcroft, Geoffrey. "The Finchley Factor." *London Review of Books* 40, no. 17 (September 13, 2018): 15–18.
Yeger, Moshe. *Toldot ha-makhlaka ha-medinit shel ha-sokhnut ha-yehudit*. Jerusalem: Mossad Bialik, 2011.
Zal'tsman, Shlomo. *Min he-avar: Zichronot u-reshumot*. Tel Aviv: Sh. Zal'tsman, 1943.
Zaslavskii, D. and St. Ivanovich. *Kadety i evrei*. Petrograd, 1916.
Zimmerman, Joshua. *Poles, Jews, and the Politics of Nationality: The Bund and the Polish Socialist Party in Late Tsarist Russia, 1892–1914*. Madison: Wisconsin University Press, 2004.
Zipperstein, Steven J. *Elusive Prophet: Ahad-Ha'am and the Origins of Zionism*. Berkeley: University of California Press, 1993.
———. "Odessa." In *The YIVO Encyclopedia of Jews in Eastern Europe*, 2 vols., edited by Gershom Hundert, 2:1277–1282. New Haven, CT: Yale University Press, 2008.
———. *Pogrom: Kishinev and the Tilt of History*. New York: Liveright Press, 2018.
Zouplna, Jan. "Beyond a One-Man Show: The Prelude of Revisionist Zionism, 1922–25." *Israel Affairs* 19, no.3 (2013): 410–432.
———. "Revisionist Zionism: Image, Reality and the Quest for Historical Narrative." *Middle Eastern Studies* 44, no. 1 (2008): 3–27.
———. "'State-Forming Zionism' and the Precedent for Leadership—T. Herzl, V. Jabotinsky, and D. Ben-Gurion." *Asian and African Studies* 13 (2004): 29–49.
———. "Vladimir Jabotinsky and the Split within the Revisionist Union: From the Boulogne Agreement to the Katowice Putsch, 1931–33." *Journal of Israeli History: Politics, Society, Culture* 24, no. 1 (2005): 35–63.

INDEX

Abdullah ibn Al-Hussein, 160
Achdut ha-Avoda Party, 198, 199–200
Achimeir, Abba, 159, 210, 216
Acre (Akko): "The Acre Fortress," 163;
  Jabotinsky interned in, 6, 163, 169;
  Jabotinsky released from, 160
Adler, Max, 55, 81
"Aesopian" language, 26, 53
Ahad-Ha'am (Asher Ginsberg), 7, 37,
  48, 57; on antisemitism, 61; compares
  Eastern and Western Jews, 36, 109; on
  Gegenwartsarbeit, 71; and Herzl, 37, 41,
  71; and negation of the Galut, 45, 50n46;
  in Odessa, 5, 17; on Palestine, 37, 84; and
  "Slavery in Freedom," 109
Aleinikov, Mikhail, 191, 192
Alexandrovsk, 127
Alexandrovsk Fortress, 23
Aliyah Bet, 217, 235
Aliyah, Second, 3, 43, 170, 210, 222
Aliyah, Third: labor brigade in, 200
Aliyah, Fourth: revisionists in, 206, 235;
  Yishuv hostility toward, 198
Allenby, Viscount Edmond (Gen.):
  campaigns of, 145–46, 155n80; in
  correspondence with Rutenberg, 135;
  forbids the Jewish Legion to fight in the
  Galilee, 162; liberates Jerusalem, 147; and
  military administration of Palestine, 161
Amery, Leopold, 126, 145
anti-Jewish riots (May 1–7, 1921), 147, 165,
  175, 238
antisemitism: and ideology, 2; Jabotinsky's
  analysis of, 17–18, 61–62, 103–11, 113–15, 117;
  in Jabotinsky's fiction, 89–91, 226; and
  Jabotinsky's politics, 9, 28, 79, 80, 196, 217,
  229, 231; prohibition of state, 104; rise of,
  9, 78–79, 110, 217; treated in *Poles and Jews*
  (1910), 110; and the Zionist movement,
  196, 119–20. *See also* asemitism; Cherikov

Affair; diaspora, Jewish; nationalism;
  pogroms; *and the names of individual
  people, places, government entities and
  political movements*
Arab nationalism: Jabotinsky's praise for,
  238; and Muslim brotherhoods, 131, 133;
  in North Africa, 132–33; in the Ottoman
  Empire, 82–84, 132; in Palestine, 158, 165. *See
  also* Arab-Jewish relations; Arabs; Palestine
Arab-Jewish relations: under British rule
  in Palestine, 157, 159–61; Jabotinsky on,
  85–86, 157–59, 168–69; separatism in, 159
Arab revolt (1936–1939), 230
Arab Riots (1920), 6, 147, 163, 175, 238
Arabs: and colonialism, 168, 174; as "enemies
  of the Zionist enterprise," 210; and
  Europeans, 131, 158; Palestinian, 3–4, 158,
  160, 171, 174, 176, 177, 180, 215; and pan-
  Arabism, 132; as policemen in Palestine,
  160; post-war prospects of, 150; and Turks,
  131–32. *See also* Orientalism
Arlosorov, Hayim, 227
Armenia, 81, 82, 68, 149
Aronson, Aron and Sarah, 135–36
Artsybachev, Mikhail (*Sanin*, 1907), 22
Asch, Sholem, 87
asemitism, 105–7
assimilation: Arab rejection of, 84; and
  Jabotinsky, 45; in Jabotinsky's fiction,
  223–26; of Jewish minority populations,
  109; of Jews in Palestine, 159; and Russian
  liberals, 54, 56, 58, 110; in Synthetic
  Zionism, 45; and Young Turks, 82
Assyrian Jewish Refugee Mule Corps. *See*
  Zionist Mule Corps, the
Australia, 145
Austria-Hungary (Austro-Hungarian
  Empire): fall of, 150; and Jabotinsky, 127,
  129; as multicultural empire, 116. *See also*
  Hungary; Vienna

Austro-Marxism, 55; Jabotinsky's elaboration on, 67–69
autonomy: Jabotinsky on, 80–82, 84, 116, 151, 235; national, 56–57, 66–67 (*see also* Austro-Marxism; Bund, the); political, 6, 7, 8, 63, 71; problems with terminology of, 67; in Turkey, 84

Babkov, Arye, 43
Bakhtin, Mikhail, *Problems of Dostoevsky's Poetics* (1929), 223
Balfour, Lord Arthur: letter (1917) of, 36
Balfour Declaration: and British in Palestine, 148, 156, 161, 167, 170; and Churchill's White Paper, 171; credit for, 125–26, 146; and the Jewish Legion, 176; and Palestinian Arabs, 171; and political legitimacy, 134, 166; and Zionists, 146, 148, 230
Basel. *See under* Herzl, Theodor; Zionist Congresses
Bauer, Otto, 55, 81. *See also* Austro-Marxism
Begin, Menachem, 11, 13n26, 159
Beilis, Mendel, 6, 95
Beilis Affair (1911–1913), 6, 79, 206; newspaper accounts of, 95, 114, 123n58; and Jabotinsky, 114–15
Béla Kun, 206
Bely, Andrei, 87
Ben-Gurion, David: and Histadrut, 200; and Jabotinsky, 2–3, 157, 196, 197–98, 199, 202; and partition of Palestine, 230; and Second Aliyah, 43, 170, 210; on Sephardim in Turkey, 83; and Soviet leadership model, 200; on Shomer movement, 153n38; and socialism, 198, 200; and statism, 3; and Zionism, 72
Ben-Yehuda, Eliezer (Eliezer Yitzhak Perlman), 83
Berdiaev, Nikolai, 78
Berdichevsky, Micah Yosef, 7
Berlin, 138; and Jabotinsky, 6, 93, 187, 193, 196; Russian émigrés in, 196, 217–18. See also *Rassvet* (1922–1934, Berlin/Paris)
Berlin, Isaiah, 1–2

Bern, 5, 16, 17, 18
Bernstein-Kogan, Yaakov, 37, 42
Betar: formation of, 9, 214n81; and *hadar*, 91, 208–9, 235, 237; militaristic character of, 208, 229; and the political right, 215; popularity in interwar Eastern Europe of, 235; as revisionist institution, 217, 229, 235; in the United States, 6; versus other European youth groups, 208, 237. *See also* militarism
Bialik, Hayim Nachman: "In the City of Slaughter" (trans. Jabotinsky, 1911), 28, 29, 108, 113; Jabotinsky's praise of, 113–14; in Jerusalem, 161; and Jewish humiliation, 105–6, 108, 113; and Kishinev, 115
Bialystok. *See* pogroms
Bickerman, Iosif, 25–26, 31–32n40
BILU, 69
Birzhevye Vedomosti [*Stock Market News*], 139
Black Hundreds, 104
Blok, Alexander, 87
"Bloody Sunday" (Revolution of 1905), 52, 162
Bolshevism: American perceptions of, 165; and Jewish émigrés, 189; and Jewish socialists, in the Yishuv, 199–200; psychology of, 189; revisionist hostility to, 195; and Slavinsky Affair, 170–71. *See also* Revolution of 1917
Brit ha-Biryonim [Band of Hoodlums], 151, 159, 217
British Mandate, 151, 171, 176, 188, 229, 234–35; call for changes in, 166; and discriminations, 161; and League of Nations, 134, 150; and political legitimacy, 160; terms of, 159–60, 170; violence in, 169
British Zionist Federation, 144
Brit Shalom, 166, 168, 238
Briusov, Vasily, 22
Brutskus, Julius (Yuly): and émigré reaction to Jabotinsky, 193–94; at Kovno Conference, 78; and *Rassvet*, 10, 43; as russified Jew, 27
Buber, Martin, 41
Bulgakov, Sergei, 78

Bund, the (Jewish Workers' Party [of Russia, Poland, and Lithuania]): and assimilation, 56; congresses of, 56, 58; and the Duma, 55, 57, 104; and national autonomy, 56, 63; origins of, 26–27; role in the Revolutionary era, 54–55; and Zionism, 55–59, 74n26. *See also under* Jabotinsky, Vladimir (nonfiction): *The Bund and Zionism*

Caliphate, the, 131–32, 134
capitalism, 45, 55, 199
censorship: and Jabotinsky's literary work, 19, 31n27, 99n52; promised end of prepublication, 66; and *Rassvet*, 212n25; in tsarist Russia, 26, 52–53, 140
Central Europe. *See* Austria-Hungary; Hungary; Vienna
Chekhov, Anton: influence in Russia of, 20; and Jabotinsky, 20, 90; Jewish stereotypes in, 88
Cherikov, Evgenii, *Jews* (1904), 87–89
Cherikov Affair (1907–1909), 6; 86–87, 88, 90, 101
Chernov, Viktor, 188
Chlenov, Yehiel: at Helsingfors, 70; on Herzl, 35, 38; and Jabotinsky, 7, 137–38; at Kovno, 78; and Palestine, 37, 42; and Uganda plan, 42; on Zionism, 44, 52
Chmelnitsky Rebellion (1648), 61
Christianity, Russian Orthodox: flagellant sect in, 115; Jewish converts to, 27
Chukovsky, Korney: on Chekhov, 20; and Cherikov Affair, 87; and Jabotinsky, 28, 32n50, 38
Churchill White Paper (1922), 157, 160, 171–72, 173, 176, 179. *See also* White Paper (1939)
Constantinople and colonialism, 158. *See also* Istanbul
Copenhagen, 137, 140
cosmopolitanism: and Cherikov Affair, 87; end of, 27; and Jabotinsky, 8, 17, 18, 218, 222, 226; versus Russian nationalism, 102
Cossacks, 88
Cowen, Joseph, 144

Danton, Georges, 96
Ha-Davar, 72
decadence: as literary movement, 19–23, 31n33, 92; moral, 90, 225, 226. *See also* cosmopolitanism
Decembrists, 103
Democratic Nationalists (Endeks), 77; antisemitism and, 98n14, 110, 179. *See also* Dmowski, Roman
Derby, Edward, 143
diaspora, Jewish, 16, antisemitism and, 79; and autonomy, 66–67; and Helsingfors, 69–71, 105, 120; Jabotinsky on, 118–19, 134; youth in, 201; Zionism and, 45–46, 57, 116, 165–66, 204, 236. *See also* Galut, the; Hebrew language
Di Tribune [*The Platform*], 140, 154n58
Dizengoff, Meir, 27, 85–86
Dmowski, Roman: antisemitism of, 121–22n38; Jabotinsky and, 79, 110, 117; plans revolt against Russia, 179
Dubnov, Semyon: on antisemitism, 61; and Jewish cultural autonomy, 63, 65, 67–69; on Jews in revolutionary France, 102; *Letters on Old and New Jewry*, 68; on nationalism, 122n40; in Odessa, 5; on the Revolution of 1905, 112, 113
Dubrovsky, N., 110
Duma [Parliament], 6, 66; antisemitism and democracy of, 78–79; count of Jewish deputies in all Dumas, 98n20; and reduced voter enfranchisement, 77; tsarist reforms to, 52, 61. *See also* Duma, first; Duma, second; Duma, third
Duma, first (1906): dispersal of, 53, 64, 77, 112; elections to, 53, 57, 63–64; Jewish delegates to, 60, 64
Duma, second (1907), 59; closed, 77; Jabotinsky's campaign for office in, 79–80; and Poland, 80, 98n14; and Zionism, 65
Duma, third (1907–1912): debate on abrogation of the Pale of Settlement in, 104; dominated by conservatives, 101; Jewish delegates to, 77; and *Rassvet*, 120n13; restrictions on Jewish representation in, 110

Eastern Europe. *See* Europe, Eastern; *and the names of individual cities and countries*
Eder, Montague, 144
Egypt: Alexandria, 134–36; British conquest of, 127, 149; Jabotinsky as journalist in, 129, 131, 139; the Jewish Legion in, 134, 145–46; and the Ottoman Empire, 83; uprisings in, 138, 139, 147; and World War I, 149; and Zionism, 169
Elmaleh, Avraham, 159
Emes, Der, 188
Eretz Yisrael: and diaspora, 45; Jabotinsky and, 79, 125; and Palestinian Arabs, 4; and Slavinsky Affair, 172; and Zionism, 16, 170. *See also* Israel; Yishuv
Estonia, 193–94
Ethiopia, 181
Etzel, 217, 235
Europe: antisemitism in, 4, 9, 217, 226, 229, 231; and imperialism, 126–27; Jabotinsky on, 54–55, 65–66; 139, 150, 168; nationalism in, 3; progress as idea in, 17; right-wing movements in, 206; "Russian Zionists" (émigrés) in, 187–89; and World War I, 126. *See also* Austria-Hungary; Eastern Europe; Western Europe; *and the names of individual cities and countries*
Europe, Eastern: Jews in, 25, 57, 69, 180; and Jewish emigration, 3–4, 34, 187; Jewish immigrants to Palestine, 187; politics in, 237; popularity of fascism in, 207; "spiritual purity" of, 36–37, and Zionism, 194, 235, 236. *See also the names of individual cities and countries*
Europe, Western: and Beilis Affair, 114; Jewish troops in armies of, 134; and Young Turks, 82. *See also* Europe; *and the names of individual cities and countries*
Evreiskaia Tribuna [*Jewish Tribune*], 188
Evreiskaia Zhizn' [*Jewish Life*], 5, 38, 42–48, 66, 81, 91–92; and Avram Idel'son, 44–46. See also *Rassvet*

fascism: contemporary understanding of, 207; German, 207; Italian, 91, 207, 208; and Jabotinsky, 2, 10, 209–10, 216, 227–28, 230, 236–37

feuilleton: definition of, 92–94; and Jabotinsky, 25, 26, 85, 92–97, 99n52
fin de siècle culture: and influence on Jabotinsky, 5, 8; scholarship on, 7. *See also* cosmopolitanism; decadence
Finland. *See* Vyborg Appeal
Florensky, Pavel, 114
France: and alliances, 131, 133, 139; in Canada, 177; cultural superiority of, 149, 158, 203; fascism in, 237; and imperialism, 127; and Jewish immigration, 187; in Morocco, 152n25; and Palestine, 134; Revolution of 1848 in, 61; and World War I, 131, 149, 150. *See also* Revolution, French; Paris
Fraynd, Der, 50n41, 128

Galilee, the, 47, 162
Gallipoli, 136–37
Galut, the, 191; negation of, 45, 50n46, 69. *See also* Ahad-Ha'am; diaspora, Jewish
Gapon, 161–62
Garibaldi, Giuseppe, 116–17, 222; as influence on Jabotinsky, 14, 31n33, 146, 164–65, 227
Garshin, Vsevolod, "Attalea Princeps" (1880), 62
Gegenwartsarbeit, 71, 82
Georgia, 67
Gepstein, Shlomo, 10, 43, 99n52, 190, 192
Germany: antisemitism in, 9, 208; and German Zionists, 137; and Jewish immigration, 187; and leftist revolution, 206; Russian-Jewish sympathy for, 137–38; and stabilization of the mark, 187; and Turkey, 149–50; and World War I, 125, 126, 137, 138, 148, 149, 150; Zionist émigrés in, 191–92. *See also* Germany, Nazi
Germany, Nazi: antisemitism in, 9, 106, 230; *Freikorps* in, 208; Jabotinsky and fascism of, 207, 237. *See also* Hitler, Adolf
Gershenzon, Mikhail, *Fates of the Jewish People,* 177; *Landmarks* (ed., 1909), 78
ghetto, Jewish, 45, 47, 109, 193, 203. *See also* pogroms
Gindin, Mikhail, 190, 191
Ginsberg, Asher. *See* Ahad-Ha'am
Gippius, Zinaida, 20

Gogol, Nikolai, *Taras Bulba* (1835), 88
Goldberg, Boris, 27
Goldstein, Alexander, 27, 43
Gorky, Maxim: *bosiak* [tramp] in works of, 21, 22; and Cherikov Affair, 87; and Jabotinsky, 20–21, 93, 220; *Mother*, 165
Grabsky, Wladislaw, 110
Great Britain: and alliances, 131; conscription in, 141–42; Foreign Office of, 139, 145, 166, 167; imperialism and, 127, 149, 177; Jabotinsky's alliance with, 36, 125–26, 138, 142–43, 180, 197, 229; Jewish immigrants in, 138, 144, 184n49; and "Jewish tailors," 141, 142; and Palestine, 134, 159–60, 229, 230; and Uganda plan, 33, 34; and World War I, 150; and Zionism, 138, 139, 140, 146–47, 156, 174, 176–77; Zionist benefactors in, 36, 126. *See also* Balfour Declaration; British Mandate; Churchill White Paper; Jewish Legion, the; Weizmann, Chaim; White Paper (1939)
Greater Actions Committee, 137, 139
Greece, 202, 209
Greenberg, Uri Zvi, 159
Grinberg [Greenberg], Hayim, 70, 75n76
Grossman, Meir, 6, 10, 154nn56–58, 190, 204, 210; *The Case Against the "Mixed" Jewish Agency*, 141; and the Jewish Legion, 139–41, 162–63; and Revisionist coup d'état, 217
Gruzenberg, Oscar, 115, 169, 206
Gruzenberg, Osip, 46, 102
gypsies, 81

Haganah [Defense], 163
Halastra [Group], 43
Hamilton, Sir Ian (Gen.), 126
Harmsworth, Alfred Charles. *See* Northcliff, Lord
Hashemite Kingdom, 176
Hasmonea, 194–95
"Hatikvah," 161
HaTzoHar [Brit Ha-Tsionim Ha-Revizionistim]. *See* Zionism, Revisionist
Haynt, 188
Hebrew language: in the diaspora, 119, 123n70, 129, 212n32; and Jabotinsky, 15–16, 27, 28, 46, 81, 89, 98n19, 113, 129, 170, 187, 216, 218, 221; and the Jewish Legion, 136, 145; in Palestine, 134, 161; resurrection of, 5, 47, 135; in schools, 68, 119, 123n70; versus Yiddish, 58, 85–86; and Zionism, 47
Hebrew University (Jerusalem), 161, 184n55
Hedin, Sven, 130
Helsingfors Conference (1906), 69–72; and *Gegenwartsarbeit*, 71; and Zionist autonomy, 64, 71
Helsinki Conference (1906), 186n88
Herzen, Alexander, 103, 228
Herzl, Theodor: and Ahad-Ha'am, 37, 71; critics of, 41–42, 44; death of, 38–39; and emigration, 42, 105, 151; and failure to secure charter for Palestine, 42, 44; faith in progress of, 26; and the feuilleton, 96–97; Jabotinsky as follower of, 40–41, 84, 92, 151, 236; Jabotinsky's views on, 34–42; Jewish identity of, 41, 92; *The Jewish State*, 16, 178, 202; and Uganda plan, 33–42, 79; and Zionism, 16, 34–35, 41, 79, 193. *See also* World Zionist Organization; Zionism, Revisionist
Hibbat Tsion [Lovers of Zion], 16, 30n7, 31–32n40; and rejection of political activity, 69–70
Histadrut (labor exchange), 11, 198; defined, 200
Hitler, Adolf, 207, 210
Holocaust, 3
Hungary, 61, 81, 114, 129, 206
Hussein Ibn Ali (Sharif of Mecca), 134

Idel'son, Avram, 1, 7, 50n47, 76n79; and Helsingfors, 69; and Jabotinsky, 63, 79, 80; and Marxism, 45; and Synthetic Zionism, 44–46
individualism: in literature, 21–22; versus fascism, 220; and Jabotinsky, 92
intelligentsia, Russian: abandonment of Jews by, 61–62; and antisemitism, 77, 101–5; and Bolshevism, 189; characteristic behavior of, 173–74; and rise of pressure politics, 53; term defined, 24. *See also* Cherikov Affair; Jewish intelligentsia; liberalism, Russian
"Iron Wall," 174–81, 186n88. *See also* militarism

Iskra, 58, 74n26
Israel, 48, 181, 195. *See also* Eretz Yisrael; Palestine; Yishuv
Istanbul, 6; and Jabotinsky, 78, 79, 80, 82, 85, 221
Italy: fascism in, 91, 207, 209, 210; Jabotinsky and, 14, 17–18, 20–21, 90, 157, 164, 221; nationalism in, 116–17; and Sephardic Jews, 203. *See also* Mussolini, Benito; Garibaldi, Giuseppe

Jabotinskaia, Chava (mother), 15, 138
Jabotinskaia, Jeanne (wife), 81, 129, 161, 187
Jabotinskaia-Kopp, Tamara (sister), 94
Jabotinsky, Eri (son), 129, 161, 167
Jabotinsky, Evgenii (father), 127–28
Jabotinsky, Vladimir: as "Altalena," 21, 93, 94, 232n22, 223; "Arab theory" of, 159; antisemitism and, 9, 28; attacks Ben-Gurion, 197–98; autobiographical fabrications of, 8; and character assassination, 105; charisma of, 141; compared to Danton, 96; death of, 6; and democracy, 65, 71, 80; education of, 80–81; and educational initiatives, 80, 94, 119; on ethno-nationalism, 111–12, 116–19; and Hebrew, 15; "hero of Jerusalem," 163; and Herzl, 33–42, 84, 92; imprisoned, 6, 23, 72; "internal politics" proposed by, 63; on Jewish heroism, 113; "Jewish pedigree" of, 15; and Jewish self-hate, 105–9; and Jewish self-reliance, 119–20; as journalist, 42–43, 81, 91–97; and languages, 81; on leftists, 198–200; and liberalism, 79, 104–5, 209–10; literary career, 18–19; mentors of, 48, 63, 79; on morality, 21, 88–89, 95, 114, 128, 176, 180–81, 224, 228, 230; move to political right, 156–57; on non-Jews, 115; and non-Zionists, 72, 116; and notion of "youth," 53–54, 65–66; philosophical contradictions of, 92, 111, 117–18, 128, 209; poetry of, 97; political agenda of, 105; political office run, 65, 79–80; political opportunism of, 62–63; and radical right, 80, 207–9; resignation of, from Zionism, 173; and revolution, 65–66; as Russian author, 87–91; scholarship on, 7–11; and the "tramp" of history (*see also* Gorky, Maxim), 164–65, 170, 227; on territorial control, 118; and Uganda plan, 33–42; utopian ideas of, 84; visits Palestine, 85–86; visits United States, 163–64; volunteers in British Army, 145; on World War I, 84, 124–26, 148–51; on Zionist legitimacy, 157, 181; Zionist rhetoric of, 95–97, 196–97. *See also under all items generally*
Jabotinsky, Vladimir (autobiography), *The Story of My Life* (1936), 221–22; "first visit" to Palestine, 85–86; on Helsingfors Conference, 70; on Herzl, 40, 43; intellectual crisis depicted in, 80; on "magnetic power" of war, 130; on Orthodox Jewry in Galicia, 108–9; on revolutionary Russia, 53–54
Jabotinsky, Vladimir (works of fiction cited): *Abroad* (*Na chuzhbine*, 1909/1922), 89, 99n52; *Blood* (*Krov*', 1901), 21–22, 31n27; "Diana," 90–91; "Edmée" (1912), 90; "Hêsped" (1905), 38–39; *It's All Right* (*Ladno*, 1902), 21–22, 31n27; *Stories* (*Rasskazy*, 1930), 188; *Samson the Nazarite* (*Samson—Nazarei*, 1926), 188, 217–21; "Squirrel," 91. *See also* Bialik, Hayim Nachman; Poe, Edgar Allan
Jabotinsky, Vladimir (works of nonfiction cited): "About the Iron Wall (We and the Arabs)" (1923), 174–77; "The Bund and Zionism" (1906), 55–57; "The Enemy of the Workers," 198; "The Ethics of the Iron Wall" (1923), 174–77; *The Five* (1936), 215–16; 222–27; "Homo Homini Lupus" ["Man Is Wolf to Man"] (1910), 111; "Horoscope" (1912), 126; "Instead of an Apology" (1912), 95, 114, 123n58; "The Iron Wall" (1923), 3, 111, 117; "Leftists," 198; "Legion" (1924), 201; "Letters on Nationalities and Districts: Jews and their Attitudes" (1911), 109; "On Jews in Russian Literature" (1908), 87; "On National Education" (1910), 108; "Our Everyday Event" (1910), 107; "Our Tasks" (1906), 66; "Political Autonomy of a National Minority" (1913), 80–81;

"Political Offensive" (1924), 200–1; "Race" (1913), 118–19; "Reactionary" (1912), 3, 116–18; *Revisionist Principles* (1929), 201; "The Revolt of the Old Men" (1936), 226; "Right and Force" (1912), 126–27; "Russian Gentleness," 87; "Sitting on the Floor" ("Sidia na polu," 1905), 39–40; "Sketches without a Title" (1905), 46; *Story of the Jewish Legion* (1927), 136, 138, 145–47, 152–53n29; "Turkey and Us," 140; *Turkey and the War*, 150–51; *What Do Revisionists Want?* (1926), 41, 195
Jabotinsky Institute (Tel Aviv), 7
Jacobson, Viktor, 137, 138, 192
Jerusalem, 6, 34, 36, 39, 119, 147, 161, 169, 204; pogrom in, 147; riots in, 163–65
Jewish Agency, 160, 171, 197
Jewish Chronicle, 144
Jewish Democratic Group, 64
Jewish emigration/immigration: barriers to, 3; and development of the Jewish sector in Palestine, 165–66; as goal of Zionism, 25–26; Jabotinsky's "obsession" with, 85–86; as "maximalist" solution, 115; open, to Palestine, 175; opposed by Arab majority in Palestine, 167; from Russia, 124; from the Soviet Union, 10; statistics on, 187; in Synthetic Zionism, 45. *See also* Eastern Europe; Europe; Ottoman Empire; Palestine; Russia; United States; Western Europe; Yishuv; *and the names of other individual countries*
Jewish identity: and the Cherikov Affair, 87–88; collective, 102; need to embrace, 108; in pre-Revolutionary Russia, 27; and russification, 16–17, 18, 27, 89
Jewish intelligentsia: and Bolshevism, 189; as émigrés, 188–89; as liberals, 79; in Odessa, 5; associated with Russian liberalism, 54; and Sephardic Jews, 203. *See also* Cherikov Affair; Intelligentsia, Russian; Liberalism, Russian
Jewish Legion, the, 47, 133–47; British role in, 133–34, 135, 136–37, 141–46; demobilized, 160, 162–63; goals of, 140, 142–43; objections to, 137–38; origins of, 6, 135–37, 143; promoting political agenda, 134;

reinstatement of, 201–2; as symbol, 146; Weizmann's praise of, 144–45. *See also* Zionist Mule Corps, the
Jewish minority, 45; 54, 59–60, 71–72; and "absorptive capacity," in Palestine, 166–67; restrictions and quotas for; 18, 78. *See also* assimilation; Helsingfors Conference
Jewish National Group, 104
Jewish nationalism: and the Bund, 57; as dependent on Russian liberals, 109–10; in Jabotinsky's fiction, 223, 226; and left-wing leadership, 58; and the Ottoman Empire, 83, 133; and Zionism, 56. *See also* Arab nationalism; autonomy
Jewish People's Group (or Party), 64, 104, 121n16
Jewish Question, 41, 103, 104
Jewish sovereignty, 3; as goal of Zionism, 25–26; theories on, 67
Jewish State Party, 141
Jewish University Society of Workmen (*Weltarbeitergenossenschaft*), 47
Jewish Workers' Party (of Russia, Poland, and Lithuania). *See* Bund, the
Jews, Ashkenazi, 203
Jews, Russian: and Ottoman Empire, 125; and self-defense, 125, 126, 134. *See also under* Jewish identity
Jews, Sephardic, 83, 202–3
Journalism: and contemporary muckrakers in the US, 24; and the gutter (yellow) press, 77, 101, 103; and internal Zionist politics, 140; Jabotinsky's early contempt for, 24, 94; liberal Russian, 103, 128–29; in Palestine, 72; praxis and, 44; role in Russian society of, 24; Russian émigrés and, 190; Russian-Jewish, 5, 43–48, 105; in Turkey, 82; and World War I, 127; in Yiddish, 128, 140. *See also* feuilleton; Jabotinsky, Vladimir; *and the names and titles of individual journalists and newspapers*
Judaism: diaspora, 67; in Eastern Europe, 36–37; and Herzl, 92; and Jabotinsky, 15; rejection of, 107–8; in Russia, 27; and Zionism, 45
Judeo-Kommuna, 189

Kadet (Constitutional Democratic) Party: and antisemitism, 102–5; and Bialystok pogrom, 60; and First Duma, 66, 112; and nationalism, 77, 101–5; political alliance with Zionists, 65; support for Jewish rights by, 54; as threat to Zionism, 104–5. *See also* assimilation
Kahn, Jacobus, *Erez Israel, das jüdische Land* (1909), 85
Katznelson, Berl, 43, 72, 83, 170, 210
Kaufman, A. E., 24, 31n38
Keren Hayesod [Land Fund], 6, 10, 163, 165, 199
Keren Kayemet, 157, 199
Keynes, John Maynard, 150
Khlysty [flagellents], 115
kibbutz movement, 170
Kiev, 135, 137
King, Joseph, 144
Kishinev. *See under* pogroms
Kitchener, Lord Horatio, 141
Kitchener's Army, 142
Klausner, Joseph, 5, 137, 159
Klinov, Yehoshua, 95
Korolenko, Vladimir, 19, 87, 88
Kovno Conference (1909), 78
Kulisher, Alexander, 10, 69, 96, 177, 179, 189, 204

Landmarks (*Vekhi*, 1909), 78
Latvia, 84, 194–95
League (or Union) for the Attainment of Full Rights for the Jews of Russia ("the League"), 6, 54–55, 59–65, 80
League of Nations, 134, 159, 229
Lebedintsev, Vsevolod, 18, 23, 28, 29
Lenin, Vladimir, 157, 230
Leskov, Nikolai, 88
Levin, Shmaryahu, 60, 63, 137
Levitan, Isaac, 102
liberalism, Russian: and antisemitism, 103–5, as "assimilators," 65; cultural initiatives of, 78; decline of, 65; and the First Duma, 113; and nationalism, 80, 101–5, 116; alliance with the League, 59–65; support of Polish independence by, 110; and "Zionist monopoly" of power, 104. *See under* Russia; *see also* Kadet Party; *Landmarks*; "League, the"

Lichtheim, Richard, 190, 204
Likud, 11
Lilienblum, Moshe Leib, 5, 17
literary clubs, Russian, 106–7
Lloyd George, David, 144
Lodge, Henry Cabot, 143n82
London: and Jabotinsky, 129, 143, 163–64, 165, 171, 188, 190, 228, 230; Jewish population of, 139, 143–44, 145. *See also* Great Britain

Manchester Guardian, 128, 144
Mandate Palestine. *See* British Mandate
Maklakov, Vasilii, 79, 101, 102, 104, 115
Mapai, 11, 222
Margolin, Moisei, 43–44
Margolina, Rakhel', 28, 32n50
Markov, Nikolai, 116, 117, 118
Marx, Karl, 227
Marxism: opposition to, in Russia, 59–60; and Synthetic Zionism, 45. *See also* Austro-Marxism
Mastermann, Charles, 126
Maxwell, John (Gen.), 136
McMahon, Sir Henry, 134
Medem, Vladimir, 58
Mediterranean Expeditionary Force, 136–37
Meyuhas, Yosef, 159
Merezhkovsky, Dmitry, "The Causes for the Decline of Contemporary Russian Literature and New Trends in It," (1892), 19–20
Middle East: and Jabotinsky, 131, 148; and Great Britain, 133–34, 150–51. *See also* Arabs; Egypt; Ottoman Empire; Palestine
Miliukov, Pavel, 66, 101, 102, 105, 115, 230, 122n47, 188
militarism: and Jabotinsky, 174, 190, 195, 206, 210, 216–17; in early twentieth century, 181; Jewish groups espousing, 151; and Pilsudski, 207; Prussian, 139; versus fascism, 210; youth groups and, 201, 206, 208, 235; Zionist objections to, 177, 235
minority nations: capitalism and, 45; experimental thinking on, 81; increasing discontent of, in Russia, 26; Jews as, 193–94; rights and responsibilities of, 3. *See also* autonomy; Jewish minority; nationalism

Mir Bozhii, 19
Mizrachi (Orthodox Zionist party), 33, 202
Monism, 86, 97; defined, 46-47
Morocco, 131–33, 158. *See also under* France
Moscow, 35, 128–29, 137, 177
Murometz, Elias, 164
Mussolini, Benito, 91, 157, 210, 215

nationalism: and antisemitism, 80, 103, 117; Jabotinsky on, 66-69, 116–19; and official recognition, 109. *See also* Arab nationalism; autonomy; Jewish nationalism; *and under the names of individual countries*
Nationalitätenstaat [state of nationalities], 109
Nazi Germany. *See* Germany, Nazi
Nein-Sagers, 33–34, 36–37
Netanyahu, Benjamin, 11
Netanyahu, Benzion, 11
New Zionist Organization (NZO), 6, 215
Nicholas II, Tsar, "Manifesto on the Improvement of the State Order" (October Manifesto), 52, 53, 73n14. *See also* Tsarist rule
Nietzsche, Friedrich, 18, 22, 130, 227
Nordau, Max, 33, 96, 171, 204
Nordau Plan, 169, 171, 173, 184n63
North Africa. *See under* Arab Nationalism; *and the names of individual countries*
Northcliff, Lord, 167, 183n44
Nuova Antologia, 20

October Manifesto. *See* Nicholas II, Tsar
Odessa: antisemitism in, 64; Jabotinsky and, 5, 42–43, 134; Jewish life in, 18, 26–27; mix of nationalities in, 5; theater in, 21–22, 31n27; and Young Turks, 82; Zionism in, 5, 26–29, 31n40, 47, 70, 125. See also *Evreiskaia Zhizn'*; Journalism; *Odesskie Novosti*; *Odesskii Listok*; pogroms
Odesskii Listok, 94
Odesskie Novosti: Jabotinsky as journalist for, 19, 21, 24; Jabotinsky's coverage for, at Basel, 33, 35; and Jabotinsky's outburst over Kishinev, 28
Ha-Olam, 124

Orientalism, 132–33
Ost-Juden, 169
Ottoman Empire: and Herzl, 34; Jabotinsky on, 82–85, 125; minorities in, 82; opposition to Jewish immigration, 33, 83–84; and Palestine, 72, 84; and World War I, 125–26, 131–33, 148–51. *See also* Arab nationalism; Sultan, Ottoman; Turkey

Pale of Settlement: educational initiatives in, 78, 80; Jabotinsky in, 80, 124; Kadet attempt to abrogate, 102, 104; pogroms in, 61. *See also* asemitism
Palestine: antisemitism in, 160, 166; anti-Zionist policies in, 160–61; center of Zionist activity, 222; and the émigré press, 190–93; fundraising for immigration to, 70; and Hebrew, 134–35, 161; and Hibbat Tsion, 16, 30n7; imperial governance of, 158; popularity of Jabotinsky, 2, 163; and Arab-Jewish conflict, 158–60, 174–78, 228–30, 238; economy of, 204; Jewish alternatives to, 4, 116; Jewish immigration and, 37, 115, 140, 160, 167, 171, 187, 226; creation of Jewish majority in, 41, 46, 118–19, 172, 175, 202; Judaizing, 48; and Kahn scandal, 85; and Keren Hayesod, 6; labor strikes in, 11; land purchase and cultivation in, 47, 72; and maximalism, 204; and Monism, 46; as national home, 64, 66, 69, 70, 144, 167, 192, 194, 203; partition of, 228, 230; and political autonomy for minorities, 8; political infighting in, 198–200, 205; and political sovereignty, 67; population of, 157; as refuge, 33, 158; and rejection of diaspora, 57; and Second Aliyah leadership, 3, 43, 62, 196; security in, 165, 201; and self-determination, 167; *shomrim* in, 85, 99n40, 126, 135; Turkey and, 83–84, 133, 140; use of violence in, 165, 168–69, 177; as utopian, 25, 231; wartime opportunism and, 133, 142, 149; and World War I, 139–40, 142, 147; youth in, 135. *See also* Ahad-Ha'am; Ben-Gurion, David; Balfour Declaration; British Mandate; Herzl, Theodor; Helsingfors Conference; Iron Wall; Jewish Legion, the; Transjordan; Uganda plan; Weizmann, Chaim; Zionism

Palestine Royal Commission. *See* Peel Commission
Pasmanik, Daniil, 43
Paris: as center for Russian emigration, 187–88; Jabotinsky in, 131; 172. *See also Rassvet* (1922–1934, Berlin/Paris)
Patterson, John Henry (Col.), 126, 130, 136, 145–46, 154n75
Peel Commission, 228, 230
Peter the Great (Emperor of Russia), 35, 169
Petliura, Semyon, 172
Pilsudski, József, 179, 207, 210, 215
Pinsker, Leo, 7, 57, 115, 193
Plehve, Count Viacheslav von, 40, 41–42
Plekhanov, Grigory, 57, 226
Poalei Tsion [Workers of Zion] Party, 57, 72, 137
Poe, Edgar Allan, "The Raven" (trans. Jabotinsky), 5, 28
Ha-Poel Ha-Tsair [Young Worker] Party, 72
pogroms: in Bialystok (1906), 60, 103, 109; in the ghetto, 61; in Homel, 113; Jabotinsky on, 45, 58–59, 62, 68, 79, 113; in Jerusalem, 147; in Kishinev (1903), 10–11, 27–28, 103, 113; non-Jewish objections to, 62; in Odessa, 27, 53, 58; in the Pale of Settlement (1905), 61; in Russia, 18, 53, 58, 113; Russian promotion of, 62
Poland [Congress Poland, Russian Poland], 2; antisemitism in, 77, 78, 80, 98n14, 101, 106, 110, 111, 117, 217; autonomy of, 67; and the Bund, 55; ethno-nationalism in, 3, 80, 111, 117; and First Duma elections, 64; independence movement in, 110–12; and minorities, 181; Russian imperialism in, 179; and Second Duma elections, 80. *See also* Dmowski, Roman; pogroms; *Poles and Jews*
Poles and Jews (1910), 110
Pro-Israël (1917), 202
propaganda: antisemitic, 103; and Jabotinsky, 52, 78–79; and the Jewish Legion, 138, 140; versus "positive press" on Zionism, 82; and *Rassvet*, 193; of Revisionism, 177; and the war effort, 143, 145
Propes, Aharon Zvi, 195
Purishkevich, Vladimir, 79, 116–17

Rassvet (1860–1861, Odessa), 192
Rassvet (1904–1917, St. Petersburg), 7, 74n26; character of, 43; Jabotinsky and, 80. *See also Evreiskaya Zhizn'*
Rassvet (1922–1934, Berlin/Paris): original mission of, 192–93; and Revisionist Zionism, 190–91; tirades against official Zionism in, 196; as transformed by Jabotinsky, 193, 196
Ravnitzky, Yehoshua, 5, 15, 25–26
Recanati, Abraham, 195–96, 202, 204
Rech', 105
Red Army, 200
Renner, Karl, 55, 67, 81. *See also* Austro-Marxism
Renner, Karl, *State and Nation*, (trans. Jabotinsky, 1906), 67–68, 81
Revolution, French, 96, 102
Revolution of 1905 ("October Revolution"), 6, 46–47; as catalyst for Zionism, 52–55, 65–66; debate on failure of, 112–13. *See also* "Bloody Sunday"; October Manifesto
Revolution of 1917, 187, 237, 190. *See also* Bolshevism
Revolutions of 1848 ("Spring of Nations"), 54, 61
Riga, 194–95, 203, 206
Rome, 5, 16; Jews in, 17–18
Rothschild, James de, 145
Rothschild, Leopold de, 142
Royal Fusiliers Battalions, 145, 155n80
Rozanov, Vasily, 22, 114
Rozanov, Vladimir, 115
Romania, 81, 187, 207
Rus', 42–43
Russia: and anarchism, 189; antisemitism in, 4, 77, 78–80; 101–4, 110–11, 114, 138; as cultural center, 4, 87; education in, 78; Jewish émigré commitment to liberation of, 189; Jews as nonterritorial in, 67; lack of Russian majority in, 109; official discrimination in, 53, 104–5; and World War I, 126, 130, 150, 237–38. *See also* Christianity, Russian Orthodox; Pogroms; Russian Imperial Army; Liberalism, Russian; Russian literature; Soviet Union, the; Tsarist rule; White Russian émigrés;

and the names of individual cities and regions
Russian Imperial Army: Jews in, 47
Russian literature: and Jews, 87–89; versus the Western canon, 88, 118. *See also* the names of individual authors and movements
Russian Revolution. *See* Revolution of 1905; Revolution of 1917
Russian Social Democrats (SD), 55
Russkie Vedomosti, 5, 128–29
Russkoye Bogatsvo, 25
Russo-Japanese War (1904), 52
Rutenberg, Pinhas, 6, 135, 137, 161–62, 163

Saltykov-Shchedrin, Mikhail, "The Golovlev Family" (1880), 62–63
Samuel, Sir Stuart, 143
Samuel, Viscount Herbert: and Arab problem, 177, as high commissioner, 159, 161, and the Jewish Legion, 142, 144; popularity of, 204; proposes Arab Agency, 197; and Transjordan, 185n81
San Remo Conference (1920), 167
Savinkov, Boris, 188
Schechtman, Joseph: on centrality of Arab problem, 174; on Arab separatism in Palestine, 159; as Jabotinsky's biographer, 7, 93, 171, 222–23; on *Chuzhbina* (1910/1922), 99n52; on emigration, 192; and *Rassvet*, 10, 191, 192; on Jabotinsky's resignation, 173; on White Russian émigrés, 189; on violence, 190; and Revisionist Zionism, 204; on "Russian-émigré Zionism," 188, 192
Schutzjuden, 201
Schwarzbard, Shlomo, 172
Second Aliyah. *See* Aliyah, Second
Seiderman, Arnold, 43
Severnye Tsvety [*Northern Flowers*], 20
Scott, C. P., 126, 144
Sebag-Montefiore, Sir Joseph, 142
Sephardim. *See* Jews, Sephardic
Sforim, Mendele Mocher, 17
Shomer movement, 135, 153n38. *See also* Palestine
Shtadlanut [Jewish intercession], 53

Shwartz, Shalom (Ben-Baruch), 70, 75n76
Sirkin, Nahum, 70
Slavinsky, Maxim, 170–71
Slavinsky Affair, 169–73, 200
Slavinsky Agreement. *See* Slavinsky Affair
Sliozberg, Henrik, 70, 72
socialism: and the Bund, 55–58; Jabotinsky and, 16, 17, 58, 156, 198–200, 206, 207; the right's rejection of, 236; and Zionist socialism, 188, 198–200. *See also* Austro-Marxism; Bolshevism; Mapai
Socialist Revolutionary movement (SR), 23, 162
Society for the Promotion of Enlightenment, 78
Sokoloff, Nahum, 61, 74n39, 126, 146, 183n42
Sologub, Fyodor, 22, 87
Soloveichik, Max, 43
Solov'ev, Vladimir, 36–37, 122n40
Sorin, Nikolai, 43, 189, 222
South Africa, 181
Soviet Russia. *See* Bolshevism; Soviet Union, the
Soviet Union, the, 216; Jewish population (1917) of, 171, 187; Jewish press in, 212n26; and émigré press in Russian, 192–93; ideological influence in Palestine of, 197–200, 206; and Russian émigrés, 188; and Slavinsky Affair, 172; strongman as leader in, 157
Spartacus League, 206
St. Petersburg: and Jabotinsky, 5, 42, 49n37; Jewish university in, 78. *See also* Cherikov Affair
Stolypin, Pyotr: and Helsingfors, 72; "necktie" of, 79; and Third Duma restrictions, 110
Storrs, Sir Ronald, 163
The Story of My Life. See under Jabotinsky, Vladimir (autobiography)
Struve, Pyotr, 79; "The Intelligentsia and the Face of the Nation," 101–2, 104–5; *Russkaia Mysl'* (*Russian Thought*), 109
Sultan, Ottoman, 16, 34, 47, 82, 132, 152n25
Suvorin, Aleksei, Jr., 42–43
Sweden, 130
Switzerland, 18, 81, 140

Sykes, Mark, 145
Sykes-Picot Agreement (1916), 133–34
symbolism: and Cherikov Affair, 87; "mystique" of, 92
syndicalism, 58
Syria, 129, 149, 169

Tabenkin, Yitzhak, 43, 72
Tel Hai, 158, 163
territorialism. See under Zionism
theater, Russian-Jewish, 23, 31n27
Tiszlaeszlár Affair (1882), 114
Transjordan: and Jabotinsky, 118, 130, 172, 185n81, 204; and the Jewish Legion, 147; made a separate state, 160, 176
Trivus, Israel, 26–27, 70, 192, 222
Trudoviki, 60; in Vyborg, 77
Trumpeldor, Joseph: death of, 147, 163; and the Jewish Legion, 6, 135–36, 143, 145–46; national loyalties of, 139; and the Zionist Mule Corps, 136–37
tsarist rule: and antisemitism, 120, 138; and independence movements, 60; mistreatment of Russian recruits, 126. See also censorship; Duma; Nicholas II; Russia; Zubatovshchina
Turgenev, Ivan: Jewish stereotypes in, 88; "Hamlet and Don Quixote," 20
Turkey: Jabotinsky on, 82–84, 149–51; and Palestine, 84, 147; and rumors of jihad, 131–32, 133; and World War I, 125, 148–51; and Zionist press, 82. See also Istanbul; Ottoman Empire; Young Turk Revolution

Uganda plan: as detour to Palestine, 34; proposed, 33–42
Ukraine, 65, 69, 189; and Jabotinsky, 79, 127–28. See also Chmelnitsky Rebellion; Slavinsky Affair
Ukrainian Central Rada, 140
United States: and Beilis Affair, 114; Jabotinsky's tours of, 183n42; Jewish emigration to, 17, 79, 187; and the Jewish Legion, 137, 145, 155n80
Ussishkin, Menachem, 1, 7, 37, 42; influence on Jabotinsky of, 47–48, 63, 64; at Kovno, 78; "Our Program" (1905), 47–48; and Young Turks, 82

Vestnik Evropy [Messenger of Europe], 81
Vienna, 79, 80–81
Vilna, 59–60, 71, 124
Vinaver, Maxim, 70, 112, 116; and Jabotinsky, 79, 105; on liberal position in the League, 61; and Struve, 102
Violence: political role of, 190. See also British Mandate
vitalism, 130
Volynsky, Akim, 20
Vozrozhdentsy, 57, 63
Vyborg Appeal, 77, 112

Warsaw, 70, 193, 203
Weizmann, Chaim, 2, 210; and the Balfour Declaration, 146; and Hebrew University, 184n55; and Herzl, 41; and the Iron Wall, 170, 176, 177–78; and Jabotinsky, 6, 10, 40, 163, 166, 169, 170, 196–97, 202; and the Jewish Legion, 138–39, 144–45; and diplomacy in Palestine, 126, 139, 156–57, 183n44, 185n79; as president of WZO, 157; and World War I, 144; opposes Zionist leadership, 138; and Zionist Executive, 205
Weizmann, Vera, 145
Western Europe. See Europe, Western; Europe; and the names of individual cities and countries
White Paper (1939), 229
white Russian émigrés, 189, 191–92
Wolf, Lucien, 142
Wolffsohn, David, 79, 85, 173
World War I: causes of, 148–151; Jabotinsky on psychology of, 130–31; outbreak of, 126–127; and Zionist neutrality, 125, 137. See also under the names of individual countries, continents and empires
World Zionist Organization (WZO), 79, 173; and funding, 205; Jabotinsky's role in, 119, 163; Jabotinsky's withdrawal from, 6, 215; and the Jewish Legion, 140; and Weizmann, 157; and public opinion, in the Young Turk Revolution, 82

Yaroslavl, 80
Yellow press. *See under* Journalism
Yiddish language, 134, 190; and the Bund, 57–58, 226; and Jabotinsky, 15, 17, 24, 85–86; newspapers in, 50n41, 128, 140, 188, 211n17; and schools, 68. *See also* Cherikov Affair; Hebrew language
Yievin, Yehoshua, 159
Yishuv, the, 170; arbitration in labor strikes in, 11; criticized by Jabotinsky, 205; as depicted in Jabotinsky's *Story of My Life*, 85–86; fundraising in the United States for, 164; and the Iron Wall, 176; and Jabotinsky's plans for increased immigration, 166, 198; morality and the legitimacy of, 157–59; and partition of Palestine, 230; political leftists in, 198, 199–200, 206; and postwar discriminations, 161; and World War I, 137. *See also* Eretz Yisrael; Palestine
Young Turk Revolution (1909), 82–85, 149
youth organizations, 208. *See also* Betar
Yudishe Folks-Tsaytung, 140
Yushkevich, Semyon, 89

Zal'tsman, Shlomo, 28–30, 93
Zangwill, Israel, 143, 144
Zeitlin, Moshe, 43
Zionism: activist, 193; and Arab question, 158–159, 174–78; and Arab-Turkish disunity, 132–33 (*see also* Ben-Gurion, David); declared illegal, 72, 79; decried by Struve, 102; and first Duma, 64–65; and second Duma, 65; Eastern European Zionists, 36, 42; as European minority nation, 193–94; general, 119, 190, 202, 210 (*see also* Herzl, Theodor); and Great Britain, 126, 138–39, 148, 159–161, 166–67; and "internal politics" of Jabotinsky, 63; and Jewish immigration to Palestine, 165–66; labor, 3, 163, 180–81, 198–99, 206, 210, 222; left-wing, 58, 156, 197, 206, 215; mass emigration, 25; militant, 2; Mizrachi, 33; newspapers (*see under* Journalism); nonsocialist, 6, 54; and non-Zionist donors, 141, 196, 210; and non-Zionists, 72, 116, 168, 206; and Odessa, 5, 29, 47, 82; as "panacea," 105–6; and Pinsker, 115; political, 16, 41, 44, 114, 168, 115–16, 178, 202, 204; and radicalism, 79; radicalizing of Jews by, 103–4; repression of, 58, 72; right-wing, 11, 156, 200; rise of, in Russia, 44, 52; Russian, 37, 41–42, 52, 83, 124, 137, 188, 192; self-determination and, 25, 167–68; as separatism, 107; and Sephardim, 83; single-shekel membership in, 44, 55, 79; "Synthetic," 41, 45–46, 69–72, 119–20, 222; and territorialism, 42; *Tsiyonut gedolah* [Zionism on a grand scale], 200; as utopianism, 25, 231; United States and, 79, 163–65 (*see also* Ussishkin, Menachem); weakened post-1905, 79; before World War I, 124–26; neutrality of, in World War I, 137–38, 146; Young Turks and, 82. *See also* Bund, the; Jewish Legion; the; Jewish nationalism; Kadet Party; the League; Palestine; Russia; Zionism, revisionist; Zionist Congresses; Zionist Executive Committee
Zionism, revisionist, 1, 2, 3, 6, 69; clashes with Labor Zionism, 198; constituencies of, 203, 206; founding conference (1925) of, 204; and funding problems, 195–96, 205–6; and Meir Grossman, 141; heterodoxy of, 195; and Jewish majority, 202; as maximalist, 204; origins of, 10, 194–95; program of, 200–1; as revision of Herzl's Zionism, 41, 204; and revisionist union, 205; and Transjordan, 172, 204. *See also* Herzl, Theodor; Zionism
Zionist Congresses: Basel (1897), 16, 230; Basel (1898), 16, 192; Basel (1903), 29, 33–40; Minsk (1902), 16; Vienna (1925), 197, 205
Zionist Executive Committee: Jabotinsky and, 6, 10, 157, 165, 166, 171–73, 190, 196, 205, 210, 236; Weizmann and, 157, 196, 210, 217. *See also* Slavinsky Affair
Zionist Mule Corps, the, 136–37
Zubatovshchina (anti-revolutionary government policy), 56

BRIAN J. HOROWITZ holds the Sizeler Family Chair in Jewish Studies at Tulane University. He is author of many articles and books on European and American Jewry, including *Empire Jews: Jewish Nationalism and Acculturation in 19th- and Early 20th-Century Russia*; *Jewish Philanthropy and Enlightenment in Late-Tsarist Russia*; *Russian Idea-Jewish Presence: Essays on Russian-Jewish Intellectual Life*; and *The Russian-Jewish Tradition: Intellectuals, Historians, Revolutionaries*.

www.ingramcontent.com/pod-product-compliance
Lightning Source LLC
Chambersburg PA
CBHW030338240426
43661CB00052B/1667